Pursuit of Profit and Preferment in Colonial North America

JOHN BRADSTREET'S QUEST

William G. Godfrey

Wilfrid Laurier University Press

Wilfrid Laurier University Press acknowledges the financial support of the Government of Canada through the Canada Book Fund for our publishing activities.

Library and Archives Canada Cataloguing in Publication

Godfrey, William G., 1941–2008

    Pursuit of profit and preferment in colonial North America : John Bradstreet's quest

Includes bibliographical references and index.

ISBN 978-1-55458-475-8 (paper)
ISBN 978-0-88920-806-3 (PDF)

1. Bradstreet, John, 1714–1774. 2. Soldiers – Canada – Biography.
3. Canada – History – 1755–1763. 4. Great Britain – Colonies – America.
I. Title.

FC384.1.B74G63   971.01'8'0924   C82-094711-3
F1030.9.B74G63

© 1982 Wilfrid Laurier University Press
Waterloo, Ontario   N2L 3C5
www.wlupress.wlu.ca

Cover design by Leslie Macredie

Every reasonable effort has been made to acquire permission for copyright material used in this text, and to acknowledge all such indebtedness accurately. Any errors and omissions called to the publisher's attention will be corrected in future printings.

No part of this publication may be reproduced, stored in a retrieval system or transmitted, in any form or by any means, without the prior consent of the publisher or a licence from The Canadian Copyright Licensing Agency (Access Copyright). For an Access Copyright licence, visit www.accesscopyright.ca or call toll free to 1-800-893-5777.

Pursuit of Profit and Preferment
in Colonial North America

JOHN BRADSTREET'S QUEST

William G. Godfrey

for Mom and Dad

CONTENTS

Preface		ix
Abbreviations		xiii
I	The Bradstreets of Nova Scotia	1
II	Emergence at Louisbourg	12
III	Disappointment and Readjustment	32
IV	Reunited with Shirley	57
V	Success with Lord Loudoun	88
VI	Triumph Despite Abercromby	115
VII	Prosperity but Little Progress	142
VIII	Preparations for Detroit	175
IX	The Great Lakes Campaign	196
X	The Last Decade	233
Conclusion		264
Bibliography		271

Preface

John Bradstreet's lengthy and active career has produced a rich harvest of contemporary opinions and historical evaluations, which have been profuse but not overly profound. His activities involved some of the major events and individuals of eighteenth-century Colonial North America. His unbridled ambition, a willingness openly to plead his own case, and penchant for elaborate justification of all his actions were bound to antagonize people. He was a man who constantly sought the rewarding applause of his contemporaries but his aggressive approach invited criticism. He received much of both. Yet, despite the wealth of documentation available, his career has never been carefully examined in a full-length study. Rather, historians have awarded Bradstreet elaborate biographical footnotes, some consideration in biographies dealing with his contemporaries, and reports on his better-known military exploits; but they have left a great deal undone and provided an inadequately sketched figure.

Admittedly the bare outlines of Bradstreet's career are fairly well known. He first emerged during the Louisbourg expedition of 1745 when his significant services to Governor William Shirley of Massachusetts and to the expedition's commander, William Pepperrell, earned him an appointment as lieutenant-governor of St. John's, Newfoundland. This colonial office when combined with his rank in the English army, which he had formally entered as an ensign in 1735, provided the basic foundation to which he hoped to add further colonial and military offices and honours. Despite his Louisbourg contribution, however, Bradstreet faded from view, only to re-emerge in Shirley's Niagara campaign of 1755. During the years of defeat which marked the first phase of the Seven Years' War, Bradstreet's activities and achievements constituted one of the few bright spots in the English military effort. Praised by Shirley and Lord Loudoun,

Bradstreet went on to earn the respect of his later commanders, James Abercromby and Jeffery Amherst. To his misfortune, an impressive record of military service from 1755 to 1763 was to be tarnished by his alleged mishandling, in 1764, of the expedition against Pontiac and by acrimonious wrangles with Thomas Gage and William Johnson. Notwithstanding the achievement of the rank of major-general in 1772, it appeared that for John Bradstreet "after 1764 the way led gently down."[1]

A study of Bradstreet based only on his dealings with these men and events appears to be justifiable and was suggested as worthwhile well over forty years ago.[2] But as his widely scattered correspondence was brought together, it became obvious that a far broader and deeper analysis could be attempted. Specifically, the utilization of his hitherto neglected correspondence with his trusted English confidant and dedicated supporter, Charles Gould, provided a rare insight into the trans-Atlantic connections and manipulations of John Bradstreet. These letters to and from Gould, housed at the National Library of Wales, when linked with the ample but also little-used material on this side of the Atlantic, shed new light on what was already known about the man. Many of the mysteries, obscurities, and unappreciated twists and turns of the "enigmatic Colonel Bradstreet['s]"[3] career finally could be brought into clearer focus. Alison G. Olson has called for studies of "the men who made Anglo-Colonial politics work—the governors, the agents, and colonists who crossed the Atlantic on private business...." Their methods of manoeuvring and their "criteria for success or failure" must be elucidated.[4] As well, "an additional dimension of historical importance" has recently been underlined by David Syrett's introduction to a useful collection of documents revealing "how patronage worked in the British military and naval establishments during the eighteenth century."[5] The problem, of course, as Leland J. Bellot discovered in his study of William Knox, is that often "only meager information" is available on the relationship between patron and client.[6] Such is not the case with Bradstreet. His correspon-

---

1. John Shy, *Toward Lexington: The Role of the British Army in the Coming of the American Revolution* (Princeton, N.J., 1965), 170.
2. See John C. Webster, "Review of *Native Stock: The Rise of the American Spirit Seen in Six Lives*," *Canadian Historical Review*, 13 (1932), 79.
3. John S. McLennan, "Review of *Louisbourg Journals, 1745*," *Canadian Historical Review*, 14 (1933), 206.
4. Alison G. Olson, "Anglo-American Politics, 1675-1775: Needs and Opportunities for Further Study," in Alison G. Olson and Richard M. Brown, eds., *Anglo-American Political Relations 1675-1775* (New Brunswick, N.J., 1970), 5. See also Stanley N. Katz, *Newcastle's New York: Anglo-American Politics, 1732-1753* (Cambridge, Mass., 1968) for an indication of the rewards of such an approach.
5. David Syrett, "The Historical Background," in Marion Balderston and David Syrett, eds., *The Lost War: Letters from British Officers during the American Revolution* (New York, 1975), 4.
6. Leland J. Bellot, *William Knox: The Life and Thought of an Eighteenth Century Imperialist* (Austin, 1977), 54-55. See also Julian Gwyn, *The Enterprising Admiral: The*

dence with Charles and King Gould, Richard Lyttleton, Jeffery Amherst, and others is substantial enough to facilitate a study which uses his career as a vehicle to examine, against the background of deteriorating mother country-colonial relations, the adjustments made and approaches used by trans-Atlantic linchpin figures in enlisting and activating the vitally necessary English patrons.[7]

A detailed treatment of Bradstreet's career and connections has an additional purpose. Like other rootless and ambitious figures, owing their primary allegiance to London while their lives were largely spent in America, he was a man on the periphery of two worlds. An Anglo-Irish-Acadian, neither of the true heartland nor of the new hinterland, Bradstreet was neither English nor American. Yet he repeatedly used his American esteem to bolster his cause in England and employed intimations of powerful friends "at home" in the mother country to awe colonial critics. His success or failure reveals a great deal about the eventual fate of the type of individual he represented, since, on both sides of the Atlantic, suspicions about and hostility towards these administrators and proponents of empire made a substantial contribution to the eventual revolution. Especially in the military sphere, his career provides an acid test of the receptivity and flexibility of the British regular officer corps to those who could be classified as somewhat irregular in social background and military expertise.[8] Moreover, many of his territorial and military schemes concerned Louisbourg, Newfoundland, Quebec, and the Great Lakes country, areas that today appear to be relegated to the periphery of Colonial North American studies. Too many scholars dealing with Colonial Canada limit their work to New France, Acadia, or Nova Scotia while the vision of their American counterparts seems to extend no further than the northern boundaries of Massachusetts and New York. Bradstreet's career can be viewed as a contribution to an early and somewhat neglected chapter in colonial Anglo-Canadian-American relations.

I am deeply indebted to many individuals and institutions for the support and encouragement given to this study. At Mount Allison

---

Personal Fortune of Admiral Sir Peter Warren (Montreal, 1974), 6, who feels the manner in which Peter Warren accumulated his wealth was not exceptional, but the documentation concerning his fortune is exceptional and for this reason alone warrants study.

7. The frequent neglect of trans-Atlantic patron-client relationships is demonstrated in a somewhat deceptively titled dissertation. John C. Guzzardo, "Sir William Johnson's Official Family: Patron and Clients in an Anglo-American Empire, 1742-1777' (Ph.D. dissertation, Syracuse University, 1975), offers a very useful study of Johnson as patron and his clients in New York but presents little substantial evidence or analysis of Johnson's relationship with his own patrons back in England. See Guzzardo, 8, 96-97, 102, and 105.

8. See Peter E. Russell, "Redcoats in the Wilderness: British Officers and Irregular Warfare in Europe and America, 1740 to 1760," *William and Mary Quarterly*, 3d Ser., 35 (1978), 629-52, for a defence of the regular officer corps serving in America. Russell praises many of Bradstreet's commanders and colleagues for their awareness of and willingness to apply irregular, frontier, military tactics. The course of Bradstreet's own career, and fate of many of his suggestions, raises questions about the validity of Russell's contentions.

University, Dean Alexander Fancy and Associate Deans John Read and Paul Bogaard have been consistently supportive, while a generous and timely grant from the Marjorie Young Bell Faculty Fund aided the final preparation for publication. Faithful typist Helen Brown worked above and beyond the call of duty, despite the limited attention given to her native Newfoundland. At Queen's University, Frederick Gibson, Donald Schurman, Klaus Hansen, John Archer, and Roger Graham all contributed to my development as a student of history. At other universities, I must thank Julian Gwyn, Alice Stewart, John Shy, Jack Bumsted, and David Galenson for their help. Archival and library workers on both sides of the Atlantic made my research enjoyable, but the staffs of the William L. Clements Library, the National Library of Wales, and the Public Archives of Canada must be singled out for special praise. My thanks go to Phillip Buckner and *Acadiensis* for permission to use a revised version of an article first published in that journal (vol. 4 [1974]). The original research was made possible by a Canada Council Doctoral Fellowship, while a final check on documentation and the opportunity for further revisions were facilitated by a Canada Council Leave Fellowship. This book has been published with the help of a grant from the Social Science Federation of Canada, using funds provided by the Social Sciences and Humanities Research Council of Canada.

My greatest debt is to George Rawlyk who first suggested John Bradstreet as a potential dissertation topic, supervised my work in a perceptive, constructive, and rewarding fashion, and encouraged the transformation of a bulky thesis into a more manageable manuscript. Like many other graduate students in history who passed through Queen's, any scholarly contribution I may have to offer was brought to fruition by George Rawlyk's stimulating scholarship and friendship. The errors and shortcomings of this work are, of course, my own responsibility. To Myrna, Marc, Evelyne, and Karam, my special thanks for living with this project for so long, perhaps too long.

Abbreviations

A.A.S.	American Antiquarian Society
B. M.	British Museum
C.S.P.	*Calendar of State Papers, Colonial Series, America and West Indies*
H.H.L.	Harvard University, Houghton Library
H.L.	Henry E. Huntington Library
Me.H.S.	Maine Historical Society
M.H.S.	Massachusetts Historical Society
N.L.W.	National Library of Wales
N.S. A.	Nova Scotia A Series
N.S.A.II	Nova Scotia Archives II
N.Y.H.S.	New-York Historical Society
N.Y.P.L.	New York Public Library
N.Y.S.L.	New York State Library
P.A.C.	Public Archives of Canada
P.A.N.S.	Public Archives of Nova Scotia
P.R.O.	Public Record Office
T.P.C.	Tredegar Park Collection
U.M.C.L.	University of Michigan, William L. Clements Library
U.M.G.L.	University of Michigan, Graduate Library

Chapter I

The Bradstreets of Nova Scotia

In March of 1716[1] "Jean Baptiste Bradstreat" was baptized at Annapolis Royal, Nova Scotia. Son of "Sieur Edmon Bradstreat lieutenant de Compagnie et d'Agathe de St Etienne de la Tour," he had been born two years earlier on "le 21 de Decembre 1714."[2] This combination of a Nova Scotia birthplace, an Anglo-Irish army officer as a father, and a member of one of Acadia's most prominent families as a mother would prove a mixed blessing to young Jean-Baptiste. It has, for example, contributed to the historical obscurity surrounding Bradstreet's early years.[3] Bradstreet himself, once his military career was underway, was very reticent about his family background and childhood. The scarcity of his comments on this period of his life might be a clue to his

---

1. The exact date is March 12, 1716. Probably this is Old Style. Except for occasions when French sources are being used, Old Style dates will be used until the English calendar change in 1752.
2. "Registres des Baptimes, mariages et Sepultures de la Parisse de St. Jean Baptiste du Port Royal," 1702-1728, M. G. 9, B. 8, vol. 24-1, 291, Public Archives of Canada, Ottawa. A slightly different version with a more correct spelling of the Bradstreet name, although with the same basic information is found in "French Register at Annapolis Royal, 1702-1728," vol. 26, 139, Public Archives of Nova Scotia, Halifax.
3. Few historians have been as perceptive as Stanley M. Pargellis, ed., *Military Affairs in North America 1748-1765* (New York, 1936), 187n., who suggested that the very active John Bradstreet of the Seven Years' War period "may be identical with that Jean Baptiste Bradstreet" born in 1714. Most scholars fall back upon an earlier biographical sketch, also contributed by Pargellis, contending that Bradstreet "either was born in Nova Scotia" around 1711 "or immigrated at an early age." See Allen Johnson, ed., *Dictionary of American Biography*, 2 (New York, 1929), 578. Examples of this approach are Arthur Pound, "John Bradstreet," in *Native Stock: The Rise of the American Spirit Seen In Six Lives* (New York, 1931), 45; Leonard W. Labaree *et al.*, eds., *The Papers of Benjamin Franklin*, 8 (New Haven, Conn., 1965), 344n.; George A. Rawlyk, *Yankees at Louisbourg* (Orono, Me., 1967), 33. George A. Rawlyk, *Nova Scotia's Massachusetts: A Study of Massachusetts—Nova Scotia Relations 1630-1784* (Montreal, 1973), 149, offers the correct information, as does William G. Godfrey, "John Bradstreet," in Francess G. Halpenny *et al.*, eds., *Dictionary of Canadian Biography*, 4 (Toronto, 1979), 83-87.

embarrassment over the lack of a British birthplace and proper English parentage. A sifting of the evidence available concerning Bradstreet's parents, Edward Bradstreet[4] and Agathe De La Tour, provides a much needed insight into his early years.

It was reported to the Queen of England in October of 1710 that Port Royal and Acadia-Nova Scotia had finally been captured from the French. Francis Nicholson, commander of the Anglo-American expedition, also expressed the hope that such "a vast large dominion as is now most happily added to your Majesty's mighty Empire in America cannot but be judged worthy your Majesty's Royall care and that of your Parliament...."[5] Such was not to be the case. Nova Scotia was to be a much neglected colony over the next few decades. This neglect was especially hard upon the English troops doing garrison duty at Annapolis, "loneliest, dullest, and dreariest of quarters."[6] At this time life in the British army was an extremely harsh experience for the rank and file and the difficulties were compounded in the overseas garrisons.[7] During the years after the conquest of Acadia, chronic complaints were heard from Annapolis about the living conditions endured by the troops stationed there.[8] Like others at this forgotten outpost, Edward Bradstreet was determined to awaken the London authorities to the problems facing the British troops garrisoned there. In consequence his name appeared on several of the memorials and petitions which flowed back to England. He was among those complaining of the small and inadequate allowance the garrison received for "fireing and candle"[9] and arguing the need of adequate provisions as well as full pay for the troops.[10] An acknowledgment of the existence of the Annapolis

---

4. He is referred to as both Edmond and Edward but in the documents bearing his signature which I have examined his name is Edward.

5. Francis Nicholson and the Council of War at Annapolis Royal to the Queen, October 1710, Great Britain, Public Record Office, *Calendar of State Papers, Colonial Series, America and West Indies 1710-June 1711* (London, 1860-19), 25, 245, hereafter cited as C.S.P.

6. John W. Fortescue, *A History of the British Army*, 2 (London, 1910), 45. The standard treatment of Nova Scotia in this period remains John B. Brebner, *New England's Outpost* (New York, 1927).

7. For examinations of the eighteenth-century English army, see Raibeart E. Scouller, *Armies of Queen Anne* (London, 1966); Franklin and Mary Wickwire, *Cornwallis: The American Adventure* (Boston, 1970), 49-78; William A. Foote, "The American Independent Companies of the British Army 1664-1764" (Ph.D. dissertation, University of California, Los Angeles, 1966), 6-47.

8. See, for example, Samuel Vetch to Dartmouth, November 16, 1711, *C.S.P.*, 26, 148-51; John Mulcaster to Council of Trade and Plantations, May 13, 1715, ibid., 28, 179-80; Vetch to Council of Trade and Plantations, February 21, 1715/16, ibid., 29, 25. See also Meeting of February 22, 1715/16, Great Britain Public Record Office, *Journal of the Commissioners for Trade and Plantations From March 1714/5 to October 1718*, 3 (London, 1924), 115.

9. "Copy of Meml. of the Lt. Govr. and other Officers of the Garrison of Annapolis, to Coll. Nicholson, relating to ye Charge of Firing &c.," November 3, 1714, M.G. 11, Nova Scotia A Series/5, 140, P.A.C, hereafter cited as N.S. A.

10. "The Memoriall of the Officers of this your Majesties Garrison of Annapolis Royall in behalf of the Troops under their Command" [1714], ibid., 227-30.

garrison came with the renewal of the officers' commissions in April of 1715, and among the officers listed was "Edward Broadstreet, Lieut."[11] In 1717 a step was taken towards a stronger British presence in Nova Scotia when the independent companies serving at Annapolis, along with those at Placentia, Newfoundland, were formed into Philipps' Regiment of Foot (later the 40th). Bradstreet was to be a lieutenant in the new unit.[12] Shortly thereafter in December of 1718, "after a long lingering sickness," Edward Bradstreet "died in his bed...."[13]

Soon after his arrival at Annapolis, Bradstreet had married into one of the first families of Acadia. Agathe De Saint-Etienne De La Tour was the granddaughter of the well-known Charles De Saint-Etienne De La Tour[14] and was a resident of Port Royal prior to its capture by the British. She had adjusted quite well to the conquest since by 1714 she was married to Edward and had commenced her campaign to become the sole recognized heir to the La Tour lands in Nova Scotia. A signover of land claims to her, which was dated "ce neufvieme novembre mille sept cent quatorze neuaveause Estille," mentioned her husband "Edmond Brastried lieutenant d'une Compagnie dans cette garnison d'Annapolis Royalle." Thus, by November 1714 she was married to Bradstreet, but the same document contains the information that they already had one son. The land was signed over to Agathe and "a son defeaux a son fils Simon Brastried."[15] It would thus appear Jean-Baptiste was the second child of the Bradstreet-La Tour marriage.[16] After the death of Edward, Agathe married again. Her choice was yet another member of the Annapolis garrison, Hugh Campbell, who appears to have died before 1730.[17]

---

11. "Garrison at Annapolis Royal, Nova Scotia, Commissions renewed at St. James' 8 Apr. 1715a," Charles Dalton, *George the First's Army 1714-1719*, 1 (London, 1910), 240. See also "A List of the Officers of Annapolis Royl. belonging to the Four Companys &c.," enclosed in Pulteney to Lords of Trade, July 16, 1715, N.S. A/7, 49.

12. "Colonel Richard Philipps' Regiment of Foot," Dalton, *George the First's Army*, 1, 312; Raymond H. R. Smythies, *Historical Records on the 40th (2nd Somersetshire) Regiment* (Devonport, Eng., 1894), 3. Although it was not until the mid-eighteenth-century that regiments were given numerical designations, Philipps' regiment will be described by its later designation, the 40th.

13. Lawrence Armstrong to the Council of Trade and Plantations, January 14, 1734/35, *C.S.P.*, 61, 353.

14. The genealogy of the family is outlined in Azarie Couillard Després, *Charles de Saint-Etienne de la Tour Gouverneur, Lieutenant-Général en Acadie et son temps 1593-1666* (Arthabaska, Quebec, 1930), 463-65. See also Clarence J. D'Entremont, "Agathe de Saint-Etienne de la Tour," in David M. Hayne and André Vachon, eds., *Dictionary of Canadian Biography*, 2 (Toronto, 1969), 590-91.

15. "Cessions et transports faits à ... Agathe de la Tour," N.S. A/22, 59-60.

16. D'Entremont, "Agathe De Saint-Etienne De La Tour," 590-91, mentioned that she had a son, Jean-Baptiste, by Edmond (Edward) Bradstreet but did not mention Simon.

17. For information about Campbell, see Charles Dalton, ed., *English Army Lists and Commission Registers, 1661-1714*, vol. 6: *1707-1714* (London, 1960), 190-92; James Campbell to James Stanhope, December 6, 1716, N.S. A/8, 41; John Doucett to Richard Philipps, November 5, 1717, ibid., 173-74; Charles Dalton, *George the First's Army 1714-1727*, 2 (London, 1912), 322. In D'Entremont, "Agathe De Saint-Etienne De La Tour,"

By this time Agathe had a well-documented claim to all of the La Tour seigneuries in Nova Scotia and set off for England to have it recognized. Governor Richard Philipps looked with disfavour upon her pretensions, describing her as "a woman, who has been wife to two subaltern Officers of the Regiment." He claimed that by "cunning address" she had persuaded her La Tour relatives "to make over their pretensions to her, on promise of some small consideration, and is goeing over to sollicite in hopes of obtaineing something of the Government in lieu thereof."[18] Agathe proved an undaunted and patient lobbyist and her pleas finally were rewarded in March of 1733/34 when the Board of Trade recommended that she be given £2000 for her seigneurial rights.[19]

In her petitions and supporting documents Agathe Campbell, as she was called in the 1730s, occasionally referred to her children. When matched with other information these references provide evidence concerning the early years of John and Simon Bradstreet. As a suspect Roman Catholic Acadian, Agathe took great pains to emphasize her acceptance of all things British. A 1733 affidavit by Mary Barton, in support of Agathe's land claims, described her as "a constant Communicant of the Church of England." Moreover, she "hath Carefully educated her five children in the same Religion."[20] Unfortunately the five children were not named, so it is uncertain how many bore the Bradstreet name and how many were the product of her second marriage. Acceptance of the Protestant faith was stressed in at least one of Agathe's petitions and, in addition, some further light was shed upon her two eldest children. In the early 1730s Agathe described herself as "a most dutiful and Loyal Subject to the Crown of Great Britain ever since the conquest of the said Province; she having embraced the Principals of the Protestant Religion before her Marriage." Her children were educated in the same religious beliefs and their loyalty was demonstrated by the fact that "her eldest" at "Nineteen Years of age is a Cadet in your Majesty's Service at Pemaquid" while "her Second Son upwards of Seventeen years old is a Cadet at Placentia."[21] This petition is not dated although the supporting affidavits with it were drawn up in June and July of 1733.[22] If the petition was drafted in 1732 or 1733, then her eldest son would have been born in 1713 or 1714, while the birthdate of her second son might be 1715 or 1716. This only roughly

---

590, James and Hugh Campbell are confused and it is stated: "Her second husband was Lieutenant James (Hugh?) Campbell."

18. Philipps to the Council of Trade and Plantations, September 2, 1730, *C.S.P.*, 37, 253.

19. D'Entremont, "Agathe De Saint-Etienne De La Tour," 591.

20. Affidavits of Mary Barton, John Welch, and William Tipton, June 23, 1733, N.S. A/22, 70.

21. "The Petition of Agatha Campbel of Port Royal now Annapolis Royal in your Majty's Province of Nova Scotia in America Widow and Relict of Mr Hugh Campbell late an Ensign in Collo. Philips Regiment there in behalf of her self and her five children" [1732 or 1733?], M.G. 11, C.O. 217/6, 199, microfilm, Reel B-1023, P.A.C.

22. Affidavits of Barton, Welch, and Tipton, ibid., 190-91.

fits Simon and John Bradstreet, although their ages make it clear that both sons were children of her first marriage to Edward Bradstreet.

The mention of the cadet sons' service at Pemaquid and Placentia is revealing. In late 1732, "a party of thirty men with two officers" had been sent from Nova Scotia to assist Colonel David Dunbar's work on Fort Frederick at Pemaquid.[23] One of the detachment was a Bradstreet, since he asked to be replaced and Lieutenant-Governor Lawrence Armstrong promised "an officer to relieve Broadstreet."[24] Quite possibly this was Simon. In the summer of 1733 the fort was evacuated and "the Garrison there posted were returned to Annapolis Royal."[25] Turning to the "Second Son" at Placentia, we find that there is clear evidence that this was John Bradstreet. Listings of the garrison stationed at Placentia, Newfoundland, in September of 1730 and in August of 1731 included among the "Private men" one "John Bradstreet."[26] At about this time it was decided to demolish the Placentia works and erect a new fortification to contain only one company. Thus, "it was thought proper to remove ye other four [companies] that were there, to take Post at Canso, where they remain at this time."[27] This explains why John Bradstreet was not included in the 1732 list;[28] in all probability he had been removed with his company to Canso. Thus the available evidence suggests that the young cadets serving with Philipps' regiment in Nova Scotia and Newfoundland were "Simon Brastried" and "Jean Baptist Bradstreat."

Once Agathe Campbell had received her £2,000 settlement in March 1733/34, she retired to Kilkenny, Ireland.[29] This rather unusual residence, at least for a La Tour, probably was chosen because relatives of her first husband, Edward Bradstreet, resided in the area.[30] One of Mrs. Campbell's first concerns was to arrange that Edward's sons, Simon and John, could follow their father in military careers. Before leaving England for Ireland she mentioned her desire to purchase commissions to King Gould, who had been appointed agent of the 40th Regiment in 1732.[31] Gould also held an appointment as deputy judge

---

23. Armstrong to Lords of Trade, November 15, 1721, N.S. A/21, 110; Col. Dunbar to Popple, August 7, 1733, N.S. A/22, 99.
24. Armstrong to Dunbar, April 21, 1732, Archibald M. MacMechan, ed., *Nova Scotia Archives II: A Calendar of Two Letter-Books and One Commission-Book in the Possession of the Government of Nova Scotia 1713-1743* (Halifax, 1900), 83, hereafter cited as *N.S.A. II.*
25. Dunbar to Popple, August 7, 1733, N.S. A/22, 99.
26. "Copy of the State of the Garrison at Placentia in Capt. Osborne's of September 25, 1730," M.G. 11, C.O. 194/9, 7-8, microfilm, Reel B-210, P.A.C.; "The Establishment and State of the Garrison at Placentia, 10th August, 1731," ibid., 100.
27. Philipps to Lords of Trade, January 24, 1731/32, N.S. A/10, 133.
28. "The State of the Garrison at Placentia," July 22, 1732, C.O. 194/9, 181-82, microfilm, Reel B-210.
29. D'Entremont, "Agathe De Saint-Etienne De La Tour," 591.
30. Land in Kilkenny county had been granted to the Bradstreet family in the era of Oliver Cromwell. For a sketchy summary of the Kilkenny Bradstreets' genealogy, see Bernard Burke and Ashworth P. Burke, *A Geneàological and Heraldic History of the Peerage and Baronetage* ... (London, 1913), 285.
31. Appointment of King Gould as "Lawfull Agent and Attorney..." for Philipps,

advocate-general, from 1723 to 1749, and both he and his son Charles were destined to be important spokesmen for the Campbell-Bradstreet interests in the years ahead. On this particular occasion, the elder Gould was quick to act when the opportunity arose. In November of 1735, he reported to Mrs. Campbell that the King had "sign'd your son Simon Bradstreet's Commission on the 5th of July last."[32] Simon's commission was as an adjutant in Richard Philipps' regiment while that of John, secured shortly thereafter, was in the same regiment but at the rank of ensign. John's appointment was slightly more difficult since the commission Gould had his eye on had been requested for another individual. As a result Gould had to persuade Colonel Philipps to substitute John Bradstreet's name for that of the original nominee. "Colonel Cavalier has been with me in behalf of the other son of Mrs. Campbell whose name is John Bradstreet," Gould explained. Bradstreet "has been a volontier in the Regiment and done Duty as such above 7 years, is about 22 years of age, and is now Doing Duty with the Regiment, and his Father it seems was an Officer in the Same and Dyed abroad which may have some weight with the King."[33] Philipps apparently accepted the substitution and was soon informed by Gould "of the Success of our application for Bradstreet to Succeed Wood as Ensign."[34] Thus were launched the careers in the 40th Regiment of Adjutant Simon Bradstreet, commissioned July 5, 1735, and Ensign John Bradstreet, commissioned August 23, 1735.[35]

At the time of their appointments both Bradstreets were in Nova Scotia; but while there is evidence of Simon's serving at Canso,[36] it is uncertain exactly where John was. Where John desired to be, however, is clear since he quickly wrote Gould requesting that a leave of absence to go to Ireland be arranged. Gould patiently explained the difficulties such a request would meet but so that "you may Spend some few months with your Mother . . . I will take care to get you Excused till the Month of August."[37] As a result John was able to spend the summer and fall of 1736 at his mother's home in Kilkenny. He was still there in late September although Gould had advised him: "you Shou'd go to your Post especially as you have not been there since you have been an officer."[38] Probably John accepted this advice and rejoined his company at Canso, but there is no evidence one way or the other since, over

---

July 22, 1732, Tredegar Park Collection, 49/2, National Library of Wales, Aberystwyth, hereafter cited as T.P.C.; Philipps' contract "with Mr. Gould for the agency of his Regiment," ibid., 103/183.

32. Gould to Mrs. Agathe Campbell, November 1, 1735, T.P.C., MS/285, 65.
33. Gould to Philipps, July 29, 1735, T.P.C., MS/284, 119.
34. Ibid., September 4, 1735, 135.
35. "State of 183 days Net Clearings of Brigadier General Philipp's Regiment from the 25th. June 1735 to the 24 December following Incl.," ibid., 178-79.
36. Simon's name repeatedly appears in "Orders from the 23rd Sept. 1735 given out by Major Paul Mascarene att Canso in Nova Scotia . . ." to December 31, 1735, N.S. A/23, 136-59.
37. Gould to Ensign John Bradstreet, March 2, 1735/36, T.P.C., MS/285, 70.
38. Ibid., July 22, 1736, 81.

the next few years, Gould's letter-books contain no correspondence with John. Judging from the tone of the correspondence with the other members of his family, one reason for John's neglect might be that Gould looked upon him as very much the younger son and considered Simon and Agathe's needs to be of primary importance.

At the request of Mrs. Campbell, Gould wrote to Lieutenant-Governor Armstrong in the spring of 1737 to arrange a leave of absence for Simon Bradstreet.[39] By October of the same year Gould had received word that Simon was at Boston "and going to Embarque for Ireland."[40] Once arrived in Ireland Simon also overstayed his leave, but in this case Gould was far more tolerant. Initially Simon had a good reason for his tardiness, since he was ill during the winter of 1737/38.[41] Then the chore of settling a number of personal matters tied him up. Gould explained his absence to the regimental commander, Philipps, and persuaded him to grant Bradstreet's "Request of Staying sometime longer at Home, upon my Assuring him, the Scituation of your Affairs made it absolutely Necessary for your so Doing."[42]

Mrs. Campbell found Gould equally cooperative on matters not relating to her sons. He sent her the eligibility form for her widow's pension and carefully instructed her on the need to have it sworn before a justice of the peace and accompanied by "a Certificate from the Minister & Church Wardens of the Parish where you are." She was to copy the form, sending one copy to Gould every year, and he could then "receive your Pension" and credit it to her account.[43] As well, Mrs. Campbell had some interests in Scotland to which Gould repeatedly referred, unfortunately in a rather vague fashion.[44] This attention to her interests was, of course, not without a price. Gould would receive the normal agent's commission but, in addition, on occasion he was able to take advantage in other ways of her carefully established personal indebtedness to him. For example, Gould heard that Agathe owned an unoccupied house at Annapolis which, he felt, could be used to store goods he was sending to Nova Scotia. Since she had "no use for it, not intending to return thither any more" he asked her to set a price and he would eagerly purchase it.[45] When Agathe replied that £40 had been offered for the house, Gould told her he could not think of buying at that high a price. While claiming the sale was now out of the question, he went on to describe the house as "quite out of Repair: in a Ruinous condition" and tried to drive the price down.[46] He continued in this vein for several letters arguing that the house was "in a perishing Condition and allmost ready to tumble down," but invariably conclud-

---

39. Gould to Mrs. Campbell, April 14, 1737, T.P.C., MS/285, 90.
40. Ibid., October 5, 1737, T.P.C., MS/284, 217.
41. Gould to Simon Bradstreet, February 20, 1737/38, T.P.C., MS/284, 256.
42. Ibid., June 5, 1738, T.P.C., MS/286, 5.
43. Gould to Mrs. Campbell, November 1, 1735, T.P.C., MS/285, 65.
44. Ibid., April 14, 1737, 90.
45. Ibid.
46. Ibid., October 15, 1737, T.P.C., MS/284, 217.

ing such letters with the reminder that he did not "neglect any opportunity of Serving you or your Sons."[47] In December of 1737 Agathe yielded and received the considerably reduced price of £10, credited to her account, and Gould received her Annapolis home.[48] There is some significance in this transaction because it was more than a case of a good businessman driving a hard bargain. This was an excellent indication of the way Gould operated with many of his clients. He made clear in his letters and in his actions his continuing involvement with the protection of their interests, but eventually the clients could expect that ways and means would be found by which they could be of service to him.

Simon Bradstreet was about to discover how he too could serve King Gould. During Bradstreet's stay in Ireland he asked Gould to arrange the exchange of his adjutant's commission in the 40th for rank as an ensign in another regiment. Gould stressed how hard he tried to fulfill this request, but that his efforts were not blessed with success.[49] It was only after Simon had departed for Nova Scotia that Gould was able to secure him an ensign's commission in the 40th dated March 22, 1739/40.[50] Nevertheless, dedicated lobbying had been carried out and reported to Simon. In return for Gould's efforts Simon was willing to pursue other activities besides his military career upon his return to Nova Scotia. When he rejoined his company at Canso he had the additional chore of handling the trade goods of King Gould. This was revealed in a May 1739 letter from Gould to an officer stationed in Newfoundland. Apparently there had been difficulty selling some of his goods in Newfoundland so Gould advised that they should be shipped "to Mr. Simon Bradstreet at Canso, who is lately gone from hence to that place, and with whom I have agreed for them."[51]

Obviously, by the time both Bradstreets had left their mother in Ireland to return to Nova Scotia, a vital link had been forged with King Gould. This relationship worked both ways. As Agathe Campbell discovered, Gould's interest and concern were tremendously helpful, but at times higher interest than an agent's commission was desired by Gould. So her sons, Simon more so than John at this point, were learning that while Gould would be ever vigilant concerning the advancement of their careers, they in return could further his interests by handling his trade goods at Canso. To rise through the ranks they needed this connection in England while he needed friends in Nova Scotia to market his goods. Aspirations intertwined in what all parties hoped would be a mutually profitable enterprise.

---

47. Ibid., November 25, 1737, 226.
48. Beamish Murdoch, *A History of Nova Scotia or Acadia*, 1 (Halifax, 1865), 525; William A. Calnek and Alfred W. Savary, *History of the County of Annapolis* (Toronto, 1897), 90; Gould to Mrs. Campbell, December 27, 1737, T.P.C., MS/284, 230.
49. Gould to Simon Bradstreet, November 14, 1738, T.P.C., MS/286, 64; ibid., December 16, 1738, 78.
50. Account of Simon Bradstreet, T.P.C., MS/258, 148.
51. Gould to ? Cope, May 3, 1739, T.P.C., MS/286, 143.

This examination of the Bradstreet-Campbell-Gould relationship is of crucial importance if the early Nova Scotia years, and particularly the origins, of John Bradstreet are to be understood. Historians who have touched upon Bradstreet's career have not bothered to clear away the clouds of mystery surrounding these years. Moreover, those who have made brief comments upon this period of his life have confused matters even more by mistakenly linking him with another John Bradstreet who was also in Nova Scotia in the 1720s and 1730s. While all other pieces of the Bradstreet puzzle fall neatly into place, the complete and accurate picture will not emerge until this other John Bradstreet is fitted in. It has been suggested that he was the same Bradstreet who went on to fame at Louisbourg and Frontenac.[52] However, an examination of his activities reveals that this was an entirely different John Bradstreet, although the two men were related.

As early as 1717 he is mentioned as a cadet who had served for several years in Nova Scotia;[53] his military career continued as he gained an ensign's rank in March of 1724/25[54] and then a lieutenant's commission in 1733.[55] At the same time he became quite knowledgeable about the "clandestine trade' between Nova Scotia and Ile Royale, urging the Board of Trade to clamp down on it and being appointed by Philipps at one point to control it.[56] Several times he visited Cape Breton as a representative of the Nova Scotian government to complain about French activities among the Indians and to discuss the return of English deserters who had fled to the island.[57] Service in the 40th Regiment meant Bradstreet depended on King Gould to handle his pay[58] and it is in Gould's detailed accounts kept for the two officers that conclusive evidence is found of two separate John Bradstreets. Bradstreet received an appointment as justice of the peace at Canso in July of 1739 but by December of the same year Richard Philipps

---

52. See Pound, "John Bradstreet," 47; Dalton, *George the First's Army*, 2, 323.

53. Doucett to Philipps, November 5, 1717, N.S. A/8, 174.

54. His commission as ensign was dated March 12, 1724/25. See Dalton, *George the First's Army*, 2, 322.

55. Account of "Ensign John Bradstreet now Lieutenant," T.P.C., MS/257, 69.

56. Philipps to the Council of Trade and Plantations, September 27, 1720, *C.S.P.*, 32, 151; "Proceedings of Hibbert Newton and Capt. Bradstreet ... ," ibid., 34, 419; "Report on Clandestine Trade With Louisbourg," by Hibbert Newton and John Bradstreet, August 30, 1725, Adam Shortt *et al.*, eds., *Documents Relating to Currency, Exchange and Finance in Nova Scotia with Prefatory Documents 1675-1758* (Ottawa, 1933), 158; Meeting of March 24, 1725/26, *Journal of the Commissioners for Trade and Plantations*, 5, 228-29; John Bradstreet to the Council of Trade and Plantations [Mar. 24], 1725/26, C.O. 217/4, 306-307, microfilm, Reel B-1022.

57. Armstrong to St. Ovide de Brouillan, August 12, 1725, *C.S.P.*, 34, 415; "Instructions of Mr. Newton and Capt. Bradstreet on above mission," ibid., 416; "Proceedings of Hibbert Newton and Capt. Bradstreet with the Governor of Cape Breton," August 19, 1725, ibid., 417-19; Frances Conolly to Philipps, September 17, 1728, N.S. A/17, 300-302.

58. See, for example, Account of "Ensign John Bradstreet now Lieutenant," T.P.C., MS/257, 69.

received word that "Mr. John Bradstreet a Lieutenant in the Regiment under my Command Died there the 4th November last."[59]

Bradstreet left a widow and several children at Canso when he died[60] and it is at this point that a linkage with the other John Bradstreet takes place. Because not only were the two men related, in that they were cousins,[61] but Ensign John Bradstreet was to marry the widow of Lieutenant John Bradstreet. Their marriage to the same woman was to confuse considerably the delineation of their respective offspring. It has been suggested that what was in reality Mrs. Mary Bradstreet's second marriage, to the John Bradstreet who eventually was to achieve major-general's rank in the British army, produced four children: Samuel, Agatha, Martha, and Elizabeth.[62] A more plausible explanation is that both Samuel and Elizabeth were the children of Mary's marriage to the Lieutenant John Bradstreet who died in 1739. The whole matter is convincingly clarified by one of the descendants of the lady involved in both marriages. Christopher Aldridge reported that Mary Aldridge had "been married to Lieut. John Bradstreet of the 40th Regt: she had by him a Son, Major Samuel Bradstreet of the 40th and Miss Elizabeth Bradstreet." Left a widow, Mary (Aldridge) Bradstreet married the John Bradstreet destined to become a general in the British army and "two daughters, Mrs. Agatha Buttar and Miss Martha Bradstreet," were the children of this marriage.[63]

Disentangling the Bradstreets of Nova Scotia is a complicated and yet very necessary task. In a sense it merely transforms one of many historical suggestions, a suggestion previously based upon pure speculation, into a positive assertion. Thus there appears conclusive evidence that John Bradstreet was born at Annapolis Royal in 1714 and that the John Bradstreet active in the 1720s and 1730s was an entirely different person. Even more important is the illumination which a knowledge of Bradstreet's background sheds upon the actions and problems of the

---

59. *N.S.A. II*, 179; Murdoch, *A History of Nova Scotia*, 1, 528; Philipps to Sir William Yonge, December 13, 1739, T.P.C., MS/286, 209.

60. Gould to Simon Bradstreet, March 20, 1740/41, T.P.C., MS/286, 277.

61. Gould to Ensign John Bradstreet, July 6, 1736, T.P.C., MS/284, 81. Gould refers to the leave of absence secured for "your Cousin Lieutenant Bradstreet."

62. This is what Benson J. Lossing, the biographer of Philip Schuyler, claims in a note which he signed and dated in Edmund B. O'Callaghan, ed., *Commisary Wilson's Orderly Book: Expedition of the British Army Under Maj. Gen. Jeffery Amherst Against Ticonderoga and Crown Point* (Albany, 1857), 8. This copy is held by the New York State Library at Albany.

63. "A Book containing an account written in the hand of Major Christopher Aldridge, giving information for the benefit of Sir Charles Morgan relating to the financial affairs of the Bradstreet family," c. 1809, T.P.C. 128/1730. For confirmation by an American descendant of Major-General John Bradstreet, see "A Bundle of Old Papers... 1894," Misc. Mss, Taber, 8 and 18, New-York Historical Society, New York City. This American relative, Sydney R. Taber by name, also identifies Mary Aldridge as the wife of both Bradstreets. He states: "The general's wife had previously married his cousin Sir John Bradstreet, Bart. of Ireland, by whom she had two children:—Elizabeth, who became the wife of Peter Livius, a Canadian jurist who is referred to later, and Major Samuel Bradstreet...." Taber is incorrect about the baronetage. The above-mentioned Peter Livius became Chief Justice of the colony of Quebec in 1777.

man in his later career. Service in a regiment which was stationed in a neglected colony gave him a taste of the life of a regular in the British army. In addition, the frontier conditions of Nova Scotia prepared Bradstreet for the irregularities and special problems found in the North American service. An awareness of the way in which the British army operated was balanced by a first-hand experience of frontier necessities. His later success in meeting the transportation problems of the army in the American theatre and in working with the irregular bateau-men of New York undoubtedly derived in part from his Nova Scotia experience. On the other hand, his Acadian-Nova Scotian background could have been a real liability to his future career. It becomes clear that Bradstreet was not regarded as a colonial American and yet he never won full acceptance as an "Englishman" either. On several occasions his English colleagues in arms frowned upon his colonial approach. New Englanders, in at least one instance, suspected him of French sympathies, no doubt because of his mother and his French contacts at Louisbourg. There are other examples of a lack of cooperation on the part of the colonials simply because he was regarded as another condescending English regular officer. Caught between two stools, Bradstreet downgraded or ignored his Nova Scotia background and spoke with repetitious rapture of his friends "at home" in England. But realizing that, at times, a colonial expertise could help his cause, he was not above stressing his American experience and friends as well. Throughout his career Bradstreet was to emphasize alternately his English connections or the colonial esteem he claimed to enjoy, depending upon which suited his immediate needs. But the Acadian background and Nova Scotia birth were never mentioned.[64] Yet it was probably these which most profoundly influenced John Bradstreet. It was a somewhat intangible legacy, but the La Tour spirit of adventure and aggressive opportunism, so evident in his mother Agathe De La Tour, were to shape and animate his entire career.

---

64. A similar case of reluctance to reveal his antecedents for fear of jeopardizing his career is found in J. F. W. DesBarres. See Geraint N. D. Evans, *Uncommon Obdurate: The Several Public Careers of J. R. W. DesBarres* (Toronto, 1969), 3n.

Chapter II

Emergence at Louisbourg

At first glance service in the Canso garrison of Richard Philipps' 40th Regiment does not seem the most advantageous way to build a successful military career. Yet both Simon and John Bradstreet, each in a quite different fashion, were to reap considerable benefit from the years spent at this declining fishing village. With good reason both men, by the winter of 1740/41, were reluctant to leave their Canso posting. King Gould confidently assured Simon that "You nor your Brother need not be under any Apprehension of your being removed from Canso as it is both your desires to stay there, I will mention it to Govr. Cosby as You desire."[1] These early years of the 1740s were to bring Simon the financial resources and loyalty of "friends at home" which combined to achieve his rapid rise in the British army.[2] These were also profitable years for John in monetary terms, but his indiscretions and failure to appreciate and utilize properly his old-world "friends" prevented him from achieving higher military rank. However, where influential words were lacking, dramatic actions might be substituted. The years at Canso provided John with a knowledge of "fortress Louisbourg" which could prove of immense value in the event of a French-English war. This expertise, and the military accomplishments it facilitated, were to be the key to his fame and fortune.

In the mid-1730s great importance was attached to the revenues produced by the booming fishery in the Canso area. In addition Canso was thought to be "the key to this part of North America,"[3] functioning as a barrier to French ambitions in Nova Scotia. Within a few years,

---
1. Gould to Simon Bradstreet, March 20, 1740/41, T.P.C., MS/286, 278, N.L.W.
2. See ibid. for an example of Gould's concern.
3. Armstrong to Council of Trade and Plantations, December 8,1735, *C.S.P.*, 62, 133.

however, it became clear that both the economic and military positions of Canso were on the verge of total deterioration. Captain Peter Warren, in 1739, described "the English Fishery at Canceaux" as "much decayed, in proportion to the improvement and increase of the French Fishery within these Ten Years past." Warren felt the vastly expanded French fishery was causing the shrinkage of the undefended, and thus easily intimidated, English fishery.[4] There were, of course, many other factors involved in the wastage of the Canso fishery: the poor quality of the fish, the migratory habits of the cod, the change caused by direct operations from New England ports such as Marblehead and Gloucester. In addition, a report on the fishery in 1741 pointed out that "Before the Warr with Spain, the Fish was generally carried to the Different parts of that Kingdom," but with this market closed off only the West Indies and New England were left open for the sale of the fish.[5] Loss of this important market must have been a damaging blow to the Canso fishery.

In terms of defences, Canso had never been fortified properly. Lieutenant-Governor Armstrong urged the construction of adequate fortifications in 1735,[6] but no action was taken. Four years later, Peter Warren described the "*Garrison at Canseaux* if it can be called so" as "in a *most miserable condition*, not One Gun Mounted, nor a Barrack fit for a soldier to live in, there are now there Four Companies of Thirty Men each."[7] In addition to the one hundred and twenty soldiers, some of whom had their families with them at Canso, there was a handful of families who resided there permanently. In 1739 it was estimated that there were nine or ten such families,[8] while in 1741 there were "at present but four Familys in Canso besides the Troops."[9] This population was swollen during the summer fishing season when the New Englanders arrived. In 1742, for example, there were 25 sloops and schooners, all from New England, involved in the Canso fishery. These boats were manned by a total of 119 men.[10]

Despite the small population, the shrinking fishery, and the miserable state of the troops, there were various profitable enterprises possible at Canso. As early as 1734 there was evidence of at least two such operations. It was reported that residents did not want for taverns

---

4. "A State of the French Fishery at Cape Bretoon in June 1739," by Peter Warren, July 9, 1793, C.O. 218/8, 49, microfilm, Reel B-1024, P.A.C.

5. "Queries and Answers relating to the Trade and Fishery at Canso, and parts adjacent in Nova Scotia," in Burrish to Hill, November 24, 1741, N.S. A/25, 146, P.A.C.

6. Armstrong to Council of Trade and Plantations, September 17, 1735, *C.S.P.*, 62, 65.

7. "A State of the French Fishery at Cape Bretoon in June 1739," by Peter Warren, July 9, 1739, C.O., 217/8, 49, microfilm, Reel B-1024, P.A.C.

8. "Letter from Captn Temple West... inclosing his Answer to ye Heads of Enquiry (sent him in April last) concerning the Fishery at Canceau for this year 1739," ibid., 54.

9. "Queries and Answers relating to the Trade and Fishery at Canso...," in Burrish to Hill, November 24, 1741, N.S. A/25, 145.

10. "State of the Cod Fishery at Canso for the Year 1742," in Burrish to Hill, December 22, 1742, ibid., 259.

since "there are five or six in Canso, four of which are kept by the four serjeants of the companies."[11] Moreover, when the naval captain assigned the task of reporting on Canso's fishery and trade pressed the commander of the troops stationed there concerning another activity, the answer received was so defensive as to raise the possibility, and probability, of another more illicit operation. Captain Charles Cotterell asked Captain Christopher Aldridge, future father-in-law of John Bradstreet, about trading activities of the officers under his command. Aldridge replied brusquely "that he did not know that any Captn. of a ship of warr had any business with the officers there, if at home they had suspition of their trading why did not their commanding officers send them orders as they thought proper on that occasion."[12] Apparently trade and the Canso garrison's needs were sufficiently lucrative to provoke evasive responses from those stationed at the post.

At this time, thoughts of providing the isolated garrisons of Nova Scotia "with Necessarys" were very much on the mind of King Gould, agent of the 40th Regiment in London. In 1734 and 1735 he was trying to work out a provisioning scheme with Samuel Cottnam and William Shirreff, residents of Annapolis Royal, Nova Scotia. In a long letter, written in June of 1735, he thanked them "for your Interesting yourselves in my Proposal of Supplying the Garrisons with Necessarys" and outlined his plan. Gould proposed that "every Gentleman" wanting supplies should let him know this year what he wanted for the following year. Gould would then "Consider where and in what Country those goods can be bought Cheapest" and purchase them himself. To ship them to Nova Scotia, he continued:

> We know that there are men of War sent every Year to Canso, and perhaps the next Year I may desire my Friend who is a Member of Parliament to ask for that Station, which he wou'd do purely to Serve me, and my Brother may be his Lieutenant; But besides if this Don't take, We shall be able by Cloathing & Recruits, which will be wanting every year, to make a Cargo for a Small Vessell Directly to Annapolis, and if I find this Scheme upon a Tryal of a Year or Two turn out to advantage. I wou'd have a vessell of my own, which I wou'd keep on purpose for this Service, and to take in a Loading of Fish at Canso for the Streights or other Parts where I can always by Merchants here who have Obligations to me, have the Preference of a Loading of Merchandize Directly to London.

To complete the scheme an agent was required in Boston since there were "some Commoditys which perhaps are to be had nowhere so Cheap as at N:E:."[13] Two years later an arrangement was worked out with Christopher Kilby, a Boston merchant, whereby the "Gentlemen

---

11. Charles Cotterell to Council of Trade and Plantations, April 23, 1734, *C.S.P.*, 61, 396.

12. Ibid., 397. For further information about Aldridge, see William G. Godfrey, "Christopher Aldridge Sr.," in Frances G. Halpenny et al., *Dictionary of Canadian Biography*, 3 (Toronto, 1974), 8-9.

13. Gould to William Shirreff and Samuel Cottnam, June 1, 1735, T.P.C., MS/285, 61; Gould to Cottnam, August 8, 1734, T.P.C., MS/285, 42.

of Nova Scotia" were to be supplied "with such Necessarys as they may want from thence."[14]

While the trade does not appear to have developed into a lucrative enough proposition to justify Gould's arranging a vessel solely concerned with it, it must have turned a reasonable profit, since his letter-books reveal a continuing involvement and interest until the early 1740s. At Annapolis Royal, Shirreff emerged with the major responsibility for handling Gould's goods. Canso was a problem, however, because of the short sojourn of many officers there. Taking advantage of his friendship with the former Canso commandant, Captain Christopher Aldridge, who was then in England, Gould wrote in March of 1737/38 to Aldridge's son, Lieutenant Christopher Aldridge, at Canso, asking him to oversee goods which were soon to arrive. Gould explained that "yr. Father giving me Encouragement, I have taken the Liberty to Consign those goods to you, and desire you will dispose of them to ye best Advantage for my Interest and be pleas'd to Charge Commission for yr. trouble, and make me as quick remittances as you can."[15] This was only a temporary arrangement and Gould seemed quite relieved when Simon Bradstreet, a person far better known to him, took up his Canso posting in the spring of 1739.

Over the next few years Gould repeatedly expressed his enthusiastic appreciation for Simon Bradstreet's careful handling of the wine, linens, and other goods consigned to him.[16] His letters to Simon invariably included this sort of comment: "As to the Sale of the Wines and all of the other Matters You have done for me I am very well Satisfied that thou art a very honest fellow; And one of the best the Country Affords." Naturally, these same letters stressed that Gould missed no opportunity of getting Simon "preferr'd." Personal advice was also directed to Simon. Gould counselled: "Pray be a good Oeconomist and get out of Debt as soon as you can, and be sure not to Marry in the Country if you are that way Dispos'd We can get you a Girl here with some Crop and I'm sure You'll meet with none there."[17] By the time he left Canso to return to England in the fall of 1742, Simon probably had accumulated a store of "obligations" as well as a reasonable financial state, both of which could now be drawn upon. He had served Gould well and Gould would now serve him.

In the same period Gould's correspondence with Simon's younger brother, John, who was also at Canso, has a quite different tone. While Simon appears to have confined himself to marketing Gould's goods within Nova Scotia, John was very much involved in the illegal New England trade with Louisbourg and was developing business connections in New England rather than Old England. As a result, the ties

---

14. Gould to Christopher Kilby, April 6, 1737, T.P.C., MS/285, 89.
15. Gould to Lieutenant Christopher Aldridge, March 4, 1737/38, T.P.C., MS/284, 252; Gould to Shirreff, March 4, 1737/38, T.P.C. MS/284, 251-52.
16. Gould to Simon Bradstreet, March 15, 1739/40, T.P.C., MS/284, 229; March 20, 1740/41, T.P.C. MS/286, 278; and March 15, 1741/42, T.P.C., MS/287, 68.
17. Ibid., March 20, 1740/41, T.P.C., MS/286, 278.

between Gould and himself were weakened considerably. John relied on Gould to collect his pay and subsistence allowance and sort out his credits or debts with other officers serving in Nova Scotia, and that was the extent of their business dealings. Even in performing these limited tasks there was a noticeably uncooperative and critical attitude revealed in some of Gould's comments. Gould was disturbed by a letter received from John concerning "the Payment of a Fire and Candle Bill drawn by Captain Mitford in your favour from the 25th of August 1742." He felt the request was "not altogether so reasonable, as I might expect from you" since the fire and candle payment would not be received from the War Office until Christmas of 1743. If in the interval, as it was now March of 1741/42, Philipps should die, Gould ran the risk of losing "every farthing of it, for another Agent wou'd be appointed and receive the Money." Despite his reservations, in this instance Gould agreed to accept the bill.[18] On another occasion, however, he was even more scathing in his criticism and refused outright Bradstreet's bill. This second incident concerned money owed Bradstreet by Lieutenant William Strahorn of Canso. Strahorn was in debt to Bradstreet and arranged that his subsistence pay and any favourable balance in his account should be paid to Bradstreet by Gould.[19] This agreement was made in October of 1741 but by the following spring Strahorn had died. Bradstreet then drew up a bill "upon the Pay and Arrears of Lieutenant Strahorn in favour of Francis Borland." A very upset Gould declined to honour it, explaining: "I am Surprized at your Request, for you must know or might have been inform'd if you had asked the Question, that what is due to a Deceased person cannot be legally paid without an Administration." Gould concluded the letter with two further interesting remarks. Firstly, since Simon was coming to England in the fall of 1742 he would do nothing about seeking letters of administration concerning Strahorn's pay until the elder brother arrived and advised "what will be proper to be done." Secondly, in answer to anxiety expressed by Bradstreet, Gould assured him: "As To your preferment you need not be under any Apprehension of any Injustice being done you by Sir Your most humble Servant."[20] Clearly Gould continued to regard Simon as very much the senior Bradstreet in all matters. In addition, John's apprehensions concerning his chance of promotion by means of Gould's influence were probably quite valid. Somehow he had drifted away from his English contact and would suffer for it.

Because of the limited amount of evidence available it is difficult to explain the gap which was opening between John Bradstreet and King Gould. It might have been a natural result of Gould's tendency to regard Simon's advancement as his primary concern. No doubt the ill-considered and risky bills submitted by John also helped to sour the relationship. But on one of the few occasions when Gould wrote to

---

18. Gould to John Bradstreet, March 15, 1741/42, T.P.C., MS/287, 67-68.
19. William Strahorn to Gould, October 25, 1741, T.P.C., 128/400.
20. Gould to John Bradstreet, August 10, 1742, T.P.C., MS/287, 124.

Bradstreet in a very personal vein, there is a clue concerning what might have been the root cause of the disenchantment. Rumours of John Bradstreet's involvement in illicit trading activities had been carried across the Atlantic and caused Gould to write:

> I cannot conclude this Letter without giving you my thoughts upon your being Engag'd in Trade; as it may at one time or other be of Dangerous Consequence to you, and very probably by some ill natur'd person, be a complaint against you: several complaints of this kind have lately been made of Officers in the Army, as well as those in the Navy, which has been mentioned in Parliament and not long since: an Officer who was Tryed here upon several Articles Exhibited against him; and it appearing upon the Tryal that he had been concerned in Trade, altho' it was not one of the Articles Alledged against him; The King taking notice of it in the Proceedings; Order'd him to be Suspended, Declaring his mind that he should look upon every Officer engag'd in Trade as a Peddlar.... What I mentioned above about Trade, keep to your self and don't think that I have any other meaning then Guarding you against those who don't wish you well. And as soon as you can Conveniently wind up your Bottom Knock off.[21]

Several points should be made about this letter. Apparently Gould did not regard the activities of Simon Bradstreet as trading ventures, but merely as the sale of his products for cash or credit. He seemed to view this as a legitimate enterprise. Furthermore, one would have to surmise that Simon did not become involved in the illegitimate activity of trading since no such warning was penned for his benefit. It appears that John alone of the two brothers was involved in "trade." Moreover, when Gould spoke of "trade" to an officer stationed at Canso, Nova Scotia, it can be assumed almost automatically that he was referring to the trade with the fortress in the French colony of Ile Royale, Louisbourg. The nature of the trade and the participants in it must be carefully established because historians, such as Guy Frégault and J. S. McLennan, have been unaware that the Canso base was used by more than one Bradstreet for more than one purpose. Both these scholars employ the same French sources in discussing the Louisbourg trade of the early 1740s. Since these sources only mention a Bradstreet, albeit misspelled, who was a British officer at Canso without specifying any first name, they do the same. Thus, they consider the trade, but can only say it was conducted by an officer named Bradstreet.[22] This could have been either Simon or John, but Gould's letter and the implications it contains can be used to establish John Bradstreet as the Louisbourg trader. Further evidence for awarding this dubious distinction to John, rather than Simon, can be found in the Louisbourg officials' discussion of their English contact at Canso in 1743, after Simon left and John remained. In addition, Simon's obvious lack of first-hand knowledge concerning Louisbourg was to be demonstrated in 1744.

---

21. Ibid., March 15, 1741/42, 68.
22. Guy Frégault, *Francois Bigot: Administrateur Francais*, 1 (Montreal, 1948), 143; John S. McLennan, *Louisbourg from its Foundation to its Fall* (London, 1918), 103.

It is not surprising that documentation concerning this New England trade with Louisbourg is far from plentiful. For the British subjects involved in it there were considerable profits to be gained, but there were also the risks of confiscation by over-zealous British naval officers or, worse yet, damaged reputations if full disclosure of the extent of the trade and the names of participants should leak out. On the other hand, because this trade was essential to Ile Royale, the French were reasonably open about its existence. The colonial authorities, both at home and in Louisbourg, even were willing to give official approval to the importation of certain products.[23] Nevertheless, despite their acknowledgment of the trade, it is too much to expect that the French records would list every trading transaction with New England and the name of every visiting trader. Thus, there is only one detailed description of a trading visit by Bradstreet, in 1741, although the tone of the report on his activities leaves the impression that he was well known at Louisbourg, possibly because of numerous unrecorded visits. Bradstreet, at least initially, was in good company in taking advantage of this profitable enterprise. In 1737, for example, that respected British naval officer, Peter Warren, arranged with Peter Faneuil, successful Boston merchant, to ship a cargo of foodstuffs to Louisbourg.[24] Two years later Nova Scotia's Lieutenant-Governor Armstrong sent a schooner loaded with flour to Louisbourg. Along with it came a letter asking the Ile Royale authorities "de permettre la vente des ces farines pour payer des provisions dont il avoit besoin."[25] Where Bradstreet perhaps overstepped the line was in the extent and the timing of his trade.

In October of 1741 Du Quesnel, Governor of Ile Royale, reported the arrival from Canso of "le Sieur Brastrit," whom he described as a relative "de plusieurs officiers icy." These undoubtedly were La Tours related to his mother. Du Quesnel continued that he made the visitor very welcome and, with the agreement of Bigot, gave permission to Bradstreet "de vendre la goelette dans laquelle il est venu." This money was then used to purchase rum and molasses and "d'affreter un batteau pour emporter a Canceau avec luy les effets qu'il a achetés."[26] Du Quesnel estimated that in total Bradstreet spent over two thousand crowns.[27] The following year this entire transaction with "Sr. Brastrie officier de la garrison de Canceau" was approved of by Maurepas.[28] Admittedly, mention of the relatives and the warm welcome is not clear evidence establishing that Bradstreet was well known at Louisbourg and a frequent visitor. Yet, when coupled with Gould's letter, written in

---

23. Frégault, *Francois Bigot*, 1, 95.
24. Julian Gwyn, "Money Lending in New England: The Case of Admiral Sir Peter Warren and His Heirs 1739-1805," *New England Quarterly*, 64 (1971), 120.
25. Forant and Bigot to Maurepas, November 9, 1739, M.G. 1 Series C¹¹B/21, 18-19, P.A.C.
26. Du Quesnel to Maurepas, October 19, 1741, M.G. 1, Series C¹¹B/23, 64.
27. See ibid. Du Quesnel said that "il a laissé icy plus de deux mil escus en argent."
28. Maurepas to Du Quesnel, June 6, 1742, M.G. 1, Archives des Colonies, Series B/74, part 3, 559-60, P.A.C.

winter a few months later, perhaps it is a useful hint. Surely Gould would not write Bradstreet such a lengthy warning purely on the basis of one visit to Louisbourg. There must have been other equally elaborate trading visits which explain Gould's sermon and Du Quesnel's report.

Furthermore, the elaborate scale of Bradstreet's operation at Louisbourg is rather obvious. Selling a boat and returning laden with goods from the French fortress was no minor trading venture. It was business on a large scale and revealed that Bradstreet's finances had advanced considerably beyond the level normally associated with a lowly ensign in the British army. Equally obvious were the excellent contacts he enjoyed through relatives. Perhaps also there were individuals at Louisbourg who regarded Bradstreet as an excellent contact with the New England market. In June of 1742 Bigot found provisions running low at Louisbourg and made arrangements for an English vessel to sail to New England to purchase supplies. This effort involved cooperation with a Canso contact, since Bigot mentioned the individual entrusted with this task "a associé a son voyage un anglais de cancau moyennant quoi j'espere qu'il ne sera pas confisqué."[29] Both J. S. McLennan and Guy Frégault surmise the Canso connection to be Bradstreet,[30] and this seems a reasonable assumption. Again in August of 1743 when Louisbourg supplies were in a depleted state, Bigot dispatched Du Vivier to Canso "pour engager quelques anglais conus a partir pour baston" and mentioned an officer at Canso with whom various arrangements concerning provisions were usually made.[31] Once more, there is a good possibility that this was John Bradstreet.

It is rather ironic that as late as 1743 goods still were moving through Canso to Louisbourg since within a few short months, in May of 1744, Canso was to be the first target hit and captured by the Louisbourg French. This time factor should be considered carefully because it ties in with the indiscretion of John Bradstreet. To be involved in the Louisbourg trade in the late 1730s was not nearly as risky as it had become by 1742 and 1743. The early 1740s were the correct time, as King Gould had put it, to "wind up your Bottom" and "Knock off." In view of the deteriorating relations between England and France it was simply not the proper time to trade with someone against whom you soon would be warring. In the eyes of the Old World it was a time to clamp down on clandestine trade, not expand it. Thus, the continued linkage of Bradstreet with this sort of activity could only hurt him. It seems at best indiscreet, at worst foolhardy, for him to have allowed any hint to surface concerning his continuing involvement. But Bradstreet was in a real sense a citizen of two worlds. What looked like an indiscretion in Old England, and severely undermined any chance of promotion in the British army, was still an acceptable practice in New England

---

29. Bigot to Maurepas, June 18, 1742, C¹¹B/24, 90.
30. McLennan, *Louisbourg*, 103; Frégault, *Francois Bigot*, 1, 143.
31. Bigot to Maurepas, August 12, 1743, C¹¹B/25, 112-13.

and continued to be a profitable undertaking despite the risks involved. As the two mother countries moved towards hostilities, instead of the number of New England ships trading at Louisbourg declining, it actually was increasing. While forty-nine ships arrived at Louisbourg in 1739 from New England and Acadia, there were sixty-seven in 1742, and in 1743 this number increased to seventy-eight.[32] Bradstreet might have been out of touch with British feelings concerning the Louisbourg trade, but this was because he was too much attuned to New England aspirations and actions in relation to dealings with the French. Of course there were individuals and groups in New England who already regarded Louisbourg as a menace,[33] but if war broke out between England and France and Louisbourg was revealed or portrayed as a serious threat to New England, Bradstreet could adjust quickly to this change by turning his knowledge of the fortress acquired during the trading visits into a vital asset to be used against the French. Indeed, he might use the emerging New England antagonism towards Louisbourg to bolster his position in the colonies and to restore his credibility and reputation in the mother country.

As the winter of 1743/44 set in, the Canso post, at which Bradstreet was still stationed, remained as vulnerable to military attack as Peter Warren had found it in 1739. It still had "no Guns mounted no Batterys no Caste no Shot no Baracks."[34] The four companies stationed there were under strength, numbering only eighty-seven "poorly armed and badly trained" soldiers.[35] When the element of surprise is added to the garrison's ill-prepared condition, since word of a state of war between Britain and France had not even reached Canso, it is easy to understand how the French attack on this post, in May of 1744, resulted in its quick surrender. Among the officers and men captured by the French force was Ensign John Bradstreet. But even as the articles of capitulation were being drawn up, the position of Bradstreet as no ordinary English officer was emerging. His schooner had been captured and in the capitulation terms it was immediately pressed into service. The residents of Canso were promised "tout ce qui luy appartiendra et a lad Garnizon leur restra il sera chargé dans la goelette du Sr. Jean Brastreck" and transported to Louisbourg.[36] It was the first of a series of tasks assigned Bradstreet and his schooner which transformed the next few months from a captivity to a business-as-usual situation, at least for him, if not for his captured colleagues.

---

32. See chart, "Shipping of L'Ile Royale" in McLennan, *Louisbourg*, 382.
33. For an analysis of the Massachusetts perception of Louisbourg in the mid-1740s, see Samuel E. D. Shortt, "Conflict and Identity in Massachusetts: The Louisbourg Expedition of 1745," *Social History*, 5, (1972), 165-85.
34. Robert Young to Board of Trade, December 6, 1743, N.S. A/26, 54.
35. Rawlyk, *Yankees at Louisbourg*, 5. The background of the Canso attack as well as the entire Louisbourg campaign are given detailed attention in Rawlyk's study.
36. "Copies des articles de Capitulation accordée par M. Duchambon à M. Patrick Heron...," $C^{11}B/25$, 45.

In June 1744 a shortage of food caused the Louisbourg officials to put out feelers to Governor William Shirley about an exchange of prisoners. Such an arrangement would remove the burden of feeding the Canso captives, among whom were included wives and children as well as soldiers, and strengthen Louisbourg, since French troops imprisoned in Massachusetts would be gained in return. John Bradstreet was to sail to Boston and deliver Governor Du Quesnel's letter suggesting such an exchange. In addition, Bradstreet was instructed by his fellow officers to inform Major Christopher Aldridge, who was once more the Canso commandant although absent at the time of its capture, of the "State and Condition of the men that remains here." In the event of Aldridge's absence Bradstreet was to acquaint Governor Shirley with their food needs, which was their major problem.[37] Along with Bradstreet's schooner went another boat under a flag of truce, manned by "five Men-prisoners" and carrying some of the wives and children captured at Canso. Entrusted to Bradstreet's care were "Major Aldridge's Wife and family, and fourteen lame incurable Soldiers of the Canso Companies."[38]

Both boats arrived safely at Boston by July 6, but it was to be roughly a month and a half before Bradstreet completed his assignment and left Boston to return to Louisbourg. The delay was caused by Governor Shirley's suspicions about which side really would benefit from an exchange of prisoners, as well as his reluctance to meet the request of the captured Canso officers to arrange provisions for themselves, the troops, and their families at Louisbourg. The latter was resolved in mid-July when the Massachusetts Council approved a list of provisions which were to be purchased and transported to Louisbourg by John Bradstreet. However, these were intended only "for the Subsistence of the English officers and their familys."[39] No supplies were arranged for the remainder of the troops because Shirley felt it to be "an unprecedented and dangerous thing to supply 'em with provisions in the Enemy's Country where there is a scarcity of Provisions for the support of the Inhabitants & what would probably prevent their being releas'd before the Term of their Capitulation was expir'd."[40] The Governor was also very suspicious of the suggested prisoner exchange. While he wanted to secure the release of the English troops at Louisbourg so that they could serve at Annapolis Royal, he did not want to waste his French prisoners on an exchange which might secure only aged and infirm soldiers, and women and children. He therefore spelled out in detail to Du Quesnel the types of exchanges he could accept. To begin

---

37. Patrick Heron, Thomas Prendergast, Christopher Aldridge Jr., and Samuel Cottnam to Ensign John Bradstreet, June 19, 1744, N.S. A/26, 101.
38. William Shirley to Duke of Newcastle, July 7, 1744, Charles H. Lincoln, ed., *Correspondence of William Shirley*, 1 (New York, 1912), 132.
39. "An Account of Provisions Mr. Bradstreet desires for the Officers and Families that were taken at Canso," N.S. A/26, 122-23.
40. Shirley to Lords of Trade, July 25, 1744, Lincoln, *Shirley Correspondence*, 1, 136.

with he made it clear that the "invalid Soldiers and five old Cripples" the Ile Royale governor had already sent could not be exchanged for "an equal Number of able bodied Men taken upon our Coasts in the Actual Commission of Hostilities, who are Prisoners for the whole Continuance of the War." Likewise no exchange should be expected for the women and children who, in any case, "would have been a Charge and Inconvenience to you." What Shirley proposed was that the ninety French prisoners of war he possessed be exchanged for all the Canso officers, men, and other English prisoners. Admitting that "you have a greater Number of English Prisoners than I have of French," Shirley promised to make good the difference as soon as more French captives were brought in or secured from Rhode Island. He then went on to discuss variations of this plan but in all cases it was made clear he was willing to give up his prisoners only for the able-bodied Canso officers and men.[41]

Should Du Quesnel agree with Shirley's proposals, he was to send word "by Mr. Bradstreets Schooner or any other Vessel that you shall choose."[42] But for Bradstreet to return with Du Quesnel's comments, he first had to get back to Louisbourg, and this posed a bit of a problem because of Shirley's hard-nosed bargaining over prisoners. Bradstreet had expected that French prisoners exchanged for the English he had brought from Louisbourg "would be able to carry the Vessell back again,"[43] but Shirley felt compelled to give up only three of his French prisoners,[44] whom he probably regarded as the exchange for the five able-bodied men who had manned the boat accompanying Bradstreet under a flag of truce. As a result Bradstreet found himself "without Sailors suffishent to Navegate the Vessell back againe" and requested permission "to ship two hands on board said Vessell as English Marinours."[45] The New England delays were not repeated at Ile Royale. A little over a month later, on September 21, there arrived at Boston the Canso officers and men, "with other prisoners of War to the amount of 340 from Louisbourg in Three Flaggs of Truce."[46] The problem of provisions must have dictated Du Quesnel's speedy acquiescence with the terms of exchange offered by Shirley. But while the French governor's quick answer limited Bradstreet's Louisbourg stay on this occasion to only a matter of a few weeks, and Bradstreet had passed more of his "Louisbourg captivity" on the high seas and at Boston than at Louisbourg, he was very aware of conditions in the French fortress at this time. When this awareness was linked with his

---

41. Shirley to Du Quesnel, July 26, 1744, vol. 12, doc. #24, P.A.N.S.
42. Ibid.
43. John Bradstreet to Shirley, August 14, 1744, "Baxter Papers," *Documentary History of the State of Maine*, 11 (Portland, Me., 1908), 300.
44. Shirley to Du Quesnel, July 26, 1744, vol. 12, doc. #24, P.A.N.S.
45. John Bradstreet to Shirley, August 14, 1744 "Baxter Papers," *Documentary History of... Maine*, 11, 300.
46. Shirley to Lords of Admiralty, September 22, 1744, M.G. 12, A, Adm. 1/3817, n.p., microfilm, Reel B-2987, P.A.C.

knowledge of Ile Royale accumulated over the years during his several visits,[47] it converted him from a message bearer to a knowledgeable advisor of the Massachusetts governor, William Shirley.

The very day the returned prisoners reached Boston, two of them provided Shirley with a written report concerning activities at Louisbourg. Lieutenant George Ryal, who ironically had been left at Canso with a sloop in the summer of 1743 to cut off the illegal trade, and Ensign John Bradstreet, former participant in said trade, gave an account of a fleet recently arrived at Louisbourg which included a number of East India merchant ships and other well-armed vessels.[48] Naturally the presence of such French naval strength at Louisbourg was quite alarming to Shirley. It meant that the remaining British post in Nova Scotia, Annapolis Royal, was in a precarious position; it easily could be bottled up and captured by such a fleet, and, even worse, Boston and New England shipping could be threatened and harassed. Shirley had the consolation of knowing that the fleet was to depart for France in October or November, but it was clear that, if Louisbourg continued to be used by the French as a powerful naval centre, it was a serious threat to the New England colonies. The immediate response by the Massachusetts governor was to make every effort to guarantee that Annapolis would not fall. But obviously the best protection for Annapolis, and indeed for all New England, was the capture of Louisbourg.[49]

Shirley passed this "Intelligence" concerning Louisbourg on to the admiralty office in England, describing Bradstreet and Ryal as "both Competent Judges in the Matters contain'd in their inclosed Information."[50] One of these "Competent Judges," John Bradstreet, was quick to detect the drift of Shirley's mind as well as New England's increasing apprehension about Louisbourg. In December 1744, if Bradstreet's own journal of the Louisbourg campaign can be trusted, he had drafted and presented to Shirley a plan for an attack on the French stronghold.[51] The general proposal for an attack on Louisbourg had been in the air for a number of years, but considerable credit for the

---

47. As might be expected, in later years Bradstreet was silent about his trading ventures at Louisbourg. In 1757 when he was called before a Council-of-War which wanted to explore his knowledge of the fortress, he stated only that prior to 1745 "he was at Louisbourg in 1736, 1738" and "in 1744." See "At a Council of War held at Head Quarters in the Town of Halifax in Nova Scotia on Saturday the 23rd of July 1757," W.O. 34/101, 99, microfilm, Reel 1429, University of Michigan Graduate Library, Ann Arbor.

48. Shirley to Lords of Admiralty, September 22, 1744, Adm. 1/3817, n.p., microfilm, Reel B-2987; John Bradstreet and George Ryal to Shirley, September 21, 1744, ibid.; George A. Wood, *William Shirley: Governor of Massachusetts, 1741-1756* 1 (New York, 1940), 232-33.

49. See Rawlyk, *Yankees at Louisbourg*, 26-30; and Wood, *William Shirley*, 1, 232-36.

50. Shirley to Lords of Admiralty, September 22, 1744, Adm. 1/3817, n.p., microfilm, Reel B-2987.

51. "Tenth Journal Colonel John Bradstreet," Louis E. De Forest, ed., *Louisbourg Journals, 1745* (New York, 1943), 171, hereafter cited as "Colonel John Bradstreet's Journal."

specific proposal brought forward at this time must be given to Bradstreet. Even allowing for the tendency of Bradstreet to exaggerate his role and contribution in his own statements, it is clear from the comments of William Pepperrell,[52] eventual land commander of the expedition, Peter Warren,[53] naval commander, and William Shirley,[54] the power behind the entire campaign, that Bradstreet was an enthusiastic, influential, and possibly the first advocate of the attack.

While there is clear evidence of Bradstreet being an early advocate of the attack, his sole authorship of the master plan for the assault is less certain. A plan was passed on to the Massachusetts General Court by Governor Shirley in January 1744/45, of which William Vaughan claimed to be the author. But G. A. Wood feels the plan "was perhaps suggested chiefly by Bradstreet,"[55] while G. A. Rawlyk raises the possibility that "the plan placed in Shirley's hands by Vaughan was originally drafted by Bradstreet and then revised by Vaughan."[56] Given the fact that Vaughan had never visited Louisbourg but only talked with the former prisoners and other visitors, it is highly probable that Bradstreet's intimate knowledge, whether passed on to Vaughan orally or in a written form, provided the core of the plan around which Vaughan could build the final presentation. In any case the initial scheme was not accepted by the General Court. It was only after petitions and pressure that the Court reconsidered the plan, which had now evolved into a more detailed proposal. A committee of the General Court, originally established to consider the scheme, heard testimony from Bradstreet and others concerning the feasibility of the attack and finally passed a resolution approving it. Careful political manoeuvring by Vaughan and Shirley had brought some members of the General Court around to support the project and on January 25, 1744/45, this body approved the committee's resolution by a one-vote margin.[57]

Organization of the expedition commenced immediately and naturally the choice of a commanding officer was a high priority. As an ensign in the British army, barely turned thirty years of age, it might be assumed that John Bradstreet was foolishly vain to have any pretensions concerning that particular appointment. Yet Bradstreet maintained in his journal,[58] and even as late as eleven years after the Louisbourg action,[59] that Shirley offered him the command. But Shirley was "addicted to cajolery" since he extended the same offer to Benning Wentworth, Lieutenant-Governor of New Hampshire, and

---

52. William Pepperrell to Newcastle, June 19, 1745, vol. 19, n.p., P.A.N.S.
53. Peter Warren to Duke of Newcastle, June 18, 1745, ibid.
54. Abstract of a Letter from Gov. Shirley to his Grace the Duke of New Castle—Louisbourg 1745—" in "Colonel John Bradstreet's Journal," De Forest, *Louisbourg Journals*, 177.
55. Wood, *William Shirley*, 1, 246-47.
56. Rawlyk, *Yankees at Louisbourg*, 34.
57. For a detailed explanation of the plan and its approval, see ibid., 33-40.
58. "Colonel John Bradstreet's Journal," De Forest, *Louisbourg Journals*, 171.
59. Memorial of John Bradstreet to Lord Loudoun [September 1756], Loudoun Papers, LO 5183, Huntington Library, San Marino.

Peter Warren.⁶⁰ By this gesture he hoped to win their interest and support but in the case of Bradstreet the manoeuvre almost backfired. When Shirley withdrew the offer, explaining to Bradstreet that William Pepperrell was to command since "the men Cou'd not be rais'd but under the Command of a Native of New England,"⁶¹ Bradstreet was ready to wash his hands of the entire expedition. Although he was commissioned as second colonel and captain of the second company of the First Massachusetts Regiment in February of 1744/45,⁶² Bradstreet had not as yet decided to join the assault. When the Massachusetts Council heard of his reluctance it passed a unanimous motion, on March 14, 1744/45, "that his Excellency, be desir'd to offer him all Suitable Encouragement for his engaging therein."⁶³ According to Bradstreet's journal, the concession Shirley made was that "Sir William Pepperell should be advis'd by me, well knowing how impossible it was to Suceed under the Conduct of People Ignorant of the least Military Branch necessary in such an undertaking."⁶⁴ By 1756 this concession had been expanded into a requirement that "the Sole direction of the Expedition should be in your Memorialest."⁶⁵

Regardless of which of these descriptions presents the totally accurate picture of Bradstreet's position, it is clear that he joined the expedition in a key advisory capacity. But was the offer of such a position all the inducement required? Perhaps he was demanding and receiving a higher price for his services. As the expedition progressed Shirley wrote to Pepperrell concerning Bradstreet's contribution: "I wish you would be as strong and particular in your next to me in favour of him as you can with justice."⁶⁶ What Shirley would do with favourable comments concerning Bradstreet is fairly obvious. These were to be passed on to the home authorities and could be of major importance in Bradstreet's preferment as a British officer. Thus, while Bradstreet accepted the loss of the original rank promised him by Shirley and joined the expedition, in return he expected Shirley to be lavish in praise of his deeds. By means of the Louisbourg expedition Bradstreet hoped to arrange a well-orchestrated chorus of praise carefully directed at the ears of British officialdom. But although several of his actions during the campaign were contributions of the highest order,

---

60. Byron Fairchild, *Messrs. William Pepperrell: Merchants at Piscataqua* (Ithaca, N.Y., 1954), 174.

61. Memorial of John Bradstreet to Lord Loudoun [September 1756], Loudoun Papers, LO 5283.

62. "A Register Of all the Commissions in the Army under Command of the Hon. General Pepperrell, in the Expedition against Cape Breton, 1745," New England Historic-Genealogical Society, *The New England Historical and Genealogical Register and Antiquarian Journal*, 24 (Boston, 1870), 368.

63. "Colonel John Bradstreet's Journal," De Forest, *Louisbourg Journals*, 177.

64. Ibid., 172.

65. Memorial of John Bradstreet to Lord Loudoun [September 1756], Loudoun Papers, LO 5183.

66. Shirley to Pepperrell, May 22, 1745, "Pepperrell Papers," Massachusetts Historical Society, *Collections*, 6th Ser., 10 (Boston, 1899), 207.

he was to discover that suspicions of his non-New England background and jealousy caused by his driving ambition were to arouse a mixture of critical comments and generous acknowledgments concerning his performance.

At the end of March 1744/45, the expedition sailed from New England for the Canso rendezvous, where most of April was to be spent. At Canso the New Englanders were joined by a squadron of the British navy under the command of Peter Warren. At this point Bradstreet was functioning as one of the Pepperrell's key officers, since the Massachusetts commander explained to the newly arrived Warren that "Col. Bradstreet, will communicate to you the plan of the operation proposed, and deliver you a plan of this place."[67] As might be expected, duties as a liaison officer, however vital, were not the only chores the impetuous Bradstreet wanted to be assigned. After the successful landing in Gabarus Bay, the first important target was the Grand Battery. Bradstreet was to lead a force of 500 men against it but "the French thought proper to save me that Trouble, by deserting it."[68] Already, in the planning of this attack, bitterness towards Bradstreet had emerged. A combination of fears for the safety of a company of his New Hampshiremen, who were supposed to serve in the assault, as well as a hatred for Bradstreet, caused Captain Thomas Waldron to label the plan "a Mad Headlong Ignorant Scheem."[69]

The French abandonment of the Grand Battery deprived Bradstreet of immediate glory, or possible embarrassment if the New Hampshire company had refused to serve under him, but it also revealed his vital contribution to the planning of the entire expedition. He had noted that the Grand Battery was in an exposed position because of an over-looking high hill, which might cause the French to desert it "immediately on the approach of an Enemy by Land, to avoid being taken."[70] Should this occur, Bradstreet planned to turn the battery's guns against Louisbourg itself. To accomplish this, special shot would be needed, since the Grand Battery cannons were forty-two pounders while the expedition's largest siege cannon were only twenty-two pounders.[71] In addition, workmen were required to drill out the captured cannon since undoubtedly the French would spike them. Owing to his advice, both needs had been foreseen and provided for, Bradstreet claimed, before the expedition left Boston.[72] On the morning of May 2 the Grand Battery was discovered to be abandoned and it was immediately occupied by a small force under William Vaughan. The same day Bradstreet arrived on the scene and found his plan eminently feasible. He put in an immediate request to Pepperrell for the men and

---

67. Pepperrell to Warren, April 23, 1745, "Letters relating to the Expedition against Cape Breton," M.H.S., *Collections*, 1st Ser., 1 (Boston, 1792), 21.
68. "Colonel John Bradstreet's Journal," De Forest, *Louisbourg Journals*, 174.
69. Fairchild, *Messrs. William Pepperrell*, 176; Rawlyk, *Yankees at Louisbourg*, 80.
70. "Colonel John Bradstreet's Journal," De Forest, *Louisbourg Journals*, 172.
71. Rawlyk, *Yankees at Louisbourg*, 90.
72. "Colonel John Bradstreet's Journal," De Forest, *Louisbourg Journals*, 174.

materials to get the cannon in shape to fire upon Louisbourg. It was his hope that "We may have four 42 pounder ready to play on the town by to-morrow by 12 O'clock" and, indeed, the next day, according to a Louisbourg inhabitant, "the enemy greeted us with our own cannon."[73] It was a master stroke and considerably buoyed the spirits of the attacking New Englanders.

As these guns opened fire on Louisbourg, Pepperrell held an important Council-of-War, from which Bradstreet as well as Samuel Waldo, second in command of the expedition, were excused because of their involvement at the Grand Battery. Pepperrell raised the question of whether at this time the Louisbourg commander should be offered the opportunity to capitulate. The council was obviously reluctant to accept such a suggestion, as were the two major absentees. Samuel Waldo and Bradstreet felt "that the Govr. of Louisbourg would give a very ready answer to a summons for surrender by hanging up the messenger thereof, unless we had made a more formidable genl appearance than we have been yet able to make." Waldo reported: "Colo. Broadstreet desires me to tell yr Honr that it will be of the utmost ill consequence to ye expedition to take the least step towards a parly with the enemy untill we have gott our whole artillery in the best order to play on them"[74] Bradstreet and Waldo made clear that they felt an encirclement of Louisbourg by carefully placed batteries and a damaging bombardment were necessary before initiation of negotiations or the launching of any all-out assault. This suggestion did not deviate from the basic strategy outlined in Bradstreet's journal and it was for the most part the very approach that Pepperrell chose to take in directing the siege of Louisbourg. This is important to note for two reasons. In his journal, written several years after the Louisbourg action, Bradstreet carefully linked the strategy behind the fall of Louisbourg with his suggested plan, to make it appear that his strategic thinking was the root cause of the success. Acceptance of such a claim purely on the basis of his journal is very risky since, writing after the event and with the advantage of hindsight, he merely could have taken every successful manoeuvre and portrayed it as his own brilliant suggestion. However, the letters of Waldo, containing as they do both his and Bradstreet's thoughts concerning the way in which the siege should be conducted, and written while the action was in progress, provide clear evidence that both men made a solid contribution to the successful strategy behind the Louisbourg victory.

A second important point concerning the strategy advocated by Waldo and Bradstreet is that they also recommended "that an attack

---

73. William Vaughan to Pepperrell, May 2, 1745, "Pepperrell Papers," M.H.S., *Collections*, 6th Ser., 10, 138; John Bradstreet to Pepperrell, May 2, 1745, ibid.; George M. Wrong, ed., *Louisbourg in 1745: The Anonymous "lettre D'un Habitant De Louisbourg"* (Toronto, 1897), 41.

74. Rawlyk, *Yankees at Louisbourg*, 102-103; Samuel Waldo to Pepperrell, May 3, 1745, "Pepperrell Papers," M.H.S., *Collections*, 6th Ser., 10, 141-42; Waldo to Pepperrell, May 3, 1745, ibid., 144.

against the Island Battery ... had best to [be] deferrd."[75] In other words, their policy of cautious encirclement and bombardment largely ignored the Island Battery and focused on the exertion of far heavier pressure from the land side and land forces than from the sea side and naval forces. On May 10 the several-times aborted assault on the Island Battery was to be attempted with Pepperrell's approval. Bradstreet had "us'd all the Means in my power to desswade them from it [the attack],"[76] and he went even further than verbal persuasion, since at the last moment he intervened and ordered the assembled volunteers to disperse. While his action might have been caused by his being perceptive enough to realize the costly toll in casualties such an attack would take, more likely it was the result of his strong commitment to a strategy which rendered such an attack unnecessary. It appears totally unlikely that his actions were taken because he was a sympathizer with the French cause.

Nevertheless, the latter explanation was the one which swept through the camp. The rumour spread through the ranks of a traitor within the New England force who was frustrating the effort against Louisbourg. The finger of guilt was pointed at Bradstreet, since he had thwarted the attack on the Island Battery. Further spice was added by reports that he had been seen entering and leaving Louisbourg. By the day following Bradstreet's unfortunate intervention, the stories reached Peter Warren prompting him to write Pepperrell: "For God's sake, Sir, put a stop to that disagreeable and ill-grounded suspicion that some unthinking people have pretended (for I can think it no other) to conceive of Collonel Broadstreet, it may otherwise be of fatal consequence to the expedition."[77] Pepperrell was already acting to investigate the rumours since at a Council-of-War, held the same day as Warren's letter, the matter was thoroughly discussed. At the meeting Bradstreet was completely exonerated and a Lieutenant-Colonel Chandler, who "had been guilty of great imprudence in entertaining and reporting such surmizes with the least reasonable foundations therefor," was forced to apologize. In clearing Bradstreet the council spoke of "his zeal for the success of the expedition" and "his active and prudent behavior on all occasions."[78] These laudatory comments appear warranted both by his actual performance at Louisbourg and in view of the attempt he was making to rescue his career in the British army. He had to perform with zeal and vigour to offset the criticisms and suspicions arising from his pre-war activities which created such fertile ground for the anti-Bradstreet rumours to grow among the New Englanders. After all, he did speak French, he was not a New Englander, he was known as a former trader with Louisbourg, and he did have

---

75. Ibid.
76. "Colonel John Bradstreet's Journal," De Forest, *Louisbourg Journals*, 175.
77. Rawlyk, *Yankees at Louisbourg*, 114; Warren to Pepperrell, May 11, 1745, "Pepperrell Papers," M.H.S., *Collections*, 6th Ser., 10, 162.
78. Council-of-War, May 11, 1745, "Pepperrell Papers," M.H.S., *Collections*, 6th Ser., 10, 18-19.

relatives on the enemy side of the line. Bradstreet's mysterious background when combined with one unfortunate action threatened to destroy all his plans and hopes.

Pepperrell seemed to sense the grave danger to Bradstreet of the accusations and tried to offset them by expressions of confidence and praise. On the day after the council meeting he informed Warren: "I have resented and taken measures to suppress the surmizes that some silly persons had propagated of Col. Bradstreet's behaviour wch am sensible was as ill grounded & prejudicial to our design here as it was injurious to him; hope shall hear no more about it."[79] Several weeks later he assured Governor Shirley of Bradstreet's innocence and contribution:

> I have had abundant experience that the surmises some persons entertained of that gentleman were entirely groundless, and cruelly injurious to him. No person in the army could possibly have behaved with more zeal, activity and judgement in the measures taken for the accomplishment of our design, which added to his particular knowledge in the circumstances of this place, justly entitle him to the esteem and thanks of every well wisher to the success of the expedition.[80]

Not only was Pepperrell willing to express in letters his respect for Bradstreet, but at Louisbourg itself important tasks continued to be assigned the controversial officer. When arrangements were being finalized for the surrender of Louisbourg, it was Bradstreet whom Pepperrell entrusted with the honour of accepting the keys to the city.[81] But even as he enjoyed the glory of leading the New England troops into Louisbourg and receiving the keys, the unfortunate Bradstreet was ensnared in yet another controversy. The surrender of the keys to the New Englanders, rather than to an officer of His Majesty's Navy, accentuated the rivalry between the representatives of the colonies and the mother country. Peter Warren had intended that one of his officers receive the keys but Pepperrell had outmanoeuvred him.[82] Despite the actual course of events, stories circulated in New England that the keys had been delivered to Warren and that Pepperrell had not sufficiently exerted himself "for the honor of New England upon this occasion." Furthermore, it was argued that one of Pepperrell's own officers had

---

79. Pepperrell to Warren, May 12, 1745, ibid., 164-65.
80. Pepperrell to Shirley, June 3, 1745, "Letters relating to the Expedition," M.H.S., *Collections*, 1st Ser., 1, 40.
81. Pepperrell to Du Chambon, June 17, 1745, M.G. 1, Archives Nationales, Series F³/50, part 1, 322, P.A.C.
82. Rawlyk, *Yankees at Louisbourg*, 149-51. Julian Gwyn disagrees with Rawlyk's contention that the New Englanders received the keys. See Julian Gwyn, "Sir Peter Warren," in Halpenny *et al.*, *Dictionary of Canadian Biography*, 3, 656. Rawlyk offers the stronger evidence and argument. Substantiation for Gwyn's contention is provided by Captain Philip Durell's remark that the French "delivered the Keys of the Town to Mr. Warren" but a recent article hints Durell's remark was an attempt to enhance the contribution to the victory made by the Royal Navy. See Douglas E. Leach, "Brothers in Arms?— Anglo-American Friction at Louisbourg, 1745-1746," *Proceedings of the Massachusetts Historical Society*, 89 (1977), 44-45.

aided in this loss of proper credit to New England's sons. The hapless Bradstreet was the suspected man once more. In an unflattering climax to his Louisbourg service the feeling was being expressed in Boston "that affairs would have been managed full as well, if he had not been there, or less regard had been paid to him."[83]

Countering such uncharitable, and largely undeserved, rumours was the chorus of praise from the leading figures connected with the expedition. Bradstreet had cultivated William Pepperrell, William Shirley, and Peter Warren very carefully and in the aftermath of victory their glowing words were designed to help achieve the prized higher rank he so eagerly sought in the British army. All three gentlemen were quick to supply the Duke of Newcastle with favourable comments on his behalf. Warren felt that Bradstreet "has been very active, and is deserving of His Majesty's favour." Shirley and Pepperrell were both stronger in his support and more specific about the reward. Shirley spoke of "his Extraordinary Activity and good Conduct" during the siege and that, in general, Bradstreet had "in every thing Exerted himself for his Majestys Service." He recommended the reward of "his good services ... with his being Sir Williams [Pepperrell's] Lieut. Colonel in the Regiment design'd to be Establish'd." Pepperrell expressed the hope that "his majesty would be graciously pleased to apoint Collo Bradstreet ... who has distinguish'd himself upon all occasions to be my Lieut Collo."[84] When these comments are linked with Bradstreet's actual contributions to the Louisbourg victory, a solid case on his behalf emerges. He had brought word to Shirley of the weakened state of the garrison, fortifications, and general condition of Louisbourg. He had been an early advocate of the attack and helped in the formulation of the proposals submitted to the Massachusetts legislators. At Louisbourg he had contributed to the shaping of the basic strategy applied during the siege and demonstrated considerable foresight and ingenuity.

Bradstreet's remarkable record of service was even further enhanced by his relative youthfulness at the time of the Louisbourg campaign. For a young man, barely thirty years of age, he seemed to move with uncanny ease into the confidence of a colonial governor and a Massachusetts general while at the same time winning the respect of the English Admiral Warren. It was a masterful performance. Admittedly, his cocky attitude, confident expectations and suggestions, and impressive knowledge of Louisbourg's strengths and weaknesses worked to his disadvantage as well as to his advantage. To the rank and

---

83. Dr. Charles Chauncy to Pepperrell, July 27, 1745, "Letters relating to the Expedition," M.H.S., *Collections*, 1st Ser., 1, 50-51.

84. Warren to Newcastle, June 18, 1745, vol. 19, n.p., P.A.N.S.; "Abstract of a Letter from Gov. Shirley to his Grace the Duke of New Castle—Louisbourg 1745—" in "Colonel John Bradstreet's Journal," De Forest, *Louisbourg Journals*, 177; Pepperrell to Newcastle, June 19, 1745, "Baxter Papers," *Documentary History of ... Maine*, 11, 301; Pepperrell to Newcastle, June 19, 1745, vol. 19, n.p., P.A.N.S.

file of the New England force, who lacked the wider and more appreciative vision of their superiors, these same traits and knowledgeability spawned rumours, suspicions, and criticisms. But, on balance, Bradstreet had made a good impression and had made it, he hoped, where it counted most. The rather indiscrete young ensign trading out of Canso had been replaced by a shrewdly opportunistic officer, fully able to handle the heady dealings with governors, admirals, and generals.

During the short span of a few years John Bradstreet had moved from being an obscure ensign doing garrison duty at neglected Canso to being an important contributor to the Louisbourg triumph who could quite legitimately aspire to a lieutenant-colonelship in the British army. The neglected fishing village seemed far behind him. And yet, in terms both of distance and time, Canso and his activities there were not that far removed. One of the basic reasons for his Louisbourg exertions had been to blot out his earlier indiscretions. Bradstreet hoped his colonial friends and deeds could overcome the old world disfavour and neglect he had encountered. Could he assume that this had been achieved when suspicions still were voiced even among his fellow colonials who should have been most aware of his zeal and contributions? Rewards for his Louisbourg endeavours were to come, but they were not the prizes for which he had hoped. His triumphant emergence at Louisbourg was viewed by some doubters as merely a re-emergence. It was a re-emergence which, in the minds of some of his detractors, was not yet far enough removed from the Canso years and Canso activities for Bradstreet's total vindication.

Chapter III

Disappointment and Readjustment

Among other things, the capture of Louisbourg in 1745 demonstrated "that there was a widening chasm developing between Britain and its New England colonies."[1] Such a development had significant implications for the career of John Bradstreet. Initially, Bradstreet was victimized by this chasm, since his plans concerning the future of Louisbourg and his own military future were totally tied to colonial aspirations and colonial friends. During the next few years, however, colonial viewpoints were to be given only token consideration. Caught between two diverging worlds, a disappointed but wiser Bradstreet moved on to Newfoundland and then "home" to England. By 1754, as he prepared to return to the colonies, bitterness and disappointment still marred all his comments about his treatment, but underneath it all a fundamental readjustment had been made in his thinking. He now knew the power of connections at home and attempted never again to allow a too-heavy dependence on colonial plans and patrons to jeopardize his career.

The day after Louisbourg's capture, June 18, Warren and Pepperrell commissioned Bradstreet "Town Major of ye City and Fortress of Louisbourg,"[2] a post which he was to hold for almost one year. Appointments such as this, however, were only temporary in the sense that the major participants in the expedition anxiously awaited word from England concerning their more permanent rewards. Late in September rumours circulated at Louisbourg about the preferment of

---

1. Rawlyk, *Yankees at Louisbourg*, 152.
2. "A Register of all the Commissions in the Army under the Command of the Hon. General Pepperrell, in the Expedition against Cape Breton, 1745," *New England Historical and Genealogical Register and Antiquarian Journal*, 24, 378.

various individuals. It was reported that Warren was to be governor of Louisbourg and "Rear Admiral of the Blue," while Pepperrell "is Made Baronet of Great Britton as also Col. of a Regiment Here, and I—Broadstreet Leut Col., and that Shirley is to have the Care of the Other Regiment."[3] In the cases of Warren, Pepperrell, and Shirley, these early whisperings were essentially correct. But in Bradstreet's case, suggestions of the fulfillment of his desire for rank as a lieutenant-colonel were totally incorrect. Indeed, because of manipulations in England a commission as major was also denied him. Apparently it was intended that Bradstreet should be appointed lieutenant-colonel of Shirley's new regiment, "which his Majesty was graciously pleas'd to Consent to, but by some means or mistake the late Colonel Elison Obtained the Commission." Then, Bradstreet claimed, "his Majesty Sign'd a Commission for Your Memorialists being Major to the said Regiment." This too slipped through his fingers when, in the words of William Shirley, "his Elder Brother then present in England, who has not the least pretensions to that Post, found means to supplant him and obtain it for himself." Fortunately for Bradstreet the new regimental commanders, Pepperrell and Shirley, did not have all of their officers appointed in England but were provided with a number of blank commissions which they could dispense as they saw fit. It was Pepperrell's generosity rather than any commission direct from Britain which eventually allowed Bradstreet to replace his old ensign's commission, given up in November of 1745, by a captain's commission in Pepperrell's new regiment.[4]

Nonetheless, while others were being given generous rewards for their Louisbourg contributions, Bradstreet watched with mounting frustration as his own lofty expectations were not realized. Instead of a significant honour, a lieutenant-colonelship, or a major's commission, he was left with only a captain's rank, and even that was gained only because of Pepperrell's friendship. Bradstreet's damaged ego must have received a further blow when it was realized that this complete neglect was only partially the result of a mistake on the part of the English authorities. In the case of both the loss of the lieutenant-colonel and major's ranks, it became obvious that Bradstreet was totally lacking a friend in key places to protect his interests. In fact, there is the distinct possibility that his old "friend" King Gould, in collusion with Simon Bradstreet, had a hand in arranging John's rebuff.

While John was attempting to gain promotion by his deeds on the field of battle, Simon was proceeding to the same goal by a more careful and more successful route. At the time of his return to England in 1742

---

3. "First Journal," De Forest, *Louisbourg Journals*, 45.
4. Memorial of John Bradstreet to Lord Loudoun [September 1756], Loudon Papers, LO 5183, Huntington Library; Shirley [to Fox] January 13, 1756, M.G. 12, W.O.1/1 pt. 1, 3, P.A.C.; Newcastle to Shirley and Pepperrell, September 11, 1745, vol. 13$^{1}/_{2}$, doc. #1, P.A.N.S.; "Mr. Gould's Schedule to his further Answer," T.P.C., 103/760, N.L.W.

Simon had held two commissions, as adjutant and ensign, in Philipps' regiment. He drew pay for both positions until May of 1744 when he sold them for a total of £600 and purchased the rank of lieutenant in Lieutenant-General Henry Harrison's regiment. Naturally Gould handled these transactions and faithfully recorded the details in his account books. Less than a year later, on March 21, 1744/45, Gould arranged another leap in rank for Simon when he smoothed the way for the purchase of a captain's commission.[5]

By this time, of course, Simon's brother John had turned his far more extensive knowledge of Louisbourg into a valuable asset and was very much involved in the projected New England attack on Cape Breton. Since Simon's commission as captain was in Philipps' regiment which was still stationed in Nova Scotia and Newfoundland, there was a real possibility that the brothers soon would be reunited. While Louisbourg was still under siege, Shirley passed on word "to let Col. [John] Bradstreet know yt. his brother has got a company, wch he is now recruiting for and will soon raise for Newfoundland."[6] A few months later Simon Bradstreet was given the task of delivering some recruits to Paul Mascarene at Annapolis Royal. In preparation for this journey Gould explained to Mascarene that "Captain Bradstreet is my ffriend and too assure he is yours and hath served himself so on all occasions."[7] Obviously, the close friendship of Gould and Simon continued. But before he could leave for Nova Scotia, another opportunity for preferment arose which Simon was quick to snatch. Since officers were being appointed for the new regiments of Shirley and Pepperrell, some delightful plums were ready to be taken. Accordingly, when the list of Shirley's officers was released early in September, it included "Captain Simon Bradstreet of Lt. Genl. Philipps's to be Major, and Captain of a Company" with his commission dated September 1, 1745. Gould wrote to Mascarene concerning the change in plans necessitated by Bradstreet's promotion but other than mentioning Simon's change in rank no further comment was offered.[8] Thus it is uncertain just what role Gould played in the promotion. But for Gould to have arranged that the name of his friend Simon Bradstreet be slipped in to replace that of John Bradstreet on the major's commission was not out of line with his earlier practices, since one such substitution had launched the career of John Bradstreet himself. And moreover, such a favour was a logical culmination of his close friendship with the elder Bradstreet. Hence Major Simon Bradstreet sailed for Louisbourg where his brother John sat seething with resentment at his hard treatment. Ironically the ship *Rousby* sank off Cape Breton in December of 1745 and among the

---

5. Accounts of Simon Bradstreet, T.P.C., MS/262, 75 and 136, N.L.W.
6. Shirley to Pepperrell, May 22, 1745, "Pepperrell Papers," M.H.S., *Collections*, 6th Ser. 10, 207.
7. King Gould to Mascarene, August 15, 1745, T.P.C., MS/287, n.p.
8. W. Yonge to the Secretary to Lord Harrington, September 7, 1745, R.G. 22, B. 3, Louisbourg Restoration Project, n.p., microfilm, Reel B-331, P.A.C.; King Gould to Mascarene, October 21, 1745, T.P.C., MS/287, n.p.

unfortunates who drowned was Simon, "brother to Mr. Pepperrell's Lieutenant Colonel," John Bradstreet.[9] There is no evidence that John was particularly saddened by his brother's abrupt, and perhaps fitting, demise.

The same winter of 1745/46 took a dreadful toll among the New Englanders stationed at Louisbourg with an estimated 1,200 of them perishing because of an epidemic.[10] For John Bradstreet it must have been a doubly harsh winter. He remained at Louisbourg performing town major's duties but holding only a provincial lieutenant-colonel's commission as his real rank. This commission would be lost in the spring when the provincials returned to New England and their regiments were disbanded. As the winter deepened so did his desperation. It was becoming obvious that he who had contributed so much to the Louisbourg triumph was either forgotten or being deliberately passed over. He could still hope that Pepperrell would fill in one of the blank commissions in his favour, but no doubt the higher ranks had been awarded in England and only the lower positions were left free.[11] Somehow all Bradstreet's plans and hopes had gone astray. For the true hero and man of action, there appeared to be one simple way to escape from this incredible situation. An even more daring stroke, an even more convincing triumph, with himself as not only the architect but one of the leaders, was required. The capture of Louisbourg had to be followed by an immediate campaign against Canada. Quebec must be reduced by a force led by John Bradstreet.

The proposal to attack Quebec was on the minds of many men at this time.[12] However, Bradstreet's suggestion is interesting not only because it pointed to the past but also because it was a further indication of what was to be a happy knack he enjoyed throughout his career. He was continually able to take schemes that were very much in the air, whether it be an assault on Louisbourg in 1744 or New Orleans in 1770, add to them what appeared to be a detailed knowledge of the project's requirements, and give the impression that the wheels already had been set in motion for its successful conclusion. On some occasions this hyperactive hard sell was totally successful. At other times it was not.

---

9. Warren and Pepperrell to Newcastle, January 18, 1745/46, vol. 19, 43, P.A.N.S.; Pepperrell and Warren to Shirley, January 28, 1745/46, "Pepperrell Papers," M.H.S., *Collections*, 6th Ser., 10, 44; "The Petition of Anna Elizabetha Bradstreet, Widow of Simon Bradstreet Esqr. late Major to Colonel Shirley's Regiment of Foot" [1746], M.G. 23, A 2, Chatham MSS, Bundle 73, 211, P.A.C.

10. Rawlyk, *Yankees at Louisbourg*, 157.

11. Actually Pepperrell had blank commissions for two captains, eleven lieutenants, and four ensigns. See Newcastle to Shirley and Pepperrell, September 11, 1745, vol. 13½, doc. #1, P.A.N.S.

12. Shirley suggested such an attack as early as October 1745. See Shirley to Newcastle, October 29, 1745, Lincoln, *Shirley Correspondence*, 1, 284. Peter J. Bower, "Louisbourg, the Chimera, 1745-48," in National Museum of Man, History Division, *Papers and Abstracts For a Symposium On Ile Royale During The French Regime* (Ottawa, 1972), 21, mentions that Newcastle received "numerous suggestions urging such an expedition from the principals involved in the attack on Louisbourg."

This proposed attack on Canada fits the latter category. But even with its eventual failure it starkly reveals the unhappy predicament into which Bradstreet had fallen by this time. An attack on Canada fitted well the colonial view of Louisbourg. To Shirley and Pepperrell in particular, after its capture Louisbourg was to be "integrated into the British colonial system as a place to settle and trade," and as a base "leading to the expulsion of France from North America."[13] Bradstreet held a similar view of the fortress.

Bradstreet's Louisbourg plans and position, along with the general colonial hopes relating to the fortress' utilization and development, were about to be challenged. By June of 1746 Pepperrell and Warren had both departed from Louisbourg and Commodore Charles Knowles arrived to serve as governor of Cape Breton. Several of the new commander's first actions gave cause for considerable alarm to the already-distraught Bradstreet. Early in June, Bradstreet wrote to Pepperrell that he continued "to doe Town Majors Duty & he [Knowles] is Prety Sivile to Me." Before he finished this letter, however, Knowles sent for and informed Bradstreet that he was relieved as town major "& desir'd I would make up my Act. of Cole, for he would Endever to get it Cheper, (that is he Intends to doe it himself)." At one stroke, the last major military function of Bradstreet and the profitable side line he had developed by providing fuel for the garrison were abruptly ended. Knowles was also concerned about the extensive rum trade in which his New England officers engaged. Not surprisingly, the same day after his meeting with Knowles, Bradstreet ordered a Mr. Ward "to take the Rum away, for the Devil is to Pay here, & I believe if Possible will be Worse yet."[14] Bradstreet's service under Charles Knowles was obviously going to be a far more difficult proposition than it had been under Warren and Pepperrell.

To remedy this situation Bradstreet was writing to "my Dr. & Good friend Mr. Warren"[15] as well as to Governor Shirley, but his greatest reliance was on Pepperrell. Already during February of the past winter he had engaged in recruitment activities on behalf of Pepperrell's new regiment, persuading some of the New Englanders to enlist in this regular regiment when their provincial units were disbanded. By June it appears that Bradstreet himself was an officer in this regiment, since he asked Pepperrell to "Pray keep my Commissions with you." The commissions referred to were probably those of a captain and adjutant.[16] But Bradstreet did not want to be restricted to this rank in

---

13. Bower, "Louisbourg, the Chimera," 31.
14. Bradstreet to Pepperrell, June 9, 1746, Belknap Papers, 61 C 59, Massachusetts Historical Society, Boston; Bradstreet to Pepperrell, June 9, 1746, ibid., 61 1C 61; McLennan, *Louisbourg*, 175.
15. Bradstreet to Pepperrell, June 9, 1746, Belknap Papers, 61 C 59. Several months earlier, Bradstreet had written directly to Newcastle, outlining in considerable detail his Louisbourg contribution and his plight in terms of his rank, or lack thereof, in the army. See Bradstreet to Newcastle, April 8, 1746, Newcastle Papers, Add. MSS 32,707/34-35, British Museum, London.
16. Pepperrell to Shirley, February 28, 1745/46, Lincoln, *Shirley Correspondence*, 1,

Disappointment and Readjustment

Pepperrell's regiment. The idea of an attack on Quebec had congealed in his mind and he wanted his regimental commander's support in securing his own regiment to participate in the proposed campaign.

Judging from the frequent references to a Canada expedition in his June 1746 letters to Pepperrell, a memorandum written by Bradstreet concerning "Cannady" must have been drafted in the spring or early summer of this year.[17] It contained a particularly interesting picture of Quebec City which Bradstreet described as composed of two towns. "One is call'd the upper & the other the Lower Town. The upper has a Sod wall of about 8 or 9 feet high [which] goes round from the Citedel to the Intendents house, the Lower Town has nothing Round it." He went on to pinpoint the weakness of the fortress "on ye land Side of the Town" where it "is a fine plaine & Nothing to Interrupt ye Men from Marching up to the Town." Since an attack on Quebec that summer was unlikely, "I am of opinion that they might be kept Destitute of all manner of Supplyes & Even put it out of their powers of Sending one Vessell out of the River by our haveing 6 or 7 good 60 gun ships goe up the River with some Small tenders as high as is Necessary for them to anquer Safely out of Danger of the Winds, & Sea & there pas the Summer." It is uncertain to whom Bradstreet offered this memorandum, although Pepperrell was a logical recipient since it was to him that Bradstreet spelled out further details of his specific role. In addition, he several times wrote to Shirley concerning "my Inclenation of goeing to Canada"[18] and no doubt the document was exposed to the governor's view as well. Regardless of who the intended reader was, the point was made that Bradstreet was an authority, of sorts, on Quebec and not the type of person to be left out of such an expedition.

Throughout the month of June, Pepperrell was bombarded with reminders and suggestions from Bradstreet concerning the Canada expedition, suggestions which became increasingly far-fetched and unrealistic. He assured Pepperrell that "Numbers of our Officers have tould me they would Raize Men for me, & that they would goe with me." To aid recruitment he had instructed "Mr. Borland to furnish Major Titcomb wth. 3 or four hundred Pound old tenour if I should be so lucky as to be Establish'd or Even apointed to help on the Inlestments, till I should arrive my Self." For purposes of recruitment Bradstreet promised to come to Massachusetts immediately, if Pepperrell considered such a move wise, and had no doubt at all that "wth. my friends help & the Expense I would be at mySelf" a regiment could be completed very quickly. But while Bradstreet was emphasizing the ease

---

309n.; Bradstreet to Pepperrell, June 9, 1746, Belknap Papers, 61 C 59. In "Memorial of John Bradstreet to Lord Loudoun [September 1756]," Loudoun Papers, LO 5183, Bradstreet mentions that as his reward for his efforts at Louisbourg he "Obtain'd nothing more than a Company & adjutant in the 51st [Pepperrell's] Regiment and the year following Lieut. Govr. of St. Johns in Newfoundland."

17. See "Collo. Bradstreets Memorandm about Cannady & ye Island of Cape Breton" [1746], Belknap Papers, 61 C 68.

18. Bradstreet to Pepperrell, June 16, 1746, ibid., 61 C 62.

with which a regiment could be raised for service under him, he was, as usual, riding off in all directions before a glimmer of approval had been received. All his actions were contingent upon "the Sertainty of you & my friends Doeing Something for me for Canada." This was not a very solid assumption to build upon, but to the desperate Bradstreet it was the only salvation remaining. Consequently he proceeded to add further wrinkles to the expedition proposals. He suggested "that it would not be amiss to take from five hundred to a thousand of the young Men of Nova Scotia with us which would Infalebly in Case of any Accident, Secoure the Rest to his Majestys Interest, & that I would Engage to doe it in three weeks or less with five hundred Men."[19] Clearly the risks and difficulties involved in recruiting Acadians for service in the British army rendered such a suggestion totally unacceptable.

Bradstreet's letters made abundantly apparent his readiness to plunge into a Canadian campaign. If approved, this would have allowed his departure from Louisbourg to take the form of a heroic advance into a new adventure rather than an ignoble retreat from the new realities at Cape Breton. However, in the event that the expedition, or a role for him in it, did not materialize, Bradstreet still wanted to leave Louisbourg. He felt "that if I should be left hear God only knows what would be the Event of it." But he was careful to link his fate at Louisbourg, and the difficulties caused by the arrival of British officialdom in the form of Knowles, with the common problems and discouragements the New Englanders were then encountering there. Emphasis was placed on the great changes wrought at Louisbourg since Pepperrell's departure, changes to the disadvantage of New Englanders. He reported that "I never saw Such an alteration in a place in my Life, nothing but Dejected Countenances to be Seen among the Poor Inhabitants & many others, Such strict order never was Ever yet Seen." Houses were being pulled down and people turned "out of the Town, Vessells out of the harbour." So extensive was the damage that Bradstreet believed "it will be Deficult to get Vessels to come hear soon." All this, of course, ran directly counter to the colonial desire to convert Louisbourg into a settlement and trading centre. As Bradstreet stressed, "this I must Say the New England People find a Sisible Change to their Disadvantage."[20]

By the summer of 1746 the hopes of Bradstreet, as well as those of Pepperrell and Shirley, concerning the proper development of Louisbourg and the need to follow up its capture with an attack on Quebec, had been undermined. As Governor of Cape Breton, Charles Knowles unleashed a stream of letters making clear to the home authorities that Louisbourg was of precious little value as a British fortress and that Cape Breton's potential for settlement was sadly restricted.[21] In addi-

---

19. Ibid., June 9, 1746, 61 C 59. See also Ibid., 61 C 61, written the same day, where some of the same points are repeated and ibid., June 16, 1746, 61 C 62.
20. Ibid., June 9, 1746, 61 C 59; ibid., June 16, 1746, 61 C 62.
21. Bower, "Louisbourg, the Chimera," 24-27.

tion, while a divided British government approved an expedition against Canada in 1746, it was to be conducted largely by British regulars with the colonial forces limited to an auxiliary role. Recruitment among the colonials for such an expedition would be difficult, and even to Bradstreet it probably held only a limited attraction. This proposed expedition was never to materialize, however, as it was beset by a series of difficulties and order changes in the summer and fall of 1746, and then abandoned by the Cabinet in early January of 1746/47. The decision to cancel the attack on Canada had direct implications for Louisbourg's future. If the Cabinet members supporting the attack, among whom the Duke of Bedford and William Pitt were the most prominent, were willing to give ground on this question, they were probably about to yield and become equally flexible concerning Cape Breton. Thus Louisbourg was about to become "a pawn in peace negotiations"[22] which were to culminate in its return to the French. Such a course was contrary to the colonial desires and apprehensions expressed by Pepperrell and Shirley and seconded so enthusiastically by John Bradstreet.

As the summer of 1746 wore on and the Canada expedition failed to take shape, Bradstreet's fortunes appeared ready to hit rock bottom. Compounding all his difficulties was a bout of sickness which put him "very much out of order for three weeks" and caused him to fear for the life of his spouse, Mary, since "my poor Wife has been Exceeding Ille & is now at Deaths Door." Even the support of one of his strongest colonial patrons appeared to have vanished. Bradstreet confessed his fears to Pepperrell that "I have great Reason to believe Mr. S_____ y [Shirley] is not my friend & that I need not expect any favour from him, I am satisfied I deserve Better from his hands if he would reflect but a Little." Bradstreet had assumed that the vacant major's rank in Shirley's regiment, caused "by the Death of my Brother," would be offered to him.[23] Instead, already upset about commissions in his regiment being awarded to officers in England, including Simon Bradstreet, who would be of little help in recruiting colonials,[24] Governor Shirley ignored John Bradstreet in favour of Captain John Littlehales. In all probability Shirley was punishing John for the deeds of Simon. Ironically Simon's capture of a major's rank in Shirley's regiment caused one disappointing setback to his brother and now John found himself hurt once more by the same action.

Evidently Shirley at this point was unaware of the bitter cleavage between the Bradstreet brothers which had opened shortly before Simon's death. As well, John Bradstreet was unaware of the Governor's

---

22. Arthur H. Buffinton, "The Canada Expedition of 1746: Its Relation to British Politics," *American Historical Review*, 45 (1939-1940), 570-79; Bower, "Louisbourg, the Chimera," 28.

23. Bradstreet to Pepperrell, July 20, 1746, John S. H. Fogg Collection, vol. 7, n.p., Maine Historical Society, Portland.

24. John A. Schutz, *William Shirley: King's Governor of Massachusetts* (Chapel Hill, N.C., 1961), 110-11.

displeasure at the way in which commissions in his regiment had been dispensed in England. Pondering this latest snub, Bradstreet, in a revealing exercise, attempted to portray Shirley's hostility as caused by his own over-enthusiastic loyalty to Pepperrell. He suspected that his fall from grace was chiefly because of "Mr. Waldoes Representations of mye Conduct in regard of the Inlesting & sundry other things Last winter in favour of you [Pepperrell]."[25] Possibly there was some truth in this suggestion. Waldo was very much in the Shirley camp at this time, despite his later defection, and the competition for recruits between agents of Shirley and Pepperrell's regiments undoubtedly created some rivalry and animosity.[26] Thus, Bradstreet likely was hurt both by the activities of his brother and by his own actions on behalf of Pepperrell.

Nevertheless, John remained hopeful that these setbacks were only temporary and that his Louisbourg contributions were about to be rewarded. While confiding to his still faithful friend Pepperrell his bitter conviction that "when the work is Done you are Soone Forgotten, Which I am sorry to say is too Much my Case Here," there was a hint that his remaining allies were active. "I can but with a heart full of gratitude Return you my Sincer thanks for your kind offer & shall be Exceedingly oblig'd & sattisfied with what Ever you & my good friend Mr. Warren shall doe for me."[27] Their solicitations probably helped but it was because of the personal recommendation of Alderman William Baker of London that an acknowledgment of Bradstreet's contribution finally emerged several months later. On September 16, 1746, John Bradstreet was appointed Lieutenant-Governor of St. John's, Newfoundland.[28]

The Newfoundland appointment was an honour but, as Bradstreet was to point out several years later, it was far from lucrative in monetary terms, paying only ten shillings a day.[29] When its low financial yield was reinforced by the sinecure nature of the office, since his permanent residence in Newfoundland was not required, Bradstreet felt no immediate need to leave Louisbourg for St. John's. As well, possibilities of improving his rank in Pepperrell's regiment had emerged which Bradstreet wanted to examine fully. Lieutenant-Colonel Ryan, who had received the rank under Pepperrell which Bradstreet originally coveted, soon revealed himself as a corrupt incompetent. By the spring of the following year Knowles outlined Ryan's sins, which included selling for his own profit several commissions he was supposed to have delivered to his commanding officer, Pepperrell. Bradstreet had already

---

25. Bradstreet to Pepperrell, July 20, 1746, John S. H. Fogg Collection, vol. 7, n.p.
26. Schutz, *William Shirley*, 111.
27. Bradstreet to Pepperrell, July 20, 1746, John S. H. Fogg Collection, vol. 7, n.p.
28. "A List of Promotions for the Year 1746," *Gentleman's Magazine*, 16 (1746), 497. In Henry Fox's book of promotions and purchases, Bradstreet's appointment is dated August 24, 1746, and it is noted that the appointment was recommended by "Ald. Baker." See Holland House Papers, Add. MS 51,435/6, B.M.
29. "Colonel John Bradstreet's Journal," De Forest, *Louisbourg Journals*, 178.

Disappointment and Readjustment

made a case against Ryan to Pepperrell, describing him as "a novice in the service" whose incompetence was so great that even a completed regiment blessed with the best of troops "in two years . . . would dwindle to nothing." When Ryan was court-martialed and cashiered, both Pepperrell and Bradstreet were hopeful that John Bradstreet would secure his rank, but instead James Mercer, who was already major in the regiment, was granted the Lieutenant-Colonelship.[30]

Before leaving Louisbourg a frustrated Bradstreet initiated one final effort at gaining the higher rank in the British army which was proving so elusive. His brother-in-law, Captain Christopher Aldridge, Jr., relayed word that Pepperrell was interested in disposing of his colonel's commission and regiment. Bradstreet was quick to snatch at the opportunity, offering to pay his commander "at the rate of ten years' purchase, and you to have all the perquisites of the regiment, during its standing, or your life, which will make two thousand pounds sterling, which money shall be deposited in any bank in England, to be delivered as soon as the commission is made out, and further, that I will be at all the cost, etc. etc." He went on to point out to Pepperrell the reasons why it was wise for him to discard the burden of the regiment, arguing that a career in the army was not Sir William's primary concern and, among other troubles, the regiment could be stationed anywhere in the world which might be a considerable inconvenience. Bradstreet frankly expressed his own reasons for wanting to purchase. "The rank is what I want, and as my friends will then have it more in their power to serve me, notwithstanding it is the youngest regiment."[31] The whole effort proved abortive as Pepperrell chose to retain his regiment despite the difficulties it was causing him.[32] For a change, however, Bradstreet was experiencing a rather fortuitous frustration since, within a few years, in April 1749, Pepperrell's regiment, as well as Shirley's, were to be deactivated.[33]

If one is overly influenced by Bradstreet's exaggerated rhetoric, the picture which emerges from a consideration of his years at Louisbourg after its capture is that of a friendless creature, left with only shattered hopes of a successful military career. Yet even in his darkest moments, when his suggested schemes or cries for promotion were being ignored, there are clues that he was not without financial resources and was carefully rebuilding the old world connections which could eventually turn affairs more favourably to his advantage. For example, there are two interesting points about his attempt to purchase Pepperrell's rank and regiment. Financially, if such a transaction went

---

30. Knowles to Newcastle, April 26, 1747, vol. 19, n.p., P.A.N.S.; Bradstreet to Pepperrell, March 19, 1746/47, Usher Parsons, *The Life of Sir William Pepperrell* (Boston, 1856), 159; Pound, "John Bradstreet," 57.
31. As quoted in Parsons, *The Life of Sir William Pepperrell*, 150-51.
32. For a brief consideration of some of these regimental headaches, see Fairchild, *Messrs. William Pepperrell*, 183-84.
33. See Julian Gwyn, "The Impact of Louisbourg Upon the Economy of Massachusetts, 1745-49," in National Museum of Man, *Papers and Abstracts*, 94.

through, it required quite a sizeable amount of money. Obviously, Bradstreet could arrange to meet the price, just as earlier, when soliciting for his own regiment as a part of the Canada expedition, he had the cash necessary to stimulate recruitment. He had suffered many setbacks, but his personal wealth seemed reasonably substantial. Such healthy finances were not only the product of a captain's pay but owed a great deal to the profitable side lines first revealed at Canso and continued at Louisbourg. An involvement in the rum trade as well as arrangements with New England merchants such as Pepperrell possibly were rewarding enterprises. Even more important, providing badly needed fuel for the Louisbourg garrison proved an extremely profitable venture for him. Knowles was very disturbed by the high cost of wood and coal and, shortly after his arrival, made clear that measures were being taken to bring the costs down. One of the first measures, as Bradstreet discovered, was an attempt to force him out of fuel provisioning, since Knowles wanted to handle it himself. At this point the Governor seemed unwilling to attach openly any blame to Bradstreet for the high cost of the fuel, preferring to stress the difficulties of loading it because of the tides and the many losses and accidents caused by such problems. By August of 1747, as he left Louisbourg, however, Knowles had no inhibitions about openly accusing Bradstreet of profiting at the expense of the government. Knowles claimed he no longer permitted Bradstreet "to Plunder the Government (he having in Mr. Warren's time supplyed the Garrison with Fuel & made him pay upwards of 6000 pound & I have done it for little more than four thousand.)." Despite his pride in having curbed Bradstreet's excesses, he had not been able totally to exclude him from the fuel business. In an account detailing fuel purchases for the year 1746, Knowles stressed that the cost was "£2000 less than what it amounted to in the preceeding year." However, of the total £4152/7/4 spent, £776/15 was paid "To Capt. Bradstreet's Account for Fuel laid in by him."[34] It was business as usual for Bradstreet even under the most adverse conditions.

The second point emerging from Bradstreet's attempted purchase of Sir William's commission relates to his intriguing reference to the fact that, once equipped with a colonel's rank, "my friends will then have it more in their power to serve me." Who were these friends? The letter was written to Pepperrell, so the reference does not apply to his major colonial patron. Sir Peter Warren is a possibility, since Bradstreet considered him a loyal friend. Warren's naval career, however, meant that he would have to be absent from the mother country for considerable periods of time, while effective representation of Bradstreet's interests required a continuing presence on the London scene. Although a reconciliation with King Gould was to occur shortly, there is

---

34. Knowles to Newcastle, September 18, 1746, N.S. A/29, 30-31, P.A.C.; Bradstreet to Pepperrell, June 9, 1746, Belknap Papers, 61 C 59; Knowles to Newcastle, August 31, 1747, M.G. 11, C.O. 5/901, 260-61, P.A.C.; "Fuel Account for Louisbourg, 1746," Shortt et al., *Documents Relating to Currency*, 251.

no evidence it had taken place in 1747. Bradstreet felt he was under the "greatest obligation" for his Newfoundland appointment to Henry Fox, who had been appointed Secretary of War in May of 1746. But Fox was more likely responding to the wishes of "friends," rather than acting as a patron himself. Although definitely not a friend, Charles Knowles put his finger on a very important connection that Bradstreet enjoyed in London. He described Bradstreet as "an Implement of my *Good Friend* the Aldermans" and went on to predict that Bradstreet was going to create a fuss about the way in which Knowles had clamped down on his activities. The Cape Breton Governor warned Newcastle that Bradstreet's "representations to the Alderman may occassion Your Grace the trouble of being teazed by him, wch. is the reason of my mentioning this."[35]

The "Alderman" was William Baker, a powerful London merchant who was indeed an influential friend to have enlisted in one's cause. He has been described as "one of the foremost merchants trading with America" but his activities were not restricted to commerce. Entering parliament in 1747, with the help of the administration, he was a confidant of Newcastle and eventually became one of the Duke's respected advisors on American affairs.[36] By 1752 Bradstreet had entrusted him with a power of attorney to collect the pay of the staff officers at St. John's as well as the garrison's fire and candle allowance. In that year, because of a technical irregularity, Baker submitted a memorial on Bradstreet's behalf to collect these payments for the period from December 1748 to December 1751.[37] In all probability he had been employed in this capacity as soon as Bradstreet received his Newfoundland appointment. But other than this arrangement, little is known concerning the actual dealings between the two men. It does seem that, until King Gould's support re-emerged, Bradstreet relied heavily upon Baker. He referred to him as "my good Friend the alderman" and appointed him executor of his estate, along with Charles Gould, when he drew up his will in November of 1754.[38] Such gestures indicated a close relationship and, in addition, Knowles' comments in 1747 implied that Baker was a very interested patron of Bradstreet. Thus in the context of Bradstreet's Louisbourg service from 1745 to 1747 it is clear that he had a good connection with one of the intimates of the Newcastle administration. While the strength of the connection is uncertain, just to be linked with Baker gave an aura of respectability, and indeed prestige, to Bradstreet. A knowledge of the existence of such a link evidently was a factor which caused critics such

---

35. "Colonel John Bradstreet's Journal," De Forest, *Louisbourg Journals*, 178; Knowles to Newcastle, August 31, 1747, C.O. 5/901, 260-61, P.A.C.
36. See the biographical sketch contained in Lewis Namier and John Brooke, *The History of Parliament: The House of Commons 1754-1790*, 2 (London, 1964), 39-41.
37. Memorial of William Baker on behalf of John Bradstreet to Henry Fox, c. 1752, T.P.C., 128/402.
38. Bradstreet to King Gould, August 10, 1751, ibid., 128/404; Last Will and Testament of John Bradstreet, November 10, 1754, ibid., 128/461.

as Knowles to tread rather warily when discussing or dealing with John Bradstreet.

Despite the apparent support of William Baker in England, by the late summer of 1747 Bradstreet's position in Louisbourg had become rather precarious. Knowles' determination to curb some of Bradstreet's more lucrative endeavours had severely restricted John's activities. Moreover, the English neglect of Louisbourg, and Knowles' oft-repeated lack of faith in the possibilities of its development, revealed to the perceptive observer the increasing likelihood of Cape Breton's return to French hands. This possibility was to become a reality in the very near future. Undoubtedly disheartened at his own Louisbourg treatment and disappointments, as well as the more general English failure to capitalize upon the fortress' potentialities, Bradstreet decided to leave Cape Breton for Newfoundland. Perhaps in this temporary haven he could attempt the reconstruction of his damaged reputation and severely weakened, except for the Baker tie, old-world connections. Consequently, in August of 1747, John Bradstreet arrived at Newfoundland to begin active service as Lieutenant-Governor of St. John's.[39]

As at Canso, Bradstreet was quick to perceive the possibilities, both immediate and long range, of this out-of-the-way post. The annual reports filed concerning Newfoundland did not indicate the population of St. John's at this time, although the number of residents possibly approached 2,400 souls. Regardless of the exact population, it was large enough to support "twelve Taverns or Publick Houses" and attract merchant traders from New England and other American colonies. "Cows, Sheep and Swine" were "Annualy Imported from New England" while "from New York, Philadelphia and the American Colonies, Great Part of the Bread, Flour, Beef, Pork, Rum, Molasses, Tobacco and Lumber" was purchased.[40] Bradstreet's old friend, Sir William Pepperrell, was involved in this Newfoundland trade and he naturally received encouraging cooperation from the Lieutenant-Governor.[41] Bradstreet faithfully reported to Sir William's son, Andrew, the arrival of "one Cargo of Boards" as well as the information that "they lost the Master tells me forty sheep Coming down the Remainder I am told he has sold for five shillings apeace on Account of the Badness of them." He continued, "You May be Assur'd what ever assistance he may want on Your Account in this part of the World if he makes it known to me he shall have it."[42] Other than the obvious

---

39. Otho Hamilton to Lords of Trade and Plantations, October 31, 1747, C.O. 194/12, 51, microfilm, Reel B-211, P.A.C.

40. "Answers to the Queries contained in His Majesty's Instructions to Francis William Drake Esqr...," received with his letter dated December 26, 1750, ibid., 186-87; "Answers to the Queries Contained in His Majestys Instructions to George Bridges Rodney...," October 2, 1749, C.O. 194/25, 76, microfilm, Reel B-215.

41. Fairchild, *Messrs. William Pepperrell*, 188.

42. Bradstreet to Andrew Pepperrell, August 1, 1748, Pepperrell Papers, Book 2, n.p., Maine Historical Society.

continuing friendship such action facilitated, it is uncertain whether Bradstreet derived any further advantage, of a financial sort, from this concern for Pepperrell's interests.

Bradstreet also received a first-hand education in some of the difficulties of life in Newfoundland at this time, difficulties which were aggravated by the English government's failure, or unwillingness, to allow the development of the proper apparatus of government on the island. The need for a full-time governor was one point not lost on John Bradstreet, and his views concerning this and other governmental changes in Newfoundland were to be revealed in the 1753 proposals of Lord Baltimore. Raising questions about Newfoundland's government and furthering cementing his friendship with Pepperrell, however significant, were not the major achievements of Bradstreet's Newfoundland sojourn. More important was his careful projection of the image of a loyal servant of the Crown, by means of his letters to his English superiors. To reinforce this portrayal, he evidently also completed at this time his well-known Louisbourg journal, thus documenting his contribution to the 1745 expedition as well as his unwarranted neglect.[43] Eventually both activities were to pay handsome dividends in the form of a revitalization of King Gould's interest in Bradstreet's cause. Hence, in long-range terms, Bradstreet was taking the first steps towards regaining the support of the English patrons and friends so necessary for his advancement.

In the interval, however, his limited official correspondence during these years was carried on with the Duke of Bedford. In these few letters, faithful fulfillment of all orders by an obviously loyal and diligent Lieutenant-Governor was repeatedly stressed. Even in arranging his departure from St. John's, Bradstreet demonstrated a respectful observance of the proper procedures. As he explained to King Gould, he hoped to secure the "Kings Leave" to go to Great Britain; and, although he could receive permission for such a journey from the Newfoundland Governor, Francis William Drake, he "would much rather have his Majesty's consent."[44]

By the time Bradstreet's plans to return to the mother country had taken shape, King Gould had re-emerged as his friend and benefactor. The reasons for the elder Gould's reawakened interest are shrouded in uncertainty. But after 1750 his concern, and the ever-increasing active involvement of his son, Charles, were of tremendous significance in shaping Bradstreet's future career. Hints that the old connection with King Gould had been re-established are contained in a letter from

---

43. The journal held by the New-York Historical Society is catalogued with the suggestion that it might have been "written about 1753?" See "Retained copy of Bradstreet's Letter concerning the taking of Louisbourg," Misc. MSS, N.Y.H.S. In reprinting it in his *Louisbourg Journals*, 170-78, De Forest accepts the 1753 date. As will be suggested, however, quite possibly it was drafted earlier, during Bradstreet's Newfoundland stay.

44. Bradstreet to the Duke of Bedford, October 8, 1748, C.O. 194/25, 12-13, microfilm, Reel B-215; ibid., June 10, 1749, 28; ibid., August 10, 1750, 84; Bradstreet to King Gould, August 10, 1751, T.P.C., 128/404.

Bradstreet to Gould written in August of 1751. Letters from Gould written in February and March of 1750/51 were acknowledged and the Lieutenant-Governor confessed that "tis not possible for me to find words sufficient to express how happy I think my self in being honour'd with a Continuance of Your Favour, & must own to You I am not a Little proud of my Self when I hear from so many Hands how You have on Several occasions been pleas'd to express Yourself with respect to me." Such words of gratitude and mention of Gould's continuing favour leave the impression that this good relationship enjoyed a long life and had never suffered any serious disruption. Yet the ingratiating tone of the entire letter, carried through to its conclusion with a gift of spruce beer and assurances "that I have always had a greatfull sense of Your goodness to me," might have indicated Bradstreet's determination to paper over past differences with enthusiastic affusions concerning an abiding friendship. An indication that the two men were not as close as Bradstreet implied was contained in his interesting acknowledgement that it was "my good Friend the alderman" who was asked to secure him "the Kings Leave to goe to England this fall." Admittedly, the journey was being made "agreeable to Your [Gould's] advice"[45] but it was William Baker, not King Gould, who was chosen to make the most important arrangement.

Bradstreet must have had good reason for thinking that Gould was solidly in his camp at this point, and, as well, something must have caused Gould to be willing to convey this impression. The answer to Bradstreet's new confidence and Gould's reinvigorated interest might be found in the chronicle of neglect penned by Bradstreet in summarizing his Louisbourg contributions. In the August letter there were two further interesting comments which could be linked with his solicitations via his journal. Bradstreet thanked Gould "for this last Trouble You have been at for my advancement." Then, later in the letter, came the comment, "Mr. Rodney tells me that H:R:H: the Duke[46] was pleas'd to read my Memorial very attentively & said he thought my Care hard as likewise did Mr. Fox."[47] Is it possible that this memorial was actually Bradstreet's Louisbourg journal? If it was convincing to Fox and Cumberland, perhaps it was equally so to Gould. Moreover, is it possible that Gould actually had a hand in arranging their perusal of it? The journal, judging from statements within it, was written between April of 1749 and the fall of 1751 for the benefit of King Gould,[48] whose devotion to Simon Bradstreet and neglect of John had allowed him to drift out of touch with John's activities, and who now needed to be updated concerning his "old friend." An individual who faithfully served as Lieutenant-Governor of St. John's and who mustered such convincing arguments concerning his neglect was probably once more a respecta-

---

45. Ibid.
46. In all probability this was the Duke of Cumberland.
47. Bradstreet to King Gould, August 10, 1751, T.P.C., 128/404.
48. "Colonel John Bradstreet's Journal," De Forest, *Louisbourg Journals*, 171-78.

ble friend whose cause was well worth representing. Evidently Bradstreet's full vindication in the eyes of King Gould had been achieved by the time he left Newfoundland for England in the fall of 1751.[49]

Throughout Bradstreet's career different peaks emerged when everything seemed advantageous for the achievement of his ambitions. Yet in every instance, when he came so far and seemed so near, the prize eluded his grasp. Such was the case at Louisbourg. Such was to be the situation in England as well. Despite his praiseworthy deeds at Cape Breton, his faithful service at St. John's, the involvement of influential friends such as Gould and Baker, and the apparent interest of major figures like Cumberland and Fox, when Bradstreet prepared to return to the colonies late in 1754 he was still only Lieutenant-Governor of St. John's and Captain in a recently reactivated regiment. He had witnessed the rejection of several of his schemes and suggestions and what appeared to be the total failure of his personal solicitations.

A major disappointment came with the defeat of a proposal which grew out of his Newfoundland experience. In July 1753 the committee of the Privy Council handling colonial affairs considered a petition submitted by Frederick Calvert, Lord Baltimore, which suggested the need to appoint a full-time resident governor for the Calvert family's proprietary colony of Avalon in Newfoundland. The petition attempted to establish that the Calvert's ancient claim to the Avalon peninsula had not lapsed but remained in force; it was buttressed by various decisions and declarations over the years. Once this point had been established, the petitioner moved on to elaborate upon the governmental ills of a colony which had grown considerably in terms both of wealth and population. These descriptions of the fishery, the number of inhabitants, the inadequate administration of justice, and the problems created by a government which really only operated during the fishing season, revealed a fresh and first-hand knowledge of Newfoundland which probably had been provided to Calvert by John Bradstreet. It was pointed out that the "Fishing Admirals" had only a "Short occasional Residence in Newfoundland" in which to oversee the administration of justice and, in consequence, "the Country is for the space of 9 or 10 Months in the Year destitute of any form of Government the Military Authority and that of a few Justices of Peace only excepted." To remedy this "long interval of Anarchy and Confusion" there was

---

49. Bradstreet probably left at this time since there is no further evidence of his presence in Newfoundland after August of 1751. His signature no longer appears on troop returns. See Returns for August, 1752, C.O. 194/13, 75, microfilm, Reel B-211, which bear only the signature of his brother-in-law, Captain Christopher Aldridge. Bradstreet's arrival in England at this time and the possibility that Baker introduced him to Newcastle is perhaps borne out by Baker to Newcastle, November 22, 1751, Newcastle Papers, Add. MSS 32,725/426, in which Baker refers to the arrival of an unidentified Nova Scotian: "If Your Graces Curiosity with regard to Nova Scotia continues, & you shall be in the Country and at leisure for half an hour on Sunday morning I believe I shall have a Gentleman with me . . . who was born there & knows that Country better than any person whatever, whom I shall be proud to introduce to Your Grace, on your signifying your pleasure to that purpose."

needed "a regular and permanent form of Government supported by an Established Governor constantly resident in the province and invested with all Powers to Execute and Administer the same." The petition proceeded to suggest a specific individual as well equipped for the governor's appointment. "Your Petr hereby most humbly offers persuant to the several powers and Authoritys vested in him by his said Patent to appoint John Bradstreet Esqr a Gent of great honour and Ability and who is perfectly well acquainted with the Circumstance of the said Province he having been for several Years past by Your Majesty's Lieut Govr. of St. John's."[50] This was to be the first of many attempts by Bradstreet to secure a governorship. But whether it was the wilderness interior around Detroit, the more settled colony of New Jersey, or as in this case the rugged Avalon peninsula, all such efforts were to fail.

It should be clear that Bradstreet's recent arrival from Newfoundland and the presentation of Calvert's petition were not unrelated coincidences. The information contained in the document as well as the nomination of Bradstreet as governor point to the fact that he must have cooperated closely with Lord Baltimore on the scheme. But the well-documented case and very worthwhile suggestions were to be ignored by the English government. For complex reasons and at the behest of a variety of villains,[51] it was to be many years before Newfoundland was granted an adequate system of government. On this occasion a rather glaring flaw in the petition provided the basis for its rejection. Calvert's proposals were passed on to the Board of Trade which in turn sought the advice of "His Majesty's Attorney and Solicitor General"[52] who were quick to point out the fatal weakness of the presentation. The entire document was hinged upon the Baltimore family's claim to Avalon but the Crown's legal advisors ruled that "there is no Evidence of any Actual possession, of the Province claimed, or Exercise of any Powers of Government there, by the Baltimore family; On the contrary it is most probable that at least from the year 1638 they have been out of Possession." Since a governor could only be appointed where there was "a clear Title of Proprietorship; We are humbly of Opinion, that it is not advisable for his Majesty to comply with the said Petition."[53] Bradstreet at least had the consolation that the collapse of this scheme could be traced to the weakness of Calvert's claims rather

---

50. "The humble Petition of the Right Honourable Frederick Calvert Lord Baltimore in the Kingdom of Ireland Lord Proprietary of the Provinces of Maryland and Avalon in America," n.d. but the Privy Council committee considered the petition on July 26, 1753, C.O. 194/13, 105-10, microfilm, Reel B-211.

51. For a recent thorough study of colonial Newfoundland, see C. Grant Head, *Eighteenth Century Newfoundland: A Geographer's Perspective* (Toronto, 1976).

52. Meeting of November 14, 1753, *Journal of the Commissioners for Trade and Plantations*, 9, 454.

53. "Report of His Majtys Attorney & Solicitor Genl. upon a Petition from Ld. Baltimore . . . relative to his Claim of a Tract of land called Avalon in Newfoundland," April 5, 1754, C.O. 194/13, 143-44, microfilm, Reel B-211.

than any deficiency in the information he provided concerning Newfoundland.

Nonetheless the proposal had failed to be accepted and, as it turned out, this was only one of several rebuffs suffered by Bradstreet in England. With the help of a future Secretary at War, Charles Townshend, an abortive attempt was made to have "nine Independent Companys Regimented and that I [Bradstreet] should be the colonel."[54] In September of 1754 as the Duke of Cumberland's plan for a campaign against alleged French "encroachments" in North America was discussed and eventually approved,[55] Bradstreet naturally hoped to be fitted with a major role in it. By January the British forces were ready to sail for America but Bradstreet, who felt fortune had smiled upon him "when this expedition was first meditated," found himself "placed in an inactive state on this occasion" and by-passed once more. He was to sail to America with Braddock's troops but all that awaited him was his old captain's rank in the now reactivated 51st Regiment commanded by Pepperrell, while he obviously had aspired to a more important position. Just what he hoped for is not clear but the perceptive prediction that "I fear his Majestys European Regulars will not answer the great & many good purposes for which they are intended when they get to America"[56] possibly revealed that a heavier reliance upon colonial irregulars and the appointment of senior officers possessing an expertise in colonial warfare, such as himself, was what he had in mind.

While the reasons behind the frustration of his quest for a civil appointment in Newfoundland were fairly straightforward, the consistent failure of his military requests is not so easily explained. He admitted that he was guilty of past errors and personal faults and, no doubt, his abrasively ambitious approach hurt his cause at times. Linked with this was his continual return to "the success I had against Louisbourg" and the repeated description of himself as "the Person who laid the Plan for attacking Louisbourg" and "the principal person in Conducting the Siege."[57] While there was a limited validity to such claims, it was by now a distant triumph, if a triumph at all. While the colonies took obvious pride in it and the British populace had rejoiced momentarily at its capture, to Newcastle and other officials the fall of the fortress in the mid-forties had jeopardized their peace negotiations

---

54. Bradstreet to Charles Gould, October 20, 1762, T.P.C., 128/76. See also Charles Gould to Bradstreet, June 12, 1761, ibid, 128/92 in which Bradstreet is advised, "You will, I assume, take the first opportunity of Congratulating (upon the Strength of your Acquaintance, whilst in England) the new Secretary at War Mr. Charles Townsend." See also "A Scheme for the Improvement & Employment of His Majesty's Forces in America," by Charles Townshend for Newcastle, September 13, 1754, Newcastle Papers, Add. MSS 32,736/515-18.

55. Dominick Graham, "The Planning of the Beausejour Operation and the Approaches to War in 1755," *New England Quarterly*, 61 (1968), 554-55.

56. Bradstreet to King Gould, January 7, 1755, T.P.C., 128/4; Bradstreet to Charles Gould, December 2, 1754, ibid., 128/3.

57. Bradstreet to ?, November 27, 1753, Louisbourg Restoration Project, n.p., microfilm, Reel B-3311; Bradstreet to King Gould, January 7, 1755, T.P.C., 128/4.

with France. This same Newcastle remained in power in 1754 and was unlikely to be impressed by actions obscured by the passage of almost a decade, actions which he never had appreciated in the first place. Bradstreet's reaching back to Louisbourg graphically revealed the difficulties facing the ambitious citizen of two different worlds. In other ways as well his problem of keeping a foot in both camps was demonstrated. The British government with which he dealt was in a state of turmoil and consequently colonial plans and suggestions were very much a secondary consideration. The Duke of Bedford, with whom Bradstreet had corresponded while in Newfoundland, had resigned as Secretary of State in 1751, and was replaced by Lord Holdernesse. This change meant that in the post-1750 period in this department Bradstreet was dealing with a person unknown to him. Even more serious, and at a higher level, Henry Pelham died in March of 1754. While his brother, the Duke of Newcastle, promptly assumed his treasury office, "the question of who was to hold the key office of leader of the House of Commons remained unsettled and occupied the attention of politicians for the next three years."[58] As Bradstreet was to discover again, in the period after the Seven Years' War, political upheaval in Great Britain meant colonial neglect. On the individual level, when major office holders in the mother country were changing or being replaced, minor colonial office seekers had to wait for the political turbulence to subside before their claims for preferment could be acted upon. A final barrier to Bradstreet's aspirations at this time was the simple fact that he was a colonial pursuing a career in the English army, and as such was of uncertain calibre. The colonials plainly were not judged to be competent enough to serve as high-ranking officers in the British army.[59] Any major expedition was to be controlled and led by British officers. After Braddock's disaster Newcastle commented, "We must certainly now set out upon a new principle—Americans must fight Americans, and regular troops must not be puffed up to their own disgrace and our miscarriage in all our operations."[60] But much time and many deeds were required before this English condescension softened and the military contributions of colonial officers, such as Bradstreet, were appreciated.

Waiting at Cork to take ship for America, in January 1755, John Bradstreet well deserved a few moments of introspection as he pondered his fate at the hands of the goddess fortune.

> I am now so far convinced of her being a capricious goddess, that should she take me by the hand again, I shall look on her favours in another light than I have hitherto; I shall not think she means to make her bountys

---

58. Lewis Namier and John Brooke, *The History of Parliament: The House of Commons 1754-1790*, 1 (London, 1964), 1. Useful studies of the Newcastle era are James A. Henretta, *"Salutary Neglect": Colonial Administration Under the Duke of Newcastle* (Princeton, N.J., 1972); Reed Browning, *The Duke of Newcastle* (New Haven, 1975).

59. See Stanley M. Pargellis, *Lord Loudoun in North America* (New Haven, 1933), 16-17.

60. As quoted in Graham, "The Planning of the Beausejour Operation," 565.

compleat: and therefore shall never grow fond of her gifts, nor place my heart upon the pleasing prospect of what I have only the expectation of; nay, should she ever be so liberal as to place riches, honours & reputation upon me, I shall endeavour to place them so in my mind, that whenever she is pleas'd to call them back, she may take them without giving me much disturbance. I no longer suffer in my minde for what is past, but have submitted, slept of murmuring, and have very nearly persuaded my self, that what ever happens ought to happen, and that it did not become me to expostulate; tho satisfied, that whatever errors I have committed, or whatever faults can be objected to me, still I have always lov'd my country, & study'd to serve it.[61]

But Bradstreet was not so willing to let fate take its course as he implied in this letter. Quite the contrary, his interests were left in the hands of very real mortals, rather than any capricious goddess, and these mortals were firmly convinced of the merits of his cause. Although Bradstreet came away from England with many failures behind him, a careful foundation for future success had been erected by means of the friendships developed and solidified during these years of apparent disappointment and resignation. William Baker still handled some of Bradstreet's finances for him[62] but other individuals had supplanted the Alderman as concerned advocates of Bradstreet's cause. By this time Sir Richard Lyttleton and Charles Gould had emerged as his true friends. In years past, King Gould, Lord Baltimore, Charles Townshend, and Henry Fox, had all been helpful, in ways varying from the very limited to the quite substantial, while in the years ahead Lord Loudoun, James Abercromby, and Jeffery Amherst were among those to contribute kind words and effective intervention on Bradstreet's behalf. But his two most consistent English champions were Lyttleton and Gould.

During preparations for the British general election of 1754, Bradstreet was active arranging support for Sir Richard Lyttleton. A short note to Charles Gould, written from Poole, reported that he had successfully "Engag'd 40 votes," while in another brief report he had secured "103 Votes this night for his Lordship."[63] This vote gathering was carried out on behalf of Lyttleton who eventually was returned unopposed as the Member of Parliament representing Poole.[64] Sir

---

61. Bradstreet to King Gould, January 7, 1755, T.P.C., 128/4.
62. For examples of Baker's attention to financial matters, see Charles Gould to Baker, March 29, 1755, T.P.C., 128/406; and Bradstreet to Charles Gould, December 2, 1754, T.P.C., 128/3.
63. Bradstreet to [Charles Gould], n.d., T.P.C. 128/1 and 128/2. Both these notes are unaddressed and undated but the National Library of Wales calendar of the Tredegar Park Collection includes them among letters from Bradstreet to Charles Gould dated 1754-1756. 128/1 was written at Poole but the place where 128/2 was written is not decipherable.
64. Lewis Namier and John Brooke, *The History of Parliament: The House of Commons 1754-1790*, 3 (London, 1964), 75. Biographical information concerning Lyttleton is derived from sketch of him contained in this study, 75-76. Rose Mary Davis, *The Good Lord Lyttleton: A Study in Eighteenth-Century Politics and Culture* (Bethlehem, Pa., 1939),

Richard (1718-1770) had combined a career in the army, which was to take him to the rank of Lieutenant-General in 1759, with a political career as member of the Commons, sitting first for Brackley from 1747 to 1754 and then for Poole from 1754 to 1761. With the help of William Pitt he was appointed Master of the Jewel Office in 1756, and held this office until he assumed the governorship of Minorca in 1762. He served in this capacity until accepting the Guernsey governorship in 1766, which he was to hold until his death. Because of his excellent relationship with Pitt,[65] Lyttleton was of crucial importance to Bradstreet during the Seven Years' War. He saw to it that a number of John's suggestions concerning the war effort, as well as requests for advancement, were placed directly in Pitt's hands for his consideration. In addition, he was instrumental in arranging at least one of Bradstreet's promotions and kept a careful watch for any other rewards which might be gained for his colonial friend.[66] To Bradstreet's misfortune, ill health forced Lyttleton to go abroad by 1760,[67] and after this date his effectiveness was severely handicapped, although his interest in Bradstreet's career remained strong.

Although extremely significant, Lyttleton's greatest contributions on Bradstreet's behalf were limited to the period from 1754 to 1760. Charles Gould, on the other hand, first met Bradstreet during his visit to England in the 1750s and was destined to serve faithfully his interests for the remainder of John's life. He then handled the General's estate, and all the thorny problems connected with it, until his own death in 1806. Born in 1726, Charles, the eldest son of King Gould, after studies at Westminster and Oxford was admitted to Lincoln's Inn in 1743 and called to the bar in 1750. His legal training provided an excellent background for first assisting and then succeeding his father, in 1749, as Deputy Judge Advocate-General. Actually, Charles was already functioning as Judge Advocate-General since his nominal superior, Thomas Morgan, allowed him to carry out all the duties associated with the office. In 1769 with the death of Morgan, Gould succeeded him as Judge Advocate-General. This was a logical step both in view of Charles' long service in the office and the fact that he had married Morgan's daughter, Jane, in 1758. As his career progressed,

---

provides considerable information concerning the Lyttleton family. Since she deals with the career of Lyttleton's brother, Lord George Lyttleton, Sir Richard makes only rare appearances.

65. Pitt to Bute, February 4, 1757, Romney Sedgwick, ed., "Letters from William Pitt to Lord Bute, 1755-1758," in Richard Pares and A. J. P. Taylor, eds., *Essays Presented to Sir Lewis Namier* (London, 1956), 119, in which Pitt comments, "The unexampled injury done Sir Richard Lyttleton if he is left out of the promotion, astonishes me."

66. See, for example, Richard Lyttleton to Charles Gould, c. 1757, T.P.C., 128/33; and Bradstreet to Charles Gould, September 12, 1757, T.P.C., 128/30, in which Bradstreet states, "Since my leaving England I have received many kind letters from Sir Richard Lyttleton and in the last he gave me hopes of my being soon consider'd for my services to my Country and this day we have the account here of Mr Pitts being Secretary of State with whome I know he is well...."

67. Namier and Brooke, *History of Parliament*, 3, 75.

honours accumulated: "K.C. in 1754, and Oxford D.C.L. in 1773, a knighthood in 1779, a baronetcy in 1792, and a Privy Councillorship in 1802." Offsetting some of these successes was his early failure to launch a political career. In 1756 and again in 1759 Thomas Morgan applied to Newcastle on Gould's behalf for a Commons seat, but both applications were unsuccessful. In 1778, however, he entered the House and sat until his death, representing first Brecon and then Breconshire. Gould's fortune was considerably enhanced in 1792 when his wife inherited the Morgan estates of Ruperva and Tredegar, since her brothers had died without children, and it was at this time that he changed his name to Sir Charles Morgan.[68]

Gould was just settling into the office of Deputy Judge Advocate-General when Bradstreet first met him in the early 1750s. His official duties appear to have consisted of preparing the annual Mutiny Bill and Articles of War for parliamentary consideration,[69] as well as pointing out to the War Office, and officers abroad, the proper procedures and any irregularities in court-martials they contemplated conducting or had already completed. The powers of the office were obviously limited and, when the minor nature of Gould's appointment is linked with his lack of political success in the 1750s, it is at first difficult to fathom his utility to Bradstreet. Gould himself reminded Bradstreet, "As to Politicks, you know I swim only on the Surface."[70] This might have been true, but he was swimming in the very restricted pond of London officialdom and it was here that his value emerged. Because of the activities of his office, Gould was in constant communication with senior officials of the War Office and senior army officers. He had his finger on the pulse of English military activities and, through his personal acquaintances at the War Office, possibly could capitalize on any changes or proposals to the advantage and interest of Bradstreet. In addition to the access he enjoyed to this major government department, Gould's presence in the corridors of power allowed him to assess the various political changes, whether in the wind or already accomplished, and then instruct Bradstreet how best he could adjust to these governmental fluctuations in order to protect or advance his fortunes. As a legalistic member of the English bureaucracy there were other ways in which Gould was to be an invaluable aid to Bradstreet. His civil service background enabled him to cut quickly through the bureaucratic maze and place Bradstreet's requests in the proper hands. Furthermore, his legal training caused him to hone carefully his friend's submissions into reasonably precise and balanced presentations. Bradstreet's various petitions and memorials were polished by

---

68. Frederick B. Wiener, *Civilians Under Military Justice: The British Practice since 1689, Especially in North America* (Chicago, 1967), 175-76. Wiener offers a very laudatory treatment of Gould's career as Deputy and then Judge Advocate-General. Namier and Brooke, *History of Parliament*, 2, 522-23, also provide biographical details concerning Gould.
69. Wiener, *Civilians Under Military Justice*, 10.
70. Charles Gould to Bradstreet, December 18, 1754, T.P.C., 128/14.

Gould, placed in the hands of key officials, and, most important of all, presented at the best possible moment.

Bradstreet was quick to recognize and express appreciative acknowledgements of Charles Gould's immense value. But the relationship was substantially different from that of John with Charles' father, King Gould. In the case of John Bradstreet and Charles Gould there appeared to be a friendship founded on mutual respect and genuine amicability, unlike the more business-like arrangement with King Gould. In his letters to the elder Gould, John referred to an abiding friendship, but there was a certain cloying artificiality to these expressions, and a careful distance seemed to be observed between the two men. While King Gould was cautiously addressed as "Sir," John wrote to "Dear Charles" in a far more sincere and open fashion. As he made his departure from England, John rather laboriously and formally thanked King Gould; while at the same time in a free and friendly style he communicated his final wishes to Charles, underlining the need "to communicate to me from time to time what ever happens either of consequence to the publick, which concerns my Self, or is agreeable to You." For his part, Charles was quick to make clear his willingness to serve a friend in what was to be the first of a long chain of reports concerning the state of Bradstreet's cause.[71] Of course, the elder Gould was getting on in years (he was to die in July of 1756),[72] and Bradstreet might have been realistically arranging stronger ties with Charles bearing this in mind. But John appeared quite sincere when he bade farewell to Charles Gould with the words, "Heavens bless you, keep your health, the rest will follow; such talents which God has given You never fail making the Man an ornament to his Country & a blessing to his friends & relations."[73] Although he never saw him again, Charles Gould was to answer with over five decades of faithful service to John Bradstreet, his immediate family, and his descendants.

Bradstreet's career was steeped in contradiction and irony but at no time were these characteristics more evident than during the years from 1745 to 1755. As Bradstreet took leave of England Charles Gould was a close friend and committed patron; yet it had been the neglect, whether unintentional or quite deliberate, of Gould's father which originally had threatened Bradstreet's rise in the army. Not only had he gained the support of Charles Gould during his years in England, but Sir Richard Lyttleton also was won over by the justice of his cause. Henry Fox, Lord Baltimore, and Charles Townshend, moreover, were willing to at least extend a helping hand. Apparently Bradstreet had a real capacity for making friends and enlisting patrons. Just a few years earlier, however, the same Bradstreet demonstrated a fumbling inept-

---

71. See Bradstreet to King Gould, January 7, 1755, T.P.C., 128/4; Bradstreet to Charles Gould, December 2, 1754, T.P.C., 128/3; Charles Gould to Bradstreet, December 18, 1754, T.P.C., 128/14.
72. Wiener, *Civilians Under Military Justice*, 174n.
73. Bradstreet to Charles Gould, January 9, 1755, T.P.C., 128/5.

ness in such efforts. Charles Knowles had quickly become his sarcastic and critical opponent; William Shirley had withdrawn his support from the key advisor whose earlier activities had been particularly praiseworthy. And even Bradstreet's own brother, Simon, had been sufficiently inhospitable to displace John and frustrate his aspirations for a higher military rank as his proper Louisbourg reward. At the same time, as his friends and relatives turned against him and a shrill desperation emerged in Bradstreet's letters, he did not allow such misfortunes to lead to his sterile acquiescence. He showed amazing recuperative powers and an ability to make thoughtful adjustments which were to combine to meet such adversities with an immediate counter-attack. Although obviously disappointed at his hard treatment, he was quick to respond with imaginative suggestions concerning a Canada expedition, a Newfoundland governorship, and a major role in what became Braddock's ill-fated expedition against the French in America.

While these proposals were rejected and his immediate gains appeared quite limited, when viewed within the wider perspective of his future achievements, it becomes clear that these years could be considered an extremely useful apprenticeship period for John Bradstreet. He had learned the need to publicize his deeds, but such statements of his own case were carefully substantiated, properly balanced so as to make clear his plight and pretensions as well as a certain humble resignation, and delivered into significantly influential hands. The experiences with Knowles and Shirley must have impressed upon him the need for faithful fulfillment of assigned duties and the constant cultivation of superiors in England as well as comanding officers in the field. The twists and turns of his own career must have convinced him that this was the way of the world, and a perceptive awareness of the drift of men and ideas was necessary if full advantage was to be taken of such changes. Thus, Shirley's animosity was used to strengthen Pepperrell's friendship; New England's disappointment with conditions in conquered Louisbourg was blended into Bradstreet's own disenchantment; a proposed expedition or appointment was carefully fitted to his talents and qualifications. In other words, he had acquired the knack of constantly keeping abreast of the suggested policies or aspirations of those in authority in order to accentuate his own utility and continually demonstrate the need for the enlistment of his expertise. It was a much more polished, discrete, and aware John Bradstreet who sailed for the American colonies in 1755.

The very fact of his return to America revealed one further, but very fundamental, reality which had been driven home quite forcefully to the now forty-year-old Bradstreet during the past decade. He was a colonial and not an Englishman. In the past this colonial background had proved a major liability; it handicapped him in his search for higher office. It also restricted him to colonial patrons when mother country supporters were needed, and it emasculated his thinking to such an extent that conceptions concerning the utility of Louisbourg, the governmental needs of Newfoundland, and the military needs of English America were formulated largely from the American vantage point with insufficient consideration allowed to the mother-country viewpoint. Nevertheless, rather than turning away from England with resentment, Bradstreet was going to attempt to meet the problems created by his Nova Scotia birth and childhood by bridging the chasm, taking full advantage of his trans-Atlantic connections and knowledge, and even, at times, playing one world off against the other. It was a delicate undertaking which was already underway before he left England. In a prophetic comment Bradstreet pointed out to King Gould that his military neglect in England "must be in a great measure attended with the loss of that consideration which I was in possession of in the people of America."[74] In other words, the old world must appreciate the sensitivities of the new world, in this case its respect for John Bradstreet. However, on the other side of the ocean Bradstreet made no secret of the "Easie Access"[75] he enjoyed in London through various powerful patrons. This recognition and manipulation of the distance between mother country and colony, when linked with an awareness of their common fears revealed during the Seven Years' War, might yet bring Bradstreet the success and recognition he so deeply desired.

---

74. Bradstreet to King Gould, January 7, 1755, T.P.C., 128/4.
75. I borrow the expression from Stanley N. Katz, "An Easie Access: Anglo-American Politics in New York, 1732-1753" (Ph.D. dissertation, Harvard University, 1961).

Chapter IV

Reunited with Shirley

During the American preliminaries to the Seven Years' War, the career of John Bradstreet demonstrated a blending of duty and possible profit.[1] An interesting intermixture of mother-country and colonial aspirations and fears concerning the French empire in North America presented Bradstreet with the opportunity to offer territorial and economic proposals. These hopes for the English conquest and development of the Great Lakes region could only be achieved by the collapse of New France. The rapid emergence of such schemes was to occur shortly after Bradstreet joined the campaign against Niagara led by his one time friend and patron, Governor William Shirley of Massachusetts. If such suggestions were carried through successfully, Bradstreet had an excellent chance to obtain both financial rewards and military promotions. The colonies' territorial desires, and personal gains for Bradstreet, meshed perfectly with military duties performed in order to alleviate apprehensions felt by Great Britain concerning French "encroachments" in the Great Lakes area, as well as in the Ohio valley and the Nova Scotia peninsula. But such an intricately staged production could never materialize without a cooperative commanding officer, willing to give full rein to Bradstreet's ambitions and assign him the duties which could be employed so advantageously. In this respect William Shirley proved a real asset and more than compensated for his Louisbourg actions, or lack of actions, relating to Bradstreet. However, Shirley's influence was declining and a better-informed and more aware Bradstreet was extremely careful not to link his own fortune too closely with that of the much-maligned Shirley. The Mas-

---

1. Julian Gwyn, "Prize Money and Rising Expectations: Admiral Warren's Personal Fortune," *Social History*, 4 (1971), 87, argues that for Peter Warren, "war was the natural blending of duty and profit."

sachusetts governor's brief command of the English army in America, from 1755 to 1756, has been described as the "years of defeat." But for John Bradstreet, common apprehensions about the French menace, when joined to his own dynamic actions, his cautious cooperation with Shirley, and his helpful friends at home, were to make 1755 and 1756 years of solid achievement.

In March of 1755, after an eight-weeks passage, Bradstreet arrived in America with the fleet bearing Major-General Edward Braddock's troops.[2] These British regulars came at a rather critical moment since, while French-English relations were deteriorating in Europe, in the colonies hostilities had already begun. Virginia was the destination of this first contingent of regulars but it was not the only colony threatened by the French. Further north, Massachusetts, and more specifically its governor, William Shirley, felt the need for defensive precautions and limited offensive operations against French Canada. A year earlier, in 1754, Shirley had led an expedition into the Kennebec region and constructed several posts, including Fort Halifax, for defensive purposes. His activities were accepted and even applauded by some of his English superiors willing to embark on a war policy. With this encouragement and rather vague instructions "to take advantage of French weaknesses in the northern region to restore boundaries," Shirley moved on to larger considerations. For 1755 he had in mind at least two projects: one a cooperative venture with Charles Lawrence, Lieutenant-Governor of Nova Scotia, against Fort Beausejour, and the other an attack on "Carthage" itself, Crown Point. The arrival of Braddock to assume command of American defence changed the emphasis of the Shirley proposals. Braddock met with the colonial representatives at Alexandria, Virginia, in April of 1755. Plans were finalized for the English major-general to lead an expedition against Fort Duquesne, while the provincial army provided by the northern colonies was to be directed against Crown Point and Niagara.[3] It was decided that William Johnson was to command the Crown Point undertaking while Shirley was to direct the Niagara attack. Braddock also named William Shirley as his second-in-command over the British forces in North America.[4]

Well before the Alexandria conference, Bradstreet had already left Virginia. Prior to his departure he met with Braddock at Williamsburg at which time, although he was received "very politely," there was "not one word of any further rank of being imploy'd in any other way than

---

2. Bradstreet to Charles Gould, March 14, 1756, T.P.C., 128/6, N.L.W.

3. John A. Schutz, "Imperialism in Massachusetts during the Governorship of William Shirley, 1741-1745," *Huntington Library Quarterly*, 23 (1960), 228-31; Schutz, *William Shirley*, 187-89; Minutes of Council, Alexandria, April 14, 1755, C.O. 5/46-1, 25-30, P.A.C.

4. This arrangement was apparently quite satisfactory to both Johnson and Shirley and was concluded with a great deal of friendship and respect being expressed by each for the other. See Lawrence H. Gipson, *The British Empire Before the American Revolution* (New York, 1958-1970), 6, 137.

that of Captain." As a result, on the same day as this meeting, March 14, 1755, he set out to rejoin his regiment, the 51st, in New York, feeling that he was "now really reduced so low on this side the water in expectation of rank." In England also his quest for higher rank was not going well. Although "Your Friends... wished for a Promotion, that might have vacated a Majority in your favour," no such acceptable opening emerged. Service in the 51st Regiment was not a totally bleak proposition, however, since although Bradstreet heard it was composed "of all sorts of people" and indeed discovered it to include "the worst of troops upon earth,"[5] its military inadequacies served to highlight his own competence and experience. The regiment was slated for service in Shirley's Niagara campaign and no doubt the militarily inexperienced Massachusetts governor, totally lacking any professional staff,[6] was quite relieved when the knowledgeable veteran, John Bradstreet, joined his command. Shirley's confidence in Bradstreet was revealed by the way in which he quickly entrusted the recently arrived captain with elaborate duties at Oswego, an outpost which was the key to the entire Niagara expedition.

In 1755 Oswego had at least a threefold value to English America. Economically, it had long functioned as a centre for the profitable fur trade, developed by various New York interests, which challenged the French fur trade enterprises in the Great Lakes and more westerly regions. Growing out of its trading-post value was the diplomatic role it played among the surrounding Six Nations Indians. It was here that the English came into continuous contact with the Iroquois and worked to enlist their support in any confrontation with the French. If the outright support of all of the Six Nations was not possible, Oswego at least served the purpose of a listening post, useful in the detection of changing Indian moods and the impact French overtures were having upon the various tribes. In a military sense, the friendly Indians congregating at Oswego provided valuable information about French military movements and plans in the Great Lakes area. In addition, the Lake Ontario outpost was the vital base needed for the launching of an attack on Niagara or for any English campaign on the Great Lakes.

Realizing the importance of Oswego, Shirley wasted no time in reinforcing the post, strengthening its fortifications, and making the changes necessary if it was to accommodate the forces directed against Niagara. All of these chores were assigned to his old Louisbourg advisor, John Bradstreet. Bradstreet was ordered "immediately to proceed with two Companies of Sir William Pepperrell's Regiment" to reinforce the Oswego garrison. On his journey up to Lake Ontario he was "to make the best observations" possible "of the Rivers and Country from Schenactady to Oswego," noting the distances and any difficulties

---

5. Bradstreet to Charles Gould, March 14, 1755, T.P.C., 128/6; Charles Gould to Bradstreet, April 18, 1755, T.P.C. 128/16; Bradstreet to Charles Gould, June 1, 1755, T.P.C., 128/7.
6. See Schutz, *William Shirley*, 198.

encountered, and informing Shirley concerning these matters "as soon as possible." Once arrived at the post, he was to survey "the Forts and Works," draw up a plan including what he felt to be the needed fortification alterations, and "immediately to set about such Repairs or new Works as shall appear to You to be necessary for the immediate Defence of the Fort, and which may soon be effected and without great Expence." For the proper defence of Oswego as well as to facilitate any offensive launched from there, Bradstreet was "to get the best intelligence you can of the Navigation on the Lake Ontario." Finally, he was reminded "to treat all Indians, who shall come to Trade at Oswego; with Kindness."[7] Of the various instructions, this last was probably the most pleasing to Bradstreet. The other tasks were rather pedestrian preparations, behind-the-lines assignments which Bradstreet continually claimed to be inadequate employment of his talents. Activities as an Indian diplomat were far more to his liking. He fancied himself an Indian authority "par excellence" and made every possible effort to stress his abilities in this regard. To his misfortune his competence as a boat-builder and mover of men and materials was to overshadow the more glamorous Indian activities and make him a vital cog behind the lines rather than an active participant at the front. While the instructions made clear that at this point Bradstreet's talents as a competent organizer and officer equipped to handle preparations for the supply and movement of men were recognized, he at least had the consolation that the same orders revealed his commanding officer's total confidence in his recommendations and actions. He appeared to have regained the solid support of William Shirley. As a result, temporary acceptance of the largely mundane duties handed him might further gratify Shirley and pave the way for the assignment of the more active role which Bradstreet desired.

After reaching Oswego on May 27, Bradstreet plunged into the strengthening of the post as well as the drafting of numerous letters concerning the Great Lakes theatre of war. To Braddock and the colonial governors he dispatched word that information first secured when he and William Johnson had questioned a French deserter on May 16,[8] during a brief visit by Bradstreet at Mount Johnson, was now verified by his findings at Oswego. They had learned that the French had sent a force of 950 men to the Ohio to meet Braddock's army. Once arrived at Oswego this was confirmed in Bradstreet's conversations with Indians and by the activity of the French bateaux moving on Lake Ontario. At the same time Bradstreet provided the first of many suggestions concerning the proper handling of Indian affairs. He reported the presence of "many Indians here," their careful watch on "the proceedings between the French and us," and the need to give

---

7. Instructions to Captain John Bradstreet of Sir William Pepperrell's regiment from William Shirley, 1755, ref. #3406, New York State Library, Albany.

8. "Examination of Jean Silvestre & Wife," May 16, 1755, James Sullivan *et al.*, *The Papers of Sir William Johnson* (Albany, 1921-1961), 1, 508.

"Provisions to such as are in Real Want, and well chosen Presents to the principal People." With such a policy "great Good might, & I believe would result." A copy of this account was enclosed in another letter written the same day to Governor Shirley. Some very accurate observations about the route recently traversed were added for the benefit of his commander. Bradstreet's journey to Oswego had convinced him that it was going to be extremely difficult to move an army with any amount of speed and with adequate provisions to the Lake Ontario post. Furthermore, there was a real danger of the supply line being severed by hostile Indian parties unless troops were stationed at key positions such as the Great Carrying Place. Turning to Indian affairs, he reported "that I have engag'd the principal Chief of the Miscisage Indians who came here to trade, to go to Colonel Johnson's; & at his request have sent a Belt of Wampum to his Nation, who live on the North Side of the Lake; they are a numerous Nation, and live in Friendship with the Six Nations, and certain I am, if I had Authority, with proper presents and provisions, I could engage many Indians to go to the Westward with us."[9] Shirley was aware, and Bradstreet must have known as well, that Johnson had authority over the Indians in this region. Yet by hinting at the contribution the Indians could make to Shirley's Niagara expedition, Bradstreet hoped to overcome any scruples the Massachusetts governor might have had about encroaching on Johnson's domain. Moreover, while Bradstreet's request appeared to be very minor, it was to prove one of many sources of friction which developed between Shirley and Johnson. It was one which was to be magnified considerably by Bradstreet's repeated and open assertions of his pretensions to a major role in Great Lakes Indian diplomacy.

As Bradstreet's desire for a particular position unfolded, he offered his proposals at different levels in different ways. To the governors and Braddock he made a limited suggestion concerning gifts, to Shirley the specific need of augmented authority was presented, while to the Secretary of State for the southern department, Sir Thomas Robinson, the full dimensions of his plan were unravelled. After only three days at Oswego, on May 30, the perceptive and resourceful Bradstreet penned an elaborate analysis of the state of Oswego and the proper approach which should be taken by Great Britain to meet effectively the French threat in the Great Lakes area. "I find the Fort, or Trading House so trifling, and the Situation so bad, that any additional works would be throwing Money away," he wrote. For the present he was merely erecting "some Palisades round the back of it" and clearing the woods for about a "Musket Shot round." It is interesting that this critical assessment of the post's defences was submitted to the home authorities before Bradstreet bothered to provide Shirley with the same distressing information. He might have assumed that his commander was all

---

9. Bradstreet to the Colonial Governors, May 29, 1755, ibid., 547-48; Bradstreet to Shirley, May 29, 1755, ibid., 549-50.

too well aware of Oswego's shortcomings. But it also could have been an early indication that Bradstreet was very aware of his being obliged to serve two masters, his immediate field commander, and the more powerful authorities at home. Placed in such a predicament he had no compunctions about passing on information which put his immediate superior in a rather unfortunate position but which might enhance his own position in the eyes of the authorities who held power. His letter to Robinson then mentioned the progress of the boat-building ordered by Shirley and summarized the information garnered about French movements across the lakes which, Bradstreet reported, was so alarming that he had sent "an Express to the General, and to the respective Governors from New York to Virginia." The obviously zealous servant of the Crown came now to the heart of his proposals. He spoke of the Indian presence at Oswego, emphasizing the need "to Treat them properly & take the Necessary Measures to attach them to Us" while bemoaning the "Scandalous... Manner in which the Trade is now carried on here, & I am really Surpriz'd the Indians have not long Since destroyed the Traders, & plundered the Place; And it is clear that half the Indian Trade has been lost within these Five Years."

Having made his point, Bradstreet went on to report that the French had established a post between Fort Frontenac and Montreal to stimulate trade and were angling for Indian permission to establish another one on the south side of Lake Ontario, halfway between Oswego and Niagara. Because of the difficulties of provisioning their garrisons, they had the foresight to establish permanent settlements where there was good land available, at Detroit, for example. To counter this activity Bradstreet proposed a British settlement at the site midway between Niagara and Oswego, near present-day Rochester, which the French had proposed to develop. "Gerondequast," as it was called, had good, cleared land and could be a self-sufficient settlement within a year. As to the problems of Indian sovereignty and recruiting of settlers, Bradstreet had "not the least Doubt, but the Indians will permit the English to build a Fort & Trading House there, & sell those lands I have mentioned for a Settlement at a reasonable Rate, & believe the most of the People belonging to the two Regiments designed for Service this Way, would gladly settle theron, and many come there from different Parts of the Colonies for a small Encouragement." In a neat summation of his various proposals and their objective, he concluded that "there is no other Way to Secure the Six Nations, to His Majesty's Interest, rendering the Expence of Garrisons Supportable & effectually put an End to the French Power amongst the Indians, than Securing this Place Gerondequast, Settling the lands above-mentioned, Securing Niagara, & breaking up the French Settlement at the Detroit."[10]

Coming from an individual who was only recently arrived on the Lake Ontario frontier, Bradstreet's report was comprehensive and

---

10. Bradstreet to Sir Thomas Robinson, May 30, 1755, C.O. 5/46-2, 515-20.

penetrating. Admittedly, to some it would be far from pleasing. An experienced Indian diplomat such as William Johnson could find much to criticize in Bradstreet's proposed intrusions on Iroquois territory. The complexities of securing Indian agreement to any such settlement as "Gerondequast" were numerous, since it involved the touchy question of Indian sovereignty, and Bradstreet's hope of an easily arranged purchase was too optimistically simple.[11] As well, Bradstreet's shafts concerning the mishandling of English relations with the Indians and his suggestions concerning proper approaches could only be interpreted as a calculated indictment of Johnson's performance and an outright effort either to supplant him as Indian superintendent or at least to undermine his authority. Such a manoeuvre on Bradstreet's part was extremely premature and bound to alienate Johnson's supporters and friends in New York. Bradstreet's over-eager search for personal aggrandizement and advancement rushed him into such indiscrete statements and revealed an unusual insensitivity to the realities of colonial New York.

While this challenge to Johnson's authority was a rather jarring note upon which to inaugurate his return to the colonies, the general economic and territorial points made in Bradstreet's presentation to Robinson were far more compatible with colonial feelings. He called for the countering of French influence in the Great Lakes area by a vigorous trade and settlement policy, an expansionist approach from which the colonies, and probably Bradstreet as well, stood to gain. Similar desires and hopes were being expressed by other major colonial figures, such as Thomas Pownall and William Shirley.[12] Bradstreet's old ability to adjust quickly to the realities and possibilities of a new posting, be it Canso, Louisbourg, St. John's, or Oswego, was readily apparent. Despite his years in England, in the short space of a few months after his return to America he sensed colonial anxieties and hopes for the Great Lakes area and formulated proposals which were very much in step with the opinions expressed by expansionists such as Shirley and Pownall. Moreover, it is noteworthy that all three individuals were aware of trans-Atlantic realities. They offered proposals and pursued careers that were dependent upon a certain amount of unity, in terms of aspiration and response, between mother country and colony. In this instance considerable further time and effort was to be expended before English and American interests were to be fully roused and adequate contributions, in terms of manpower and finances, were forthcoming.

---

11. Johnson revealed his sensitivity to Indian sovereignty when he objected to the construction of storehouse forts at the Great Carrying Place before Indian consent was secured. Despite his objections the posts were built. See Theodore Thayer, "The Army Contractors for the Niagara Campaign, 1755-1756," *William and Mary Quarterly*, 3d Ser., 14 (1957), 38.

12. See "Considerations Upon the Scite, Interests, and Service of North America" (1755), by Thomas Pownall, Pargellis, *Military Affairs*, 158-66; Shirley to Robinson, August 12, 1755, Lincoln, *Shirley Correspondence*, 2, 228.

Until such grand plans for the Great Lakes area gained total approval and support, Bradstreet had to content himself with the implementation of Shirley's instructions concerning Oswego. But he did not rest content with these duties. He was continually on the watch for a more active role and made clear, at least to Charles Gould in England, his impatience with his present responsibilities. Early in June he outlined to his London friend the boat-building, troop-training, and "talking politicks with all sorts of Indians," in which he was engaged at Oswego. He also expressed his "anxiety and indignation" at the helpless position in which he found himself as he watched "the French pass the place with colours flying and Drums beating to oppose my General." His helplessness, he felt, was caused by "my not having weight enough to get leave to be employ'd in a service that would prevent the great opposition the ffrench are like to make on the Ohio."[13] This impatience increased as the month of June wore on. It became clear that Bradstreet's predictions about the difficulties of moving Shirley's forces to Oswego were proving only too accurate. While Bradstreet's boat-building[14] went on at a busy pace, Governor Shirley was making only slow and limited progress getting under way on the route to Oswego. As a result, in answering a letter received from Shirley which had been written on June 15, Bradstreet carefully presented his commander with a proposal for an immediate strike at Niagara. Although Bradstreet had been informed by Indians that Niagara was going to be reinforced by "several hundred men" who were to construct a fort, the post "at this time has but a very small garrison and no works going on." At Oswego, however, he felt the three companies already there were soon to be "fit for immediate Service" and adequate bateaux transportation could be arranged quickly. Thus, he informed Shirley, "If I should receive Your orders to proceed farther I may set out that moment." Having established Niagara's vulnerability, the adequacy of preparations at Oswego, and his personal readiness, Bradstreet proceeded with the details of his proposal. If "You find You cannot be here in time put it into my hands, [to attack Niagara] with the three companys now here and the Jersey troops, and were the two company now at the Carrying place sent here they would be sufficient to protect this place."[15]

No indication of Shirley's reply exists, although the proposal obviously was not accepted. At least one possible reason for its rejection is fairly evident, however. Shirley probably felt the limited manpower needs envisaged by Bradstreet as necessary for the attack were far from sufficient. At this time he was actively pressing the need to increase the Niagara forces to no fewer than 2,400 men. Without this large a force,

---

13. Bradstreet to Charles Gould, June 1, 1755, T.P.C., 128/7.
14. Bradstreet to Shirley, June ? [1755], Colonel John Bradstreet Manuscripts, American Antiquarian Society (A.A.S.), Worcester. Bradstreet comments on the further orders, dated June 8, which he had received concerning the construction of another schooner and row galley.
15. Bradstreet to Shirley [June 1755], ibid.

he argued, the expedition's chances of success were severely restricted. In consequence, he was redirecting troops originally intended for service under Johnson against Crown Point into his Niagara expedition, while offering profuse justification for such action to Johnson and Sir Thomas Robinson. For Shirley to have approved Bradstreet's Niagara assault with only 500 New Jersey troops and five companies, two of which were to remain at Oswego for its protection, when he himself was stressing that at least 2,400 men were needed for success against Niagara, was totally out of the question. To be sure, Bradstreet's proposal concerning the actual size of the attacking force roughly corresponded with the attacking force proposed by Shirley after he reached Oswego. But the important difference in their conceptions of manpower needs emerged in the contrast between the two companies Bradstreet was going to leave behind for Oswego's protection and the "700 Effective men" advocated by Shirley.[16] While Bradstreet might be able to carry off a quick strike at Niagara, his plan left Oswego very vulnerable to a French attack from their Fort Frontenac base. French success in such an attack, while Bradstreet was engaged at Niagara, would wipe out the English bridgehead on Lake Ontario, and cut off the supplies of Bradstreet's Niagara force, perhaps leading to its easy capture. To his credit, Bradstreet was quite correct about Shirley's late arrival at Oswego making a 1755 attack on Niagara a doubtful proposition. However, Shirley's cautious approach and apparent rejection of an immediate thrust against Niagara was equally correct in that maintenance of reasonable strength at Oswego temporarily preserved the only base the English possessed on the Great Lakes.

In early July menacing French manoeuvres in the Oswego area revealed their increasing concern about English activities at the Lake Ontario post. In meeting this threat Bradstreet offered a rapid response and was equally quick to file full reports concerning his achievement on this occasion. On July 7 he heard of a force numbering 500 French and 200 Indians heading toward Oswego. He sent two of his loyal Indians to the enemy encampment, which was approximately four to eight miles east of Oswego,[17] to inquire concerning the reasons the Indians had for joining in such an attack and also to ascertain to what nations they belonged. It was stressed that the Oswego commander wanted to know precisely what nations were involved in the campaign so that when the inevitable retaliation of English arms came there would be no damage done to innocent tribes. According to Bradstreet this approach so intimidated them that "the Indians were extremely obliged to me for the regard I had for them and that I might be assured they would not act against the English, and several left the French

---

16. See Shirley to Johnson, May 31, 1755, Lincoln, *Shirley Correspondence*, 2, 179-82; Shirley to Robinson, June 20, 1755, ibid., 195-99; Minutes of Council-of-War at Oswego, September 18, 1755, ibid., 268.

17. Gipson, *The British Empire Before the American Revolution*, 6, 154, has the encampment four miles east of Oswego, while a letter quoted in Frank H. Severance, *An Old Frontier of France*, 2 (New York, 1917), 119, places it "within eight miles" of Oswego.

directly & the rest next day" until only thirty remained. This desertion proved so discouraging to the French that they decided it was best to return to their bateaux and push on to Niagara. The "Scandalous manner" in which the French quickly retreated under cover of night, Bradstreet claimed, "has brought upon them the contempt of all the Indians here, & I shall take care to have it well known to all the Nations on and about the Lakes in a very short time so it may be productive of great good."[18] This detailed description of Bradstreet's vigilant defence of Oswego and his skills in dealing with the Indians was sent off to Secretary of State Thomas Robinson two days after the events occurred. Not only was word soon carried to England concerning Bradstreet's deeds, but the colonies were informed as well. At the end of July a letter from Oswego, dated July 9, 1755, appeared in the *Pennsylvania Gazette* outlining the now considerably inflated threat to the post. It was reported that a force of "1000 European troops, and a large body of Indians" had encamped near Oswego and were planning "to attack this place." They abandoned such plans when their spies "informed them of the preparations Captain Bradstreet had made to receive them."[19] While the real extent of the French threat is debatable,[20] Bradstreet's letters and the newspaper account are revealing indications of the elaborate coverage all his deeds were to receive. A short message, carried less than ten miles from the post, had evolved into a quite significant declaration, important to Oswego's preservation and as proof of Bradstreet's abilities.

There were other Oswego activities which enjoyed equally wide-ranging coverage. Bradstreet had mentioned to Robinson the progress of his boat-building efforts, with one little schooner in the water by the tenth of July and "one of the large ones" due for launching in two days. The promised launching took place on July 13 and, according to the *Halifax Gazette*, the accompanying ceremonies quite impressed the large number of Indians in attendance. The new vessel was introduced to Lake Ontario with the firing of "three Cannons as she went off, which gave great Pleasure to the Indians." This report also hinted that the elaborate ceremonies were quite deliberately intended to impress the Indians. In concluding its commentary the point was made that "the Traders there agree, they were entirely ignorant of Indian Affairs till now." Not only was Bradstreet adding supposedly new wrinkles to Indian diplomacy but the same article recorded his ability to use the older and better-known tool of rhetoric on the natives. He took advantage of the presence of visitors from distant Indian nations to deliver "a Speech relative to the Times." His eloquence sparked the reply that "He had effectually open'd their Eyes, & that they would no longer be

---

18. Bradstreet to Robinson, July 10, 1755, C.O. 5/46-2, 528-31.
19. As quoted in Severance, *An Old Frontier of France*, 2, 119. Severance speculates Bradstreet himself might have written the letter, but it seems more likely, judging from some of the comments contained in it, that it was drafted by one of the naval officers sent to Oswego to man the boats Bradstreet had under construction.
20. Gipson, *The British Empire Before the American Revolution*, 6, 154.

Tools to the French, but would live in strict Friendship & botherly Love with the English; &, if necessary, die with them." Among the interested readers of such reports on Bradstreet's exploits were his friends in England. Early in October Charles Gould wrote, "Tho' I have not lately had the pleasure of a Line from You, I read your name in the Papers, as having made a Speech to an Assembly of Indians with Success."[21] Aware of the value in having his name constantly before the public, Bradstreet was converting his service at isolated Oswego into a series of well-known achievements.

While Bradstreet attempted to strengthen Oswego and enlist Indian support, the French were preparing a substantial assault on it. Throughout July the Canadian Governor, Vaudreuil, sent brigades to Fort Frontenac and hoped to have a force assembled to strike at Oswego by August 25.[22] The attack was to be led by Baron Dieskau but eventually it was postponed because of his September defeat by Johnson's forces in the Lake Champlain region. In the interval, however, the massing French troops represented a serious threat to Oswego. In mid-July three companies of the New Jersey recruits arrived on Lake Ontario[23] but the main English forces, under Shirley, still struggled over the treacherous route from Albany to Oswego.[24] Bradstreet grew increasingly apprehensive about Shirley's slow progress, sensing that something was afoot on the French side of Lake Ontario.[25] However, the Massachusetts governor was unable to accelerate the plodding pace of his forces. Suffering from a shortage of provisions and increasingly apprehensive about a French-Indian ambush, Shirley's worries increased further with word, early in August, of Braddock's defeat. New responsibilities were now thrust upon him as commander of all English forces in North America.[26] As Shirley finally neared Oswego, Bradstreet found his worst fears confirmed by an Indian who described to him the French preparations at Frontenac. On August 17 Bradstreet sent off an urgent message to Shirley summarizing this "Intelligence from Cadaraqui [Frontenac]." According to his Indian source there were presently 600 French troops at Frontenac in addition to "a large Number of Irregulars." Once additional troops and "a considerable Body of Indians" reached the French fort, these forces were going to link up with 500 men from Fort Niagara, who were to be

---

21. Bradstreet to Robinson, July 10, 1755, C.O. 5/46-2, 531; *Halifax Gazette*, August 23, 1755; Charles Gould to Bradstreet, October 6, 1755, T.P.C., 128/19.
22. Vaudreuil to the Minister, July 24, 1755, Richard A. Preston and Leopold Lamontagne, *Royal Fort Frontenac* (Toronto, 1958), 248.
23. Bradstreet to Shirley, July 20, 1755, Bradstreet MSS.
24. For a description of the many difficulties experienced by Shirley's army in making this journey, see Schutz, *William Shirley*, 208-209; Thayer, "The Army Contractors for the Niagara Campaign," 38-39.
25. Bradstreet to [Shirley] [July] 24, 1755, Bradstreet MSS.
26. Schutz, *William Shirley*, 209. It is interesting that upon hearing of Braddock's defeat, the vigilant Charles Gould wrote Bradstreet that "I shall be glad if any thing shall arise out of it in Your favour." See Charles Gould to Bradstreet, August 27, 1755, T.P.C., 128/17.

accompanied by further Indians, for a combined assault on Oswego. Shirley received this letter the same day it was written and within twenty-four hours he had arrived at Oswego.[27]

Shirley's much-delayed arrival on Lake Ontario brought not only relief to Oswego but rewards, both in terms of rank and praise, to Bradstreet. On August 22, the Captain was appointed Adjutant-General for the Niagara expedition and given rank as Brevet Major by Shirley. In addition, while Shirley was distressed at the state in which he found Oswego, he made clear to Robinson that no blame should be attached to Bradstreet for its condition. "I found it, notwithstanding Captain Bradstreet, the Commandant, had done everything, that an active, able officer in his Situation could do, in a very defenceless Condition."[28] The promotion and the kind words must have been considerably gratifying to Bradstreet, especially since they had been won by his activities in the field rather than by arrangement of his friends "at home." Apparently he now served under a commander appreciative of his contributions and, as Shirley's future actions were to reveal, willing to take full advantage of Bradstreet's talents. However, Bradstreet's gains were not matched by any English gains against the French. Shirley had yet to prove himself as a commander and until he did so Bradstreet, while offering vigorous cooperation, was careful not to place excessive reliance on Shirley's support. Once before, at Louisbourg, Bradstreet had become too dependent on colonial patrons and had suffered for it. While accepting Shirley's favours and working with him he rarely expressed any praise for the abilities, military or otherwise, of his commander.

Such a cautious silence proved rather fortunate since Shirley's military capabilities, or lack of them according to his critics, were about to be revealed. He was now faced with the choice of immediately pushing on to strike at Niagara or remaining at Oswego and putting it in shape to meet the French forces gathering at Frontenac. He chose to attempt both and, in the final analysis, was totally successful at neither. The weak condition of his Lake Ontario base caused the momentary postponement of the Niagara assault in favour of the strengthening of Oswego. Shirley proposed to construct two additional forts because of the exposed position of the original post. This work, he felt, had to be well advanced before the Niagara attack could be launched. Oswego was the vital base of his entire Niagara expedition and there was a pressing "necessity of it's being secur'd, as soon as possible, against any Sudden Attempt of the French from Fort Frontenac, with which it hath been threaten'd."[29] In mid-September the strengthening of Oswego's fortifications was far enough advanced for Shirley to consider seriously

---

27. Bradstreet to Shirley, August 17, 1755, C.O. 5/46-1, 128; Shirley to Robinson, September 19, 1755, Lincoln, *Shirley Correspondence*, 2, 261.

28. "A List of Commissions Issued by General Shirley in North America," W.O. 1/1, pt. 1, 35, P.A.C.; Shirley to Robinson, September 19, 1755, Lincoln, *Shirley Correspondence*, 2, 262.

29. Shirley to Robinson, September 19, 1755, Lincoln, *Shirley Correspondence*, 2, 263.

the attack on Niagara. By this time he also had reports on the strength of Niagara and Frontenac. Apparently buoyed by this information, Shirley called a Council-of-War on September 18 to consider the reports and his own suggestions. Leaving 700 men to defend Oswego, Shirely intended to lead the remainder of his 1,376 effectives, "besides the Albany Men [bateau-men] and Indians, and a Train of Artillery," against Niagara. These proposals were unanimously accepted by the Council.[30]

Preparations began immediately with the selection of the soldiers who were to proceed to Niagara and the loading of artillery, ordnance stores, and part of the provisions on board the sloops *Ontario* and *Oswego*,[31] which had been constructed under Bradstreet's directions. The "immoderate Rains, and tempestuous Weather upon the Lake" played havoc with the expedition since such weather "much retarded our Works, and increas'd the Number of the Sick." It caused the bateau-men and Indians to state bluntly that it was too late in the season "for the Men to go now to Niagara in Battoes," while among his officers Shirley noted a "considerable Uneasiness" concerning the expedition. In consequence, the Massachusetts governor reconvened the Council "for their further Opinion and Advice" about the Niagara campaign. At this Council-of-War, held on September 27, the necessity of postponement was debated. Major John Bradstreet took a leading role emphasizing that at this time of year the French forces which had journeyed further westward were probably returning to Niagara, and the large number of French reinforcements which had moved to the enemy post was well known. Furthermore, the bateau-men, so important to any Niagara attack, were tied up with the chore of bringing provisions from Albany to Oswego. Without their expertise "the Soldiers cannot conduct the Battoes to Niagara thro' so ruff Water, as is now generally five days in six upon the Lake." Deferring to Bradstreet's judgment and listing a number of other reservations, the Council resolved that it was "unanimously and clearly of opinion that it would be much more advisable for his Excellency to defer making any Attempt, either against Niagara or Cadaraqui until the next year."[32] Shirley recognized the general uneasiness in the camp as well as the many other problems and decided to abandon his "intention to proceed thither."

In reporting this decision to Sir Thomas Robinson he brought forward a new priority. The Council, in setting back the Niagara attack, also postponed a Frontenac expedition, and Shirley now made an attack upon Fort Frontenac the first step in his projected spring cam-

---

30. Minutes of Council-of-War, Oswego, September 18, 1755, ibid., 264-68.
31. "A Review of the Military Operations in North-America, from the Commencement of the French Hostilities on the Frontiers of Virginia in 1753, To the Surrender of Oswego, on the 14th of August 1756; in a Letter to a Nobleman," September 20, 1756, Massachusetts Historical Society, *Collections*, 1st Ser., 7 (Boston, 1846), 119.
32. Shirley to Robinson, September 28, 1755, Lincoln, *Shirley Correspondence*, 2, 289; Minutes of Council-of-War, Oswego, September 27, 1755, ibid., 290-91.

paign. He proposed first to capture Fort Frontenac and then launch a western sweep against Forts Toronto, Niagara, Presqu'Isle, Pontchartrain (Detroit), and Michilimackinac. He argued that "the Execution of this Scheme will open an Entrance for the English into the most distant parts of the Country of the Western or far Nations of Indians (as they are frequently call'd) it will put it into their Power to secure those two great, essential points, the carrying on an exclusive Trade with those Indians, and thereby fixing them absolutely in the Interest of the English." Clearly, Bradstreet and Shirley thought alike on the merits and methods of English mastery of the Great Lakes. An even more visible sign of the confidence and cooperation now existing between the two men emerged concerning Fort Frontenac. Shirley was "determined to begin the Operations of the next Year with attempting the Reduction of Fort Frontenac." The man assigned the all-important task of capturing "the Key"[33] to Lake Ontario was John Bradstreet.

While Fort Frontenac had supplanted Niagara as the leading target in Shirley's next campaign, the one unvarying constant in any Lake Ontario proposals was the successful English maintenance of Oswego. Consequently the defensive preparations now were redoubled. Work on Fort Ontario, on the east side of the Oswego River, was resumed while the September 27 Council also felt it "very expedient to erect a Work as soon as may be on the Eminence West of the Old Fort."[34] Declining manpower, Indian harassment, and inadequate provisions were to combine during the approaching winter to retard much of this work. Near the end of October Shirley withdrew from Oswego, leaving the garrison under the command of Lieutenant-Colonel James Mercer. By this time the Governor apparently felt that the defensive precautions were well advanced and adequate provisioning arrangements had been made. He was to be disappointed on both counts. Shirley also made arrangements which were quite pleasing to John Bradstreet and which should have kept him reasonably active during the winter. Bradstreet was ordered to Albany where he was to grant furloughs on Shirley's behalf and supervise the enlistment necessary to bring Shirley and Pepperrell's regiments up to full strength. Construction of the "Whale Boats" to be used in the spring as well as any additional barracks which might be immediately needed at Schenectady and Albany was also entrusted to him. Shirley's confidence in Bradstreet, as well as his appreciation of his efforts, were revealed in the Governor's request to hear "from time to time his Sentiments upon every point of his Majesty's Service," and the fact that the orders were addressed to the apparently promoted Lieutenant-Colonel Bradstreet. Shirley was contemplating raising two new regiments and he had

---

33. Shirley to Robinson, September 28, 1755, Lincoln, *Shirley Correspondence*, 2, 289-98.

34. Minutes of Council-of-War, Oswego, September 27, 1755, Lincoln, *Shirley Correspondence*, 2, 291. See also "A Review of the Military Operations in North-America," M.H.S., *Collections*, 1st Ser., 7, 123.

already conferred upon Bradstreet a lieutenant-colonel's rank in one of them.[35] Shirley himself now retired to Boston to deal with his neglected duties as Massachusetts governor and to defend the outcome of the Niagara expedition.

The campaign had not been the great success anticipated. While Johnson's repulse of a French force under Baron Dieskau early in September had not been followed up with a push on Crown Point, it at least appeared more successful than Shirley's Niagara effort. In New York, moreover, there existed a faction which was determined to exaggerate Shirley's failure and, if possible, secure his removal. Matters such as the boundary difficulties of Massachusetts Bay and New York, the tradition of Albany neutrality and the resulting profitable contraband trade which had been badly disrupted by Shirley, his methods in arranging contractors for the expedition, and the growing animosity between Johnson and Shirley over a variety of questions all contributed to a feeling in certain quarters that Shirley must be replaced.[36] The Governor of New York fired one of the opening guns in this colonial power play in November of 1755. Sir Charles Hardy pleaded for the appointment of "some more able & experienc'd General," hopefully a "General Officer." Of course, he claimed, it was not his intention "to insinuate anything to the Prejudice of General Shirley, from any hasty misguided Opinion. Your Lordship has enjoin'd me to be sincere, and as a lover of Truth I cannot be otherways, & think it my Duty to tell you, that it is a Task far beyond our present General's Abilities."[37] The criticisms of Shirley were to grow increasingly sharper in tone until Hardy's missive does appear as the statement of a "lover of Truth."[38]

If these complaints were acted upon and Shirley was replaced as the commander of the English forces in America, there were significant implications for John Bradstreet. The critics of the Massachusetts governor linked Bradstreet with Shirley because of his role in one of

---

35. Shirley to Bradstreet, November 28, 1755, Bradstreet MSS; Shirley [to Fox], January 13, 1756, W.O. 1/1, pt. 1, 4; Goldsbrow Banyar to William Johnson, November 18, 1755, Sullivan et al., *Johnson Papers*, 2, 309.

36. Gipson, *The British Empire Before the American Revolution*, 6, 143-45, 187. Gipson emphasizes the conspiracy against Shirley which was supposedly directed by a clique including Thomas Pownall, James DeLancey, Oliver DeLancey, Goldsbrow Banyar, Peter Wraxall, and Daniel Claus, among others. Surprisingly, although the Johnson-Shirley clash over Indian affairs is frequently mentioned as one of the disagreements between them, only the activities of John Henry Lydius are usually examined and Bradstreet is ignored. Yet, as will be demonstrated, Bradstreet's interventions in Indian matters were a very real source of concern to Johnson and his supporters. For recent examples of Bradstreet's neglect, see David L. Salay, "The William Johnson—William Shirley Dispute: Origins, Course, and Consequences" (M.A. thesis, Vanderbilt University, 1972), 83-96; Milton W. Hamilton, *Sir William Johnson: Colonial America, 1715-1763* (Port Washington, N.Y., 1976).

37. Sir Charles Hardy to Lord Halifax, November 27, 1755, in Pargellis, *Military Affairs*, 151.

38. "Extracts from Letters of G____l Ab____y to his friends in London from his first landing at New York till 8th Octr. 1756," Chatham MSS, Bundle 95, 62, P.A.C.

the bitter difficulties which had arisen between Shirley and William Johnson. While Shirley's many enemies were aroused by a number of different grievances, Bradstreet was only openly involved in the limited questions of Indian affairs and Shirley's relations with William Johnson. It was here that Bradstreet, by his ambitious activities, contributed to the provocation of the criticism and eventual demise of his commander.

While Bradstreet's personal involvement in this controversy undoubtedly increased the friction, it is clear that the clash concerning authority over the Six Nations was not new. In 1746 and 1747 Shirley had attempted to extend Massachusetts influence over the Iroquois by means of his agent in the Albany area, John Henry Lydius, a merchant and Indian trader. By the late summer of 1747 Johnson had responded to this challenge and secured Shirley's repudiation of Lydius.[39] It was obviously a sensitive matter, at least to Johnson, and in view of this and the confirmation of Johnson's authority over the Iroquois by Braddock in 1755, it seemed foolish of Shirley to reopen this sore spot during the Niagara campaign. Yet he did just that, not only by means of Lydius but with the help of John Bradstreet as well. The activities of John Henry Lydius were met head-on by William Johnson. Reports reached Johnson in June of 1755 "that Lydius had been privately persuading [Indians to go to] Niagara with: him and Govr: Shirley." On June 21, Johnson confronted Lydius with this information and the accused replied by showing him "Govr: Shirley's Orders [for] what he had done." Johnson immediately forbade him to "interfere any further with the Indians."[40] Meanwhile John Bradstreet had arrived at Oswego and was liberally dispensing suggestions concerning proper management of the Indians. General Braddock took it upon himself to remind Shirley, and hopefully in turn Bradstreet, of Johnson's pre-eminence in Indian matters. He pointed out to Shirley that he was disturbed by a letter received from Bradstreet requesting provisions and presents for the Indians. Funds for such needs were supposed to be handled by Johnson since he had "unlimited Credit for that Purpose," and Braddock suggested that "some Mistake must consequently have arisen wch. you will very much oblige me to remove."[41] But Bradstreet's Indian activities were no mistake since he was quite deliberately trying to carve out his own niche as an Indian authority. Moreover, Braddock's sudden removal from the scene in July, leaving Shirley in command, meant that Bradstreet's ambitions remained unbridled, if not deliberately encouraged, by Shirley.

Bradstreet continued to outline his prowess among the Indians to his English friends, in hopeful expectation of an appointment which

---

39. See Nicholas Varga, "New York Government and Politics During the Mid-Eighteenth Century" (Ph.D. dissertation, Fordham University, 1960), 414.
40. "[The Secretary for Indian Affairs his Note in the proceedings at the Conference between the Indians & Col. Johnson] at Mount Johnson [21st June 1755]," in Sullivan *et al.*, *Johnson Papers*, 1, 644-45.
41. Edward Braddock to Shirley, June 22, 1755, in ibid., 645.

would utilize his abilities. He informed Charles Gould that he knew "more of the far Nations of Indians which are of such importance than any English Man of common Sense" and reminded King Gould that he was "not only a Sachem of the Six Nations of Indians but a great favourite with weight and influence among them." In discussing the many contributions which Bradstreet had made to the English cause, Governor Shirley was also willing to support Bradstreet's Indian pretensions. He mentioned to Henry Fox how Bradstreet succeeded "in gaining a general influence among the Northern and Western Indians."[42] Shirley's comment provided a clue as to exactly what Bradstreet was aiming at, since his description of Bradstreet's sphere of influence matched perfectly with the suspicions held by some of Johnson's supporters concerning Bradstreet's desires. Shirley spoke of Bradstreet's influence among the "Northern and Western Indians," a careful distinction, since an appointment as Indian superintendent over these tribes meant that Johnson did not necessarily have to be removed. Rather his terms of authority simply could be clarified, allowing Bradstreet's appointment, and clearing the way for both men to serve as Indian superintendents over neighbouring but different tribes and regions. That this was exactly what Bradstreet had in mind was borne out by an analysis of Bradstreet's ambitions offered to Johnson by his friend Goldsbrow Banyar. "He now aims," Banyar wrote concerning Bradstreet, "at the Superintendency of Indian affairs at least as to the foreign & uppermost 3 of the five Nations. It's said the Commission to you should be of a different Nature, I suppose to make room for other Persons."[43]

This letter was a clear indication that by mid-November of 1755 Bradstreet's Indian aspirations, and the challenge they presented to William Johnson, were well known to Johnson and his supporters. In view of the suspicions then embittering the relations between Shirley and Johnson it was natural that the Johnson camp suspected Shirley to be at the root of these machinations. Thus, in the attempt to discredit Shirley, Bradstreet's Indian pretensions also came under fire. One of the criticisms Sir Charles Hardy offered about his Massachusetts counterpart concerned Shirley's use of agents to erode Johnson's influence among the Indians. Hardy was outspoken in his defence of Johnson, bluntly stating that "if the Indians are not commited to the care of Johnson, and him supported in it, I shall have great doubt of our being able to have that Dependance on their sincere Services, so necessary for the good of these Countries." He then turned to "the Persons Mr. Shirley employs" and characterized them as "meer ignorant Tools." Selecting John Bradstreet as a prime example, he continued, "I must observe to your Lordship that his [Shirley's] principal Indian Ambassador is Mr. Broadstreet, who never saw one of the

---

42. Bradstreet to Charles Gould, December 25, 1755 T.P.C., 128/8; Bradstreet to King Gould, March 9, 1756, T.P.C., 128/26; Shirley [to Fox], January 13, 1756, W.O. 1/1 pt. 1, 4.
43. Banyar to Johnson, November 18, 1755, in Sullivan *et al.*, *Johnson Papers*, 2, 309.

Castles till his going this year to Oswego, and now takes upon him to know more than any-body in this Country."[44] Critical words such as these, when presented to English officials who were in the process of replacing William Shirley by Lord Loudoun, were very damaging to Bradstreet and his friends' solicitations concerning an Indian appointment.

While his Indian aspirations were apparently being frustrated by Johnson's supporters, Bradstreet discovered that even the brevet major and lieutenant-colonel's ranks conferred upon him by Shirley were not to receive home approval. Shirley promoted him before seeing his own commission, merely assuming he was empowered to do so. Upon inspection "of my present Commission," the Massachusetts governor doubted that he had the authority and, as a result, both promotions were endangered. To extricate himself and Bradstreet from this unhappy situation, Shirley wrote a long letter explaining his apparent mistake to Henry Fox, Secretary of State for the southern department at the time of the letter but, until October of 1755, Secretary of War. Shirley outlined Bradstreet's entire career, praising his Louisbourg services, pointing out his neglect and the manipulations of his brother Simon, and stressing his contributions to Oswego's defence and to the Niagara expedition generally. Shirley concluded by mentioning the confusion surrounding the promotions, and particularly the lieutenant-colonel's rank, "which I beg leave to recommend to be confirmed to him." The recommendation was, of course, contingent upon the old plan for the raising of two new regiments still being operative.[45] Bradstreet was aware of Shirley's letter and possibly even encouraged him to write it since he passed its contents, or a copy of the letter itself, along to Charles Gould. It was natural, with his influence over the Indians being questioned and a possible loss in rank looming, that Bradstreet turned to his English friends for help. Even here there were difficulties, since he was worried that some of "my thoughts freely & candidly [put] upon paper & sent . . . home to my Friends" had not brought approval or even an acknowledgment. He was particularly concerned that Sir Richard Lyttleton had not responded to his letters.[46]

Charles Gould was rather pessimistic concerning all of Bradstreet's various enclosures. Two of the gentlemen to whom Bradstreet addressed items, "whatever may be their inclination, their present Connections are such, as will hardly suit with their forwarding your Promotion being both strongly engaged in the opposition." Who the "two Gentlemen" were is uncertain. One of them was probably Sir Richard Lyttleton, since he had emerged gradually as a supporter of William Pitt, openly entering the opposition when he voted against the administration in November of 1755 and then participating in a sharp exchange with Pitt's rival, Henry Fox, in December of the same year. The other

---

44. Hardy to Halifax, November 27, 1755, in Pargellis, *Military Affairs*, 152.
45. Shirley [to Fox], January 13, 1756, W.O. I/1 pt. 1, 3-4.
46. Bradstreet to Charles Gould, December 25, 1755, T.P.C., 128/8.

possibility was William Pitt himself, since he had come out in "open opposition" on November 13 and had been dismissed from the administration seven days later.[47] Regardless of the actual identity of these men it was clear that no help was to be expected from them. In keeping with the discouraging tone of Gould's letter, his remarks concerning the recommendation offered by Shirley on Bradstreet's behalf were equally disappointing. He wished he was able to congratulate Bradstreet on the commissions given by Shirley "being confirmed: but I am fearful, that will not be the Case." He felt that the "Strong Recommendation" contained in Shirley's letter "will not have the Weight, you may have flattered Yourself: not in any derogation from Your Merit, but as that Gentlemen from what part of his Conduct, I am not informed is no longer in great esteem here." Not only had Shirley's prestige fallen but he himself was being recalled, since Lord Loudoun was going with "full power to America" to replace him. But it was at this point that the one ray of hope contained in the entire letter emerged. Charles' father, King Gould, had taken advantage of a visit with the new commander, Lord Loudoun, "to mention You." It appeared that "his Lordship was not unacquainted with your name and your Activity" although "he had not then been spoke to by any one Person on your behalf." Charles Gould then cautioned Bradstreet not to "rely too much on what may be done on this side of the Water" and expressed his hopes for Bradstreet's prosperity under Loudoun, since "his Complacency and affability you are not ignorant of; and I think he will not be backward in rewarding merit."[48] By the time this letter reached Bradstreet, if six to eight weeks are allowed for its conveyance, it must have been late May. Thus, the news of Shirley's replacement by Loudoun came as no surprise. Already in late April rumours circulated that "the Earl of Loudoun, the Earl of Home, and Col. Abercromby are going to America, to take upon them the Command of our Forces there."[49] At least in this respect the letter merely confirmed what had been rumoured, but in other ways, despite the immediate depressing reports it contained, it was a valuable aid to Bradstreet. Gould's comments impressed upon him the total disfavour into which Governor Shirley had fallen in England. This was valuable information since it added a new dimension to the colonial attacks on Shirley and the not unusual replacement of a lawyer-governor by a more qualified military figure as commander of the English forces in America. Had his vision been restricted to colonial realities, only the colonial animosities and attacks on the Massachusetts governor would have been known to him. Gould's remarks were a salient indication of how far from grace Shirley had fallen in England as well. Once this letter had been received it must have been clear to Bradstreet that any further reliance on Shirley was

---

47. Charles Gould to Bradstreet, March 29, 1755, T.P.C., 128/22; Namier and Brooke, *History of Parliament*, 3, 75, 292.
48. Charles Gould to Bradstreet, March 29, 1756, T.P.C., 128/22.
49. *Boston Evening Post*, April 26, 1756.

out of the question. The letter was also helpful to Bradstreet in another way since it made clear that the political turmoil in England checked any immediate chance of advancement by that route. However, careful cultivation of Loudoun on behalf of Bradstreet was already initiated and this opening could be followed up by Bradstreet's quick adjustment and cooperation with the new commander.

While these behind-the-scenes battles were raging, and the letters outlining political rather than military maoeuvres criss-crossed the Atlantic, all was not totally quiet on the Lake Ontario front. Although the commander of the French forces in America, the Marquis de Montcalm, assessed the winter of 1755-1756 as "fairly quiet," he did mention one significant action. This was an attack in March, under de Levis, which was carried out against Fort Bull, one of the posts guarding the supply route to Oswego. The English outpost fell easily and the "little garrison was put to the edge of the sword." This loss was the culmination of a series of winter actions in which Indian and Canadian war parties roamed the area south of Oswego, attempting to close its supply route. As spring approached, Oswego was in an extremely precarious position and badly in need of relief. By early March Bradstreet had journeyed to Boston where, "like an obedient Soldier & a good Christian I waite for orders & submit to fate."[50] A little over a week later he received his orders, which had as one of their major priorities the relief of Oswego.

On March 17, 1756, Governor Shirley placed all the bateau-men[51] involved in Oswego's provisioning under the command of Lieutenant-Colonel Bradstreet. He was authorized to assume control over all aspects of the transportation of men and provisions from Albany to Oswego; everything from the construction of bateaux through to the delivery of goods to Oswego was placed directly in his hands. Shirley proposed that Bradstreet engage 2,000 bateau-men, to be divided into companies of 500 men each. These duties required the "general Direction of one Officer well Skill'd in the many Branches of this important Trust" and, as Shirley explained to Henry Fox, "I have been oblig'd to constitute a New Officer (Lt. Colonel Bradstreet) to

---

50. Montcalm to Madame la Marquise de Montcalm, May 19, 1756, "Montcalm Correspondence," Government of Canada, *Report of the Public Archives for the Year 1929* (Ottawa, 1930), 42; George F. G. Stanley, *New France: The Last Phase 1744-1760* (Toronto, 1968), 140-41; Bradstreet to Charles Gould, March 9, 1756, T.P.C., 128/9.

51. The bateau-men, apparently largely drawn from the Albany, Schenectady, and Mohawk River area, were a breed apart. Their "grousing, strikes... desertions... unquenchable thirsts... insatiable appetites" and willingness to rifle any cargo made them, to say the least, rather difficult to command. Not surprisingly, many English officers found them impossible to work with; but Bradstreet developed an excellent rapport with them, no doubt at least in part because of his own reckless disposition and Nova Scotia frontier background. For brief glimpses of these colourful frontiersmen, see Charles R. Canedy III, "An Entrepreneurial History of The New York Frontier, 1739-1776" (Ph.D. dissertation, Case Western Reserve University, 1967), 42-43, 96; Douglas E. Leach, *Arms For Empire: A Military History of the British Colonies in North America, 1607-1763* (New York, 1973), 409-10n.

superintend this business." In addition to these new responsibilities, and the rank as lieutenant-colonel which had almost eluded him, Bradstreet was given secret instructions. He was to proceed "as soon as may be with Two Hundred Whaleboats, and the Same Number of Battoes all loaded with provisions and stores" for the relief of Oswego. Once arrived at the Lake Ontario base he was to select as much in the way of men, boats, provisions, and ammunition as he thought necessary "and therewith to proceed to Fort Frontenac alias Cadasaqui, and there to use your best endeavours to bring off, set fire to, or in any manner destroy the Same, and any other works or building adjacent to it." Had Shirley known the beleagured state of the Oswego garrison he would have realized the immense difficulty of breaking through to Lake Ontario, let alone immediately launching an offensive. Lieutenant-Colonel Mercer was "threatened on both sides, but as yet not attacked" by what he termed "a great number of scouting Indians."[52]

Bradstreet plunged into his new duties with his usual energy. By early April he was able to report from Albany that "I have this day got of the remainder of the two hundred whaleboats and many battoos and I shall get the rest of and myself gone in three days." He also referred to the "private instructions" given him by Shirley, emphasizing the need for more men if these orders were to be carried out successfully, since a "sudden and quick push" was necessary to make "the success pritty certain before the French get there." Once enroute to Oswego the many problems encountered caused the gradual withering of his hopes for a "sudden and quick push." True to his prediction, however, by April 9 Bradstreet was moving towards Oswego, but already difficulties had emerged. Worried about the possibility of a sudden attack he wrote William Johnson requesting Indian protection and scouting help for his bateaux convoy.[53] Johnson provided reassuring words, not actions,[54] but despite this Bradstreet and the bateau-men pushed on and the convoy finally arrived at Oswego on May 16.[55] The post had gained a temporary reprieve.

Bradstreet's late arrival, when linked with the Oswego garrison's weakened condition and the incomplete state of the fortifications, made it obvious that the intended attack on Fort Frontenac was out of the question. Fortunately, an engineer, Patrick Mackellar, had accom-

---

52. "Instructions For Lieut: Colo. Bradstreet," March 17, 1756, C.O. 5/47-1, 72-76; Shirley to Fox, May 7, 1756, in Lincoln, *Shirley Correspondence*, 2, 443; "Governor William Shirley of Massachusetts Secret Instructions to Lt.-Col. Bradstreet," March 17, 1756, in Preston and Lamontagne, *Royal Fort Frontenac*, 249; James F. Mercer to William Williams, April 7, 1756, in Sullivan *et al.*, *Johnson Papers*, 9, 422.

53. [Bradstreet] to Shirley, April 6, 1756, Bradstreet MSS; Bradstreet to Johnson, April 9, 1756, in Sullivan *et al.*, *Johnson Papers*, 9, 423-24.

54. See Bradstreet to Johnson, April 14, 1756, in Sullivan *et al.*, *Johnson Papers*, 9, 430; Shirley to Johnson, April 17, 1756, in ibid., 434; Johnson to Shirley, April 22, 1756, in ibid., 439.

55. "A Journal of the Transactions at Oswego from the 16th of May to the 14th of August 1756," by Patrick Mackellar, in Pargellis, *Military Affairs*, 187.

panied the supply convoy and he promptly set to work surveying the defences and initiating limited improvements to the various Oswego forts. Bradstreet himself did not tarry long on Lake Ontario since by the morning of May 18 he was on his way back to Schenectady with the bateaux. To maintain Oswego all manner of provisions, weapons, and tools as well as equipment for the English vessels supposedly patrolling and controlling Lake Ontario were necessary. To meet these needs another convoy was assembled and on July 1 Bradstreet led these 600 bateaux into Oswego "with Provisions for the Garrison and Guns and Rigging for the Vessels."[56] The supply lines to Oswego had been successfully reopened and the post could function once more as the English base on Lake Ontario. Considerable credit for its relief and the continuation of its provisioning rested with John Bradstreet, and he certainly was not one to let any opportunity pass without his contribution receiving its proper acknowledgement. Yet both he and his superior officers, who usually reported such noteworthy actions, were strangely silent. Perhaps organizing and leading the bateaux convoys kept him so fully occupied that he had little time for the customary elaborate report. More likely, however, the quiet pause was because of the tense uneasiness surrounding what had now become officially acknowledged: Shirley's replacement by Lord Loudoun. While Bradstreet moved up and down the route to Oswego an unusual vacuum emerged at the uppermost level of the English forces in America as the command changed hands. In June the colonies awaited the arrival of Lord Loudoun with his major staff officers, General James Abercromby and Colonel Daniel Webb. The subordinate officers were first on the scene, since Webb arrived at New York on June 7, and Abercromby on June 15. They were at Albany on June 25 and Abercromby took over the command from Shirley, holding it until Loudoun reached Albany on July 20.[57] A bitter Governor William Shirley returned to Boston where a tremendous welcome greeted him as he was "received with all possible Demonstrations of Joy."[58] Amidst such an atmosphere of suspicion and change Bradstreet busied himself with his assigned duties and bided his time.

Unfortunately for Oswego, while the English marked time, postponing major offensive and defensive decisions until consideration by the new commander, there was no such neglectful indecision on the French side of the lines. In May French activity in the Oswego region had been intensified by the dispatch of Captain de Villiers with 700 Canadians and Indians. His force was to harass the enemy and watch "his movements towards the river Chouaguen." By June the French felt that the main British attack would be directed against Crown Point, and, thus, a French-Indian diversionary attack upon Oswego might be

---

56. Ibid., 188-89, 200.
57. Robert Hunter Morris to Horatio Sharpe, October 8, 1756, in Lincoln, *Shirley Correspondence*, 2, 578-80.
58. *Boston Evening Post*, August 16, 1756.

attempted with reasonable chance of success. While diversionary it was to be launched "in such a way that the defensive could be changed into offensive, according to circumstances." At the end of June, after considerable debate, the decision was made to lay siege to Oswego. Rigaud de Vaudreuil, Governor of Trois Rivières, was sent with a colonial and Indian force "to assume command of Sieur de Villiers' Camp, established At Niaouré bay about 15 leagues from Chouaguen." Montcalm arrived at Frontenac on July 29 and on August 4 left for Niaouré and the command of the Oswego enterprise.[59]

Bradstreet was the first to test this new French strength around Oswego. On July 3 he left the Lake Ontario post for Schenectady with his train of bateaux. The convoy was rather bulky, consisting of 350 bateaux and about 1,000 bateau-men. Bradstreet therefore divided it into three divisions, placing himself in command of the first unit. The various segments were separated from each other once enroute because of the difficulties of keeping close order with such an irregular force. Thus it was the advance division under Bradstreet which wandered into an ambush set up by de Villiers' men about eight miles from Oswego. The French-Indian force, consisting of about 450 Canadians, 180 regulars, and 100 Indians, was waiting on the north side of the river. They let a few bateaux pass and then struck, hitting the portion of the convoy which included Bradstreet and about 300 bateau-men. When the firing commenced Bradstreet led six men to a small island near the enemy; he hoped that such a move would keep the French-Indian force from crossing the river. Once there, he beat back an attack of twenty foes and was joined by more of his own men. A second and a third attempt at storming the island was made, but Bradstreet and his increasing but still outnumbered force stood their ground. This stubborn stance gave the remaining bateau-men time to get ashore on the south side of the river. Bradstreet now led the island force to the safe shore as well. Here he heard that the French were fording the river approximately a mile away. He took 250 men to this spot to try to catch the enemy in mid-stream. Finding about 400 had already crossed and were ensconced in a thick swampy area, he abandoned any idea of a slow advance from tree to tree and ordered a direct charge. Bradstreet himself took the lead in this headlong attack and the opposing ranks broke under it. Keeping up a steady fire, the French withdrew to the river and crossed it. At the river "the Battoemen having now a fair View of them, took them down fast; and here it was that the Enemy sustained their greatest loss." By now the remaining portions of the convoy were at hand as was a force of about 100 from Onondaga under Captain Patten. Definitely outnumbered, the French began a retreat. A scouting party sent to check the north bank found de Villiers' men had

---

59. "Journal of the Siege of Chouaguen," in Edmund B. O'Callaghan, ed., *The Documentary History of the State of New York*, 1 (Albany, 1850), 316-17. Chouaguen was the French name for Oswego.

withdrawn "in the utmost Haste and Confusion, for they had left behind their Picks, Blankets, and Provisions."[60]

Although the French had been beaten off it appears that it was the English under Bradstreet who took the heavier losses. In the three-hour engagement, the English reports counted 20 men killed and 24 wounded among Bradstreet's force while estimating that the French dead numbered over 100. However, on the French side there was a quite different description of what was considered a "successful action." The French commander, de Villiers, apparently reported that the English lost 300 killed or wounded, while "we lost in this affair a colony officer, six Canadians and colony soldiers and one Indian."[61] If only each side's own dead and wounded counts are accepted as accurate, and their estimates of losses suffered by the other side are ignored, then Bradstreet's forces had suffered far more casualties. On the other hand, despite the nature of the surprise attack, Bradstreet's bateaux convoy had not been cut to ribbons but had remained intact, with the bateau-men suffering relatively light losses, given their unpreparedness. Furthermore Bradstreet's major responsibility, running supplies into Oswego, already was completed before the action took place, so the French ambush did not disrupt the provisioning of Oswego. Rather, as the *New York Mercury* pointed out, it demonstrated the wisdom "of taking large numbers of Battoemen into the service." The action proved that given leadership such as that offered by Bradstreet, the bateau-men were capable of withstanding French attacks and, even in the face of sizeable enemy forces, could keep open the supply route to Oswego.

Considering the action as a significant triumph, the *New York Mercury* reported, and at times repeated, every detail of the battle. Bradstreet's "active, brave and circumspect Behaviour" as well as his "Gallantry and Conduct" were lavishly applauded.[62] Naturally, Bradstreet was pleased with the attention given to his heroic deeds in the colonial press, but, as usual, he took care that the mother country also was fully informed. A few days after he arrived at Albany he wrote Charles Gould about the action. Bradstreet claimed to have been very aware of the French presence on the way up to Oswego but decided not to engage them at this time because "what I was intrusted with [was] of infinite consequence & great Value & I did not think proper to engage on such unequal terms." On his return, however, he had, "gain'd a compleat

---

60. "Mackellar's Journal," in Pargellis, *Military Affairs*, 200; "Niles's History of the Indian and French Wars," M.H.S., *Collections*, 4th Ser., 5 (Boston, 1861), 417-18; "A Review of Military Operations in North-America," M.H.S., *Collections*, 1st Ser., 7, 155-56; *New York Mercury*, July 26, 1756, in O'Callaghan, *The Documentary History of the State of New York*, 1, 313-14.

61. Shirley to Fox, July 26, 1756, in Lincoln, *Shirley Correspondence*, 2, 489; Edward P. Hamilton, ed., *Adventure in the Wilderness: The American Journals of Louis Antoine de Bougainville 1756-1760* (Norman, Oklahoma, 1964), 6.

62. *New York Mercury*, August 2, 1756, in O'Callaghan, *The Documentary History of the State of New York*, 1, 313; *New York Mercury*, July 26 and August 2, 1756, in ibid., 313-14.

Victory." The letter assessed briefly the enemy strength and then the discussion of the battle was closed quickly with Bradstreet's comments, "It does not become me to give a particular account of this Action, being too personally concern'd in every part of it, therefore leave it to be told by those who were Eye Witness of all my behaviour during the several actions."[63] While the false humility can be discounted, Bradstreet obviously was confident that detailed accounts of the battle, and his role in it, would not be lacking in England. One such account was soon dispatched to Henry Fox by Bradstreet's former colleague and commanding officer. After a long description of the engagement, William Shirley commented, "It is agreed, that through the whole of this action, Captain Bradstreet behaved with good Conduct as well as Gallantry, and I must in Justice to him Observe, that the transportation of the provisions and Stores this Spring to Oswego, (upon which the preservation of the place hath so much depended) is Chiefly owing to his indefatigable Activity and Singular good Management in his Command."[64] Although removed from his command by this time, it was not surprising that Shirley reported to Fox one of the few decisive military triumphs associated with his tenure of office. Bradstreet, after all, had been chosen by Shirley and was acting on his orders and so it was natural for Shirley to place great store on his victory and at the same time perhaps share some of the credit for Bradstreet's achievement. Association of himself with Bradstreet's success might be the first step to his own vindication. Shirley's laudatory comments are interesting for another reason as well. His willingness to praise Bradstreet was no doubt facilitated by his belief that Bradstreet was still a supporter of his cause. During the month of July, Bradstreet's impatience with the inactivity of his new superior officers and his comments to Shirley on this matter caused Shirley's confidence in Bradstreet's continued loyalty to grow. He was soon to be somewhat disillusioned by his former colleague.

At first it appeared that Bradstreet was not going to do well in the exchange of commanders, since his temporary superior, James Abercromby, seemed to discount both the value of Bradstreet's advice and his bateau-men. Upon reaching Albany on July 12, 1756, Bradstreet informed Abercromby that he had learned, from the few prisoners taken in the recent action, of French preparations at Frontenac for an attack on Oswego.[65] At a Council-of-War on July 16 a report from Mackellar concerning the weak defences of Oswego as well as Brad-

---

63. Bradstreet to Charles Gould, July 14, 1756, T.P.C., 128/10.
64. Shirley to Fox, July 26, 1756, in Lincoln, *Shirley Correspondence*, 2, 490.
65. "Niles's History of the Indian and French Wars," M.H.S., *Collections*, 4th Ser., 5, 418; Morris to Sharpe, October 8, 1756, in Lincoln, *Shirley Correspondence*, 2, 580. Morris' letter states that Bradstreet arrived in Albany and informed Abercromby of the threat to Oswego on July 12, while Guy Frégault, *Canada: The War of the Conquest* (Toronto, 1969; originally published Montreal, 1955), 128, has his arrival on July 10. "A Review of Military Operations in North-America," M.H.S., *Collections*, 1st Ser., 7, 156, has Bradstreet at Schenectady on July 11 and at Albany on July 12.

street's evidence of the French threat to the post were considered. It was decided that "a Regiment should forthwith march to Reinforce that Garrison, and put the works in a posture of defence." Despite the Council's decision, however, Abercromby appeared in no hurry to speed up the arrangements to get the designated regiment, the 44th, moving. Moreover, shortly after Bradstreet's return Abercromby gave orders for the discharge of 400 bateau-men.[66] Competence and courage in battle were apparently rewarded by dismissal. An irritated Bradstreet waited impatiently to return to Oswego but lacked, among other things, even the money necessary to pay the bateau-men. He confided to Shirley that "I should have set out some Days ago for Oswego with the 48th Regiment[67] and Col. Webb, but no care being taken to send Provisions for them to Schenectada, they cannot move 'till a large Quantity is sent there, which I fear will take some time for want of Waggons." Bradstreet felt that Oswego was being neglected since "by all Appearances nothing will be done that Way without the French make it a Visit," and this he still considered a real possibility. As the French made final preparations for the Oswego assault, Bradstreet apprehensively waited for a British move, and in Albany a wrangle between the new contractor and the old Shirley appointees further snarled the necessary provisions.[68] In terms of leadership, Abercromby appeared willing to postpone all action until the new Commander-in-Chief arrived. Lord Loudoun reached Albany on July 29 and the wheels began to turn again, but on the same day Montcalm arrived at Fort Frontenac and prepared to assume command of the Oswego campaign. When the 44th Regiment finally moved on August 12 Oswego was already under fire. It was too late. As Bradstreet had predicted, the delays proved costly and Oswego fell to the French on August 14.[69]

General Abercromby's comments during the summer of 1756 indicated who was going to shoulder the blame for the Oswego disaster. In July he expressed surprise at the state of the defences of the region. Among the neglected posts he felt "the one which wants the most and is of the most importance is Oswego, which is surprizing, as it was so long last year Mr. Shirley's Residence." By August 10 he had warmed to his subject and noted that "things are far from being in the Situation Mr.

---

66. Council-of-War held at Albany, July 16, 1756, in Sullivan *et al.*, *Johnson Papers*, 9, 486; "A Review of Military Operations in North-America," M.H.S., *Collections*, 1st Ser., 7, 158.

67. Bradstreet probably meant the 44th.

68. Bradstreet to Shirley, July 16, 1756, C.O. 5/46-2, 470; ibid., July 24, 1756, 471; "State of the Dispute Concerning the Provisions for Transporting the 44th Regiment to Oswego and the true Cause of the Delay of it's Imbarcation," contained in a letter of Shirley, September 16, 1756, 472-75.

69. For a detailed report of the siege of Oswego, see "Journal of the Siege of Chouaguen," in O'Callaghan, ed., *The Documentary History of the State of New York*, 1, 315-19; William L. Grant, "The Capture of Oswego by Montcalm in 1756: A Study in Naval Power," *Proceedings and Transactions of the Royal Society of Canada*, 3rd Ser., 8 (1914), 193-214.

Shirley and his Creatures have represented them to be in." After the fall of Oswego, he wrote that Shirley had not indicated the dangerous position of the post. Abercromby maintained that the former commander "never said anything of the weakness of Oswego, on the contrary he never apprehended anything from that Quarter."[70] This was to a great extent the same argument produced by Lord Loudoun.[71] Shirley was the root cause of this setback. Shirley himself was quick to reply to these charges with explanations to Loudoun and the British authorities. There were a number of friends who also rallied to Shirley's side, pointing out such obvious facts as the ample warnings of Bradstreet and Mackellar and the long delay in dispatching the 44th Regiment.[72]

Among the "friends" who did not rush to the defence of Governor Shirley was John Bradstreet. As late as July 24, while expressing his reservations about the inactivity of his new superiors, Bradstreet still appeared loyal to Shirley. He commented on the "gloomy Aspect" of the proposed move against Crown Point created by the failure to secure cooperation between regular and provincial units. Bradstreet felt that "this would not have happen'd had your Excellency continu'd here, and taken the Command upon you, as in that Case they would have consented to the Regulars joining them." The sincerity of Bradstreet's words becomes very doubtful when his comments to his English friend on the same problem are considered. Ten days before this letter to Shirley he had written to Charles Gould that "seven thousand Americans are set out for Crown Point, they will nether have Regulars nor Indians with them." As a result of this lack of cooperation, Bradstreet predicted that "the Accounts You will receive from thence will be bad." On this occasion there was no mention of Shirley's unique ability to cope with such a problem. Instead Bradstreet went on to comment: "Lord Louden is much wanted here, who is daily expected."[73] Clearly Bradstreet was tailoring his remarks to suit the inclinations of his

---

70. "Extracts from the Letters of G____ l Ab____ y to his friend in London," Chatham MSS, Bundle 95, 58-63.

71. The British authorities noted Loudoun's strong attack on Shirley. One evaluation of the controversy stated: "The whole therefore of the Evidence on one Side was to be drawn out of Lord Loudoun's Letters. In these indeed are contained very severe accusations of Mr. Shirley." See "Memorandum relating to the charges against Mr. Shirley," n.d., ibid., Bundle 76, 27-28.

72. Some historians appear to have divided along virtually the same lines as the contemporary sources they quote. Consider for example Pargellis and Gipson. Stanley M. Pargellis, *Lord Loudoun In North America* (New Haven, 1933), 161, is influenced by Loudoun's correspondence and makes basically the same point as Abercromby; the "most discreditable" feature of Shirley's handling of the Oswego defence was the small "amount of information . . . passed on to his successors." Lawrence H. Gipson, *The British Empire Before the American Revolution*, 6, 209, relies heavily on "A Review of Military Operations in North-America" which was written by a defender of Shirley. Hence, he concludes that Loudoun's effort to fasten upon Shirley "the blame for the loss of Oswego cannot be substantiated."

73. Bradstreet to Shirley, July 24, 1756, C.O. 5/46-2, 471; Bradstreet to Charles Gould, July 14, 1756, T.P.C., 128/10.

listener. Such tangled loyalties were sorted out after Loudoun arrived, on July 29, to take over the command from Abercromby. Loudoun's criticisms of Governor Shirley boomed out once Oswego had fallen, and Bradstreet could see the danger to his own position should his ties with Shirley be continued. After the fall of this Lake Ontario post he wrote the Massachusetts governor "with a heavy heart" stating, "I pitty your Excellency greatly knowing how much the loss of this important & expensive place must Afflict You." But in this same letter he let slip several indications that he had successfully adjusted to Loudoun's takeover of the command. Despite the recent disaster on Lake Ontario Bradstreet sensed the possibility that Shirley's original plans could still be followed through. If Oswego was recovered the English forces could "go on with the first Scheme,[74] which from the little knowledge I have of Lord Loudoun and the two other General Officers I am in great hopes we shall." Then in concluding this letter, Bradstreet expressed unconcealed pleasure at his new friendship with one of Loudoun's major staff officers. "Could a Man be happy at this time I should be so under the Command of General Web, he being extremely obliging to me and as I find him both Sensible & Active."[75] Apparently Bradstreet's "heavy heart" at Shirley's misfortune was considerably buoyed by the prospects of his own survival, and indeed prosperity, under his new superiors. Ironically, evidence of Webb's incompetence was to become an integral part of Shirley's Oswego defence. Hence Bradstreet's excellent relationship with Webb was to prove of increasing importance in the deteriorioation of his relationship with Shirley.

As soon as Shirley had received word of Oswego's loss he had begun preparations to meet the charges which he knew would be hurled against him concerning the inadequacy of the post. Naturally, in preparing his case, he had turned to Bradstreet, as one intimately aware of Oswego's conditions and the actions of Abercromby and Loudoun in defending the post. On August 30 he had written to his former colleague expressing his regrets that Oswego had fallen despite Bradstreet's "Activity & good Conduct" and his "Viligance & good Management." After having voiced his fears about the blame being fastened upon himself, Shirley outlined how Bradstreet could help his cause. He wanted an account of the state of Oswego's "Works & Troops" as well as the chief causes of the setback, "& particularly what alteration in the Matter it might have made if the 44th Regiment, & a body of 1000 of your Batteau Men had been there with yourself at the head of them, when the French came agst the Forts."

Playing upon Bradstreet's vanity the letter attempted to secure his cooperation. But in addition to the flattering phraseology, Shirley tempted Bradstreet with more tangible incentives. He reminded him that "With regard to Ld. Loudoun, I have already repeatedly recommended you to him in the strongest Terms, I possibly can" and, in

---

74. Probably the attack on Fort Frontenac.
75. [Bradstreet] to Shirley, August 19, 1756, Loudoun Papers, LO 1523, H.L.

addition, Shirley promised, "on my arrival at home you may depend upon my Weight & credits being employ'd in doing you Justice, & all the Service in my Power."[76] It was alluring bait but it brought no response from Bradstreet. Nevertheless, Shirley drafted and sent to Loudoun, on September 4, the first of many vindications of his conduct. This statement revealed one of the key points in Shirley's defence: namely, that Bradstreet had provided ample warning of the French threat to Oswego and had the 44th Regiment, under Webb, moved immediately to the relief of the post its fall would have been averted. To support his argument, Shirley drew upon Bradstreet's letters of July 16 and July 24, which had been drafted when the latter was somewhat disillusioned by Abercromby's conduct.[77]

By this point it must have been clear to both Bradstreet and Shirley that the vindication of the Massachusetts governor could only be achieved at the expense of Webb, Abercromby, and at least partially, Loudoun. Bradstreet simply could not get involved in such a crusade since it jeopardized his own position under Loudoun. In addition, as Gould's comments at the end of March indicated, there was far more behind Shirley's downfall than Oswego's loss. For many reasons his cause was in obvious decline and it was foolhardy for Bradstreet to sink with it. On his part, Shirley must have recognized the risks Bradstreet ran if he should provide damaging evidence against his new colleagues. Yet he kept increasing pressure on Bradstreet to try to get his support, offering persuasive reminders of possible rewards. On September 7, 1756, he again wrote Bradstreet requesting information about Oswego's condition, the 44th's movements, and the dispute over provisions. "I had the pleasure of supping with your Mrs. Bradstreet and your family at the Province house two days ago and they were all well," he concluded. "Once more adieu and depend upon all friendship in my power to do you in England, particularly with regard to the Indian affairs." Even the revival of Bradstreet's old hope of an Indian appointment failed to bring a response. "Not knowing but that my two last Letters to you may have miscarry'd thro the hurry and Confusion," a perplexed Shirley made one last effort at regaining Bradstreet's support before leaving for England. He still desired "as full and Explicit an Acct. as possible of the State of His Majy's Service from the day of your return to Schenectady in July last, by the first opportunity." Assurances were offered concerning "my Esteem of and Attachmt. to you" and Shirley promised upon his arrival in England to present "your distinguish'd services in their just light to H.R.H. the Duke, and making the strongest Impressions in your favour upon him."[78] It was all to no avail. Ten years earlier as Bradstreet waited at Louisbourg for rewards which never materialized, Shirley had deserted him. In September of 1756, a

---

76. Shirley to Bradstreet, August 30, 1756, Loudoun Papers, LO 1627.
77. Shirley to Loudoun, September 4, 1756, in Lincoln, *Shirley Correspondence*, 2, 540.
78. Shirley to Bradstreet, September 7, 1756, Loudoun Papers, LO 1719; ibid., September 14, 1756, LO 1807.

strangely quiet Bradstreet watched at Albany as the wheel came full circle, to the misfortune of that same William Shirley.

Service under Shirley had allowed Bradstreet to blend the diligent performance of assigned military duties with his own personal quest for glory, advancement, and possible economic profit. But when it became clear that Shirley had changed from a helpful asset to a cumbersome liability, the threat that this posed to Bradstreet's obligations to his new commander and his own personal survival caused his rapid adjustment to the new realities. An appreciation of Bradstreet's motivations, actions, and adjustments sheds considerable light on his survival of the command transfer from Shirley to Loudoun, when he appeared to be a vulnerable victim caught in the crossfire between the two men. Stanley Pargellis attempts to explain Bradstreet's success by viewing him as an exception to the general rule of Shirley's miscalculation and inadequacy. Thus, Shirley, who was "seldom a good judge of men, made perhaps the wisest appointment of his career" in assigning responsibility for the bateau-men to Bradstreet. Moreover, Bradstreet's work alone, "of all that Shirley authorized, won the unqualified praise of Shirley's successors."[79] The implication of such comments is that by virtue of his meritorious service alone, Bradstreet won the continuing respect of his commanding officers, in this case Shirley and Loudoun. That there was considerable merit in many of Bradstreet's deeds during the period from the spring of 1755 to the summer of 1756 is undeniable. His general observations to Robinson concerning the Great Lakes theatre of war and his suggestions and comments offered to Shirley at different stages of the Niagara campaign were for the most part quite valuable. In May, June, and July of 1755, his presence and preparations at Oswego undoubtedly helped shore up its defenses and temporarily preserved the post, while his opening of its supply lines the following spring demonstrated considerable ability and courage. His successful organization and capable leadership of the bateau-men shone like a beacon amidst the welter of plodding disorganization and indecisive leadership which generally marked the Niagara campaign. Partially offsetting these contributions were some pardonable lapses in judgment and action. Despite Bradstreet's efforts the Oswego defences were in a far from first-rate condition by August of 1755, and perhaps his time and effort spent upon boat building and Indian diplomacy could have been better employed in the initiation of a more careful examination and rebuilding of Oswego's fortifications. Instead Bradstreet discarded such an approach as a waste of money and contented himself with temporary measures. In his defence, he was not an engineer and naturally avoided a task such as this, which he was not equipped to handle, while plunging into Indian affairs, where he obviously felt himself eminently qualified. Furthermore, given the limited manpower available to Bradstreet, in terms of carpenters and

---

79. Pargellis, *Lord Loudoun*, 156.

workmen, and the emphasis in Shirley's orders on boat construction and careful expenditure of funds, an ambitious scheme of fortification construction was probably out of the question. In other areas, Bradstreet appears more open to attack. Some of his schemes, such as the proposed immediate thrust against Niagara and the challenge to Johnson's Indian authority, were hastily conceived and overly ambitious. Yet in the former case, Bradstreet was quite correct that chances of mounting a successful Niagara attack were being frittered away by the slow movement of Shirley to Oswego. His proposal, while extremely risky, was the only chance for Niagara's capture that season. In the latter case, it is doubtful that Bradstreet's removal from the controversy over Indian management would have healed the Johnson-Shirley rupture. Bradstreet was merely adding further fuel to the fire. The Indian issue was an old sore point between Johnson and Shirley to which were now added many further causes of friction in which Bradstreet was not involved. Bradstreet's involvement in Indian diplomacy, while premature on his part and extremely exasperating to the Johnson camp, was a realistic necessity at Oswego. It was, furthermore, a policy sanctioned by Shirley's orders and inclinations.

On balance, Bradstreet had made a praiseworthy contribution while serving under Shirley. But there was far more than his competent performance involved in his emergence from this campaign relatively unscathed by the vicious attacks on his former colleague and commander, Governor Shirley. His easy transition from Shirley to Loudoun was facilitated by his personal merit but this in turn had been established, and more important embellished, by Bradstreet's persistent wringing of maximum exposure from all his actions. While in many instances an undeniable contribution was being made, Bradstreet drafted elaborate reports, at times spiced with limited exaggeration, for the benefit of his superiors both in England and in America. When these were linked with reports in the colonial press and letters to his friends at home, they resulted in a most favourable public and private portrayal of almost all his activities. Once an image of himself as the zealous servant of the Crown and indispensable man of action had been established, Bradstreet's friends in London had no hesitation about presenting his cause to the powers that be. Thus Lord Loudoun, who was "not unacquainted with your name and your activity" was approached on Bradstreet's behalf by King Gould before the new commander left England. This publicizing of Bradstreet's deeds and the lobbying of his London friends were just as important as the heroic deeds themselves in allowing him to escape the discredit heaped upon Shirley. Judged by his well-reported services during the Niagara campaign, his adjustment to Shirley's demise, and his espousal and probable eventual capitalization upon the Great Lakes' economic possibilities, John Bradstreet had done very well for a man who just eighteen months earlier could hope only for employment in no other way "than that of Captain."

Chapter V

Success with Lord Loudoun

In explaining the distressing course of the war in North America some of the regular officers newly arrived from England were not only critical of Governor William Shirley's military failures but were openly contemptuous of the military abilities of Americans. James Abercromby assessed the colonials as "not true New England chips of the old Block, but most of them are little better than Riffraff—their officers little better."[1] Apparently the time was not ripe for the talents of colonial officers to be appreciated or for any of their schemes and suggestions to be accepted and applied. Yet for at least one of these colonials, John Bradstreet, this period of service under Lord Loudoun was to witness repeated demonstrations of Loudoun's confidence in his abilities. Indeed, Bradstreet's manipulation of individual contacts on both sides of the Atlantic, and his mastery of the inclinations of the two worlds, proved so adequate that by the time of Loudoun's recall Bradstreet's most recent promotions, arranged in England, conflicted with one of his daring colonial plans which had won Loudoun's approval. It was one of the rare moments in Bradstreet's career when all circumstances combined in his favour and the prospects of a successful military career for an Anglo-Acadian, a somewhat irregular regular, seemed excellent.

Bradstreet's success under Loudoun is particularly surprising in view of the fact that a number of his new commander's accusations and suspicions about Shirley's conduct might have been equally applicable to that of Bradstreet. For example, Loudoun accused Shirley of allowing the "King's battoes" and Oswego's magazines to be used for "mer-

---

1. "Extracts from Letters of G____ l Ab____ y to his friend in London from his first landing at New York till 8 Octr 1756," Chatham MSS, Bundle 95, 62, P.A.C. For a discussion of the disharmony between regulars and provincials, see Alan Rogers, *Empire and Liberty: American Resistance to British Authority, 1755-1763* (Berkeley, 1974), 59-74.

chants' goods sent up there by his friends to dispose of to the Indians."[2] Although Loudoun's words applied to the summer of 1755, when Bradstreet was not in charge of the bateaux, it is difficult to imagine him passing up such an opportunity once it presented itself. By January of 1758, in fact, rumours in England about Bradstreet's involvement in trading activities caused considerable discomfort to Charles Gould.[3] Moreover, well before this date, Bradstreet had befriended a New Yorker who provided an invaluable connection with the Albany merchant community.

It had been during the winter of 1755-1756 that the friendship was first forged upon which the American wealth of John Bradstreet was to be built. At this time Bradstreet made Philip Schuyler his secretary and deputy, and thus began the "profitable connection" which was to last for almost twenty years.[4] The Schuyler family first settled at Albany around 1650 and had a history of involvement in the fur trade and Indian affairs. Philip Schuyler was active in the family's Albany mercantile endeavours and was to become a prominent New York landowner and politician. He was a member of the colonial élite and enjoyed all the political and economic advantages associated with such a position.[5] In the mid-fifties Schuyler had been encouraged to seek an army commission and so he entered the employ of John Bradstreet.[6]

The immediate economic consequences of the entrée Schuyler provided Bradstreet in provincial New York are unfortunately not visible.[7] But when Bradstreet's Indian aspirations are linked with the new contacts he enjoyed through Schuyler with the Albany merchant community, some worthwhile speculation can be offered. At Mount Johnson Bradstreet saw the immensely profitable little empire Sir William Johnson had carved out of the wilderness. It was quite clear that through "the fur trade of the new world Johnson had come to be a man of power and influence."[8] Bradstreet's Oswego activities and hopes of

---

2. Loudoun to Fox, August 20, 1756, quoted in William H. Smith, "The Pelham Papers—Loss of Oswego," *Papers of the American Historical Association*, 4 (1889), Pt. 4, 377-78.

3. See note dated January 17,1758, attached to a copy of Charles Gould to Bradstreet, December 27, 1757, T.P.C. 128/32, N.L.W.

4. Don R. Gerlach, *Philip Schuyler and the American Revolution in New York, 1733-1777* (Lincoln, Nebraska, 1964), 20 and 23; Benson J. Lossing, *The Life and Times of Philip Schuyler*, 1 (New York, 1872), 130.

5. Patricia U. Bonomi, *A Factious People: Politics and Society in Colonial New York* (New York, 1971), 64-66, 263.

6. Gerlach, *Philip Schuyler*, 11.

7. The Schuyler Papers housed at New York Public Library are particular disappointing in this respect since material concerning the Bradstreet-Schuyler relationship is largely limited to boxes 9 and 10 and contains little on their economic affairs during this early period or, indeed, during the entire period of their friendship. The very closeness of their relationship, since Bradstreet lived with Schuyler and his family at Albany for considerable periods of time, might be one reason for the lack of any extensive correspondence between the two men since it made letter writing unnecessary.

8. Wilbur R. Jacobs, *Wilderness Politics and Indian Gifts: The Northern Colonial Frontier, 1748-1763* (Lincoln, Nebraska, 1966), 78-79. Jacobs offers a detailed description of

an Indian superintendency were probably an attempt to duplicate Johnson's success. Oswego and other points such as Detroit and "Gerondequast" would make admirable trading posts where Bradstreet could oversee the exchange of Albany goods for Indian furs and reap considerable profits. There is evidence that at least one trader, Johan Herkimer, enjoyed Bradstreet's protection in selling his rum to the Indians,[9] but documentation is lacking concerning Bradstreet's role as a friend of Albany merchant-traders and a trader himself. It may be suggested, however, since not only was Bradstreet's presence at Oswego an inviting opportunity to participate in trading activities, but his later appointment as bateaux-commander placed him in an even better position. When his proposals concerning the fur trade and Indians of the Great Lakes region are matched with the cooperative protection and help his military positions offered, and the further useful linkage of Philip Schuyler with the Albany merchant-traders is made, the sketchy outlines emerge of profitable enterprises perhaps tapped by John Bradstreet.

Nevertheless, as Loudoun took stock of his predecessor's term of office, it was always Shirley and rarely Bradstreet whose actions were questioned. One of the headaches which Loudoun inherited from Shirley concerned the many overdue accounts which the Massachusetts Governor had neglected to pay or the British government had disallowed because of improper procedures. Some of these accounts were to remain unsettled until 1769.[10] Of more immediate consequence, the situation naturally made Loudoun quite leery about risking payment of bills accumulated under Shirley which might not be accepted by the home authorities. One of the most expensive legacies of Shirley's command was the cost of the bateau-men enlisted by Bradstreet. But while disallowing other claims, Loudoun proved both considerate and cooperative in allowing Bradstreet to meet the expenses of the bateaux service. On August 7, 1756, shortly after Loudoun assumed the command, Bradstreet submitted a request to his new commander for an additional £9,000 sterling since the recently granted sum of £4,800, New York currency, was not sufficient to meet the wages and other expenses of the bateau-men. He also asked for £142 sterling for "the company of Pioneers [who] are desirous of having their Accounts settled and to be paid of." Both requests were granted by warrants from Lord Loudoun dated the same day.[11] Over the next few months the bateau-men gradually were paid off and left the service. The last date

---

Mount Johnson which not only contained Sir William's home but also a blockhouse, sheephouse, mill, ladehouse, aqueduct, stable, storehouse, council house, and small shelters for visitors.

9. Horatio Gates to Johnson, August 8, 1755, in Sullivan *et al.*, *Johnson Papers*, 2, 534-35.

10. Pargellis, *Lord Loudoun*, 139.

11. Memorials of John Bradstreet to Lord Loudoun, August 7, 1756, Loudoun Papers, LO 1536 (1 and 2), H.L.; "Account of Money paid by John Bradstreet to the several Companies of Batteau-Men ... in 1756," T.P.C., 128/414.

of service for the few remaining companies was December 4, by which time Bradstreet had paid out the sizeable amount of £77,666/6/3, New York currency. The lion's share of this expenditure was by warrants from Lord Loudoun with only approximately £20,000 having been covered by warrants issued during Shirley's term of office.[12] In handling such a large amount of money, Bradstreet weeded out exaggerated or false claims. For example, he explained to Loudoun his strong objections to an account submitted by James Fairservice. He felt the pay demanded by Fairservice for himself and his company was far in excess of what was actually warranted by their time in the service. Such concern for protection of the English treasury, particularly after the many excesses of Shirley's term of office, must have pleased Lord Loudoun, and was probably a factor in Bradstreet's being able to report to Charles Gould that his administration of "the Battoe service" had won "the approbation & satisfaction of all parties."[13]

There were other signs indicating the excellent rapport which was developing between Bradstreet and his new superiors. The friendship with Webb continued to prosper since Bradstreet described himself "extremely oblig'd to that General who made me one of his Family during the time I was with him and upon all occasions shew'd me great civility."[14] In addition, Loudoun demonstrated a continuing willingness to approve suggestions emanating from Bradstreet. In one instance, Bradstreet was concerned that widows of the bateau-men who had perished while in the service might be deprived of their husbands' pay. The cost of securing letters of administration in order to "receive the ballance due to their Husbands" was so high that it would "come to half the money" actually owed them. As a result, he suggested that Loudoun accept all affidavits "of their being the lawful Wife of the Person whoes wages they claim" sworn before any city mayor. After considering Bradstreet's memorial on this matter, and "the distressed Condition of the Widows," permission was granted for Bradstreet's proposed procedure.[15]

Amidst such an encouraging atmosphere Bradstreet moved quickly to capitalize upon the apparent esteem he now enjoyed. Even though all was going well he still recognized the uncertainty surrounding his future role and rank. His position as bateaux-commander would vanish in December of 1756 with the disbanding of the various bateau companies. Thus while admitting to Charles Gould that "I am so happy as to stand well with my Lord Loudoun & the Generals Abercromby &

---

12. Bradstreet had £15,000 sterling equal to £25,714/5/8 New York currency so this £77,666/6/3 New York currency probably was the equivalent of between £45,000 to £50,000 sterling.

13. "Objections to Fairservices Account" by John Bradstreet [October 1756], Loudoun Papers, LO 3236; Bradstreet to Charles Gould, November 25, 1756, T.P.C., 128/12.

14. Ibid., September 25, 1756, T.P.C., 128/11.

15. Bradstreet's memorial to Loudoun, November 22, 1756, Loudoun Papers, LO 2267. Included with the memorial is the favourable reply to it dated the same day.

Webb," he immediately added that "what is to become of me this Winter I know not but expect to hear soon." Moreover, another one of the promotions awarded him by Shirley had not been followed through by confirmation from the War Office. The Massachusetts Governor had promised to use "his utmost endavours to Obtain by his Majesty's Favour, the rank of Lieut. Collo."[16] but Bradstreet remained a captain. In order to clarify his position, in September of 1756 Bradstreet drafted and presented to Lord Loudoun a memorial summarizing his services and clearly expressing his aspirations for a higher rank.

Beginning with his 1735 purchase of an ensign's commission in Philipps' regiment,[17] Bradstreet proceeded to outline the high points of his entire career. In 1744, "he Pland the Expedition against Cape Briton and engag'd the Several Colonies that were concern'd in its reduction to undertake it." Shirley, he claimed, originally intended him as the commander of the attempt on Louisbourg but eventually decided upon Pepperrell, as a native New Englander, although "the Sole direction of the Expedition" remained in Bradstreet's hands. His services won the praise of Pepperrell, Shirley, and Warren, but, Bradstreet reported, his deserved rewards as lieutenant-colonel and then major eluded him because of mistakes and his brother's activities. As a result he was provided with only a captain and adjutant's commissions and the appointment as Lieutenant-Governor of St. John's, Newfoundland. Leaping ahead to 1755, Bradstreet then turned to a consideration of his most recent exploits. His dispatch in taking up his Oswego posting was recounted as well as his successful defence of the post against the threatened attack of "600 Men 200 of which were Indians." His Oswego activities had earned him "the Approbation of General Shirley & the Publick in this part of the World." Realizing how unimpressive the recently recalled, and possibly disgraced, Shirley's approval had become, Bradstreet was careful to couple it with the American esteem he claimed to enjoy. The latter approach was a ploy used earlier in his quest for advancement and one which was destined to re-emerge repeatedly in future solicitations. He noted his appointment over the bateau-men, which was not accompanied by "pay or any kind of Advantage" except Shirley's commitment to secure him a lieutenant-colonelship, "a Rank he had often attempted to procure your Memorialist for his past Services to his Country." Loudoun's attention was drawn to Bradstreet's successful relief of Oswego and the "Compleat Victory over a body of about 700 French & Indians" which had "attack'd him the 3d July last." In concluding his memorial Brad-

---

16. Bradstreet to Charles Gould, November 25, 1756, T.P.C., 128/12; Memorial of Bradstreet to Loudoun [September 1756], Loudoun Papers, LO 5183.

17. Memorial of Bradstreet to Loudoun [September 1756], Loudoun Papers, LO 5183. It is interesting that Bradstreet claimed to be only fifteen years of age when he purchased the ensign's commission. This might have been a simple miscalculation on his part, although there is the possibility that vagueness and confusion about his Nova Scotia birth, his Acadian mother, and his best-forgotten Nova Scotian deeds were deliberately achieved by such a slip.

street offered several reasons justifying such a lengthy submission at that particular moment. Since Loudoun was "upon the spot" he could easily verify "every Particular herein set forth." More important, Bradstreet was confident, "from your known disposition" that Lord Loudoun "will no longer, than what may be necessary, suffer your Memorialist to remain in his present Rank of Capt. but Grant him such further Rank in the Army as it shall really appear to your Lordship his Services to the Publick intitle him to or represent him in such a light to his Royal Highness as he may hereafter meet with his favour & Protection."

By September of 1756 Lord Loudoun had become quite familiar with the Bradstreet case. In London he had been aware of Bradstreet's activities and reminded of his merit by King Gould. And then in North America once settled in his command, he had placed in his hands Bradstreet's very selective and carefully phrased presentation. It underlined Bradstreet's successes, ignored his failures or embarrassments except where they strengthened a case for his neglect, and worked in the praise of major figures, even that offered by Shirley. The memorial stressed that an obviously concerned and considerate Lord Loudoun could scarcely fail to recognize such heroic deeds and the respect they had won for Bradstreet among an admiring American public.

Bradstreet's memorial represented the culmination of the effort launched the previous winter by his friends in London. It was aimed at generally facilitating his advancement and, more particularly, his adjustment to Shirley's dismissal and Loudoun's takeover of the command. In achieving this end it was, of course, linked with his zealous service, his capable handling of the bateau-men, and perhaps even his ambivalent attitude toward Shirley. Designed to secure Loudoun's support and utilization of Bradstreet, the effort was a total success. Bradstreet won Loudoun's confidence and, early in 1757, reported the triumph to Charles Gould. "I have the good Fortune to be well with his Lordship upon no other foot than his being made sensible how much I had served the Publick before he came, from what he has seen & believes I can do." Indicating his desire to use Bradstreet's talents, Loudoun had ordered him to Boston "to provide many things which are necessary for the Ensuing Campaign." While Bradstreet attached considerable importance to his own deeds and presentation in winning Loudoun over, other comments in the same letter revealed his continuing awareness that his fate was still decided in Britain as well as in North America. He had heard "of almost a total change in the Ministry," which could only be for the better since "never was a time when it was more wanted."[18] The change to which he referred was the formation, in November of 1756, of the Pitt-Devonshire administration. Bradstreet watched the new ministry with great interest because of the opportunities it presented to his friend Sir Richard Lyttleton, and indirectly

---

18. Bradstreet to Charles Gould, January 22, 1757, T.P.C., 128/13.

to himself. Lyttleton accepted the position as Master of the Jewel Office the same month Pitt came to power[19] and while the office itself was of a minor nature, his access to and friendship with Pitt could prove extremely useful to Bradstreet. While hoping for helpful ministerial friends, Bradstreet was also determined that full credit be given in England for his American deeds. On this count, he felt Gould had rather disappointed him. "I am sorry to find you pass over in Silence the action I had with the french & Indians the last summer, and I fear therefore it has been misrepresented at home by some evil minded person," he complained. "I assure you it has done me great honor all over this Continent and if any thing is rong I should be glad to know it that it might be set rite, Lord Loudoun told me he would mention it to my advantage when he first came to Albany."[20] In prodding his friends, just as in petitioning his commanding officer, no opportunity to stress his contributions was allowed to pass. The American esteem, the support of Loudoun, and the heroic deeds themselves were all drawn upon to stimulate Gould's interest and activity. Bradstreet's basic message was simplistically straightforward but his delivery of it was of considerable complexity, in that it attempted to harness on his behalf the responses of the American public, his commander in America, his friends in England, and his superiors in the English government.

There was a pressing need for such extraordinary efforts because in the winter of 1756-1757 rather than achieving an immediate promotion, Bradstreet came dangerously close to losing even his rank as a captain on active service. The decision had been made to disband Shirley and Pepperrell's regiments, the 50th and 51st.[21] With his role as an active captain about to be replaced by half-pay inactivity, Bradstreet was in an embarrassing predicament from which Loudoun quickly rescued him. On March 8, 1757, his new commander bestowed upon him a captain's commission in the 60th Regiment, the Royal Americans. In addition, by this time Bradstreet was deeply involved in the special chores assigned him by Loudoun relating to the preparations for the coming campaign. To carry out these duties, which amounted to functioning as a virtual quartermaster, Bradstreet was apparently designated by Loudoun as a personal "aide-de-camp."[22]

Throughout the months of March and April, 1757, Bradstreet was active in Boston arranging to meet the various needs of the next campaign. One of the problems with which he dealt concerned the poor quality of the cannon balls produced by the New Englanders. In some cases they were of such brittle composition that they broke like

---

19. Namier and Brooke, *History of Parliament*, 3, 75.
20. Bradstreet to Charles Gould, January 22, 1757, T.P.C., 128/13.
21. This was done despite Shirley's objections in London. See Shirley to Pitt, January 1757, Chatham MSS, Bundle 56, 62-63.
22. "List of Commissions Granted by His Excellency the Rt Honble The Earl of Loudoun," in Pargellis, *Military Affairs*, 364; Lewis Butler, *The Annals of the King's Royal Rifle Corps*, 1 (London, 1913), 348; Gipson, *The British Empire Before the American Revolution*, 7, 236.

glass.[23] Bradstreet saw to it, "with difficulty & time" he reported, that "the people with whom I contracted for the Shot . . . Cast them fit for service." With this chore completed and the tools and carriages also arranged for, he provided storehouses for these supplies and started "to Collect, examine & sort every thing properly." He had also privately made inquiries concerning the number of "Sloops & Schooners" available for Loudoun's use, and assured him "that Your Lordship cannot be at a loss for any number You may have occasion for, and, I think, at a cheaper rate than the Publick were ever served in America." This interest in the protection of the "Publick purse" was to become a much repeated theme in Bradstreet's reports of his provisioning activities. For Abercromby's benefit he outlined how he had outwitted the rum merchants of Boston. He had purchased "20,000 gallons of Rum at the lowest price" as soon as the order was received. Realizing that the Boston merchants expected Loudoun to order a huge quantity of rum and they "were prepared to raise the price upon the first notice," Bradstreet struck first. With the cooperation of "Messrs. Bethune," rum was purchased, ostensibly for shipment to Newfoundland, "in so few hours that they had not time even to suspect what we were about." The merchants, aware that they had been outfoxed, now watched carefully for further purchases and, Bradstreet predicted, they "will certainly raise the price if the same caution is not observ'd." His vigilance extended even to the purchase of water casks which he bought for "less than the Common price." In terms of general purchasing practices Bradstreet was elated "to find my Lord is putting an end to all Jobbing & five pr. Cent commissions as he will certainly therby make a saving to the Publick of 25 pr. Cent in every thing purchas'd in America."[24] This changeover meant that contractors, charging a five per cent commission, would no longer be employed by the Crown. Instead, direct purchasing was to be handled by officers such as Bradstreet. In theory, as Bradstreet pointed out, it could result in real savings. In practice, there was the danger that the officer entrusted with such purchasing powers could pocket as much money as the dishonest contractors. In considering his praise for the new system there is reason to suspect that Bradstreet's over-emphasized zeal for the protection of the treasury might have been occasioned by the profits he himself was able to siphon off.[25]

While his motives may have been somewhat uncertain, his immediate effectiveness, in meeting all the demands of Abercromby and Loudoun, was more open to assessment. In evaluating his actual effectiveness it is obvious that Bradstreet tended to exaggerate what must be regarded as a contribution of some consequence. The speed with which

---

23. Pargellis, *Lord Loudoun*, 236n.
24. Bradstreet to Loudoun, March 1, 1757, Loudoun Papers, LO 3022; Bradstreet to Abercromby, March 28, 1757, Loudoun Papers, LO 3196.
25. See, for example, John R. Alden, *General Gage in America* (Baton Rouge, Louisiana, 1948), 73, for allegations concerning Bradstreet's corruption.

he assembled transports desired by Loudoun provides an excellent example of effective action, although it may not have been quite as effective as Bradstreet implied. On March 12 Abercromby wrote Bradstreet, on Loudoun's behalf, instructing him to arrange "double deck'd Vessels for Transportation of Troops, to the Amount of Sixteen hundred tuns." He was to appraise the value of the vessels in case of their loss and place on board them the various tools, lumber, and regimental accoutrements. They were then to be dispatched to a rendezvous a few miles distant from New York City, on the Jersey shore. Receiving these orders on the evening of March 18, Bradstreet replied the next day that "I shall not lose one moment in executing his Lordships commands in the best manner I can." Just two days later he wrote Lord Loudoun that the arrangement of the transports, "as near to the Tonnage You directed as possible," was completed. Bradstreet was in the process of fitting them out and hoped to see the last of them sail by March 27. As it turned out, things did not proceed as smoothly as the optimistic Bradstreet thought or desired. On March 28 he reported that in the week just passed only one day had been suitable for the work of fitting the ships. Writing on a Monday, Bradstreet now predicted "a fair prospect of their leaving... on Thursday or Friday next." On March 31 and April 4, however, the ships were still loading and it was not until April 6 that they finally sailed. Bradstreet explained the last delay to be the result of the "badness of the Weather & continual Easterly winds"[26] and, no doubt, this was a quite legitimate excuse. Some of the other delays were perhaps avoidable but this should not obscure the fact that in the space of approximately three weeks Bradstreet had diligently fulfilled his orders. The arranging of transports and their outfitting had been handled successfully without any hesitation on his part and, at least in the case of the rum and water casks loaded on board, at below the price which might have been normally exacted. There was considerable merit in Bradstreet's efficiency of organization. Yet what was annoying was his tendency to overstate his case. In doing so he ran the risk of personal embarrassment if his optimistic pronouncements could not be carried out. It was a risk and yet, as at other stages of his career, it was a risk he apparently felt well worth taking in order to impress upon Loudoun his indefatigable zeal.

Bradstreet was still at Boston on April 18 arranging additional transports, although several days earlier he had promised to report to Loudoun at New York "as soon as possible after having paid of the

---

26. Abercromby to Bradstreet, March 12, 1757, W.O. 34/58, 1-2, microfilm, Reel 152 (2), U.M.G.L.; Bradstreet to [Abercromby], March 19, 1757, Loudoun Papers, LO 3102; Bradstreet to Loudoun, March 21, 1757, Loudoun Papers, LO 3123 A; Bradstreet to Abercromby, March 28, 1757, Loudoun Papers, LO 3196; "Contents... Ship't by order of John Bradstreet Esqr. on board the several Transport vessells on his Majesty's Service," March 31, 1757, Loudoun Papers, LO 4354; "A List of, together with the quantity of the Several things shipt on Board the Several transports in the Harbour of Boston April 4th, 1757 for the use of his Majestys Troops by Jno Bradstreet Esq.," Loudoun Papers, LO 3286; Bradstreet to Loudoun, April 11, 1757, Loudoun Papers, LO 336; ibid., April 7, 1757, LO 3313.

accounts."[27] Up to this point Loudoun had intended assembling these transports at New York prior to launching the main thrust of his campaign which was to be an attack on Quebec. By the end of the month approximately thirty transports, including those chartered and outfitted by Bradstreet, were waiting in the harbour. However, on May 1 orders arrived from Pitt which significantly altered Loudoun's plans. William Pitt, who was taking an increasingly active role in the direction of the war effort, wanted Loudoun to hit Louisbourg first; and his instructions directed his American commander to proceed against the Cape Breton fortress. In England, however, the Duke of Cumberland continued to support Loudoun's Quebec proposal. To add to the confusion, Pitt himself was dismissed from the government by the King on April 6. As a result, on July 9 Loudoun received instructions which allowed him discretion in the choice of targets. By this time Loudoun's regiments were assembling at Halifax and linking up with the naval support dispatched from England. There followed "weeks of indecision" as unfavourable weather, rumours of strong French naval reinforcements arriving at Louisbourg, and a lack of sufficient further naval support from a ministry naturally unsympathetic to the projects of the recently displaced Pitt combined to hobble the entire campaign.[28]

Because of the many problems encountered, Lord Loudoun called a Council-of-War which began its Halifax deliberations on July 23 and reached a decision on July 31.[29] Even the basic question under consideration by the Council was not totally clear since, while it was initially charged with deciding whether a Louisbourg attack was advisable at this late date, by July 31 the question posed was whether Louisbourg or Quebec should be the target of the attack. On Monday morning of July 25, while the former question was still under consideration, John Bradstreet was summoned to testify.[30] In answering the Council's questions Bradstreet revealed himself as a person reasonably well acquainted with Louisbourg. As a man "Bred to the Land" but with "some connection with the Sea" he was in a position to appreciate the serious problems involved in a Louisbourg assault. He chose not to elaborate upon the fact that his naval experience, other than several trans-Atlantic passages, was largely limited to trading voyages into Louisbourg harbour. Bradstreet reported to the Council that he had visited Louisbourg in 1736, 1738, 1744, and again in 1745. Carefully omitted or conveniently forgotten were his various trading visits such as that of 1741. He continued that he had remained at Louisbourg from 1745 to

---

27. "Contract made with the Owners of Transports taken up at Boston," April 18, 1757, ref. # 2253, N.Y.S.L.; Bradstreet to Loudoun, April 14, 1757, Loudoun Papers, LO 3355.

28. Pargellis, *Lord Loudoun*, 236-39; Gipson, *The British Empire Before the American Revolution*, 92-94; Basil Williams, *The Whig Supremacy, 1714-1760*, 2d ed. (Oxford, 1962), 355.

29. "At a Council of War held at Head Quarters in the Town of Halifax in Nova Scotia on Saturday the 23rd of July 1757," W.O. 34/101, 92-119, microfilm, Reel 1429.

30. Pargellis, *Lord Loudoun*, 240-41.

1747 and at the time of his departure "it was an Irregular Fortification." The masonry was in extremely poor condition and, except for the citadel, the fortifications were "over looked in every Part, from different Highth."

Bradstreet was then questioned about his knowledge of any new works completed at the fortress since the time of his departure. Although he was willing to speculate upon what the French might have done once Louisbourg was regained, he admitted his ignorance concerning this matter. His answer to the basic question of whether a Louisbourg attack was feasible "in the Present season" was quite clear. "That he thinks that the Season will yet Admitt of Two Months Good Weather to carry it on."[31] As it turned out Bradstreet was offering a minority opinion since the majority of the officers testifying felt English naval strength was insufficient to deal with the French vessels in Louisbourg harbour. Moreover, it was felt that the treacherous fall weather would make a successful siege impossible. Fearful that cancellation of the Louisbourg attack and a total failure to move against Quebec could lead to charges of disobeying his orders, Loudoun felt compelled to rephrase the question addressed to the Council.[32] On July 31 it was asked whether Louisbourg or Quebec should be attacked and the Council unanimously agreed "That the Attack shou'd be on Louisbourg."[33] Loudoun's new resolve to push the attack was severely shaken within a few days. As the regiments waited for favourable weather, on August 4 Admiral Francis Holburne, commanding the naval portion of the expedition, passed on "exact information of the strength of the French fleet" at Louisbourg as well as his opinion that the attack had no chance of success. Discouraged by the naval superiority of the French and disturbed by the many other difficulties which had marred the campaign, such as the bad weather and ministerial instability in England, Loudoun cancelled the attack and sullenly returned to New York.[34]

Abandonment of the assault was probably a disappointment to Bradstreet, but further ministerial changes in England softened some of his discontent over the Louisbourg fiasco. Early in July Pitt returned to power through a coalition with Newcastle.[35] Word of this alliance passed quickly to Halifax where Bradstreet greeted the news with considerable pleasure. "We are inform'd here that the Duke of New Castle & Mr. Pitt are good Friends and are settled in the Administration of publick affairs for a confirmation of which I am not a little impatient." At this point Bradstreet appeared unaware of the imminent collapse of the entire effort against Louisbourg. By August 15, how-

---

31. "At a Council of War ... July 1757," W.O. 34/101, 99-103, microfilm, Reel 1429. For a discussion of the Council, see Gipson, *The British Empire Before the American Revolution*, 7, 108-12.

32. Pargellis, *Lord Loudoun*, 241.

33. "At a Council of War ... July 1757," W.O. 34/101, 119, microfilm, Reel 1429.

34. Pargellis, *Lord Loudoun*, 242.

35. Namier and Brooke, *History of Parliament*, 3, 293.

ever, the campaign had been abandoned and Bradstreet was ordered to Albany "with all imaginable dispatch to prepare Waggons, Battoes, etc."[36] As Loudoun's campaign plan collapsed, however, another was being formulated by Bradstreet. This effort was to be made in London rather than in the American theatre of war and was designed to capitalize upon Sir Richard Lyttleton's friendship with William Pitt.

The opening salvo of the new campaign was fired by Bradstreet on August 15 in a letter to Lyttleton. Although he knew full well that Pitt was already back in power, Bradstreet pretended that he was ignorant of the matter. "Where fore should your friends be in the administration again" he declared, "of which I am not without hopes, be pleas'd to make a favourable mention of me to them & stand my Godfather in any way or ways they may think proper to intrust & employ me." Since Bradstreet felt that in his present position he was "realy of little real service" he proceeded to outline, for the benefit of his "Godfather" and the latter's friends, three different positions which admirably fitted his talents and inclinations as well as the needs of the flagging English military effort in North America. Bradstreet argued that if he was appointed as governor of one of the American colonies it would provide him with the rank governors enjoyed when "they act with the Army" and he could make a real contribution leading "the Troops raised by the Colony I was set Over." Should his lack of experience or the lack of a vacant position be raised in objection to such an appointment, Bradstreet felt both could be overcome. After all, he had already served St. John's, Newfoundland, for "Twelve Years as Lieut Governor" and, furthermore, "there can be no great impropriety in removing Governor Belcher of the New Jerseys who has not been able to act for several Years from age & infirmities." If this scheme was not acceptable, the imaginative Bradstreet was ready with another.

In battling the French in America it had become clear to him that "the Indians & Canadians" were the enemy's "life, spirit & principal dependence." Military success against such an irregular foe required irregular adjustments by the English. Consequently, Bradstreet promised that if given the orders in thirty days he could organize "a Body of well chosen Rangers, regimented & properly appointed" who could be "of infinite use" in the type of war being fought in the colonies. A force of rangers comprised not only "the best & cheapest Troops the King could have" but, in addition, such a contingent could strike quickly in "all parts of the Back Country, which Regular Troops cannot." The use of rangers was an idea much under discussion at this time,[37] but as usual Bradstreet was one of the earliest to articulate it, press it home, and twist it to his own advantage. He admitted that there were approxi-

---

36. Bradstreet to Charles Gould, August 6, 1757, T.P.C., 128/27; ibid., August 21, 1757, 128/28; Bradstreet to Sir Richard Lyttleton, August 15, 1757, Chatham MSS, Bundle 95, 172.

37. Ibid., 172-74. John R. Cuneo, *Robert Rogers of the Rangers* (New York, 1959), 60-61, discusses the same proposal offered by Lieutenant-Colonel Thomas Gage in November of 1757, which was accepted by Loudoun.

mately 800 scattered rangers already in the service but they needed to be formed into one unit and put under proper direction—that is, under the command of John Bradstreet. In the event that he was not given the governorship or the command of a ranger regiment, Bradstreet, in a short postscript, put forward his final suggestion. Because of his "knowledge of the country" he could be of considerable utility in "Transporting Troops &c. & preparing every thing necessary for an army in the best & cheapest manner & with dispatch." If there was nothing else, apparently he could be persuaded to become Quartermaster-General.[38]

In fact, by 1757, Bradstreet had appropriated the responsibilities, if not the rank, of quartermaster-general. By means of his transportation and provisioning activities he had continually demonstrated his value to both Shirley and Loudoun. Additionally, the realities of office-seeking precluded certain appointments, at least at this moment. For example, an appointment as governor of one of the American colonies was a plum desired by many more qualified office-seekers who possessed even better placed patrons than those enjoyed by Bradstreet. His own limited stature and the competitiveness for such offices made his New Jersey suggestion rather unrealistic. Likewise the command of a regiment, and the colonel's rank it entailed was somewhat beyond the grasp of a lowly captain. He could perhaps hope to leap over the rank of major to a lieutenant-colonelship, but to be immediately appointed as regimental colonel over the heads of other claimants, armed with seniority and a record of steady progress through the ranks, was highly unlikely. Although continually thirsting for the more prestigious and active appointment, Bradstreet was to discover that when advancement came it was more in line with his proven abilities than his visionary schemes.

While recent English ministerial changes made it a suitable time to press such requests for his promotion, in terms of the actual progress of the war in America Bradstreet appeared to be choosing a most inopportune moment to plead his case. Not only had Loudoun's Louisbourg campaign miscarried, but in August Fort William Henry had fallen to the French forces under Montcalm. The latter defeat, Bradstreet admitted to Gould, was widely considered to have been caused by the negligence and incompetence of his friend, General Webb.[39] But Bradstreet again demonstrated a capacity for disentanglement and dissociation from such defeats, and at the same time actually turned them to his advantage. While bemoaning these setbacks and the sad course of the war, he offered elaborate suggestions aimed at rescuing the situation and, of course, facilitating his own advancement. Sir

---

38. Bradstreet to Lyttleton, August 15, 1757, Chatham MSS, Bundle 95, 174-75.
39. Bradstreet to Charles Gould, September 5, 1757, T.P.C., 128/29. King Gould had died in July of 1756 so this, and any future mention of Gould, refers to Charles. For a consideration of Webb's blunders leading to the loss of Fort William Henry, see Pargellis, *Lord Loudoun*, 243-50.

Richard Lyttleton was the recipient of these proposals but Bradstreet kept Charles Gould fully informed as well, expecting that Gould would ascertain whether Lyttleton had received his schemes and had liked them.

As he returned from Halifax to Boston and then on to Albany, the intelligence about the disaster at Fort William Henry reached him. Bradstreet became increasingly agitated about the "afflicting, nay alarming" and indeed "shocking state North America is reduced to since this War." On September 5, by which time he had reached Albany, a prayer was offered "that Heaven may be graciously pleas'd to send us better times."[40] While petitioning the Almighty, Bradstreet was also preparing more concrete proposals for the benefit of William Pitt, proposals which were designed to turn the tide of war in England's favour. At this time he provided Lyttleton with a detailed consideration of the American situation and was quite explicit about the person for whom it was really intended. "Should Your friend Mr. Pitt be in the Administration be pleas'd to lay this before him and assure him it is not wrote prematurely but well digested and founded upon much experience." Obviously confident of the merits of his plan, Bradstreet was careful not to appear too presumptuous. Portraying himself as still innocently unaware of recent English political changes he added a note of humility. If Pitt was not in power Lyttleton was to use the submission as he saw fit, but Bradstreet hoped "that my name is not mention'd lest umbrage might be taken at a person of so little consequence giving his thoughts so freely or medling at any rate with matters of so much importance."

Then Bradstreet harked back to a letter written to Lyttleton in January of 1756.[41] He reminded Lyttleton that in it he had estimated the annual value of the fur trade to the French to be "about 170,000 pounds sterling." He had suggested that about "ten or fifteen per cent" of this sum be placed "into proper hands" and then immediately used to supply the Indians "in exchange for those Furs & Skins." Such an approach "if properly manag'd, [would] be the ruin of the people of Canada." Obviously the "proper hands" intended for this money were those of John Bradstreet, and it was also clear that this attempt to win over the Indians had formed a part of Bradstreet's old effort to supplant Sir William Johnson as Indian superintendent over the area north and west of the Great Lakes. But this attempt had failed, partially at least because of the alert response of Johnson and his friends. Bradstreet himself, although for reasons other than his failure to secure an Indian appointment, admitted how impractical his plan had become by September of 1757. Because of the setbacks suffered in the

---

40. Bradstreet to Gould, August 21, 1757, T.P.C., 128/28; September 5, 1757, T.P.C., 128/29.

41. This letter was probably one of the items discussed in Gould to Bradstreet, March 29, 1756, T.P.C., 128/22, written several months after Lyttleton had openly entered the opposition.

Lake Ontario region, particularly the loss of Oswego, and the wavering if not openly hostile attitude of the Six Nations, Bradstreet now felt the British could rescue the area by means of only one action. They could recover control "by making War against the Western Indians and immediately carrying it into the heart of their Country and persevere untill You oblige them to sue for peace." Once subdued, the regular fur trade should be resumed, but with the British substituted for the French.

Elaborating upon his call for an immediate attack, Bradstreet continued, "I say, this is the time to attack them and if well manag'd, well tim'd & kept Secret the Fort at Cataraque, the Naval Force they took at Oswego and what they had of their own together with the Fort at Neagara, the Settlement at Detroit & even Fort Dusquane &ca must fall into your hands in the run of next Summer." Who could carry out such a campaign? "Four thousand Men, well chosen, well appointed & provided with every necessary requisite for that service with capacity, application and diligence at their head would be sufficient to surmount all difficulties and succeed to the honor & interest of Great Britain & her colonies." Such a successful thrust "would immediately strike of all communication & commerce with the French." In addition, it would have profound repercussions upon Indian alliances in the Great Lakes area. "By a stroke of this kind the Five Nations would return to You, and I doubt not but several other Nations of Indians would desert the French & submit the instant they saw a sufficient Force to destroy them well appointed & conducted into the heart of their Country and that the whole would follow their example soon after suffering by the War and seeing the French Forts and Settlements taken & distroy'd upon the Lakes." With himself at the head of such an expedition, winning battles and supervising an English takeover of the profitable fur trade of the French, Bradstreet must have envisaged tremendous financial gains as well as grand military victories leading to his prosperity and promotion. But while this proposed campaign fitted his aspirations like a glove he was aware that his own well-argued priorities were not necessarily the same as those of the British government. In England there was the real possibility that other campaign approaches were under consideration. Bradstreet was realistic enough to see that his proposed western thrust, while personally advantageous and a useful campaign in the over-all war effort, was in English eyes perhaps secondary in importance to the reduction of Canada itself. He recognized the limited nature of his proposal, and the danger of an overcommitment to one plan which might exclude him from a major role if another approach was adopted. He therefore turned his attention to a general campaign against Canada and his possible role in it.

The link allowing this apparently contradictory switchover to a discussion of a three-pronged campaign aimed at the capture of Quebec, rather than a sudden strike westward, was found in the fact that Bradstreet had based his initial proposal on the assumption that "nothing more is intended the next Season than to attempt the taking

Louisbourg." However, Bradstreet then proceeded to make clear that given adequate naval support and significantly augmented land forces, far more than Louisbourg's capture and a Great Lakes campaign could be attempted. Bradstreet felt that up to that point in the war complete mobilization of the mother country's and colonies' resources, particularly in terms of manpower, had not taken place. The war had been fought only "sparingly" despite the fact that it was being waged against "a handfull of people to what you are, comparitively speaking, who live in an inhospitable Country, subject to almost insurmountable difficulties every Day and at best poorly provided with the necessarys of life, while You on the contrary Inhabit an immence tract of fine Country fill'd with able body'd Men which produces in the greatest abundance every conveniency of life man can desire and at the same time every Man desirous of making a bold push to distroy the common Enemy." By picturing the American colonies as well worth defending and New France as ripe for conquest, and adding a fervent American desire to destroy Quebec once and for all, Bradstreet hoped to achieve an all-out military effort by the mother country which would bring Canada to her knees. To do this Bradstreet estimated 46,000 men, including both regulars and provincials, were needed as well as "a superior Fleet to what the French can conveniently send," which must arrive at Halifax by the "middle of April or first of May next." Once these forces were assembled, a three-pronged assault against Canada was to be launched. One of 30,000 men, "including two thirds of the Regular troops," was to reduce Louisbourg and then move up the St. Lawrence against Quebec. "The second to consist of 10,000 including the remaining third of Regular Troops," was to march from Albany and, once word was received of the fleet's departure from Louisbourg for Quebec, it was to capture Ticonderoga and Crown Point. A linkup was to be made with the third prong of 6,000 men which had advanced from Albany to Oswego and then made its way across Lake Ontario. The combined force was then to move against Montreal where it would meet the fleet, to proceed "in a short time [with] ... the reduction of the Town of Montreal." Thus in September of 1757 John Bradstreet outlined a plan of attack which bore a striking resemblance to the basic battle plan employed by William Pitt in achieving the conquest of Canada during the campaigns of 1758, 1759, and 1760.

As he concluded his lengthy submission Bradstreet hinted at his own role in the plan as well as the way in which he proposed to integrate his initial suggestion of a western thrust with the three-pronged assault. He now referred to the third prong, designed to strike out of Oswego, as a secret operation "until executed" and one which must be conducted by "chosen Men." Furthermore, the Oswego push should be "put into the hand of a person equal to so difficult tho' so advantageous a task and the whole undertaken so early this Winter as to give time to prepare every necessary in season."[42] In order to be even more explicit,

---

42. Bradstreet to Lyttleton, September 5, 1757, Chatham MSS, Bundle 95, 179-84.

Bradstreet wrote a separate letter to Lyttleton the same day offering himself as "a candidate for the command of that part of the Forces which should go by the way of Oswego." His admirable qualifications for such an appointment were supported by the claim that it was "avowed by all degrees of People that no person in America is more capable of conducting an Inland Expedition in these parts than I am." Should his low rank in the army prove a stumbling block, Bradstreet again suggested that he be provided with the necessary higher army rank by an appointment as Governor of New Jersey succeeding the now dead Belcher. Concerning the expedition itself he was "convinced of my being able to go through with it that I will risk my reputation upon the success of it as far as the taking Montreal & all the Forts upon the Lakes & Joine the Fleet, should they reach Quebeck."[43]

It is clear that Bradstreet intended himself as the commander of the Oswego prong in the campaign aimed at the reduction of Canada. But his mention of the capture of "all the Forts upon the Lakes" when linked with his earlier call for total secrecy, chosen men, and the early commencement of the Oswego operation, provided intriguing hints that he was hopeful of executing at least a portion of his initial proposal relating to a western thrust. The possibilities of plundering the weakly defended Great Lakes posts of the French and of seizing control of their profitable fur trade empire spurred Bradstreet to activity. Should he be entrusted with the Oswego command his force eventually would move on Montreal, fulfilling its vital role in the overall English war strategy. However, there was the possibility that a portion of the troops committed to the operation were to be at least momentarily diverted to hit at targets which had limited significance to the all-important thrust into the Laurentian heartland, but which were of critical importance to the economic aspirations of John Bradstreet and other colonials. Ironically, Bradstreet had spoken of the "common Enemy" against which both colony and mother country were pitted and hinted at the American willingness to unite with the English in a total war effort. Nevertheless, the circuitous way in which he introduced, dropped, and reintroduced his Great Lakes proposals, attempting to fit them with what he recognized would be an English preoccupation with Louisbourg and Quebec, revealed that, while there was agreement on the existence of a common enemy, a real discrepancy existed between mother country and colony in terms of the route to success and the type of war being fought. To Bradstreet and many colonials it was a war to possess and develop new lands, while to English policy makers it was a war against a European power and, therefore, the destruction of armies and key fortresses was the major priority. There is some significance in the fact that Bradstreet urged the use of English regulars against Louisbourg, Ticonderoga, and Crown Point but left his Oswego thrust a totally colonial operation. He knew the type of target, the type of war the

---

43. Ibid., 176-77.

colonies preferred. While demonstrating a unique ability to present the colonial aspirations within the broader imperial context, his proposals revealed that the land and furs within the Great Lakes empire of the west, not fortresses at Quebec or Louisbourg, were the primary and immediate focus of himself and other colonial expansionists. Fortresses such as Louisbourg and Quebec, once won on the field of battle, could still be returned to France in the diplomatic chess game played by the European powers. Possession of the vaguely defined Great Lakes empire and a total restructuring of Indian alliances and trade patterns promised tangible gains to the colonies which the French would have difficulty countering even if the territory itself was eventually bartered away by England.

Once these suggestions and plans had been sent off to Sir Richard Lyttleton in England, Bradstreet was naturally anxious for reports of their safe arrival and hopefully their approval. As a result, one week after the date of these letters he wrote to Charles Gould concerning this correspondence. Since Lyttleton had recently hinted of his "being soon consider'd for my services" and it was now established that William Pitt, "with whome I know he is well," was Secretary of State, Bradstreet reported to his London friend that he had urged Lyttleton to seek the governorship of New Jersey on his behalf. Bradstreet repeated his expectation that armed with such an appointment he could play a more active military role in North America. Expressing his anxiety that his letters might go astray, he urged Gould to check with Lyttleton to see if "he has heard from me upon that head and if he has if it is like to Succeed." In addition Gould was to write Bradstreet as soon as he had anything to report on this matter. Despite Bradstreet's obvious anxiety it was not until late December that Gould replied, and then the news was not good. While Lyttleton "would with the greatest Pleasure do you any Service in his Power," the appointment of a New Jersey governor "was intirely in Lord Halifax's Department, independent of Mr. Pitt, and that he had not sufficient Interest with his Lordship to Effect your desire."[44] Had he known of a note Gould received from Lyttleton shortly after this letter was dispatched, the disheartened Bradstreet would have been considerably cheered. Lyttleton described himself "charmed with the Spirit & Enterprizing Genius of Col. Bradstreet" and noted that he had passed his "several letters" along "to Mr Pitt who has not yet returned them."[45] Despite the immediate failure to achieve the New Jersey governorship, Bradstreet's comments concerning the war in America were being examined and considered by William Pitt.

---

44. Bradstreet to Gould, September 12, 1757, T.P.C., 128/30; Gould to Bradstreet, December 27, 1757, T.P.C., 128/32.
45. Lyttleton to Gould, c. 1757, T.P.C., 128/33. This note must have been written on or after December 27, 1757, otherwise Gould would have included such encouraging information in his letter to Bradstreet written on that day. Moreover, it was probably written before January 1, 1758, when Lyttleton was able to send word of exactly what his solicitations with Pitt had gained for Bradstreet. See ibid., January 1, 1758, 128/34.

Considerable time was to pass before Bradstreet's requests and Lyttleton's efforts bore fruit and in the interval Bradstreet was not idle. While his cause was championed in England, in North America Bradstreet offered variations of his schemes to his superior officer. Paradoxically, however, although Bradstreet now emphasized colonial military targets and approaches, he continued to express real misgivings about the American contribution to the war effort. In April he had reported to his commanding officer that despite the embargo Loudoun had placed on trade with the enemy, a certain laxity prevailed in Massachusetts and New Hampshire. Bradstreet suspected that Massachusetts vessels, including "one of which is a Trader," as well as fishing boats from Cape Ann, while ostensibly sailing for Nova Scotia were to be of eventual benefit to Louisbourg. He also felt that the raising of troops promised by Massachusetts "will not be so punctually comply'd with . . . as it ought." Again in late August, as he moved to take up his Albany duties, he met a colonial unwillingness to cooperate in support of the war effort. Bradstreet was trying to procure carts for the Albany service but in Massachusetts and Connecticut the people begged off contributing because "their Hay [was] not got in nor their ground Sow'd."[46] Reconciling this colonial reluctance to contribute to the war effort with his own emphasis upon colonial priorities and a greater utilization of the colonies in waging the war proved to be a relatively easy matter for Bradstreet. As it became clear that it was to his advantage to advocate and identify with the colonial view, at least in terms of military targets and approaches, Bradstreet willingly embraced their position on these matters. At the same time colonial reluctance in responding to the English call to arms was explained as, at least in part, the product of an English failure to appreciate colonial sensitivities in conducting the war. By setting the stage in this way, Bradstreet established the need for officers who appreciated colonial aspirations and yet recognized colonial liabilities as well. At the same time such officers had to be equally aware of British priorities and adequately schooled in orthodox English military approaches. And, of course, one of the indispensable officers who possessed these qualifications, so necessary for a proper meshing of the American and English war efforts, was John Bradstreet himself.

His hopefully rewarding reconciliation of mother-country and colonial aspirations was revealed in December of 1757 when Bradstreet submitted proposals concerning the creation of a special colonial force. The suggestions aimed at a changed English military approach in order to meet North American realities. Basically it was emphasized that a greater employment of American manpower and also the selection of specially qualified officers were needed. Bradstreet argued that, given the "nature of this Country," the only chance for a successful offensive and the restoration and securing of "our Frontiers" was

---

46. **Bradstreet** to Loudoun, April 11, 1757, Loudoun Papers, LO 3336; August 27, 1757, Loudoun Papers, LO 4321.

found in an attack "by Water and through woods." But a force capable of such an undertaking was lacking. Therefore, he urged "that the Crown, during the War, establish and keep up four thousand Chosen and well regulated Men accustom'd to the Woods and management of all kinds of Boats to be form'd into Companys." What he had in mind was obviously only a variation of his old complement of bateau-men, although on a larger and more expensive scale. Recruits were to be arranged by the various colonies "in their several proportions from New Hampshire to Pensilvania." Enlistment was to be stimulated by a pay rate for the "Private Men" which was "six pence per Day over and above what a Common Soldier receives" and which was greater by the same proportion for sergeants and corporals. Instead of acknowledging that the higher pay was designed for the encouragement of recruiting, Bradstreet claimed the extra money was a necessity dictated by the heavier duties expected of the troops. They would transport themselves, and regulars if need be, from place to place in the face of "formadable and distructive" opposition from the Indian allies of the French. Thus, according to Bradstreet, what seemed at first to be an "extravagant and unnecessary" expenditure, was in reality an "oeconomy and a necessary and prudent measure." Concerning the officers commanding such a special force, he recommended that they be "Natives of this Country in General from the Peoples apprehensions and fears of Serving under European Officers." Lest his reader miss the point there were other specifications concerning the officers. Several of them must "be well acquainted with the woods, the nature of the Indians and the management of Boats."[47] In this way Bradstreet had quite deliberately fitted his background, abilities, and past actions with what appeared to be the new British military needs in North America.

While Bradstreet's proposals were a perfect justification of his own utility, they were somewhat imperfect in other ways. For one thing, he anticipated an excellent enlistment response from the American colonies. But at the time of his suggestion, Loudoun was wrestling with the problem of forcing the colonies to meet his own proposed quota of rangers intended for winter service. Not only were some colonies reluctant to provide such troops but at least one, Massachusetts, refused to allow the raising of rangers and came dangerously close to providing no men at all for the next campaign.[48] In a sense, Bradstreet had foreseen this difficulty and made arrangements to cope with it by recommending higher pay and colonial officers. In spite of this, however, it might have been difficult for Loudoun to approve the creation of such a large colonial fighting force, which would necessitate his making further manpower demands upon the various colonies, at a time when it was only with great difficulty that basic manpower commitments were being met.

47. Proposal for raising local troops, by [John Bradstreet, December 3, 1757], Loudoun Papers, LO 4164.
48. See Pargellis, *Lord Loudoun*, 273-74.

Yet Loudoun's unwillingness to accept this scheme does appear rather surprising since he has been described as one of a number of British regular officers who were experienced in irregular, frontier, or guerilla tactics, and who proved innovative and adaptable in the North American theatre.[49] But when a scheme was put forward by a colonial, who suggested employing colonials, a real reluctance quickly emerged. Thomas Gage, an undistinguished regular, could propose and gain acceptance of a light infantry unit[50] but Bradstreet's suggestions, despite Loudoun's obvious respect for his performance, met with no such easy approval. Bradstreet had done an excellent job of selling his military theories to British politicians but the regular officer corps was another matter. When Charles Townshend, several years earlier, had proposed a number of military experiments in America, he drew heavily upon Bradstreet conceptions. Townshend had proposed that the seven independent companies in South Carolina, Virginia, and New York, be combined into one regiment. This new force should then be "put under the Command of an Officer of Experience and Reputation, who has serv'd in America, where there are so many peculiar circumstances attending the manner of carrying on War." Moreover he called for the creation of an additional regiment recruited in America with an almost totally American officer corps. This was necessitated, he explained, because of "it being the opinion of those who are most conversant with the temper of that people (and it is an opinion much confirm'd by late Experience) that it would be difficult to persuade an American to list under a British officer, which difficulty it is thought would be avoided if the Commander in Chief should be appointed from hence, and the subordinate officers chosen out of the People of the Country."[51] Politicians could be persuaded, even by a colonial, but the regular officer corps serving in America, despite its professional awareness and application on occasion of wilderness tactics, continued to view with icy suspicion proposals put forward by "irregulars" such as Bradstreet.

Loudoun's condescending reservations about military schemes which relied upon the reluctant colonials, whether in command or constituting the rank and file, probably explain the initial failure to act upon Bradstreet' suggestions. An undaunted Bradstreet continued to refine his basic plan until a much altered version finally gained Loudoun's approval. In a January 4, 1758 memorial to Lord Loudoun, Bradstreet revived a suggestion first offered by William Shirley in 1755. An expedition was urged against Fort Frontenac, or Cadaraqui. By taking that post and recovering the English vessels lost when Oswego

---

49. See Peter E. Russell, "Redcoats in the Wilderness: British Officers and Irregular Warfare in Europe and America, 1740 to 1760," *William and Mary Quarterly*, 3d Ser., 35 (1978), 630, 637, 645.

50. Cuneo, *Robert Rogers*, 60-61; Russell, "Redcoats in the Wilderness," 646.

51. "A Scheme for the Improvement & Employment of His Majesty's Forces in America" by Charles Townshend for Newcastle, September 13, 1754, Newcastle Papers, Add. MSS 32,736/515-18.

fell, as well as capturing the French naval force, "many and great advantages... would arize to the British Nation and her Colonies." Bradstreet offered to raise 800 "chosen Men" at his own expense. As soon as the ice broke up in the spring of 1758 the force was to strike at Cadaraqui and, hopefully, after taking the fort return to Oswego with the plunder and all the captured French vessels. Repeating his point about the expedition's expenses, Bradstreet emphasized "That Your Memorialist does not propose to put the Publick to any expence in this enterprize should it not Succeed but to bear it wholly himself." He did request Loudoun's assistance in providing him with limited artillery support, shot, shells, powder, and cartridges, as well as spades, pick axes, shovels, and ninety whale-boats, along with ten bateaux. In addition he hoped "an Officer or Serjeant & Twelve good Men of the Artillery" could be spared for the mission. There was an excellent possibility that considerable quantities of furs and supplies would fall into Bradstreet's hands with the capture of Fort Frontenac, but he expected more than this in the way of rewards. If his effort was successful Bradstreet hoped to "be reimbursed his expenses and recommended to his Majestys Favor." Furthermore, "with respect to the Payment of the Men," Loudoun would perhaps consider "a Sum of Money to be given them when the work above-mentioned is completed."[52]

This memorial was drafted by Bradstreet on January 4, 1758, and after "a consideration of 23 days" Loudoun approved the project. An elated Bradstreet immediately wrote Gould that after the failure of all his efforts to have a Frontenac attack undertaken "at the Public expense," he finally had achieved approval of such an assault provided that he bear the expense should it fail. Triumph in this "bold and hazardous attempt," which Bradstreet stressed was "next to impracticable from the distance, difficulties and the dangers of the Indians besides the French," would bring the payment of any accumulated expenses as well as Loudoun's personal recommendation of Bradstreet "to his Majesty's Favour."[53] While Bradstreet, in his letter dated January 27, informed Gould about Loudoun's acceptance of his plan, it was not until January 31 that Loudoun gave written approval in a series of letters to Bradstreet. These letters spelled out further details relating to the Frontenac assault and also revealed that Bradstreet had other important duties to perform prior to launching his Lake Ontario adventure. He was ordered to proceed immediately to the Albany-Schenectady area where he was to supervise the construction of the bateaux needed for the next campaign. In another letter, written the same day, Loudoun gave official approval to the Frontenac assault. Expressing his faith in Bradstreet's "Secrecy Diligence and Activity and in Your knowledge of the Country," he ordered him to raise 800 men

---

52. Memorial of Bradstreet to Loudoun [January 4, 1758], Loudoun Papers, LO 6895. The same item is in W.O. 34/57, 1, microfilm, Reel 154 (1).
53. Bradstreet to Gould, January 27, 1758, T.P.C., 128/35.

for an attack on Fort Frontenac. Such a thrust was intended to divert the enemy, make the English masters of Lake Ontario, sever French communications with the western Indians, and regain the vessels taken at Oswego. The men recruited for this task were to assemble at Schenectady in the first week of March, moving against Frontenac as soon as weather permitted. In a third letter, again dated January 31, Loudoun made clear that the expedition was to be provided with such essentials as provisions, artillery, ammunition, bateaux, and whaleboats. Loudoun reiterated Bradstreet's personal responsibility for "raising and Subsisting the said Body of Men," but he added that should Bradstreet be recalled before completing his mission, "then and in such Case the Expenses he shall have been at, in raising and Subsisting the said Body of Men, shall be borne and sustained by the Crown, in like manner as if he had Succeeded in his proposed undertaking."[54] Thus, Bradstreet's reassignment or the cancellation of the attack prior to its execution would bring full compensation for any expenses incurred by him. In view of the many reassignments and new orders already en route to America, which had been decided upon by Pitt and dispatched at the end of December, 1757, this proviso proved to be valuable protection for Bradstreet.

Both Loudoun and Bradstreet were to be directly affected by Pitt's new orders which were destined not to reach Loudoun until March of 1758. But until the arrival of these instructions both men assumed the Frontenac expedition was to proceed as planned. As a result, during the month of February Bradstreet busied himself at Albany with the construction of bateaux and preparations for his Lake Ontario thrust. At the same time Loudoun informed Pitt that he had assigned Bradstreet the task of building and manning the bateaux necessary for the next campaign. He also mentioned his approval of Bradstreet's proposed early spring assault on Fort Frontenac, explaining the various conditions and promised rewards surrounding the enterprise.[55]

Bradstreet's preparations and Loudoun's approving explanation of the Frontenac attack were rendered futile on March 10 when Pitt's letters reached Loudoun. The British commander was recalled to England and in Pitt's orders to Loudoun's successor, Major-General James Abercromby, Bradstreet was assigned duties in the southern colonies.[56] At first the new orders seemed a severe set-back to Bradstreet in that they totally precluded his cherished Frontenac scheme. They were even more of a blow to Lord Loudoun in that he was

---

54. Loudoun to Bradstreet, January 31, 1758, W.O. 34/58, 3, 5, 6, microfilm, Reel 154 (2).

55. Bradstreet to Loudoun, February 7, 1758, Loudoun Papers, LO 5552; February 13, 1758, Loudoun Papers, LO 5575; February 20, 1758, Loudoun Papers, LO 5635; Loudoun to Pitt, February 16, 1758, in Gertrude S. Kimball, ed., *Correspondence of William Pitt when Secretary of State with Colonial Governors and Military and Naval Commissioners in America*, 1 (New York, 1906), 194.

56. Pargellis, *Lord Loudoun*, 277; Pitt to Abercromby, December 30, 1757, in Kimball, *Pitt Correspondence*, 1, 146.

relieved of his command and returned to England, with his record blotted by inactivity and military defeat. Unlike his commander, Bradstreet was under no such cloud. On the contrary, he received a certain amount of recognition for his valued service. His initial disappointment at the failure to bring to fruition his latest plan was more than offset by a higher rank and new appointment. Bradstreet's friends in England had been quite active on his behalf and with their help his star continued to rise in the American theatre of war. In late December of 1757, at the same time as Loudoun was being supplanted by James Abercromby, Bradstreet finally won the promotion to lieutenant-colonel he so deeply coveted as well as one of the appointments Sir Richard Lyttleton had been urged to seek for him. On December 27, 1757, a message from the War Office to Pitt's secretaries confirmed a number of Promotions including that of "Captain John Bradstreet... to be a Deputy Quarter Master General of His Majesty's Forces in North America and to take Rank as Lieutenant Colonel of Foot."[57]

The role played by Lyttleton in bringing about Bradstreet's promotion and appointment was revealed a few days later. With obvious satisfaction he reported to Charles Gould his "pleasure to acquaint you that I have obtained for our Friend Bradstreet the Rank of *Lt. Col in the Kings Service*, as Deputy Quarter Master General for America." While advising Gould that he could possibly inform Bradstreet of the promotion, he hastened to add that Gould should not "mention any part of what I have acquainted you with to any body in England, and desire he [Bradstreet] will say nothing of it till he receives his Commission or a notification of it from Authority."[58] The secrecy surrounding Bradstreet's upward movement in rank appears at first a somewhat mystifying precaution on Lyttleton's part. On more careful scrutiny, however, it may be that such an approach was a calculated attempt to avoid the objections which might be raised against the promotion of an individual such as Bradstreet. Repeatedly throughout his career, the words of praise Bradstreet sought and received from his commanders and friends were contradicted by the damning accusations of his activities hurled by his critics and enemies. That such was possibly the case at this moment was revealed in a summarizing notation penned by Charles Gould. In a reminder to himself, dated January 17, 1758, which was written on a copy of a December letter to Bradstreet, Gould noted that he had this day congratulated Bradstreet on his new offices, "which he owed to Sr. Rd. Lyttleton." This same January 17 letter to Bradstreet, according to Gould's summary, also had contained a "hint about Trade, wch. had been represented to his disadvantage."[59] Once more, apparently, rumours of Bradstreet's involvement in illicit trading ac-

---

57. Barrington to secretaries to William Pitt, December 27, 1757, Louisbourg Restoration Project, n.p., microfilm, Reel B-3311, P.A.C.
58. Lyttleton to Gould, January 1, 1758, T.P.C., 128/34.
59. This note is attached to a copy of Gould to Bradstreet, December 27, 1757, T.P.C., 128/32.

tivities had crossed the Atlantic, creating discomfort for his friends. Bradstreet had carefully attempted to portray even the most minor contribution to his commander, Lord Loudoun, in the best possible light. He had also devoted much attention to the preparation of an analysis of British military needs in America. Yet despite these activities and the sympathetic presentation of his case by allies at "home," the rumours and insinuations stalking a mysterious man who was neither totally British nor totally American threatened to frustrate his quest for higher office.

With the recall of his commanding officer and his own promotion, the period of John Bradstreet's service under Lord Loudoun had abruptly ended. It had begun with cautious moves aimed at Bradstreet's survival and finished with approving rewards for his acknowledged contribution to the British cause in the Seven Years' War. During the span of roughly a year and a half, Bradstreet had adjusted successfully to the immediate realities of service under Loudoun as well as to the more distant and ever fluctuating desires of major figures in the political arena of mid-eighteenth century England. In North America his diligent service and persistent petitions had brought him to the threshold of what he obviously considered to be a campaign of major importance both to himself and Great Britain. He had won Loudoun's respect for his abilities and support for his adventurous Frontenac expedition. These gains, however, appeared dashed by William Pitt's decision to remove Loudoun. But while very much involved in New World military matters, Bradstreet had never allowed himself to be isolated from Old World currents and preoccupations. English contacts and patrons, such as Gould and Lyttleton, had been kept fully informed of his activities and they in turn, by advice and action, faithfully supported his cause at "home."

In protecting and advancing his interests, Bradstreet's English friends had been provided with considerable ammunition in the form of his praiseworthy actions in the North American conflict. There seems little doubt that Bradstreet had emerged as a real asset to Lord Loudoun. His expertise with the bateau-men, his organizational abilities in terms of provisioning the forces, constructing boats, and arranging troop transports had proved his worth to his commander. His perceptive grasp of colonial desires and sensitivities, particularly when they fitted his own, if fully appreciated by Loudoun could have helped considerably in unravelling some of the thorny problems found in a command composed of British regulars and American provincials. At the same time, and at a higher level, Bradstreet was further solidifying and adding to his contribution to the English war effort. He was submitting recommendations concerning the future direction of the war which were factors in the shaping of English war policies. Admittedly other individuals, both in 1757 and over the long years of Anglo-French rivalry in North America, had offered similar proposals for the conquest of New France, employing practically the same invasion routes. Likewise his other proposals to raise a ranger regiment, or launch an expedition for which he would bear the cost in the event of failure, were not unique to John Bradstreet. Where his suggestions differed was in the timing of his presentations and their well-executed exposure to those in key positions of authority. He was alert to the constantly shifting vagaries of war in America and frequently was adept enough to pounce upon and quickly crystallize the adjustment in orthodox military approaches necessary to meet the new need. Moreover, Bradstreet's opportunistic watch on the English political scene allowed him to submit his more elaborate considerations dealing with the overall direction of the war effort at the right time. His suggestions appeared at the precise moment when a new administration was assuming power, prepared to sweep out the old policies and seek new solutions in order to change the course of a war which up to 1758 had witnessed defeat after defeat. In addition to the properly timed emergence of his proposals Bradstreet wanted them channelled into the proper hands. The desired recipient of his plans was neither the once helpful Henry Fox, now in temporary eclipse because of Pitt, nor the once powerful Duke of Cumberland, now in disgrace because of his European defeats. Rather it was William Pitt, rightly regarded by Bradstreet as the supreme arbiter of English war policies, whom he hoped to influence. Through Lyttleton's friendship with Pitt, and Sir Richard's excellent relationship with Lord Ligonier, the figurehead Commander-in-Chief who had replaced Cumberland, Bradstreet's hopes of laying his plans before the great were translated into reality. While similar plans may have been drafted by others for Pitt's benefit, in the case of Bradstreet there is considerable evidence that his well-timed and carefully directed proposals struck home. There were undoubtedly other influences at work upon William Pitt but the thoughts of John Bradstreet definitely received his consideration and probably were a factor in his final decisions concerning the course of the war in America.[60]

To even attract the attention, let alone to influence major English statesmen such as Pitt, was a considerable triumph for John Bradstreet. His military talents and actual military contributions might be questioned but his talents as a successful propagandizer and justifier of his own cause before the Anglo-American world were definitely first rate. Indeed, he not only caught the public eye of two worlds but he was able to knit together the aspirations and needs of the rapidly diverging Anglo-American worlds in which he found himself. At this point in his career he demonstrated a rare ability to articulate American sensi-

---

60. Pargellis, *Lord Loudoun*, 343, summarizes some of Bradstreet's comments to Lyttleton and argues that Bradstreet's criticism of the way in which the war was handled was a factor working upon Pitt to the extent that these criticisms influenced him in his decision to recall Loudoun. Rex Whitworth, *Field Marshall Lord Ligonier: A Story of the British Army, 1702-1770* (Oxford, 1958), 237, mentions that in drawing up his plans for the 1758 campaign Ligonier was influenced by many suggestions, including those offered by his "great friend" Sir Richard Lyttleton who presented him with John Bradstreet's ideas.

tivities and desires while not ignoring English military priorities and aims in order to present a final picture of basic compatibility. Of course much of this effort was designed to strengthen his own position as the indispensably valuable man who could appreciate both the English and American perspectives. At other times in his career this attempt to bridge the widening gulf between colonies and mother country had resulted in discouraging failure. On this occasion it appeared a resounding success. While some "evil minded person" might utter remarks concerning his illicit activities, in late 1757 his unique value and contribution far outweighed such shortcomings. Obviously Pitt was impressed with his worth and assigned him heavier responsibilities as a result. Without knowing Bradstreet personally, the prickly and hypercritical James Wolfe, shortly after his arrival in America, offered what was probably the prevailing English view of Bradstreet as "an extraordinary man" particularly "for the battues and for expeditions."[61] John Bradstreet had made himself a respected military figure both in England and in America. As Britain's victorious war years dawned, the stage had been set for his greatest military moment, the capture of Fort Frontenac.

---

61. James Wolfe to Lord George Sackville, May 24, 1758, Beckles Willson, *The Life and Letters of James Wolfe* (London, 1909), 369.

Chapter VI

Triumph Despite Abercromby

Although Major-General James Abercromby commanded the British forces in North America for less than a year, he was connected with several significant military actions. This year, 1758, witnessed "a notable recession of the French tide in North America" as British victories at Louisbourg, Fort Duquesne, and Frontenac dealt "French power . . . a shattering blow from which it never was able to recover." It was Abercromby's misfortune, however, to be linked with none of these victories but rather to be blamed for the major setback handed to the English forces by the French at Ticonderoga. To others went the credit for the military gains on Cape Breton and in the North American interior. At Louisbourg Jeffery Amherst plodded to success, urged on by his impetuous subordinate James Wolfe. In the Ohio, John Forbes cautiously and methodically built "a Road to Victory"[1] at Fort Duquesne. On Lake Ontario, John Bradstreet finally was permitted to launch his daring strike at Cadaraqui which earned him laurels as the conqueror of Fort Frontenac. For Bradstreet it was a year of glory, but his activities were not limited to Frontenac. Considerable praise also came his way because of the efficient performance of his bateaux duties as well as his notable attempts to rescue the British military effort at Ticonderoga.[2]

During the course of the war Bradstreet had found it necessary to adjust quickly to command changeovers. In the case of James Abercromby's assumption of responsibility for the British forces in North

---

1. Gipson, *The British Empire Before the American Revolution*, 7, 167, 179, 247-86.
2. This is one of the few periods of Bradstreet's career given considerable attention by historians. See for example, John W. Shy, "James Abercromby and The Campaign of 1758" (M.A. thesis, University of Vermont, 1957), 59-60; Gipson, *The British Empire Before the American Revolution*, 7, 236-47; Stanley, *New France: The Last Phase, 1744-1760*, 186; Fortescue, *A History of the British Army*, 2, 344; Butler, *The Annals of the King's Royal Rifle Corps*, 1, 61-62.

America, Bradstreet's transition was aided considerably by Pitt's apparent respect for his contribution. In appointing and instructing Abercromby, Pitt mentioned Bradstreet's promotion to lieutenant-colonel and "His Majesty's Pleasure" that he "should be employed as Deputy Quarter Master General, under Brigadier Forbes, in the Southern Colonies." Notwithstanding the clarity of these instructions, Abercromby dared to commit what has been termed "an inspired piece of disobedience."[3] Because of his own knowledge of Bradstreet's unique abilities Abercromby was determined to utilize him in the Ticonderoga attack, which Abercromby was to direct personally, rather than allow him to take up the new appointment under Forbes in the southern colonies.

Shortly after Pitt's orders and Abercromby's inclinations were revealed, a gloating Bradstreet commented on the pleasing dilemma brought on by the quite different ways in which his superiors proposed to use his talents. "I find myself set down to serve this Campaign to the Southward but neither General Abercromby or any one else who are to serve this way are for letting me go fearing the great preparations necessary to be made to transport a large Number of Troops from hence to Canada cannot be executed in time by any other person and how it will be determin'd I cannot say—I am willing to go any where."[4] Within the month after the arrival of Pitt's instructions, Bradstreet's role had been determined by Abercromby. He was to remain at Albany continuing the construction of bateaux, the recruitment of bateaumen, and other preparations for the approaching campaign against Ticonderoga. These were the duties originally assigned him by Lord Loudoun and were responsibilities which had been linked with the Frontenac assault; an assault which, if Bradstreet can be believed, had not been totally abandoned. Apparently he was not willing to give up the idea of an attack across Lake Ontario. Consequently at a Council-of-War in March of 1758[5] he sought renewed approval for the attack. There were many objections to his proposal but it was finally rescued by one of the more enlightened and respected regular officers. Lord George Howe "highly approved of the scheme; remov'd every objection, and obtained the assent of the general [Abercromby], to its being carried into execution, as soon as our army had made an establishment on the north side of Lake George."[6] Thus, Pitt's failure to mention a

---

3. Pitt to Abercromby, December 30, 1757, in Kimball, *Pitt Correspondence*, 1, 146; Owen A. Sherrard, *Lord Chatham: Pitt and the Seven Years' War* (London, 1955), 287.

4. Bradstreet to Gould, March 13, 1758, T.P.C., 128/36, N.L.W.

5. Lossing, *The Life and Times of Philip Schuyler*, 1, 146.

6. [John Bradstreet], *An Impartial Account of Lieut. Col. Bradstreet's Expedition to Fort Frontenac* (London, 1759), 2. In a later edition of this work, Ernest C. Kyte, ed., *An Impartial Account of Lieut. Col. Bradstreet's Expedition To Fort Frontenac* (Toronto, 1940), authorship of the account is credited to Bradstreet. This appears a reasonable assumption since at times the account paraphrases some of Bradstreet's correspondence with Sir Thomas Robinson and James Abercromby. The tone and style are also quite similar to Bradstreet's. What is disconcerting is that no clear mention of the writing of the book or

Frontenac assault in his outline of the 1758 campaign and his transfer of Bradstreet to the south were overcome by Abercromby's immediate needs and Bradstreet's persistent effort.

The Frontenac attack remained alive with this conditional and clearly hesitant approval; but the Ticonderoga campaign took priority over it. Bradstreet plunged into the preparations for the latter thrust and soon was informing Abercromby of the work completed and problems encountered. Despite difficulties caused by inexperienced workmen, 250 bateaux were produced at Albany before the end of March and 1,200 completions were promised by mid-May. Slow recruitment of bateau-men to man the vessels was offset somewhat by Abercromby's acceptance of a higher pay scale suggested by Bradstreet. In planning the complicated movement of troops, equipment, and provisions along the Hudson River and then overland to what once had been Fort William Henry on Lake George, Abercromby again turned to Bradstreet for advice. In reply, a detailed outline was offered of the time it would take, the number of bateaux, wagons, and ox carts needed, and the mechanics of the operation at the various portages.[7]

The movement of the necessary materials up the Hudson River was soon underway, but a scarcity of wagons, ox carts, teams, and drivers slowed Abercromby's campaign, thereby rendering an early attack on Ticonderoga impossible. Reporting to Pitt concerning the state of his preparations as of May 22, 1758, Abercromby outlined the problems which had emerged and, in passing, made several references to Bradstreet's contribution in the face of these difficulties. This might have been Abercromby's way of justifying his failure to carry out Pitt's orders to transfer Bradstreet to the south. A suspiciously long portion of his May 22 letter was devoted to an explanation of his decision to keep Bradstreet at Albany. Yet it does appear that on the occasions when he referred to Bradstreet's special talents Abercromby was quite sincere. He underlined the urgent need of bateaux if the campaign was to succeed and he linked their construction and proper utilization with Bradstreet's own inclinations and abilities. Abercromby explained to Pitt that Bradstreet had collected the materials and carpenters and was well into the construction of bateaux ordered by Loudoun before "His Majesty's Commands" arrived. Consequently, "it was thought most for the King's Service, that Lieut. Colo. Bradstreet, who himself likewise desired it, shou'd finish the work he had begun." Elaborating upon

---

its publication was found in the Bradstreet-Gould correspondence. Even though such conclusive evidence is lacking, Bradstreet appears to be the author of the account. All future references are to the 1759 edition.

7. Bradstreet to Abercromby, March 13, 1758, Bradstreet MSS, A.A.S.; March 24, 1758, ibid.; Abercromby to Pitt, May 22, 1758, in Kimball, *Pitt Correspondence*, 1, 253-54; "Impressment Warrant issued to Colo. John Bradstreet by James DeLancey at Fort George in city of New York," May 17, 1758, *New York Colonial Manuscripts*, 86, 12b, N.Y.S.L.; Shy, "James Abercromby And The Campaign Of 1758," 59; "The Method how to proceed to transport provisions Artillery Stores & c. from Albany to Lake George" [April 9, 1758], Loudoun Papers, LO 6942, H.L.

Bradstreet's feelings, Abercromby explained that the Lieutenant-Colonel felt far better qualified for the bateaux work than the task of deputy quartermaster general, especially since "he was an utter stranger to the Country alloted for His Department, having never been beyond Philadelphia." The wisdom of this decision was driven home by mention of the "Dispatch" with which Bradstreet had proceeded. By May 22 he had completed the construction of 1,500 bateaux. When Abercromby discussed the recruitment of the bateau-men necessary to man these craft, he made no secret of the difficulties encountered by Bradstreet and himself. But he also made clear that Bradstreet was an excellent commander of the bateau-men who had been recruited. Once more Abercromby might have been forced into such an expression of confidence in Bradstreet's abilities because of his failure to carry out another of Pitt's appointments. Bateaux-building duties and command over the bateau-men had been assigned by Pitt to Joshua Loring, a Bostonian with privateering experience who had been commissioned captain in the Royal Navy in December 1757.[8] Bradstreet now had assumed both these responsibilities. In justification of his preference for Bradstreet over Loring, Abercromby reported Loring's own reservations "that he was not capable of Commanding so large a Body of Batteau Men, as we shall have Occasion for." As a result, Abercromby had "been obliged to leave this Charge to Lieut. Colo. Bradstreet, who, from his former Experience of them, knows best how to deal with them, which is no easy Task, for they are an unwieldy & unruly Set."[9]

Abercromby's persuasive comments clearly revealed his appreciation of Bradstreet. As it turned out, keeping Bradstreet in the north was to create problems for Forbes's southern campaign, in that John St. Clair proved an inept quartermaster substitute for Bradstreet,[10] and for Abercromby himself, in that Joshua Loring, although he had acknowledged his own limitations, still felt snubbed at the treatment received at the hands of his commander-in-chief.[11] But Pitt appeared to acquiesce in the decision. There were others, however, who were not so easily convinced of either the need for Bradstreet in the Ticonderoga campaign or the merits of his contribution. Bradstreet himself was aware of these critics' opinions and responded with his own abrasive and abusive comments. At the end of May, for Gould's benefit, he recited the litany of his recent accomplishments, touching upon the 1,500 boats constructed and the "100 days provisions for 12,000 Men" that he had moved up the Hudson. These were actions which had "gain'd me much credit with all degrees of people in America that are

---

8. See Shy, "James Abercromby And The Campaign Of 1758," 58 and 73, for information about Joshua Loring and the problems his appointment caused Abercromby.

9. Abercromby to Pitt, May 22, 1758, C.O. 5/50-1, 67-81, P.A.C., and in Kimball, *Pitt Correspondence*, 1, 248-56.

10. Sherrard, *Lord Chatham: Pitt and the Seven Years' War*, 291.

11. Shy, "James Abercromby And The Campaign Of 1758," 58 and 74.

free from Envy." Turning to his detractors he admitted, "I am sensible I am an object of their attention and in which I glory as much as I despise them and lose no opportunity of making them sensible of it."

Unfortunately his defensive criticisms extended even to those who functioned as admirable spokesmen for his cause. Abercromby had provided Pitt with a detailed description of Bradstreet's praiseworthy services, yet in his letter to Gould Bradstreet voiced reservations about the way in which the campaign was being handled. Apparently referring to his Frontenac "plan," Bradstreet argued that if his advice had been accepted the British forces would "now... be in the Enemies country." Instead he found himself still at Albany. Although everything was in readiness for the move against the French and the prospects of French reinforcements reaching Ticonderoga and Crown Point daily mounted, the delay continued. While Abercromby was not openly mentioned it is clear that Bradstreet already was disenchanted with what appeared to be an overly cautious approach on the part of his commander. Bradstreet was quite correct in contending that British delays would allow the reinforcement of the French positions in the Lake George-Champlain valley area. But his call for a "push forward as fast as possible"[12] was rather unrealistic in view of the many difficulties encountered by Abercromby; difficulties of which Bradstreet must have been fully aware. Transportation vehicles were lacking, bateaumen were scarce, provincial troops were slow in arriving, and then were inadequately equipped. And Abercromby himself, because of sickness, was forced to remain at Albany until the end of the first week in June.[13] The Lieutenant-Colonel's willingness to overlook such serious problems while over-emphasizing Abercromby's plodding nature was one of many signs of the incompatibility developing between the impetuous Bradstreet and the careful Abercromby. The General, for his part, was reasonably lavish in praise of his diligent subordinate, but Bradstreet's relationship with him was not the harmonious one hinted at in letters home to Pitt. Bradstreet felt that not enough attention was being paid to his suggestions and those being acted upon were only accepted after lengthy debate and consideration. Hence, any contribution he might make at this time would come about in spite of Abercromby's reservations and reluctance, rather than because of his helpful cooperation.

Preparations continued throughout the month of June, and in early July all was ready for the attempt on Ticonderoga. On July 5, 1758, the British encampment at Lake George was the scene of great activity as "the Tents were struck; and all the Troops, amounting to 6367 Regulars, Officers & Bateau-Men embarked in about 900 Batteaux & 135 Whale Boats." The entire force, which consisted of roughly 16,000 men when the provincial troops were included, moved up Lake George in four columns, led by Robert Rogers' rangers, Thomas Gage's light

---

12. Bradstreet to Gould, May 31, 1758, T.P.C., 128/37.
13. Shy, "James Abercromby And The Campaign Of 1758," 60 and 76.

infantry, and John Bradstreet's bateau-men.[14] The designated landing place, at the foot of Lake George on the western shore, was reached in the early morning of July 6. Bradstreet was with an advance party which landed so quickly in the early morning hours that the French fled leaving 100 tents and a good deal of baggage. Apparently, "no sooner did they observe us than they struck their tents, but had not time to carry them off before Col. Bradstreet landed."[15] The main force then disembarked, formed into four columns, and began the march against the "advanced-Guard" positions of the French.

Up to this point all had gone smoothly and not a causalty had been suffered. Then the entire operation began to break down. The virtually impassable woods played havoc with the various columns, confusing both guides and soldiers. Worse yet the "right Center Column" led by Lord Howe, stumbled into a French force and in the ensuing skirmish Howe was killed. Along with other casualties suffered in the sporadic fighting of this day, this loss, a very serious one in view of Howe's abilities and the respect he commanded among both regulars and provincials, caused considerable confusion in the ranks. After an uneasy night spent "under Arms," Abercromby ordered the dispersed and disorganized army back to the landing place to regroup. Fatigue, the terrain, and problems of supply had all taken their toll, making such a reorganization the only practicable course.[16]

The significance of the loss of his second-in-command was now driven home to Abercromby. In plotting his army's next move he could no longer turn to Lord Howe for advice. To whom could he turn? Thomas Gage was now second to Abercromby but his previous wilderness experience was limited to service in Braddock's disaster, and no evidence can be found of advice, wise or otherwise, emerging from this quarter. It was Bradstreet who, according to John Shy, "took up the slack left by the dealth of Howe."[17] Perhaps it would be a little more accurate to suggest that at this point John Bradstreet conceived an alternative battle plan which, after persistent pleading, he was able to sell to his commander.

The original battle plan called for the British forces to follow a rather circuitous route, keeping to the west and then north of the winding river which eventually flowed into Lake Champlain, at which point Ticonderoga was situated. The more direct route was to cross to the east bank of the river and follow a direct portage road to a sawmill and bridge located about one and a half miles from Ticonderoga. At this

---

14. Abercromby to Pitt, July 12, 1758, C.O. 5/50-1, 204, and in Kimball, *Pitt Correspondence*, 1, 297; Gipson, *The British Empire Before the American Revolution*, 7, 218.

15. *Gentleman's Magazine*, 28 (1758), 445.

16. Abercromby to Pitt, July 12, 1758, in Kimball, *Pitt Correspondence*, 1, 298; Shy, "James Abercromby And The Campaign Of 1758," 115.

17. Shy's "James Abercromby And The Campaign Of 1758," 115 and 160, and his *Toward Lexington: The Role of the British Army in the Coming of the American Revolution* (Princeton, N.J., 1965), 130, mention the strange failure of Gage to emerge at this crucial moment as a strong second-in-command and key advisor of Abercromby.

point the river could be crossed again, allowing the British forces to assemble on its northern, Ticonderoga, side. Initially it had been assumed that the longer route was necessary because the more direct path would be strongly defended by the French. It now appeared that this was not the case. As a result, according to Joshua Loring, who should have been if anything a hostile witness to Bradstreet because of the way he had been displaced by him, Bradstreet "begged" Abercromby to give him four or five thousand men. With this force he proposed to move up the portage road, and to take possession of the sawmill and rebuild the bridge if necessary.[18]

Abercromby's report to Pitt concerning the use of this direct approach to Ticonderoga gave no indication that the suggestion was Bradstreet's or that he had been hesitant about accepting it. He merely wrote that at eight-o'clock on the morning of July 7 he returned to the landing place. At eleven o'clock the same morning he had "sent off Lieut. Colo. Bradstreet with the 44th. Regiment, 6 companies of the 1st. Battalion of Royal Americans, the Batteau Men and a Body of Rangers, & Provincials to take Possession of the Saw Mill, within two Miles of Ticonderoga, which he soon effected."[19] Loring's more detailed description of the situation makes clear that the suggestion for this new approach came from Bradstreet and adds some interesting information about Abercromby's actual reluctance to accept the plan. It was only "after Soliciting the thing for a Long time, & being Backt by Severall of the Officers in the Army" that Bradstreet "was at last permitted to go."[20]

After winning this battle at headquarters Bradstreet successfully executed his plan. The destroyed mill and bridge were soon in British hands as the French withdrew in the face of his advancing force. Another bridge was constructed promptly and in the early afternoon Bradstreet relayed word of his success to Abercromby. In addition, Bradstreet requested his commander's permission to continue the advance in order to attack Ticonderoga itself. Without taking "the least Notice" of Bradstreet's request for permission to move to the attack, Abercromby instead immediately advanced with the rest of the troops to the sawmill position. John Shy has pointed out that if, as Loring suggested, Bradstreet did seek approval to push on, it was "properly refused" by Abercromby. Within Ticonderoga the estimated 6,000 French regulars and Canadians, who were about to be strengthened by 3,000 further troops, were more than a match for the several thousand colonials and less than two regular regiments under Bradstreet's command. On the other hand, at the time of Bradstreet's call for a strike at Ticonderoga, the French were feverishly labouring to complete their encircling entrenchments while Lévis and the reinforcements were

---

18. Joshua Loring to Pitt, August 19, 1758, Chatham MSS, Bundle 96, 68, P.A.C.; Shy, "James Abercromby And The Campaign Of 1758," 116.
19. Abercromby to Pitt, July 12, 1758, in Kimball, *Pitt Correspondence*, 1, 299.
20. Loring to Pitt, August 19, 1758, Chatham MSS, Bundle 96, 68.

several hours away.²¹ It was actually the best possible moment to move against the fort.

Precious time was needed by the French and Abercromby provided it with his decision to reunite his forces and camp for the night within two miles of the French fort. The attempt on Ticonderoga had veered dangerously close to total collapse only to be righted and temporarily rescued in large part by the perceptive suggestion and swift action of John Bradstreet. There was good reason for Bradstreet's being relatively pleased with the role he had played up to that point. Nevertheless, if there had been a golden moment when Ticonderoga could have been taken, it was when Bradstreet had urged the attack. By the evening of July 7, this moment had passed.

Surprisingly, Abercromby threw caution to the wind the next day and decided to hurl his forces against Ticonderoga immediately. Early in the morning of July 8 a report from his chief engineer convinced him of the weakness of the French entrenchments. The "practicability of Carrying those Works, if attacked before they were finished" led Abercromby to the decision "to storm them that very Day."²² A letter in *Gentleman's Magazine* vividly described the bloody battle as the French "who were entirely under cover of a breastwork, six feet thick, kept incessant and heavy fire upon us from their swivels and small arms, mowing down our brave officers and men by hundreds."²³ Six successive times the British forces surged to the attack only to be beaten back. The solid strength of the now completed entrenchments had been greatly underestimated. Behind them the French successfully withstood the repeated attacks, aided no doubt by the costly British failure to bring forward the supporting artillery which remained unused in the rear. At one point, using boats loaded with troops, Bradstreet attempted to strike at the fortress from the river side, but this imaginative effort was also beaten back.²⁴

In the early evening, after suffering "the loss of 1610 Regulars 334 Provincials killed and wounded," Abercromby called a halt to the assault and ordered a withdrawal, first to the sawmill position and by the morning of July 9 to the landing place.²⁵ In this retreat from Ticonderoga, just as in the advance on the French fort, Bradstreet emerged for a moment of heroic distinction. Panic and confusion, fanned by reports that the French had captured the bateaux at the landing place, threatened to turn an orderly withdrawal and embarkation into a disorganized and disastrous rush for the boats. Bradstreet

---

21. Ibid.; Abercromby to Pitt, July 12, 1758, in Kimball, *Pitt Correspondence*, 1, 299; Shy, "James Abercromby And The Campaign Of 1758," 116-19; Stanley, *New France: The Last Phase*, 178-79.
22. Abercromby to Pitt, July 12, 1758, in Kimball, *Pitt Correspondence*, 1, 299.
23. *Gentleman's Magazine*, 28 (1758), 446.
24. Detailed descriptions of the attack are contained in Butler, *The Annals of the King's Royal Rifle Corps*, 1, 58-60; Shy, "James Abercromby And The Campaign Of 1758," 121-31; Gipson, *The British Empire Before the American Revolution*, 7, 218-32.
25. Abercromby to Pitt, July 12, 1758, in Kimball, *Pitt Correspondence*, 1, 300-301.

quickly took command at the landing place and established a strong guard over the boats to prevent anyone from attempting a premature entry and departure.[26] On the morning of July 9 after the orderly embarkation preserved by Bradstreet's calm intervention had been carried out, the British forces moved down Lake George, arriving by evening of the same day at the old site of Fort William Henry. It was obvious that Abercromby's campaign against Ticonderoga had failed dismally.

Almost immediately complaints were heard concerning the way in which the campaign had been conducted. It soon became clear that Abercromby, perhaps rightly so, was going to receive most of the blame.[27] The report of the action offered to the British public in the pages of *Gentleman's Magazine* openly recited the commander's sins. It spoke of a "pannic at the head quarters," the ignorance concerning the enemy breastworks, the folly of the unsupported frontal assault, and the hasty abandonment of what still could have been a successful siege as an army of "near 14,000 men" retreated "from an enemy not above 3,000."[28] As might be expected, Bradstreet wasted no time in joining this chorus of condemnation. "I must now tell you," he wrote Gould, "that after my having transported & convey'd an Army of 16,000 Men full of helths & Spirits with every requisit for War and driving 1100 Men from an advance Guard and one of 1200 from another and the whole Army assembl'd within a mile of the Enemy the want of knowlidge in the C_____f hath sacrifis'd about 2000 Men kill'd & wounded and shamefully deserted with the remainder that night."[29]

While Bradstreet was obviously disappointed at the outcome of the campaign and his commander's blunders, the same letter gave a clear indication that his old ability to capitalize upon even the severest of setbacks still remained. He now had been assigned, he reported to Gould, "a separate Command with 3500 Men and one of the most difficult and hazardous undertakings that can well be in this part of the world." But he was at pains to make clear that this secret assignment and the positions of importance he had enjoyed in the Ticonderoga campaign should not mislead his British friends. "And pray dont immagine it [the various positions of authority] proceeds from my being in favor at head Quarters for it is really the contrary." The attempt on Fort Frontenac so long advocated by Bradstreet was the "hazardous undertaking" upon which he was now launched, but gaining approval for his latest plan had been no easy matter.

After the army's return down Lake George on July 9, Bradstreet reported, he sought permission "to prosecute the plan before con-

---

26. Bradstreet's action is mentioned in Gipson, *The British Empire Before the American Revolution*, 7, 231; Butler, *The Annals of the King's Royal Rifle Corps*, 1, 60; and Shy, "James Abercromby And The Campaign Of 1758," 132-33.

27. For a critical evaluation of Abercromby's performance, see Gipson, *The British Empire Before the American Revolution*, 7, 233. A more balanced assessment is offered by Shy, "James Abercromby And The Campaign Of 1758," 166-67.

28. *Gentleman's Magazine*, 28 (1758), 446.

29. Bradstreet to Gould, July 17, 1758, T.P.C., 128/38.

cluded at Albany," namely, the reduction of Fort Frontenac. "From the ruling gentleman in power" however, "he was again oppos'd." Fearful lest the "influence of his opponents" might lead to his plan's rejection, he pushed for a Council-of-War and presented his arguments concerning the probable success of such an operation. "Many after the warmest opposition, reluctantly approv'd, and finally by a majority it was carried in the affirmative, and a report drawn up in favour of the scheme."[30] By contrast, in reporting to Pitt concerning his decision to allow Bradstreet to proceed against Fort Frontenac, Abercromby gave no indication that it had been the subject of heated debate. In a very matter-of-fact way he outlined his apprehensions about the possibility of a French offensive down the Mohawk against Albany. To protect against such a move he had dispatched substantial reinforcements to the commander of that region, Brigadier-General John Stanwix. Furthermore, in conjunction with this defensive precaution he had allowed Bradstreet to lead 3,600 men against Fort Frontenac.[31]

At a formal Council-of-War on July 13, the day after this letter was written, these decisions were given the final stamp of approval. The sparse summary of this meeting gives only a slight indication that Bradstreet's proposal was the subject of lengthy debate and determined opposition. While the reinforcement of Stanwix was "unanimously agreed in the Affirmative" with no qualification, the Frontenac assault was "agreed in the Affirmative, provided there is no apparent reason to the Contrary, when the troops assemble at the Great Carrying Place."[32] This lack of substantial evidence verifying Bradstreet's charge of headquarters hostility and persistent opposition is disconcerting. Yet in view of Bradstreet's open admission to Gould that he was not loved by all at headquarters, it seems likely that his proposals met some opposition. Possibly the bickering was simply not deemed worthy of inclusion in minutes and letters. The interesting point about this probable attempt to block his suggestion, by direct action or indirect qualifications, was that this opposition was aimed at one of the few survivors of Ticonderoga who had emerged with distinction. So deep was the dislike aroused by Bradstreet that even after his emergence from a virtually flawless performance there was an apparent willingness to ignore his contributions and deny the merits of his proposals. It was not to be the last occasion when a Bradstreet triumph was met with indifferent neglect at best or with hostile obstructionism at worst.

At this particular time, however, Abercromby was far from indifferent to Bradstreet and his venture.[33] The Commander-in-Chief made quite clear to Pitt his approval of, and thus his responsibility for, the

---

30. [Bradstreet], *An Impartial Account*, 3.
31. Abercromby to Pitt, July 12, 1758, in Kimball, *Pitt Correspondence*, 1, 301.
32. "At A Council of War, Held In Camp On The Banks Of Lake George On Thursday The 13th of July, 1758," in Preston and Lamontagne, *Royal Fort Frontenac*, 256.
33. See his expression of "Trust & Confidence in Your Zeal and Activity" in Abercromby to Bradstreet, July 13, 1758, ibid., 256-58.

risky Frontenac attempt. He watched with interest and encouragement its progress, and openly expressed his reliance upon the resourceful Bradstreet once the deed had been done. There is no evidence that the headquarters hostility of which Bradstreet complained emanated from his commander. Yet in his *Impartial Account*, published after Frontenac's fall, Bradstreet turned to evidence such as Abercromby's instructions in an attempt to establish his commander's half-hearted and uncooperative attitude. "By the instructions ... received from the general," Bradstreet claimed, "he was left the sole judge of the probability of succeeding, and whether, if on his arrival at the great carrying place, he should, from the intelligence he might there receive from the Indians, judge it prudent to proceed." In this way, the final decision, to proceed or not to proceed across Lake Ontario, was up to Bradstreet, and "the entire burthen of the event of the expedition was thrown upon" his shoulders.[34] Admittedly, the instructions did leave a final decision to be made. With his troops Bradstreet was "to advance to Lake Ontario, to watch the Motions of the Enemy and by giving them Battle, if found adviseable, prevent their attempted Inroad on the Mohawk River; or otherwise if found practicable to attempt the reduction of Fort Frontenac, and destroy the Shipping at Cadaraqui."[35] But the major concern of Abercromby and the July 13 Council-of-War centred on a possible French thrust down the Mohawk. Defending against this threat was quite naturally regarded as the first priority of any troops in the Mohawk-Lake Ontario area, including those under Bradstreet. In addition, if such a thrust did materialize it would automatically force an alteration or abandonment of the Frontenac plan. Thus, the instructions were merely a realistic analysis of the situation in the Lake Ontario sector. They were designed to provide the flexibility necessary for the immediate defence of the area and the possible attack on Frontenac. For these reasons, Bradstreet's suspicions that they were designed to shift to his shoulders responsibility for any defeat appear unfounded.

The execution of Abercromby's instructions commenced the day after they were drafted. On July 14 the troops, one regiment per day, began to move out of the Fort William Henry camp. Within ten days they all had arrived at Schenectady and were "Ready to go up the Mohawk River to morrow morning by day Light." In moving his provisions onward from Schenectady Bradstreet encountered a shortage of "carriages" but other than that things went rather well. The route to be followed was well known to him since it was the same trek he had made while provisioning Oswego in 1755 and 1756. From Schenectady the forces proceeded for approximately sixty unobstructed miles up the Mohawk River. By July 30 this distance had

---

34. [Bradstreet], *An Impartial Account*, 50.
35. Abercromby to Bradstreet, July 13, 1758, in Preston and Lamontagne, *Royal Fort Frontenac*, 257.

been covered and the troops "arrived at the Little Carriing Place and unloaded the Battoas and Got the Prvisons in Waggons to the other side of the Caring Place which is about three Quarters of a mile over." On August 1 the journey was resumed and after covering forty-four further miles many of the troops arrived at the Great Carrying Place. By August 10 "the rear of the army arrived" and final preparations could be made for the proposed Frontenac attack.[36]

Apparently confident that no French offensive was in the offing, Stanwix issued orders on August 11 detaching approximately three thousand men from his command and assigning them to Bradstreet's expedition. It was to be largely a colonial force composed of the Massachusetts battalions of Colonels Williams and Doty, Colonel De-Lancey's New York regiment, Colonel Johnson's New Jersey battalion, and Colonel Babcock's Rhode Island battalion. In addition there were to be 27 regular artillerymen, 154 regular troops, 60 rangers, 300 bateau-men, and approximately 40 Indians, which gave a total strength of roughly 3,100.[37] Numerically it appeared a quite substantial force, but despite the size it was a disappointment to Bradstreet in several major respects.

The presence of only forty Indians made it clear that the promised Indian support had failed to materialize. On this occasion, however, Sir William Johnson cannot be blamed. He appears to have done everything possible to enlist Iroquois support, but their faith in British power had been severely shaken by the recent French victories. The Indians were wavering to such an extent that Vaudreuil tried to take advantage of what he termed the "favorable disposition of the Five Nations" by dispatching de Longueuil to confer with them. As a result, at the very time that Johnson, on behalf of Bradstreet's expedition, was appealing to the Iroquois for help, they were conducting negotiations with a French representative.[38] Not surprisingly, Johnson's personal persuasion and the efforts of his emissaries brought only about 150 Indians to the Great Carrying Place, of whom 42 were willing to serve. To Bradstreet it was "a glaring proof" of the Six Nations' "general disaffection to our interest."[39]

---

36. [Bradstreet], *An Impartial Account*, 4 and 6; "A Journal of An Expedition Against Canaday by Moses Dorr Ensin of Capt. Parkers Company," *New York History*, 16 (1935), 455; Bradstreet to Abercromby, July 24, 1758, Abercromby Papers, AB 472, H.L.

37. [Bradstreet], *An Impartial Account*, 6-7. For a detailed breakdown, see "Return of His Majesty's Troops detached from the Oneida Station, 15th August 1758 under the Command of Lieut. Colo. John Bradstreet," C.O. 5/40-2, 370. The return listed 70 Indians but the final count was closer to 40.

38. Vaudreuil to Massiac, September 2, 1758, in Edmund B. O'Callaghan, ed., *Documents Relative to the Colonial History of the State of New York*, 10 (Albany, 1858), 822, cited hereafter as *N.Y.C.D.*; Note of August 10-12, 1758, in Hamilton, *Bougainville's Journal*, 262-63, mentions the return of de Longueuil from his mission.

39. An Indian Council, July 22, 1758, in Sullivan *et al.*, *Johnson Papers*, 9, 953; Instructions for Thomas Butler, August 6, 1758, ibid., 966-67; [Bradstreet], *An Impartial Account*, 10.

Among the provincials there was also an inclination to avoid, if at all possible, the hazardous mission. This attitude was rather predictable since the provincials had just come through the harrowing experience of Ticonderoga and, without any real respite, had been ordered up the Mohawk. Already at Schenectady fatigue and sickness were serious problems. Bradstreet reported the desertion of 119 Jersey troops in one evening and was appalled at the "Great Disertion and Sickness." But his own dedication never flagged as he dramatically promised Abercromby that "Shou'd the Number be reduced so low that we cannot make out above a thousand Men fit to proceed to Lake Ontario with them I will do my best." Bradstreet could take consolation that the largest colonial contingent, the approximately one-thousand-man New York regiment, "behav'd well," and that large numbers of deserters were recovered, 111 on August 11 alone. Nevertheless, he was the first to admit that even as the expedition prepared to move out the mood was not good. "Sickness, Discontent, Disertion, Reluctance and want of Spirit . . . hath prevail'd throughout the whole of the Provincial Troops ordered to serve this way, except the Yorkers."[40]

The reluctance to serve, albeit for different reasons, infected not only the rank and file but the senior officers as well. A serious threat to the expedition's continuation emerged when every one of the provincial colonels refused to serve under Bradstreet. Colonels DeLancey, Babcock, Williams, Doty, and Johnson argued that according to Pitt's 1757 regulation[41] they, although only colonial officers, outranked the regularly commissioned Lieutenant-Colonel Bradstreet, and therefore could not serve under him. Actually, when Bradstreet first received rank as lieutenant-colonel he already was aware of this potential problem. Other regularly commissioned lieutenant-colonels had been given special rank over the provincial colonels so that they would not have to serve under colonials. Bradstreet had pointed this out to Gould, but no such arrangement was made for him. In securing Bradstreet's lieutenant-colonelship, Sir Richard Lyttleton also was aware of the difficulty. He assumed, however, that the colonel's commission, bestowed on Bradstreet by Governor William Shirley in the 1745 Louisbourg campaign, would be respected by the provincials and would provide his friend with the necessary seniority. Now the problem came to a head as, Bradstreet reported to Abercromby, the provincial colonels refused to "admit of my provincial Commision as Colo. in 1745."[42] Fortunately for Bradstreet the strong intervention of General

---

40. "George Metcalfe's Diary of Expedition against Canada, Schenectady and various places, 26 May—25 August 1758," ref. # 12564, N.Y.S.L.; Bradstreet to Abercromby, August 6, 1758, W.O. 34/57, 3, microfilm, Reel 154 (1), U.M.G.L.; "A Journal . . . By Moses Dorr," 456; Bradstreet to Abercromby, August 15, 1758, W.O. 34/57, 4, microfilm, Reel 154 (1).

41. For an explanation of this attempt to give provincial officers some ranking privileges, see Pargellis, *Lord Loudoun*, 92-93.

42. Bradstreet to Gould, March 13, 1758, T.P.C., 128/36; Lyttleton to Gould, Jan 1, 1758, T. P.C., 128/34; Bradstreet to Abercromby, August 15, 1758, W.O. 34/57, 4, microfilm, Reel 154 (1).

Stanwix and the limited cooperation of the balky colonels rescued the situation. Stanwix ordered the designated provincial units to proceed on the expedition without their colonels. At first there were fears that the colonials would refuse this command but "the provincial Colonels settled that affair so amongst their men that I [Stanwix] had no trouble about it."[43]

After the adjustments forced by these various difficulties had been made, the men, on August 13, were drawn up and reviewed "By the General & Colo. Bradstreet and ordered to Get redy to march to morrow morning by Six o clock and then after Prayers Dismissed."[44] The next day the first units began the journey which was to take them down Wood Creek to Lake Oneida, across the lake into the Oneida River, thence to the Onondaga (sometimes called the Oswego) which emptied into Lake Ontario. On the map the region appears easily traversed; in reality there were several major barriers. The first of these was Wood Creek itself which, at least in the area of Fort Bull and Fort Newport, was too shallow for the heavily laden bateaux. As a result, for the better part of the first three days the force was "imployed in Loading and floating the Battoas out of a Small Brook into Wood Creek."[45] The bateaux were floated and given a start down the Creek by damming it at intervals "and whenever a sufficient quantity of water is gather'd the sluic is open'd, which conveys them to the next dam."[46] By August 16 the last of the force was launched down the Creek. Oneida Lake was reached on August 17 and four days later the troops had arrived at Oswego and Lake Ontario. There was one setback in that a scouting party carrying detailed information about the strength of the entire expedition encountered French Indians near Oswego. Two of the party were scalped and valuable information fell into French hands to be quickly relayed to DeNoyan, the commander of Frontenac. The French commandant in turn passed the word on to Vaudreuil who was informed of the dangerous situation on August 26. The Quebec Governor dispatched a relief force of 1,500 men the next day.[47] For Bradstreet it was now a race against time.

On August 22 the army of roughly 3,100 men set out upon Lake Ontario in 123 bateaux and 95 whaleboats. Of necessity they had to keep close to shore so that in the event of a high wind or rough water they quickly could find refuge. On August 25 Fort Frontenac was sighted.[48] In 1755 the defences of the fort had been in such a state of

---

43. Stanwix to Abercromby, August 20, 1758, as quoted in Gipson, *The British Empire Before the American Revolution*, 7, 240-41.
44. "A Journal ... By Moses Dorr," 457.
45. Benjamin Bass, "Account of the Capture of Fort Frontenac By the Detachment Under the Command of Col. Bradstreet," *New York History*, 16 (1935), 449.
46. [Bradstreet], *An Impartial Account*, 11.
47. Vaudreuil to Massiac, September 2, 1758, in O'Callaghan, *N.Y.C.D.*, 10, 823; ibid., 826-27, also contains the information captured by the French: "Colonel Bradstreet's Instructions to the Commander of a Scouting Party," and "General Orders"; [Bradstreet], *An Impartial Account*, 20.
48. There is certainly no paucity of material describing the attack on Frontenac, and

deterioration that "when one of the guns ... is discharged the whole fort shakes,"[49] and this state of affairs had not improved to any great extent in the intervening three years. With a defending garrison of only about 110 men, the French obviously were not expecting an attack and the fort was in no position to withstand a siege.[50] Even the naval power, which the French had employed to control Lake Ontario, was virtually useless at this time. Only two of the barks were armed while four or five others were not even rigged.[51] For the moment everything was in Bradstreet's favour and, in typical fashion, he acted quickly.

By the evening of August 25 Bradstreet had landed his troops, and the following day the artillery was brought ashore. That morning, August 26, he reconnoitred the grounds surrounding the fort and decided that orthodox siege tactics had to be abandoned. Because of the lack of time, the absence of sufficient entrenchment tools, and "only seventy rounds of ammunition for each piece of cannon," it was clear to him that "formal approaches at the distance of several hundred yards, agreeable to the custom and practice of modern attacks, would never have given room to hope for success." Instead he proposed to open two positions as close to the fort as possible. One was an "old breastwork" about 250 yards south of the fort and the other, to the west, was "a spot very advantageously situated, at about one hundred and fifty yards distant" from Frontenac's walls. From these positions the fort was an easy target for the artillery. Taking no chances Bradstreet personally led the advancing troops as first one group occupied the enemy entrenchment in the early evening, and then, under cover of night, another force under Bradstreet's supervision moved into the more westerly position.[52] Once the guns were operable, sporadic shelling commenced. The French returned a largely ineffective fire while British shells proved more damaging, one landing near the magazine and setting off "a quantity of gun-powder." At daylight the fort came under heavier artillery fire and DeNoyan, the commandant, sensed the hopelessness of his position. After a Council-of-War agreed with his assessment of the situation, capitulation was decided upon. Firing ceased and by eight in the morning discussions commenced. Bradstreet informed DeNoyan that if he surrendered immediately the garrison could keep their money and clothing and, after their removal to Albany as prisoners of war, they would be exchanged as soon as possible. The

---

the various letters and journals agree almost completely with the descriptions provided by Bradstreet himself. See for example, Peter Jaquet to D. Normandie, August 30, 1758, Chatham MSS, Bundle 96, 77-78; Lieutenant MacAulay to Horatio Gates, August 30, 1758, C.O. 5/50-2, 371-72; Bradstreet to Abercromby, August 31, 1758, C.O. 5/50-2, 374-75; Butler to Johnson, August 28, 1758, in Sullivan et al., *Johnson Papers*, 2, 889-90; Henry I. Wendell to Johnson, September 4, 1758, in ibid. 894-95.

49. Adjutant Malartic to D'Argenson, October 6, 1755, in Preston and Lamontagne, *Royal Fort Frontenac*, 248.
50. Vaudreuil to Massiac, September 2, 1758, in O'Callaghan, *N.Y.C.D.*, 10, 822.
51. Hamilton, *Bougainville's Journal*, 275.
52. [Bradstreet], *An Impartial Account*, 31, 33, and 53.

impatient Bradstreet's demand for an answer within ten minutes brought DeNoyan's quick acceptance of the terms.[53]

Fort Frontenac had fallen on August 27 and on this same day the French relief force left Lachine. Bradstreet must have realized that by this time word of the English move against Frontenac had reached Quebec and relief was likely on the way. As a result, his stay at Frontenac could only be of short duration. His apprehension further increased when he learned from the captured garrison that an army of 4,000 Canadians and 1,000 Indians was supposedly on the march from Montreal, intending an invasion of the Mohawk region. The rumour was reinforced by evidence that "the garrison had been imployed in baking bread for this army, upwards of a fortnight."[54] This rumour of an invading force and the preparations to receive it probably stemmed from the abortive operation proposed at an earlier date by Vaudreuil. In mid-June he had planned to send a force of 1,600 under Lévis and Rigaud de Vaudreuil out of Frontenac on a mission of terror into the Mohawk and Hudson valleys. However, as Abercromby had committed himself to an attack on Ticonderoga, increasing pressures placed on Vaudreuil by Montcalm had forced the abandonment of "this Don Quixotry." The force instead had been rerouted to the aid of Ticonderoga.[55]

Very aware of the exposed position of his own force and his troops' weaknesses, Bradstreet was in no mood to do further battle with any French force, whether it was an invading army or a relief column, Consequently, the garrison's capitulation terms were altered, an elaborate ruse was attempted, and preparations to withdraw commenced. Recognizing the difficulty of carrying the captured garrison and women and children with him in a rapid retreat, Bradstreet secured DeNoyan's agreement to new terms which allowed all the French captives to return on their own to Montreal. Departing around noon, only hours after the fort had fallen, they were provided with a special pass from Bradstreet. This pass was needed, it was deviously explained to them, so that they would not be stopped by another British army of invasion which was supposedly on the move against Fort LaGalette on the upper St. Lawrence. By this ploy Bradstreet expected DeNoyan would relay word to the advancing French concerning this other British force. He hoped that the French would hesitate to advance beyond LaGalette for fear of putting themselves "between two fires."[56]

---

53. Vaudreuil to Massiac, September 2, 1758, in O'Callaghan, *N.Y.C.D.*, 10, 823; [Bradstreet], *An Impartial Account*, 36.
54. Ibid., 40.
55. Hamilton *Bougainville's Journal*, 211 and 221.
56. [Bradstreet], *An Impartial Account*, 41; "Conditions on which Mr. de Noyan... Commandant for the King at Fort Frontenac, proposes to surrender it to his Britannic Majesty," in O'Callaghan, *N.Y.C.D.*, 10, 826. In return, an equal number of English prisoners was eventually to be released into Abercromby's hands via the Richelieu River route.

As DeNoyan's party moved off, the burning of captured provisions and vessels commenced. A limited amount of plunder could be loaded on the bateaux but a great deal went up in smoke as the work of destruction continued in the afternoon and evening. A captured brig and schooner were pressed into use the next day and immediately dispatched for Oswego, heavily loaded with furs and other captured booty. The walls of the fort were demolished and the surrounding houses, the barracks, breastworks, fences, anything which would burn was set afire. In the afternoon of August 28 Bradstreet's troops steered their bateaux to the island opposite the fort. Here they encamped for the evening and gazed upon "the ruins of Fort Frontenac."[57]

At daybreak the next day the bateaux began the return journey to Oswego. When they arrived, late in the evening of August 30, the two loaded vessels which had been sent in advance were found "safely moor'd." They were unloaded, burned, and set adrift, as the troops quickly moved out of Oswego, continuing their journey southward. While at Oswego Bradstreet took the time to get off a report to Abercromby concerning the Frontenac triumph. It contained a very brief summary of the action and estimated the provisions and goods destroyed as being worth 800,000 livres, or £35,000 sterling.[58] The capitulation terms were sketched and Bradstreet speculated upon the beneficial impact his coup would have on Forbes's campaign against Fort Duquesne. In his opinion the destruction of Frontenac left the French troops "to the Southward and Western Garrisons" on the verge of starvation and without the vessels needed to transport themselves "home from Niagara." It was a well-written letter in terms of succinctly establishing the significance of Frontenac's fall. This was perhaps fortunate since it was this letter which quickly was passed on by Abercromby to Pitt for his perusal and then just as quickly published in the *London Gazette* and *Gentleman's Magazine*.

Retracing its steps the expedition continued the journey along the Oneida River, across the lake of the same name and into Wood Creek. Bull's Fort was reached on September 8 and it was here that the much-awaited division of the spoils took place. In an unusual burst of generosity, for which Bradstreet apologized to Gould, "all the goods" taken at Frontenac were divided "equally between Officers and Men." Furthermore, instead "of putting eight thousand pounds sterling in my Pocket, which I might have done with justice, I have not taken one Shilling but to encourage the people given it all up to them."[59] The same day Bradstreet wrote to Abercromby outlining what he hoped to accomplish in the following few days. Once the equal "distribution of

---

57. [Bradstreet], *An Impartial Account*, 42-44.

58. Bradstreet to Abercromby, August 31, 1758, C.O. 5/50-2, 374, and in W.O. 34/57, 5, microfilm, Reel 154 (1); [Bradstreet], *An Impartial Account*, 44-45. In his *Impartial Account* Bradstreet translates the 800,000 livres into £35,000 sterling.

59. Bradstreet to Gould, September 21, 1758, T.P.C., 128/40; [Bradstreet], *An Impartial Account*, 46. For a description of the division of the booty taken in this "dry-land privateering," see Leach, *Arms For Empire*, 437.

the effects we brought here from Fort Frontenack" had been completed, he intended to resume his journey in order to "deliver my Command up to Brigdr. Genl. Stanwix." This accomplished, he would proceed to Albany with the bateau-men "where I shou'd be Glad to have your Excellency's Commands for my further Conduct."[60] With such careful understatement he underlined the successful completion of his mission and his diligent expectation of further orders from his commander.

Abercromby had expectantly watched the progress of the Frontenac venture,[61] and his willingness to heap praise and congratulations upon Bradstreet peaked when the news burst concerning the Lake Ontario victory. On September 8 he received the first word of the fort's reduction, but "how true" it was, he would not "venture to assert." Within two days Bradstreet's August 31 letter had arrived, describing the triumph. At once a copy was dispatched to Pitt with the note that it contained "Confirmation of the Reduction of Cadaraqui . . . on which I sincerely congratulate you." A delighted Abercromby further explained, "I chuse to send it immediately, that no time may be lost, in communicating to you a Piece of Intelligence of that Importance."[62] His elation also was expressed to General Stanwix when he referred to "the Praises due to Lieut. Col. Bradstreet, on this Occasion, as they must be in the Mouths of everyone." Abercromby hoped "to see him meet with the Reward his Services merit." To Bradstreet personally went congratulations "most sincerely, on the Honour you have gained in the Reduction of Cadaraqui" and thanks "in my Name for the Extraordinary Zeal & Activity with which you have exerted yourself on that Occasion."[63]

The object of Abercromby's affection was strangely unresponsive to this lavish praise. Whether because the compliments did not reach Bradstreet, or because the Lieutenant-Colonel's old suspicions concerning his commander had re-emerged, or most likely a combination of both, Bradstreet only slowly and with increasing hostility moved to meet Abercromby. On September 9 he had reached the Great Carrying Place, from which he quickly departed, leaving even his bateau-men behind because of the onslaught of large numbers of Iroquois expecting to share in "the French Plunder." By September 13 Bradstreet was in Albany but apparently had not received any word from Abercromby, since he still desired "to have your Excellencys commands as to myself and the Battoemen." The next day, however, he mentioned to Charles Gould that he had been ordered to Lake George

---

60. Bradstreet to Abercromby, September 8, 1758, C.O. 5/50-2, 405, and in W.O. 34/57, 6, microfilm, Reel 154 (I).

61. Abercromby to Pitt, August 19, 1758, in Kimball, *Pitt Correspondence*, 1, 323-24, and in C.O. 5/50-2, 308-309; Abercromby to Bradstreet, September 7, 1758, C.O. 5/50-2, 404.

62. Abercromby to Pitt, September 8, 1758, in Kimball, *Pitt Correspondence*, 1, 345-46; Abercromby to Pitt, September 10, 1758, C.O. 5/50-2, 373.

63. Abercromby to Stanwix, September 12, 1758, in Preston and Lamontagne, *Royal Fort Frontenac*, 265; Abercromby to Bradstreet, September 16, 1758, C.O. 5/50-2, 410.

but was somewhat unenthusiastic about the duty. "I shall have great pleasure in assisting but own I have little hopes of a bould push."[64] The cautious Abercromby no doubt was the recipient of this barb. A further hint of Bradstreet's displeasure emerged in his sluggish adherence to Abercromby's commands. Although orders had reached him by this point, he remained for a further week at Albany. The Lieutenant-Colonel justified his long stop by arguing that he had to wait for all of his bateau-men. Moreover, once arrived, these men, as well as the "pilots" for the expedition, expected "some cash ... to fit themselves out." If Abercromby provided "a Warrant for seven Hundred pounds Sterling," Bradstreet thought everyone could be satisfied. A very anxious Abercromby replied the following day, enclosing the desired £700 warrant. "I must beg that you will leave" the bateau-men, he wrote Bradstreet, "and immediately upon Receipt hereof, set out and repair hither with all possible Dispatch." Bradstreet's presence was needed at Lake George so that Abercromby could scrutinize the articles of capitulation relating to Frontenac and carry out the exchange of prisoners included as one of the terms. To the General's relief Bradstreet finally reached his Lake George encampment on September 26 and "the Execution of that Capitulation" commenced shortly thereafter.[65]

Before leaving Albany Bradstreet had penned a revealing letter to Charles Gould indicating his suspicions and reservations about Abercromby. It was rather annoying to the Lieutenant-Colonel that the packet ship carrying mail to England was sent off so quickly that he and others had missed it. No one knew the reason for its surprise departure but, according to Bradstreet, "most people are of opinion it was intended to deprive me of the honour and advantage of the great benefit the publick has receiv'd through me, which if so, time will show and perhaps some people repent."[66] The accusation appears at first sight rather ridiculous and not directed specifically at Abercromby. But a wounded British officer, recovering at Albany, made the same accusation and singled out Abercromby as being clearly responsible. Charles Lee apologized to his sister for not writing earlier, "but I really had it not in my power, as our illustrious Chief thinks it necessary to conceal from the officers of his Army the time when each packet is to sail dreading very justly that some truth might be sent over not altogether to his honour, advantage and glory." Continuing in the same vein, he labelled Abercromby a "damn'd beastly poltroon." After commenting on Bradstreet's Frontenac victory, he asserted that "if our Booby in Chief had only acted with the spirit and prudence of an old Woman,

---

64. Bradstreet to Abercromby, September 9, 1758, Abercromby Papers, AB 631, and in C.O. 5/50-2, 407; ibid., September 13, 1758, C.O. 5/50-2, 408, and in Abercromby Papers, AB 653; Bradstreet to Gould, September 14, 1758, T.P.C., 128/39.

65. Bradstreet to Abercromby, September 21, 1758, Abercromby Papers, AB 685, and in W.O. 34/57, 10, microfilm, Reel 154 (1); Abercromby to Bradstreet, September 22, 1758, C.O. 5/50-2, 412; Abercromby to Pitt, November 25, 1758, in Kimball, *Pitt Correspondence*, 1, 403.

66. Bradstreet to Gould, September 21, 1758, T.P.C., 128/40.

their whole Country must inevitably have this year been reduc'd."[67] Bradstreet also was quite willing to indicate openly his total lack of confidence in Abercromby as commander. In view of the Louisbourg and Frontenac victories he felt that there was an excellent possibility that Canada would be conquered in the next campaign. All that was needed was "a common capacity & prefering the publick Service to all other Considerations" and, above all, the proper commanding officer. "I am natuerly impatient," he told Gould, "but I assure You every day will seem ten till I hear how things are settled at Home for carrying on the Publick Service for the future here; surely such a man will be found at last."[68]

In explaining the rift between Bradstreet and his commander, probably of even more immediate importance than Abercromby's inadequacies as a manager of men and campaigns was his failure, at least in Bradstreet's mind, to capitalize upon the most important gain offered by the Frontenac victory. Both to contemporary observers and modern historians a number of major contributions were linked with Cadaraqui's fall. With one brilliant stroke Bradstreet had severed the life line of the Great Lakes empire of the French. Before this severe rupture could be repaired completely, Fort Duquesne had fallen to Forbes. The demolition of Fort Frontenac, the capture of French provisions, and the destruction of their vessels had significantly weakened the morale of the Western Indian allies of the French and had also stopped the drift of the Six Nations towards the enemy. Thus, it has been argued, Bradstreet's victory had generously contributed to the final defeat of New France.[69] In his *Impartial Account* Bradstreet outlined these contributions and historians generally appear to have accepted almost all the points he made. There is, however, one critical omission when Bradstreet's comments are compared with the scholarly evaluations. Historians largely have overlooked his claim that the Frontenac triumph "laid open to us, the easy acquisition and peacable possession of those immense and valuable tracts, which border on the Ohio, the Lakes, and the surrounding country."[70] Yet it was this particular gain and the possibilities it presented that captured Bradstreet's imagination in the weeks after his triumph. Try as he might, however, he could get no support from Abercromby when he attempted to stake out the Great Lakes empire he had so long yearned to invade and to develop.

---

67. Charles Lee to Sidney Lee, September 16, 1758, "The Lee Papers," *Collections of the New-York Historical Society For The Year 1781*, 1 (New York, 1872), 6-8.

68. Bradstreet to Gould, September 21, 1758, T.P.C., 128/40.

69. For contemporary assessments, see Hamilton, *Bougainville's Journal*, 276; Vaudreuil to Massiac, September 2, 1758, in O'Callaghan, N.Y.C.D., 10, 823. For scholarly evaluations, see Arthur H. Buffinton, "The Colonial Wars and Their Results," in Alexander C. Flick, ed., *History of the State of New York*, 2 (New York, 1933), 238-39; Gipson, *The British Empire Before the American Revolution*, 7, 245-46; Stanley, *New France: The Last Phase*, 186.

70. [Bradstreet], *An Impartial Account*, 57-58.

When Bradstreet's letters written after the capture of Frontenac are added to his comments in the *Impartial Account*, it becomes clear that he was attempting to revive his grandiose 1755 scheme concerning the Great Lakes area. Because of the setback he had inflicted on the French it was possible, according to Bradstreet, that "they will be obliged to abandon their settlements, forts, and possessions on Lake Erie, the streights of lake Huron, and the lake Superior; their trade and interest with the Indians inhabiting those countries, must consequently decay, and if a proper use is made of these advantages, may be utterly taken from them." These were the same hopes he had expressed to Sir Thomas Robinson and Sir Richard Lyttleton, beginning in 1755 and continuing late into 1757, when he had presented his various plans for the conquest of the Great Lakes. In 1758 he argued that "the dominion of the lakes" could be "wrested from their [French] hands"[71] by a quick follow-up campaign. As far as Bradstreet was concerned, another expedition launched against the French position at Niagara was the urgently needed sequel to his Lake Ontario victory.

Immediately after his return from Frontenac Bradstreet attempted to persuade Abercromby of the need and justification for another Great Lakes campaign. Bradstreet pressed into service evidence, unearthed during his Frontenac enterprise, that the Iroquois had been plotting with the French. He alleged that the Iroquois had committed themselves to an attack along the Mohawk River with French forces commanded by de Longeuil. Since "the whole of the five Nations" apparently were aligned with the French, he urged "that nothing but immediately taking vigorous Measures, with them will avoid the Evil Consequence of having their Principal Force against us in a short time, tho' not openly."[72]

These were serious accusations and they provoked an outraged response from Sir William Johnson, who was still charged with keeping the Iroquois loyal to the British cause. Admitting that a French-Indian attack might have been brewing he, nevertheless, did not believe the Six Nations had committed themselves to such an undertaking. "From every Circumstance by which I am able to form a Judgement," he informed Abercromby when queried about Bradstreet's assertions, "I think your Information of the present Disposition of the 5 Nations in general to be groundless and without reason." Because of pressure from the persistent Bradstreet and his own fear of further setbacks in any area under his command, Abercromby continued his suggestive questioning of Johnson about the possible Iroquois defection. An exasperated Johnson detailed his reasons for believing in the loyalty of his Indian allies and repeated "that with regard to the Intelligence you received from Col. Bradstreet of the 5 Nations having taken up the

---

71. Ibid., 55.
72. Bradstreet to Abercromby, September 8, 1758, C.O. 5/50-2, 405-406, and in W.O. 34/57, 6, microfilm, Reel 154 (1).

Hatchet against us in favour of the French I do not give Credit to it."[73] In the meantime Abercromby had limited himself to reinforcing General Stanwix while gradually accepting Johnson's evaluation. In mid-October, although commenting that "he [Bradstreet] still persists" in his original opinion, Abercromby acknowledged that perhaps Bradstreet had erred.[74]

Persuading Abercromby of Six Nations disloyalty would have provided the plausible pretext Bradstreet needed in order to justify an expedition against the French at Niagara, proceeding through or around Iroquois territory. Such a suggestion, coming on the heels of Frontenac's fall, should have had a definite appeal to Abercromby and, at least initially, he appeared willing to accept Bradstreet's reports of Iroquois treachery. Gradually, however, he yielded to the advice and evaluation offered by Johnson and it was Sir William's view that prevailed. In this rejection of Bradstreet's advice there was a double irony. Once before, his Lake Ontario aspirations had been developed at great length and presented to his friends at home only to be ignored. In no small measure they had been rejected because of the criticisms offered by Johnson and his friends concerning Bradstreet and his ally William Shirley. Sir William Johnson's prestige and power now had re-emerged as a major obstacle blocking the fulfillment of Bradstreet's schemes. Moreover, in this instance, perhaps Bradstreet had been too successful for his own good and contributed to his own defeat. Crucial to his justification of a Niagara attack was continuing evidence of the fact that the Six Nations were leaning towards the French. But Bradstreet himself had halted and reversed this tendency. Observers such as James DeLancey and George Croghan were openly hopeful that Frontenac's fall would greatly influence the hesitant Indian allies of the British, creating "a good Effect on ye Minds of ye Six Nations."[75] Their hopes were realized. Ironically enough, Bradstreet's victory at Frontenac had brought the wavering Iroquois back to their British "loyalty." Bradstreet's attack had succeeded only too well.

It was not until mid-November that Bradstreet accepted his failure to convince Abercromby of the need for a sudden strike at Niagara. "I was not without hopes," he complained to Gould, "that in three weeks after my return from Cataraqui to have been able to have wrote You three lines only to say I was on my way to Niagara with a fresh command but I had not interest enough."[76] He had "not interest enough" but at least the effort had been made. Lawrence Gipson has assumed that if only Bradstreet had been aware of the weakened state of Niagara "he would

---

73. Johnson to Abercromby, September 17, 1758, in Sullivan et al., *Johnson Papers*, 10, 6; Abercromby to Johnson, October 6, 1758, in ibid., 27-28; Abercromby to Johnson, October 13, 1758, in ibid., 41-42; Johnson to Abercromby, November 10, 1758, in ibid., 55.

74. Abercromby to Johnson, October 13, 1758, in ibid., 42.

75. James DeLancey to Johnson, September 14, 1758, in ibid., 3, 1; George Croghan to Johnson, September 21, 1758, in ibid., 4.

76. Bradstreet to Gould, November 17, 1758, T.P.C., 128/41.

doubtless have moved upon it and thereby added immeasurably to the laurels he and his troops had already won."[77] While there is no evidence that Bradstreet realized that the Niagara garrison was manned by only forty men, in reality there is good evidence that he was straining to be unleashed against Niagara and made a real effort to secure Abercromby's approval for such a mission. His proposal was not accepted because of Abercromby's caution and the pro-British response of the Iroquois brought about by Bradstreet's own Frontenac success.

By means of the suggested Niagara attack, Bradstreet hoped that economic and territorial advantages would be gained, benefitting himself personally and the American colonies generally. This potentially profitable outgrowth of his Frontenac victory has been somewhat obscured because of the historical emphasis placed upon the more obvious and immediate military advantages Frontenac contributed to the British cause. Yet to Bradstreet this potential mastery of the Great Lakes empire was one of the greatest contributions of his victory. Moreover, colonial interest in his secret expedition and applause for his success possibly reveal that other colonials, perhaps for similar reasons, were very concerned with events in the Great Lakes theatre of war. In Albany there apparently was more joy over Frontenac's fall than at the news of Louisbourg's capture.[78] In Pennsylvania after Bradstreet's victory, Edward Shippen felt the worth of colonial troops was now established since "Provincials marched into the very heart of the enemy's country and took a fortress which is the very key to all the French settlements on the Lakes."[79] Colonial newspapers such as the Boston *News-Letter*, *Weekly Advertiser*, and *Evening Post* followed Bradstreet's departure on an unknown mission with considerable interest. All three published the first news of the outcome of this expedition, which came in the form of a letter from an officer who served with Bradstreet, dated Oswego, August 30, 1758.[80] The interesting feature of this first dispatch, and the point which all three papers developed, was that the officer returned across Lake Ontario on a heavily laden vessel which had been taken from Oswego when the French captured it two years earlier.[81] Oswego, the colonial fur trading base on the Great Lakes and potential stepping stone for any territorial push westward, had been revenged. Several weeks later the Governor of Massachusetts in opening the session of the General Court took advantage of the

---

77. Gipson, *The British Empire Before the American Revolution*, 7, 246.

78. Stanley, *New France: The Last Phase*, 186. Writing from Albany Charles Lee also mentioned: "We are at present a good deal elated with the success of Mr. Bradstreet." See Charles Lee to Sidney Lee, September 16, 1758, "The Lee Papers," *N.Y.H.S. Collections 1871*, 1, 7-8.

79. As quoted in Rogers, *Empire and Liberty*, 62. For similar sentiments, see Benjamin Franklin to the Printer of the London Chronicle, May 9, 1759, in Labaree et al., *Franklin Papers*, 8, 344.

80. This much-quoted letter is probably Jaquet to Normandie, August 30, 1758, Chatham MSS, Bundle 96, 77-78.

81. *Boston News-Letter*, September 21, 1758; *Boston Evening Post*, September 18, 1758; *Boston Weekly Advertiser*, September 18, 1758.

occasion to comment upon the recent victories. The reduction of Louisbourg, Governor Thomas Pownall stated, returned "the uninterrupted Possession of the North American Seas, and the Powers of Trade are again restored to his Majesty's Subjects." But Bradstreet's triumph was regarded as fulfilling a colonial aspiration as well as regaining English territory. "By the Destruction of Fort Frontenac, and the Enemy's whole Naval Force, their Stores and Magazines at Cadaraqui," Pownall felt, "the Dominion of the Lakes, which, sooner or later, must be the Dominion of America, is again restored to the British Empire."[82]

Similar dreams of colonial expansion were revealed in Pownall's "Dominion of the Lakes" and Bradstreet's "dominion of the lakes." As early as 1754 Pownall had suggested the need of English border colonies, specifically in the area south of Lake Erie. But he was destined to return to England by 1760 and his western dreams for the most part slumbered until their revival with the Vandalia scheme in 1769.[83] Bradstreet, on the other hand, first sensed the potential of the American interior in 1755 and was to continue his relentless pursuit of its proper development until his death in 1774. Only rarely, however, was he able to match his western dreams with such a golden opportunity for their achievement as that offered by his Frontenac victory. Here was one such opportunity, but he was unable to capitalize upon it. Nevertheless, it is clear that Bradstreet felt that one of the most important results of his Frontenac campaign was the trade and territorial empire to which it pointed. No doubt Thomas Pownall shared his faith in the potentialities of the "Dominion of the Lakes." No doubt there were other alert colonial expansionists who could also perceive this additional dimension of the Frontenac triumph.

Many barriers had emerged to frustrate Bradstreet in his immediate capitalization upon the gap he had opened in French defences on the Great Lakes. One of the most important stumbling blocks was Abercromby's cautious reluctance when imaginative but risky schemes were put forward by others. Thus it was some consolation for Bradstreet to learn in mid-November of Pitt's decision to replace Abercromby with General Jeffery Amherst.[84] In addition, although Bradstreet did not know it, his own efforts and those of his friends in publicizing his deeds in England were about to bring him some of the esteem he so deeply desired. His expedition was watched with anticipation by several mother-country observers. George Grenville was very upset about Howe's death and the Ticonderoga setback but expressed his "trust in

---

82. Ibid., October 9, 1758.

83. See John A. Schutz, *Thomas Pownall: British Defender of American Liberty* (Glendale, California, 1951), 48, 175, and 230.

84. Word of Abercromby's recall arrived in mid-November according to Cuneo, *Robert Rogers*, 90. Bradstreet mentioned Abercromby's preparations to go home and the expectation that Amherst would soon arrive in Bradstreet to Gould, November 17, 1758, T.P.C., 128/41.

God that Col. Bradstreet will Succeed." Pitt awaited word "of the very important Enterprize against Cadaraqui" which Bradstreet, "an Officer, who from his great Activity & Knowledge of the Country, is so well qualified for an Attempt of such Difficulty."[85] On October 30 the mail from New York arrived in London bearing Abercromby's note to Pitt concerning the Lake Ontario victory, as well as a copy of Bradstreet's August 31 letter to Abercromby describing the engagement. Promptly the next day a brief summary of the operation and Bradstreet's entire letter were published in the London Gazette.[86] Leaving nothing to chance Bradstreet also had sent two copies of this particular letter to Charles Gould, while at the same time commenting obscurely that "the whole account" of his expedition "will come better to the publick from other hands than mine"; a possible reference to his *Impartial Account*, destined for publication the next year and supposedly authored "By a Volunteer on the Expedition."[87]

On this occasion Bradstreet's own propaganda appeared at least a bit redundant. He had, if only temporarily, gained the attention of the great with his Frontenac coup. Pitt commented on the judgment, "Activity and Resolution" demonstrated by Bradstreet and instructed the new commander in America, Jeffery Amherst, to "acquaint Colo. Bradstreet with His Majesty's most particular Satisfaction in His Zeal and Bravery on this Occasion."[88] So gratified was the monarch that the "Successful Enterprise against Frontenac" was "enumerated among the great Events of the Year in the King's speech." An obviously pleased Gould reported this honour and added a description of the warm praise the triumph elicited from another important figure. "Lord Halifax, who moved the Address in the H. of Lords, insist'd on the great consequence of that Expedition, attended with so many hazards and difficulties, that nothing but the great Opinion he had long had of the Gentleman at the head of it, could have given him hopes of Surmounting them." Gould concluded, "In short, he was Copious upon the Subject, and did you justice."

Gould wasted no time in taking advantage of such openly acknowledged respect and praise. "I laid in a Claim for you at the War Office," he explained, which was aimed at securing Bradstreet's much sought colonel's rank. Lord Barrington immediately acted on the request, secured the King's consent and notified the secretary of state's office. All that remained was for Pitt to arrange the King's signature and the commission, backdated to August 20, 1758, would be sent off. In

---

85. George Grenville to Pitt, August 23, 1758, Chatham MSS, Bundle 1, 20; Pitt to Amherst, September 18, 1758, M.G. 18 L 4, Amherst Papers, Packet 22, 17-18, P.A.C., and in Kimball, *Pitt Correspondence*, 1, 354.

86. *London Gazette*, October 31, 1758. The entire letter also was published in *Gentleman's Magazine*, 28 (1758), 550.

87. Bradstreet to Gould, September 14, 1758, T.P.C., 128/39; [Bradstreet], *An Impartial Account*.

88. Pitt to Amherst, December 9, 1758, Amherst Papers, Packet 10, 7, and in Kimball, *Pitt Correspondence*, 1, 422.

gaining this promotion, which both Bradstreet and Gould must have realized was long overdue, Gould was careful to make "No mention . . . of your late Success" at Frontenac. His reasoning was that this left the way open for the bestowal of further honours more in keeping with the Frontenac achievement. The pursuit of these, he hoped, "is in better hands than mine, and will be properly rewarded." Undoubtedly, Gould expected that Lord Halifax, who "from his Speech cannot but be greatly your Friend,"[89] and Sir Richard Lyttleton, Bradstreet's consistent ally and patron, would arrange for these more proper rewards for the hero of Fort Frontenac.

There is no doubt that during the short time span encompassed by Abercromby's American command John Bradstreet had reached the pinnacle of his military career. The efficient performance of his bateaux and quartermaster duties, his Ticonderoga suggestions and actions, capped by his lightning strike at Frontenac, all combined to make him a military figure of some consequence. Both in North America and in England his deeds had won wide acclaim. Yet all this was accomplished while his commanding officer, like Shirley and Loudoun before him, gradually lost the confidence of the home authorities. Mounting criticisms and suspicions, when linked with his failure at Ticonderoga, had forced Abercromby's recall. Oswego had been merely the culmination of Shirley's demise, Louisbourg was one of many setbacks charged against Loudoun, and now Ticonderoga made its contribution to the undoing of Abercromby. The North American theatre of war was proving to be the graveyard of British commanding officers. Paradoxically, although Bradstreet was linked closely with each of these commanders and their setbacks, while their fortunes floundered his own career flourished.

Survival under such circumstances was no mean achievement. To do so with honour only added to the aura of success surrounding Bradstreet. To his credit, his persistent pleading and imaginative suggestions on more than one occasion had secured Abercromby's hesitant support. Bradstreet's greatest contributions had come to pass only after diligently extracting the clearly reluctant approval of his commanding officer. Interestingly enough, his clearly recognizable success did not lead to any noticeable willingness on the part of Bradstreet's officer colleagues to concede the brilliance or immediate acceptability of his further proposals. Rather, as the fate of his Niagara venture demonstrated, a hard look was taken at all his schemes despite his previous triumphs.

Rejection of any of his plans, of any of his merits, and of any of his cries for advancement, was something Bradstreet could not countenance or endure. Balancing his creditable insights and accomplishments was this pronounced discreditable side of the man which had clearly emerged in this period. So self-confident and self-righteous had

---

89. Gould to Bradstreet, December 8, 1758, T.P.C., 128/43.

he become that he could not accept those who would prick his ballooning self-esteem by underestimating his military brilliance. Provincial colonels who refused to serve under him, headquarters obstructionists who questioned his schemes, detractors who wondered about his bateaux and quartermaster contributions, all caused him to overemphasize his abilities while making him overly sensitive to even the smallest hint of criticism. He felt himself underrated and neglected, and bitterly lashed out at those suspected of hostility to his cause. Even when savouring his Frontenac triumph, this bitterness, this sense of persecution emerged. His dream of Great Lakes "acquisitions" had not materialized, he moaned, although "had any one measure been taken by ⎯⎯⎯⎯ ⎯⎯⎯⎯ to improve them properly, our advantages might have been multiplied almost beyond imagination; But as Col. Bradstreet was the projector of the enterprize, he was suffered to go in the name of the Lord, and to return again as well as he could; but not one step was taken, nor a single disposition ordered to secure his retreat in case of a repulse, or make a proper improvement of the conquest, if success had attended him."[90]

Despite Abercromby's weaknesses as a commander, despite other more real critics and enemies, success "had attended" John Bradstreet in 1758. Promotion to the rank of colonel had been achieved and all indications pointed to further honours in store for him. He was "not forgot" according to Charles Gould in January, 1759, and "other Rewards" were in the wind.[91] In reality, regardless of Gould's optimism, Bradstreet's future reward was to be indifferent neglect. Reasons for his resentful bitterness were soon to multiply. Ironically, Bradstreet had risen to his military apex during Britain's years of defeat. He had contributed to the turning of the tide and now as the victorious years began, his own decline commenced.

---

90. [Bradstreet], *An Impartial Account*, 58-59.
91. Gould to Bradstreet, January 12, 1759, T.P.C., 128/60.

Chapter VII

Prosperity but Little Progress

In late November of 1758 John Bradstreet resumed his duties at Albany as Deputy Quartermaster-General only to find his department, as he described it, in "great confusion, disorder & unnecessary expence to the Publick." True to form he made an immediate effort to impress upon his new commander, Jeffery Amherst, both the difficulties of his assignment and his conscientious dedication despite the problems encountered. "I think it my duty to assure you," he reported to Amherst, that "I am doing my utmost to repair the disorders and put it on such afoot as to have that branch of his Majesty's Service carry'd on with vigour, dispatch & oeconomy whenever you require it."[1] Enthusiastic expressions of his readiness to serve Amherst were to prove very necessary in the difficult years of 1759 to 1763. Bradstreet's quarrels with his fellow officers and with Albany officials, linked with periodic bouts of sickness, were to handicap considerably his service during the last campaigns in the North American theatre of war. Moreover, ministerial instability "at home" and the withdrawal of several of his English friends from their former influential positions were to deprive him of the leverage needed at this critical time. As he grew more and more disenchanted with his mundane quartermaster chores and the home government's failue to reward properly his Frontenac triumph, Bradstreet conceived scheme after scheme to rescue himself. But each was victimized by the turmoil and uncertainty of British politics as well as by his own pretentious preferences. Fortunately for him, he at least was to gain Amherst's solid support and continued to function as Deputy Quartermaster-General. In this office, with the help of able assistants such as George Coventry, Philip Schuyler, and John Glen he used the

---

1. Bradstreet to Amherst, November 28, 1758, W.O. 34/57, 14, microfilm, Reel 154 (1), U.M.G.L.

"lavish patronage" at his disposal to carve out his own little empire in colonial New York.[2]

In a sense during his 1758 service under Abercromby Bradstreet's quartermaster duties had never ceased. Although used in a different capacity at Ticonderoga and against Frontenac, officially he still was listed as Deputy Quartermaster-General and received the £182/10 per annum salary for that office. By December of 1758, however, exciting assignments like the Cadaraqui strike were behind him and all his attention was devoted to the standard quartermaster functions. During the early months of 1759 these involved the necessary preparations for the approaching spring campaign. The tasks he knew so well—bateaux building, procuring bateau-men, carpenters, "wagoners & ox team drivers," arranging horses, carriages and oxen—kept him busy at Albany.[3]

But after Frontenac such activities soon seemed insufficient to satisfy his restless and adventurous spirit. He yearned for a renewal of the attack on New France and further front line duties for himself. Early in February 1759, he eagerly awaited the arrival of instructions from home concerning the next stage of the war. Bradstreet hoped the orders would be "of the offensive kind" since a premature peace would destroy the opportunity to achieve "an end of the French in Canada," which could readily be done "if we act with common sense & spirit." His impatience was heightened, no doubt, by the desire to know how his 1758 exploits had been received in the mother country. March proved a month of reassurance as letters of congratulation arrived from Amherst and Gould, making clear "his Majestys most Gracious favour" with his Frontenac achievement as well as bringing word concerning his promotion to "Colonel in America." Encouraged by such honours, and undeterred by Amherst's decision to place "the whole business for what is to be done this way into my hands," Bradstreet was pressing for permission to execute another lightning strike against Fort St. Jean on the Richelieu River in the early spring. He confided to Gould, "I hope you will soon hear of my being gon on & succeeded in as lively an undertaking as I ever undertook and of great importance to the Nation."[4]

---

2. For brief comments on Bradstreet's "patronage empire" see Canedy, "An Entrepreneurial History Of The New York Frontier, 1739-1776," 319-20. Canedy's thesis does a good job of placing Bradstreet's departmental spending within the context of the New York colonial economy of that period. But Canedy's comments on Bradstreet personally and on some of his more controversial activities are rather limited and leave many questions unanswered.

3. "Colo. Bradstreet's Pay as Depy. Qr. Mr. Genl. in No. America—365 days from 25 Decr. 1757 to 24 Decr. 1758," T.P.C., 128/409, N.L.W.; Bradstreet to Amherst, December 23, 31, 1758, and February 26, 1759, W.O. 34/57, 15-17, 19, microfilm, Reel 154 (1).

4. Bradstreet to Gould, February 4, 1759, T.P.C., 128/44; Gould to Bradstreet, January 12, 1759, T.P.C., 128/60; Bradstreet to Gould, March 26, 1759, T.P.C., 128/45; Bradstreet to Amherst, March 4, 1759, W.O. 34/57, 20, microfilm, Reel 154 (1); Amherst to Bradstreet, March 19, 1759, W.O., 34/58, 17, microfilm, Reel 154 (1).

Although disappointed when Amherst failed to approve this attack,[5] Bradstreet had more than enough to keep him busy. Not only was he handling quartermaster preparations for Amherst's attempt on Ticonderoga but he also had to meet Brigadier-General John Prideaux's needs in the secondary attack on Niagara. In early June, as Amherst moved to his Fort Edward base and Prideaux moved towards Oswego, Bradstreet remained at Albany overseeing provisions for both armies as well as arranging the necessary bateaux and wagon transportation. With "everything coming on well" Bradstreet rejoined Amherst at his Fort Edward Camp on June 14. Within a few days of his arrival Bradstreet optimistically expressed readiness to "carry his [Amherst's] Army to the Enemy at Ticonderoga in five days if necessary with what is necessary to begin the Siege." In this he was to be thoroughly disappointed. There was a considerable delay before Amherst felt ready to launch the attack on Ticonderoga, preferring the completion of fortifications and roads prior to any advance. After a month spent handling such pressing problems as overloaded wagons and improperly moored bateaux,[6] Bradstreet must have been relieved when the journey up Lake George against Ticonderoga finally commenced.

Amherst's forces landed at the north end of Lake George on July 22 but a further four days were consumed in artillery placement and preparations for the advance. Then on July 26 the French troops remaining at Ticonderoga, estimated by Bradstreet to have been a rearguard detachment numbering only 350 men out of an original opposition of 2,500, "thought proper to set the Fort afire and go off." Thus on July 27 Ticonderoga fell to Amherst; it was a bloodless conquest. But it was a conquest which Bradstreet felt was long overdue. "I can only say 23 days we might have been here sooner, have stopt the people we found here in general and that I hope no more time will be lost to improve the panick or allow the Enemy time to get the better of our people at Quebeck, as their principal Force is there, and come and meet us and beat us back in the end."[7]

Still more time was to be lost, however. During the securing of Ticonderoga Bradstreet became increasingly exasperated at Amherst's failure to exert strong pressure in the Lake George-Lake Champlain area and thus offer badly needed support for Wolfe's attempt on Quebec. By August 5 an abandoned Crown Point also had been en-

---

5. Amherst to Stanwix, April 5, 1759, Chatham MSS, 5/213, P.A.C.; Bradstreet to Gould, June 19, 1759, T.P.C., 128/46; Huck-Sanders to Loudoun, June 19, 1759, as quoted in Gipson, *The British Empire Before the American Revolution*, 7, 360-61n.
6. "Major-General Jeffery Amherst's Journal from April 28 to June 19, 1759," in Arthur G. Doughty, ed., *Appendix To An Historical Journal Of The Campaigns In North America For The Years 1757, 1758, 1759, and 1760 By Captain John Knox*, 3 (Toronto, 1916), 32; Bradstreet to Gould, June 19, 1759, T.P.C., 128/46; Shy, *Toward Lexington*, 94; Sherrard, *Lord Chatham: Pitt and the Seven Years' War*, 334; Edmund B. O'Callaghan, ed., *Commissary Wilson's Orderly Book: Expedition of the British and Provincial Army, Under Maj. Gen. Jeffery Amherst, Against Ticonderoga and Crown Point, 1759* (Albany, 1857), 28, 69, 72.
7. Bradstreet to Gould, July 27, 1759, T.P.C., 128/48.

tered by Amherst's troops without any opposition, and word had arrived at Ticonderoga that Niagara had fallen. "The Lord has fought our Battles for us" exclaimed Bradstreet, while hoping that "he may not desert us from our advancing upon the Enemy so slowly." Yet he found it extremely difficult to agree with Amherst's overly cautious strategy. "Perhaps it is right" he mused, "but I own I am of a different opinion for we certainly are but of little use to Mr. Woolf at this distance."[8]

Adding to the frustration of the campaign's "painful slowness" were Bradstreet's gnawing fears that he would not be adequately rewarded for his Frontenac victory and that his future assignments would be restricted to quartermaster duties. In the spring he had been "happy to find the importance of taking Frontenac &ca is fully understood at Home" and without "the least doubt that I shall receive some mark of his Majestys Favor for the service I have done the Nation." By early August, however, he was growing uneasy since "I nether hear nor see the least of any other preferment for Cadaraqui." Furthermore, while emphasizing that his quartermaster diligence left both the Niagara and Lake George expeditions admirably supplied, he openly expressed his disenchantment with these duties and desire for a more active and prestigious role. "I fear I shall not be employed in any other way this Campaign [than as quartermaster] which is such a mortification as I cannot describe."[9]

The distraught Bradstreet must have been further annoyed when Amherst, once Ticonderoga and Crown Point were occupied, called a halt to what had been a very limited advance. Instead of pushing on, the British commander decided to reconstruct the Crown Point fortifications and build the vessels necessary to match French naval strength on Lake Champlain. It was not until October that his army resumed its advance, and then this movement was quickly reversed as the British forces soon returned to enter winter quarters.[10] Meanwhile in mid-August Bradstreet departed for Albany to support an advance on Quebec from the Lake Ontario front. Here he finally found the battles he craved, although they were not waged against the French.

During the summer of 1759 a more active campaign was being conducted on the Great Lakes front. Prideaux had lost his life during the siege of Niagara, which then was carried to its successful completion before the end of July by Sir William Johnson. Amherst decided that this victory should be followed up by turning the British forces in that area eastward against Quebec. Thomas Gage was appointed to succeed Prideaux with instruction to move down the St. Lawrence against Fort LaGalette, on the upper St. Lawrence not far distant from

---

8. Ibid., August 5, 1759, T.P.C., 128/49.
9. Shy, *Toward Lexington*, 94; Bradstreet to Gould, March 26, 1759, T.P.C., 128/45; ibid., August 5, 1759, T.P.C., 128/49.
10. Shy, *Toward Lexington*, 94-95; John C. Long, *Lord Jeffery Amherst: A Soldier Of The King* (New York, 1933), 118-19.

Lake Ontario, thus directly threatening Montreal. Strangely enough the easily delayed Amherst expected Gage to act with quick precision in carrying out these manoeuvres, which were complicated by the considerable distances involved. Amherst even assumed that LaGalette would be the winter quarters for Gage's forces, which were then to be "furnished from Oswego." Bradstreet immediately detected some obvious weaknesses in the plan. Such an "augmentation of the Troops to the Westward" required an increase in the number of bateaux working between Schenectady and Oswego as well as increased provisions for the troops during the campaign and in their winter quarters. Consequently, soon after these reservations were relayed to Amherst, who judged them "quite right," Bradstreet was ordered to Albany to supervise the movement of provisions to both Gage and Amherst's armies.[11]

Immediately after reaching Albany Bradstreet informed Gage that he had arrived "for a few days" to ensure that "you will not want provisions." Reassurances were needed because Gage was worried about the flow of supplies out of Albany. Because of his concern he had dispatched Major Gabriel Christie with orders to take "all measures to forward up Provisions & whatever else should be necessary for this army." On August 19 Bradstreet was taken aback by a letter from Major Christie explaining the nature of his duties. The Colonel immediately turned to Amherst for clarification of the situation. Insulted by this apparent threat to his authority, Bradstreet complained to his commander that Christie "would have me believe you have taken out of my hands the transportation of provisions &a. to the westward and put it into his." Since Amherst had mentioned nothing of the sort to him, Bradstreet made clear that he intended to ignore Christie and proceed with his duties until ordered to do otherwise.[12]

During the next few weeks matters were very tense since as soon as Christie arrived at Schenectady, determined to carry out Gage's orders, he discovered he might be prevented from doing so "by interruption of Col. Bradstreet who has Come here on hearing of my arrival." Both men fired off appeals to their commanding officers who in turn attempted to smooth things over. Initially Amherst explained to Gage that he had ordered Bradstreet to Albany "to fix every thing for the Mohawk River that no failure may happen." Two days later he wrote Bradstreet that Christie's "being Sent to Serve as Deputy Qr. Master General under Bridgr. General Gage" did not appear to interfere with Bradstreet's assigned duties, which remained "The Transportation of

---

11. Amherst to Bradstreet, August 10, 1759, C.O. 5/56-1, 241-42, P.A.C.; Bradstreet to Amherst, August 9, 1759, W.O. 34/57, 36, microfilm, Reel 154 (1). The order was given on August 16 according to Amherst's Journal, in Doughty, *Appendix To An Historical Journal*, 3, 52.

12. Bradstreet to Gage, August 18, 1759, Gage Papers, American Series/3 (A.S./3), University of Michigan Clements Library, Ann Arbor; Gage to Bradstreet, August 30, 1759, fms Eng 106, Gage Letters, Harvard Houghton Library, Cambridge; Bradstreet to Amherst, August 19, 1759, W.O. 34/57, 41-42, microfilm, Reel 154 (1).

Provisions, &ca, to both armies." However, he did hope that the two men would "both Agree & use your joint Endeavors" in this chore.[13] This somewhat vague clarification was unacceptable to Bradstreet but he bided his time for a few days before seeking a more clear-cut delineation of his authority over all quartermaster duties in the area, and thus over Christie. A direct confrontation between Bradstreet and Christie, and additional clarifying statements from Amherst and Gage, caused the dejected Christie to surrender. But as he prepared to rejoin Gage, he fired some final pessimistic comments about Bradstreet. By September 10 Amherst had advised him to follow an order by Gage recalling him to Fort Stanwix and he was about to do so. However he pointedly reminded Gage that "as the Case Stands, the Supplys and every thing else for your Army and Posts, intirely depend on him [Bradstreet] and of Course the blame must likewise fall upon him for what may be wanting."[14] If supply problems should arise and if explanations of Gage's failure to move against LaGalette were eventually needed, Christie already had provided his commander with a convenient excuse and obvious scapegoat.

It soon became clear that Bradstreet was having difficulties meeting all of Gage's provision requirements and that Gage was in "an agony of indecision" about Amherst's orders to strike at LaGalette. Whether, however, it was the supply problem linked with Bradstreet that was the root cause of Gage's "vacillation," and eventual decision to abandon any thoughts of a further offensive thrust, is another matter. Replying to a September 15 letter from Gage, in which were expressed his fears "of not being fully supply'd in time," Bradstreet balanced his confidence that the chore was well in hand with an enumeration of some of the rather serious difficulties encountered. He had not the "least doubt" that Gage's requirements would be met, but the "late Flood and great quantities of Artillery has kept the provisions back." Over the next three weeks the same confidence was to be expressed repeatedly by Bradstreet in the face of mounting snags and setbacks. Gage's "surprisingly great" demands, the contractors' failure to deliver provisions to Albany rapidly enough and in sufficient quantities, the scarcity of bateau-men, all combined to handicap seriously Bradstreet's provisioning effort. Yet at the same time such problems only slightly diminished his buoyant confidence. He remained convinced that the "posts from hence [Schenectady] to Fort Stanwix can never be in want" and had not "the least doubt about succeeding" in meeting Gage's other requirements as soon as the remaining provisions "gets into my hands."[15]

---

13. Christie to Gage, September 1, 1759, Gage Papers, A.S./3; Amherst to Gage, August 21, 1759, C.O. 5/56-2, 303; Amherst to Bradstreet, August 23, 1759, W.O. 34/58, 41, microfilm, Reel 154 (2).
14. Christie to Gage, September 10, 1759, Gage Papers, A.S./3.
15. Shy, *Toward Lexington*, 131; Bradstreet to Gage, September 21, 26, 28, and October 7, 1759, Gage Papers, A.S./3.

While Gage was obviously concerned about the state of his supplies, it would appear that his early October decision[16] to abandon the LaGalette assault was based largely on grounds other than mere provisioning problems. It has been suggested that Gage was worried about his forces being outnumbered by the French as well as by the possibility of Wolfe's failure at Quebec. Thus, because of what might be boiled down to a lack of "moral courage"[17] on his part, his forces remained at Oswego instead of pushing down the St. Lawrence. This decision considerably upset Amherst, since word of it reached him when he was finally moving northward against the French. Disappointed that "Gage had failed him" and apprehensive that without this pressure from the west he would be "walking into a trap" should Wolfe fail, Amherst felt obliged to abandon his own offensive.[18]

Not surprisingly, in defending his failure to carry out Amherst's orders, Gage fell back upon the convenient excuse suggested to him a month earlier by Gabriel Christie. When Amherst accused him of "timidity" Gage responded by attempting to fasten the blame on Bradstreet's "failure to provide adequate logistical support."[19] This appeared a rather lame excuse, particularly when offered to Amherst, since it threw into question the performance of a man who had earned Amherst's total confidence and support. The Commander-in-Chief had only recently made clear to Bradstreet that he welcomed "every thought that occurs to you tending to the good of the Service," promising to quickly act upon "such useful hints." For his part Bradstreet had been careful to keep his commander informed concerning a steady flow of provisions to Gage, thus winning expressions of Amherst's "pleasure . . . that the provision Affairs went on well." Consequently Gage's defence made no impression on Amherst. Gage had failed to carry out his orders thereby earning Amherst's immediate contempt, as well as future assignments which continued to reveal Amherst's reservations about his military abilities.[20] On the other hand, Bradstreet's quartermaster performance had been vindicated once more. But in the process the damage done to Gage's reputation was to convert Amherst's eventual successor as commander-in-chief into the most dedicated foe ever encountered by John Bradstreet.

---

16. Word of Gage's decision "not to advance any further that season" reached Amherst around October 11. See Long, *Lord Jeffery Amherst*, 112.

17. Shy, *Toward Lexington*, 131-32. See also Johnson G. Cooper, "Oswego In The French-English Struggle In North America 1720-1760" (D.S.Sc. dissertation, Syracuse University, 1961), 193, who claims Gage's belief that he "was not strong enough" to push on dictated "no further moves before winter set in." Cooper's thesis only briefly and in a very sketchy fashion, mentions Bradstreet and his activities.

18. Long, *Lord Jeffery Amherst*, 112-13.

19. Shy, *Toward Lexington*, 171.

20. Amherst to Bradstreet, September 14, 1759, W.O. 34/58, 51, microfilm, Reel 154 (2); Bradstreet to Amherst, September 12 and 25, 1759, W.O. 34/57, 57 and 64, microfilm, Reel 154 (1); Amherst to Bradstreet, September 18, 1759, ref. #6666, N.Y.S.L.; Shy, *Toward Lexington*, 132.

Despite Gage's failure to move against LaGalette and Amherst's limited gains at Ticonderoga and Crown Point, the campaign closed on a triumphant note with Wolfe's victory at Quebec. Nonetheless, as the British forces went into winter quarters at the end of October, Bradstreet could not resist the opportunity to comment on the less than satisfactory nature of the 1759 military operations. While pleased with "the extraordinary Success" at Quebec, he was at the same time "concern'd at the conquest of Canada not being Compleat." He could only speculate that a good deal left undone "that was expected to be done . . . may possibly make some stir at Home among those concern'd." For his part, Bradstreet felt that his particular assignment, "the great work of the transportation of provisions," had been capably executed so that "both Armies and Garrisons for the winter . . . have been and are well furnish'd."

While reporting this diligent execution of his quartermaster duties to Charles Gould, Bradstreet also voiced his disappointment at not receiving what he regarded as an adequate reward for his Frontenac achievement. By this point he was ready to return to England to plead personally his case and had so informed Sir Richard Lyttleton. If such an action was "thought unreasonable" and it was felt that it was best for him to remain in America, then he hoped at least a limited and immediate promotion could be arranged. The "appointment of Q M General (if nothing else is thought of for me) if not for all North America at least for the Service to be carry'd on from Albany to the westward & Northward" was the desired promotion spelled out to Gould which he also intended to mention to Lyttleton. Such an advance in rank was urgently needed to allay Bradstreet's fears that he was "to be turn'd adrift without provision at the End of the war as I was the last."[21]

Essentially the same plaintive message went off to Gould over a month later, although on this occasion the anxious Bradstreet was even more distressed because of rumours reaching him concerning mother-country displeasure at some of his errors of omission. He had heard that Pitt was "displeas'd at my not bringing all the Vessells and provisions to Oswego which I took last year at Frontenac." Greatly upset at the possible discredit of his Frontenac victory, Bradstreet wanted both Lyttleton and Gould to know that he was not responsible for the alleged blunder. Rather, "the fault was in Genl. Abercromby in opposition to my best endeavours to get his leave to bring every thing I should take there [at Frontenac] to Oswego and establish myself." After shifting the blame to his former commander, Bradstreet expressed his hopes that the rumour of Pitt's displeasure was incorrect, particularly in view of the obvious American pleasure at the completeness of his victory. "I would fane hope there is no foundation for the report" especially "when I reflect on the opinion of the whole world this way 'that so great a publick benifit to the Nation as the Success of that

---

21. Bradstreet to Gould, October 25, 1759, T.P.C., 128/50.

Enterprise could not fail of a great reward to me.'" To make him "the only Person living or dead so little encourag'd for so many extraordinary services to the publick" on the basis of such an ill-founded report, or for some other petty reasons, seemed grossly unfair to Bradstreet. He urged Gould to look into the matter to find precisely "why I am thus neglected and if there is any fault found with me at Home" since he was confident "there is none abroad." This spirited vindication closed with a repeated expression of his fears about being "turn'd adrift without any thing" and the need for at least the appointment as "Q M Genl."[22]

The fact that Bradstreet now was willing to continue to do quartermaster duties, although at a higher rank, despite previous protestations of his personal dislike for such a role, revealed an interesting change in his attitude. Possibly it was a sign of his intense fear of being overlooked and thus even an appointment in this lacklustre capacity was better than nothing. On the other hand, it might have been an indication that while lacking in status and glory, quartermaster duties offered other more lucrative prospects. An enormous amount of money had passed through Bradstreet's hands and some of it perhaps had stuck to his fingers and those of his friends. If that was the case, Bradstreet's continued quartermaster service might have protected him from criticism by allowing him to cover up any obvious departmental corruption.[23]

Particularly in 1759, Bradstreet's quartermaster expenditures involved very "considerable Sums," so considerable that Amherst warned that they "may Seem extraordinary to the Ministry unless properly Accounted for."[24] A comparison of Bradstreet's 1756, 1758, and 1759 accounts demonstrates the extraordinary level his expenditures had reached.[25] In 1756 his quartermaster department laid out £77,666/6/3, in 1758 this had dipped slightly to £70,541/8/9, while in 1759 expenses soared to £157,779/5/3.[26] Predictably Bradstreet's detailed accountings of these sums appear quite straightforward and aboveboard. Admittedly some of the Palatine families whom C. R. Canedy links with Bradstreet, the Freys and the Herkimers for example,[27] do reappear in

---

22. Ibid., December 9, 1759, T.P.C., 128/51.

23. For differing assessments of the possibility of corruption within Bradstreet's department, see Shy, *Toward Lexington*, 170; Alden, *General Gage in America*, 72; Canedy, "An Entrepreneurial History Of The New York Frontier, 1739-1776," 319.

24. Amherst to Bradstreet, December 19, 1759, W.O. 34/56, 86, microfilm, Reel 153 (2).

25. The sums quoted are New York currency rather than pounds sterling (one N.Y. £ equals £7/16 sterling). For a discussion of the difficulties involved in converting colonial currency into sterling, see Jackson T. Main, *The Social Structure of Revolutionary America* (Princeton, N.J., 1965), 289-90; and more recently John J. McCusker, *Money and Exchange in Europe and America, 1600-1775* (Chapel Hill, N.C., 1978).

26. "Account of Money paid by John Bradstreet... in 1756," T.P.C., 128/414; "Account of Money paid by Colo. John Bradstreet... in 1758," T.P.C., 128/415; "Account of Money paid by Colo. John Bradstreet... Ending the 24th December, 1759," T.P.C., 128/416.

27. Canedy, "An Entrepreneurial History Of The New York Frontier, 1739-1776," 166-67, 199.

his accounts at spaced intervals performing a variety of services. Henry Frey is found providing "Cedar Timber for Boards" as well as transporting provisions on the Mohawk River. Among the Herkimers, Joseph turns up providing ninety-five horses while Nicholas arranged wagon transportation. John and Cornelius Cuyler also emerge as frequent recipients of quartermaster spending, most notably in 1759 when they provided 1,264 oxen at a cost of £12,407/10/9.

Clearly more closely associated with Bradstreet were his trusted aides, Philip Schuyler, George Coventry, and John Glen. In the accounts Schuyler is described as "a Manager and Director to the Service in general" but in addition he had become Bradstreet's closest American confidant, as events in the near future were to reveal. Coventry is more briefly listed as "my Assistant," handling "Sundry Disbursements" amounting to £41,053/11/6 in 1759. John Glen, on the other hand, is designated only as a director of the bateaux service but he handled a multitude of chores. He supervised the impressment of bateau-men, constructed and repaired bateaux and workships, arranged "Boards Timber Nails & Carpenters' Tools," transported provisions, and supplied horses and wagons. Some idea of the extent of his services may be revealed by the fact that in 1759 he received approximately £8,500 for these various tasks.[28]

Examination of the accounts is useful in establishing the enormous amounts expended in Bradstreet's department as well as in clarifying the individuals and families in the Albany area whom he was most disposed to work with and reward. It leaves unanswered, however, the deeper question of whether the cultivation of potential friends and allies also represented a corrupt plundering of the department for the benefit of himself and these same friends. Rumours abounded concerning Bradstreet "being in cahoots with some of the shady traders, boat-builders, wagoners, and bateaumen with whom he contracted the business of his department."[29] Clear evidence substantiating Bradstreet's personal profiteering is considerably more difficult to unearth. However, at least one victim of his moral and financial deception has left a reasonably clear account of the Colonel's mode of operation. Well over a decade after Bradstreet allegedly had deprived him of proper payment for services rendered, John Lovell Jr. outlined his particular case to Thomas Gage. Lovell claimed that in 1759 Bradstreet declined to provide him with the funds necessary to pay two companies of carpenters for whom he apparently was responsible. Instead the Colonel promised to arrange "a Credit" in Boston which Lovell was to use "for the payment of another Company of Carpenters that then remained to be paid of as well as my own ballance." Upon arrival in

---

28. "Account of Money paid by Colo. John Bradstreet... Ending the 24th December, 1759" and "Account of Money paid by colo. John Bradstreet... in 1759," T.P.C., 128/416 and 128/415.

29. Canedy, "An Entrepreneurial History Of The New York Frontier, 1739-1776," 321.

Boston Lovell discovered he had been duped in that the arranged credit only covered the additional company's cost and left unpaid his own claims. As a result, Lovell charged, although Bradstreet's account claim of £21,445/18/10 was allowed by the British Treasury[30] the portion of this money owed to Lovell had not been passed on. Bradstreet had committed fraud, Lovell continued, "by makeing me charge in my accounts what was paid by Mr. Coventry his deputy and at the same time let Mr. Coventry his deputy charge the same money."[31]

This particular indictment of Bradstreet's conduct is convincing enough at least to raise the possibility of some accounts being mishandled and departmental funds being siphoned off for Bradstreet's personal benefit. Nevertheless, until other equally accurate accounts of Bradstreet's misconduct are produced it seems unwise to offer hasty judgments based on murky rumours. Obviously he was guilty of misappropriating some departmental funds but whether he did so on the lavish scale assumed by historians such as John Alden remains open to question. On the other hand, the charge that Bradstreet used departmental expenditures to create a coterie of friends and allies in upper New York, the political manipulation spoken of by Canedy, appears both valid and understandable.

It is understandable in the sense that the Albany area was far from renowned for its sympathy and support of the British war effort. On the contrary, it had a history of latent animosity towards the English which was punctuated by violent outbursts in the form of street battles between townsmen and troops, verbal denunciations, and open opposition to billeting or impressment arrangements.[32] Given such a charged atmosphere it was natural for Bradstreet to seek out and reward those who clearly supported his own actions and the British cause. As this committed circle broadened out from the Schuyler, Glen, Coventry, Herkimer, Frey, Cuyler base, it was perhaps inevitable that Bradstreet eventually chose to use some of these allies to challenge Albany officialdom, which in his mind consistently had demonstrated questionable loyalty and a continuing lack of cooperation.

As early as August of 1759 Bradstreet had complained about inadequate law enforcement in Albany which greatly handicapped the British army. The sheriff of the town was described as "one Evil minded person that has made himself popular, among the lower sort of people, by obstructing his Majesty's Service upon all occasions."[33] With such a person in office there was little chance that military requirements such as billeting could be carried out with the support of the local

---

30. Lovell was quite accurate in his figures in that Bradstreet's 1758 accounts (T.P.C., 128/415) contained an item: "Paid Carpenters for Building Battoes & Vessels and for attending the Armies to Ticonderoga & Frontenac on Lake Ontario—£21,445/18/10."
31. John Lovell Jr. to Gage, December 19, 1771, Gage Papers, A.S./108.
32. See Canedy, "An Entrepreneurial History Of The New York Frontier, 1739-1776," 9.
33. Bradstreet to James DeLancey, August 19, 1759, W.O. 34/57, 47, microfilm, Reel 154 (1).

law authorities. Rather, as Bradstreet discovered in the winter of 1759-1760, instead of facilitating matters the local authorities seemed determined to use legal means to harass him in the fulfillment of his military responsibilities. Thus in February 1760 he was informed of an indictment against himself and "one Mr. James Dow for breaking open" an Albany residence "and illegally quartering several persons" against the homeowner's "will and Consent."[34] To end such disloyal and insulting legal quibbling, Bradstreet demanded the removal of the officials involved. In suggesting new appointees he then turned to those whose loyalty and cooperative attitude were above question; and these men invariably were his own allies or their nominees.

But before removal could be attempted Bradstreet's Albany enemies had to be discredited. As usual, he seized upon every opportunity which presented itself to build a case against them while buttressing his own diligent virtue. It is clear from his accounts that Bradstreet felt certain individuals were dependable and conscientious enough in provisioning and transportation matters to be relied upon year after year. Yet there were others, he emphasized, who were willing to take advantage of the British forces whenever possible. In hiring wagons there were those who demanded exorbitant prices, who refused to notice "Sick men & lame horses being discharg'd," and who engaged in "many more irregular & improper proceedings to the prejudice of the Publick."[35]

As the spring of 1760 approached Bradstreet returned to this theme of "improper proceedings" particularly in matters of trade. Some of his accusations were rather surprising in view of the fact that several months earlier he had championed the cause of the Albany and Shenectady traders. In this vein he had informed Amherst in September of 1759 that "I am desir'd by some of the inhabitants of this city [Albany] and of the Town of Schenectady to acquaint Your Excellency that they are desirous of going to Niagara to Trade with the Indians and beg your leave and pass." By the following March his tone had changed considerably. Now such trading activities had to be curbed since they were impeding military preparations. The number of persons preparing to head west "in order to Trade with the Indians" was so considerable, and the wages they were offering to bateau-men so extravagant, that their activities threatened to "induce & carry off every good Battoe Man upon the Mohawk River which is evidently to the great prejudice of his Majesty's Service." Furthermore, the regimental sutlers also were draining off bateau-men as they loaded "their Battoes one half with Indian Goods." These critical comments concerning legal harassment in Albany, hard and unfair bargaining in transportation matters, and selfish trading interests competing with military

---

34. T. J. Kempe to Bradstreet, February 28, 1760, W.O. 34/57, 118, microfilm Reel 154 (1).
35. Bradstreet to Amherst, February 4, 1760, W.O. 34/57, 102, microfilm, Reel 154 (1).

needs might appear to be too general and imprecise to have had any impact. Yet they all served to pave the way for Bradstreet's general point that many of these difficulties in the Albany area stemmed from a "Nest of Harpies" who waited with "rapacious Claws extended,"[36] ready to serve their own interests rather than those of the Crown. For Amherst's benefit a careful picture was being drawn of an heroic Bradstreet doing continual battle with uncooperative, if not openly disloyal, enemies. Should an eventual confrontation occur, the scales already were being weighted in Bradstreet's favour.

In terms of headquarters reaction, General Jeffery Amherst seemed to accept Bradstreet's view of these various problems. Although at times he attempted to temper the Colonel's more impetuous actions and demands, in most instances he remained Bradstreet's firm supporter. Indications of this continuing confidence emerged during preparations for the 1760 campaign and were repeated throughout the year. By mid-February of 1760 Pitt's instructions had reached Amherst and he in turn informed Bradstreet of the immediate preparations which had to be launched. Essentially these involved "the construction of what number of additional Boats will be required for Lake Ontario & Champlain." Once more, this relegation to transportation duties caused him to complain "but believe Dr. Charles [Gould] it hurts to be the planner, the executer of the laborious part & others have the Opportunity of getting the honor by being in Action."[37]

Once the campaign got underway Amherst's hesitation and uncertainty were to be demonstrated anew. Already in February he had indicated to Bradstreet his own uncertainty about the direction of his main offensive thrust, whether it should be launched out of Oswego across Lake Ontario or out of Ticonderoga and up the Richelieu. Keeping both options open, he ordered Bradstreet to pay equal attention to provisioning and transportation preparations in both areas so that "if at any time hereafter the Circumstances should Induce me to march, an equal Force each way, I may not be disappointed in any of its necessary Supplies, but be able to proceed without any Obstacles." By mid-April Bradstreet was able to voice the confident expectation that nearly all the bateaux required "for both services" would be operational "by the first of May." Before the month of May elapsed Amherst decided that he would lead the major thrust out of Oswego and down the St. Lawrence while a smaller force under Colonel William Haviland traversed the Champlain-Richelieu route. The execution of this decision was soon postposed by delay after delay. Late arrival of provincial contingents, low water in the Mohawk which slowed transportation, the necessity to outfit and properly arm two sloops on Lake Ontario, all these difficulties delayed until early August the launching of what were intended to be synchronized Richelieu and St. Lawrence operations.

---

36. Ibid., September 14, 1759, and March 25 and December 7, 1760, W.O. 34/57, 58, 124, 167, microfilm, Reel 154 (1).

37. Amherst to Bradstreet, February 16, 1760, C.O. 5/57-2, 580-81; Bradstreet to Gould, February 18, 1760, T.P.C., 128/52.

Surprisingly, the usually impetuous Bradstreet took these delays in stride for a change. He offered his British friends no strong criticism of his commander's tardiness but limited himself to the observation that Gould was likely to be "surpris'd to find the Armies this way so late in taking the Field."[38] Such a rare outburst of discretion on Bradstreet's part might have been a good indication that the grounds for criticism were limited and that Amherst's slowness on this occasion was largely unavoidable.

Shortly after writing this letter, Bradstreet himself prepared to leave Albany and take to the field. Before doing so he placed his private and public correspondence in the hands of Philip Schuyler along with instructions as to how to proceed "in Case of my Decease this Campaign." Material of a private nature was to be conveyed to Bradstreet's wife Mary and two daughters who now resided in Boston. Public accounts and papers were to be retained by Schuyler who was to settle any matters arising from them "with whomsoever may be appointed for that purpose either in America or England." That he entrusted Philip Schuyler with such important materials clearly revealed the heavy reliance he now placed on his young protégé. In addition, the tone of the instructions demonstrated the rapport existing between the two men. Bradstreet referred to Schuyler's record of "faithful service to the Publick" and his own personal confidence "that I cant leave my publick accounts & papers in a more faithful hand than in yours."[39]

Little did Bradstreet know that his "Decease" and the necessity for Schuyler to execute these instructions were to come perilously close during this campaign. Ironically, it was Bradstreet's overpowering sense of duty and ceaseless diligence, rather than enemy bullets, which caused his health to collapse and brought him to death's door. Leaving Albany he journeyed towards Oswego, becoming increasingly apprehensive about the slow progress of the bateaux convoys and the inadequate amounts of provisions being moved forward to Lake Ontario. As he had predicted several months earlier the lack of skilled bateau-men severely handicapped military transportation. Their places had been taken by provincial troops whom Bradstreet described as mainly "old Men & Boys" unsuited to the task. Consequently the forty-six year old Colonel spent an exhausting month racing up and down the Oswego route "hurrying on in every Place, the Batteaus, Provisions & Stores." By early August all was ready for the army to move down the St. Lawrence but his exertions now took their toll. He was "thrown into a Rhumatic fever which has confin'd me some Days to my Bed., & has as yet little abated."[40]

---

38. Amherst to Bradstreet, February 22, 1760, C.O. 5/57-2, 471; Bradstreet to Amherst, April 15, 1760, W.O. 34/57, 131, microfilm, Reel 154 (1); Gipson, *The British Empire Before the American Revolution*, 7, 448-48; Bradstreet to Gould, June 22, 1760, T.P.C., 128/53.
39. Bradstreet to Philip Schuyler, July 6, 1760, Misc. MSS, Bradstreet, John, N.Y.H.S.; ibid., July 7, 1760, Schuyler Papers, Box 9, N.Y.P.L.
40. Bradstreet to Amherst, July 11, 1760, W.O. 34/57, 139, microfilm, Reel 154 (1); Bradstreet to Gould, August 6, 1760, T.P.C., 128/54.

As Amherst's army embarked upon the final reduction of Canada, Bradstreet remained behind, confined to his bed in Oswego and very concerned that his "Knowledge & Experience" would be sorely missed.[41] In mid-August he felt it was doubtful that he could attempt to follow Amherst and hoped only that once his health improved he could "go down the Country" inspecting the state of provisions and transportation. When Amherst received this letter he was quick to agree that if Bradstreet was well enough he should set out on such an inspection tour, and repeated his feeling that such a course would be more "essentially for the good of the Service than Your following me." Apparently the sickness lingered on, however, having now changed into some "sort of Small Pox." Thus it was not until the end of the month that Bradstreet, with somewhat exaggerated heroism, reported his departure down country: "Tho I cant stand still I set out to morrow for the Several Posts." By mid-September the journey was complete as both Bradstreet and word of Montreal's fall had reached Albany. A delighted Bradstreet congratulated Amherst on the reduction of Canada. "Heaven grant it may be true; and as no Man wishes it more Sincerely I have brought my Self to be assur'd of it and will venture to congratulate Your Excellency thereupon."[42] It was indeed true. Canada had been conquered but in the final victory Bradstreet's own role had been rather limited and perhaps might pass unnoticed.

Disappointed at his failure to share in the final glory of Canada's conquest, Bradstreet moved with new determination to seek an adequate reward both for his Frontenac victory and his over-all contribution to the British war effort. Worried that his earlier triumph might slip into the distant past, obscured by more recent victories, he poured out his fears and desires to his friends at home in hopes of sparking their renewed efforts on his behalf. Actually it was more a case of Bradstreet and his English allies pleading his cause with even greater vigour, since neither party had abandoned the continuing quest for his proper recognition. Admittedly in the winter of 1759-1760 both Sir Richard Lyttleton and Charles Gould could only advise Bradstreet to be patient and his rewards eventually would come. Bradstreet claimed such would be "an Easy task to me that has been so long us'd to it," but in the next breath could not resist suggesting an appointment as governor of New York. "If you think it right mention & push it for your old friend."[43] Patience clearly was not Bradstreet's strong point.

---

41. Ibid. Although signed by Bradstreet, this letter was written for him by a Captain Monypenny.

42. Bradstreet to Amherst, August 16, 1760, W.O. 34/57, 146, microfilm, Reel 154 (1); Amherst to Bradstreet, August 25, 1760, W.O. 34/56, 124, microfilm, Reel 153 (2); Bradstreet to Amherst, August 23, 1760, W.O. 34/57, 148, microfilm, Reel 154 (1); ibid., August 31, 1760, W.O. 34/57, 150, microfilm, Reel 154 (1); ibid., September 14, 1760, W.O. 34/57, 152, microfilm, Reel 154 (1). On August 27 Bradstreet had written to Gould: "I hope & expect to be able to walk in three or four days as I am much better." See Bradstreet to Gould, August 27, 1760, T.P.C., 128/55.

43. Ibid., February 18, 1760, T.P.C., 128/52.

Promises and advice continued to flow from England instead of promotions and awards. Gould helpfully informed Bradstreet of the proper procedures for settling his quartermaster accounts and also faithfully handled his various expenses and incomes as a regimental captain, deputy quartermaster-general, and lieutenant-governor of St. John's, Newfoundland. At the same time he could only offer optimistic reassurances concerning further appointments. "I wish you all Success," he wrote in May of 1760, "and, I think, it cannot be long, before I may give you Joy of some Step being taken in your favour. Sir Richard assures me you are not forgot." Then during the summer of 1760 Bradstreet's cause received a severe setback when his major patron, Sir Richard Lyttleton, had to leave England. According to Gould, Lyttleton had decided "to see if a more favourable Climate will assist him in the recovery of his Limbs" and was "going to Italy for two years for his health."[44] Sir Richard had functioned as Bradstreet's vital connection with the Pitt administration and his removal at this critical moment, when victory was at hand in North America and honours were about to be awarded, seemed a stunning blow to Bradstreet's hopes.

Sensing that his chances of success were deteriorating because of Lyttleton's withdrawal from London and fearful that he was indeed forgotten by the Pitt ministry, Bradstreet moved to the attack. "I have a thousand thanks to give you for your Endeavours with Sir Richard in particular," he wrote Gould in late September, "and I cant help thinking that if Mr. Pitt intends giving me any thing for my Service which have so much contributed to the reduction of Canada it must appear at the usual time of giving promotions." One month later the desperate Bradstreet was even more blunt about his reliance upon his English friend and more precise about possible rewards. He frankly reminded Gould that "my sole dependence is on you." Surely, he reasoned, now that "Canada has submitted Mr. Pitt will think of my Services," particularly "if he was inform'd how Singular they have been this Year also." He advised Gould to stress the acceptability of a regimental command or the New York governorship in lobbying Pitt. Concluding this presentation Bradstreet pointed to the disappointment an admiring colonial public, fully aware of his contribution, would feel should he be neglected. "In a word, my Dear Friend, the American world wait with impatience with respect to my Services being rewarded by Mr. Pitt and should I get nothing they will be no less Surpris'd than my Self."[45]

As on several occasions in the past Bradstreet again was attempting to employ suggestions of New World esteem to secure Old World favour. Yet at this very moment his position in both worlds was none too secure. In England his link with the Pitt ministry was severely

---

44. Gould to Bradstreet, May 8, July 12, and August 22, 1760, T.P.C., 128/61, 128/62, and 128/64.

45. Bradstreet to Gould, September 28, 1760, T.P.C., 128/56; ibid., October 23, 1760, T.P.C., 128/57. In Bradstreet MSS, A.A.S., the latter letter is erroneously identified as Bradstreet to [Philip Schuyler].

weakened, while in America Bradstreet found himself subjected to increasing criticism and forced to justify some of his deeds to Amherst. A number of thorny problems had cropped up in the Albany area, created by Bradstreet's aggressive actions and his detractors' equally aggressive responses, problems which eventually were deposited in Amherst's lap for possible settlement. Ranging from the appointment of a more acceptable postmaster to legal action brought against him by the Dutch Church members over his use of their property, Bradstreet found himself embroiled in one turbulent controversy after another. Through it all an effort was made to convince Amherst that attacks on Bradstreet and his colleagues amounted to unjustified harassment of loyal servants of His Majesty, and the General should not repudiate men who had only been doing their duty. What Bradstreet was attempting to do was to obscure totally the perhaps valid complaints and present all problems as a black and white clash between the disloyal and loyal. His constant portrayal of Albany as a community every ready "to plunder the Public"[46] helped considerably in convincing Amherst that his complaints were valid and that he and his men should be supported. The interesting contradiction in Bradstreet's position was that while employing suggestions of his American esteem to further his cause in England, in appealing for Amherst's support he was willing to openly voice his dislike for the many disloyal Americans he had encountered. In other words, American disagreements and their refusal to cooperate with him because he loyally served the Crown were used to gain Amherst's support, while at the same time American agreement and continued cooperation with the mother country were suggested as the net result of England's properly rewarding a man with whom the colonials identified and one they respected, namely John Bradstreet. Regardless of whether he had earned American favour or disfavour Bradstreet could find some way of channelling it to his own advantage.

Such self-aggrandizement and avoidance of what might have been legitimate grievances did little to solve civil-military problems. Ringing with charges and countercharges Albany remained a simmering potful of difficulties ready to boil over at any moment. In bringing these problems to a head there is no doubt that some Albany residents' antagonistic and opportunistic attitudes were heightened by the presence of John Bradstreet, whose inflexibly loyal and abruptly undiplomatic approach stirred things up even further.[47] Yet given the mul-

---

46. Detail concerning the many controversies can be found in Bradstreet to Amherst, November 23, 1760, W.O. 34/57, 159-60, microfilm, Reel 154 (1); December 6, 1760, W.O. 34/57, 166, microfilm, Reel 154 (1); Amherst to Bradstreet, December 12, 1760, W.O. 34/56, 136, microfilm, Reel 153 (2); ibid., December 28, 1760, W.O. 34/56, 140, microfilm, Reel 153 (2); Bradstreet to Amherst, December 7, 1760, W.O. 34/57, 167, microfilm, Reel 154 (1); ibid., December 21, 1760, W.O. 34/57, 168, microfilm, Reel 154 (1); Amherst to Bradstreet, January 18, 1760, W.O. 34/56, 143, microfilm, Reel 153 (2); Bradstreet to Amherst, January 10, 1762, W.O. 34/57, 226-27, microfilm, Reel 154 (1).

47. Shy, *Toward Lexington*, 169.

titude of incidents in Albany and Amherst's own experience with the headstrong Bradstreet, it is surprising that no serious attempt was made to bridle the Colonel or replace him by an officer better equipped to cope with the sensitive situation.

Indeed the Bradstreet-Amherst relationship seemed to flourish in the face of these attacks rather than to wither. In a variety of direct and indirect ways Amherst indicated his continuing confidence in and support of Bradstreet while giving no sign of any willingness to abandon the contentious Colonel. When a group of half-pay officers, including Bradstreet's assistant George Coventry, petitioned Amherst for permission to establish a settlement at Niagara, the General readily approved. Bradstreet himself was identified by Sir William Johnson as being linked with this project and the entire scheme was very much in tune with some of the proposals concerning Great Lakes development which the Colonel earlier had submitted to Sir Richard Lyttleton. Bradstreet's linkage apparently did no harm to the suggestion and might even have facilitated its consideration and approval. Eventually, however, the entire scheme was blocked by the Board of Trade which overruled Amherst's decision.[48]

Additional and more direct signs of the good relationship between the two men are readily available. When, in January of 1761, Bradstreet decided to dispatch Philip Schuyler to England to oversee the final settlement of some of his quartermaster accounts, he sought Amherst's approval for his choice. Amherst agreed with the sending of Schuyler, arranging to "procure him the first passage that should offer" and also making "a favourable mention" of him to the Lords of the Treasury. Once Schuyler reached England and set to work Amherst carefully watched the progress of the accounts, on several occasions expressing to Bradstreet his faith that Schuyler would soon inform him "of their being all passed." Interest and concern also was revealed by Amherst when, with obvious pleasure, he informed Bradstreet that his stepson, Lieutenant Samuel Bradstreet, had been promoted. Arranging for the Lieutenant to secure a company in the 40th Regiment pleased Amherst since "he was particular Recommended by You, and is very deserving of it."[49]

Admittedly there was at least one occasion when Amherst drew the line against a particular favour requested by Bradstreet, but even here he did so in such a way as to make clear his support of Bradstreet's cause. This particular incident arose when Bradstreet explained to

---

48. Canedy, "An Entrepreneurial History Of The New York Frontier, 1739-1776," 260-66; Johnson to Daniel Claus, May 20, 1761, in Sullivan et al., *Johnson Papers*, 10, 270; Shy, *Toward Lexington*, 105.

49. Bradstreet to Amherst, January 29, 1761, W.O. 34/57, 176, microfilm, Reel 154 (1); Amherst to Bradstreet, February 8, 1761, W.O. 34/56, 145, microfilm, Reel 153 (2); Bradstreet to Amherst, March 15, 1761, W.O. 34/57, 182, microfilm, Reel 154 (1); Amherst to Bradstreet, December 27, 1761, W.O. 34/56, 189, microfilm, Reel 154 (2); ibid., November 15, 1761, W.O. 34/56, 182, microfilm, Reel 153 (2); ibid., November 5, 1761, ref. #6920, N.Y.S.L.

Amherst his intention of applying through his English friends for "some mark of His Majesty's Royal favor for me for my Services in this Country." If Amherst would "do me the honor & favor to name me to Mr. Pitt to obtain the end above mention'd" it would enhance considerably the application. Amherst replied that while such an application "has my Entire Approbation, and I Wish it may be Attended with Success: All I can do to Contribute towards it is to do, what I have already done upon former occasions, to make mention of You in my Letters to Mr. Pitt, but I Cannot pretend to Write to him on purpose, which it is a fixed Rule with me never to do for any one: Several Persons have Asked the same Favor, but I have always declined it as I do not think it a proper application for me to make to the Secretary of State." Bradstreet quickly responded with "humble thanks" for Amherst's past and future mentions of his performance to Pitt since this was all that he claimed to hope for or expect.[50] Obviously he did not wish to jeopardize his position by pushing his original request any further. Nevertheless, Bradstreet had every reason to be grateful for the limited support and approval offered by Amherst on this occasion and for the more generous cooperation and confidence revealed in many other instances. His performance evidently had been satisfactory enough, his arguments convincing enough, to make Amherst a willing listener and extremely helpful supporter.

Bradstreet's success in gaining Amherst's friendship could prove very useful in championing the Colonel's cause in England. Gould constantly urged Bradstreet to keep on good terms with Amherst and push for repeated kind mentions in the commander's correspondence with Pitt, since Amherst was at this moment greatly "Esteemed" in England and considerable "attention is paid to his recommendations." These and other words of advice came from Gould as he vigorously moved to take up the slack left by Lyttleton's departure. In actuality even without Lyttleton there emerged a new link with the Pitt ministry in the person of Robert Wood, who was serving as Pitt's Undersecretary of State. Wood had been appointed to this office on the recommendation of Sir Richard Lyttleton and, as Gould discovered, was reasonably well disposed towards Lyttleton's old friends. It was after consultation with Wood that Gould submitted for Pitt's perusal a memorial stating Bradstreet's case. In early January of 1761 this reminder of the Frontenac triumph and diligent quartermaster service was placed in Pitt's hands in hopes of securing "some Mark of his [Majesty's] Royal favour." Shortly thereafter Wood informed Gould that he had been directed by Pitt to state "that he, Mr. Pitt, has a good opinion of the Memorialist, but that every thing of this kind must pass thro' General Amherst."[51]

---

50. Bradstreet to Amherst, March 23, 1761, W.O. 34/56, 182, microfilm, Reel 154 (1); Amherst to Bradstreet, March 29, 1761, W.O. 34/56, 151, microfilm, Reel 153 (2); Bradstreet to Amherst, April 1, 1761, W.O. 34/57, 184, microfilm, Reel 154 (1).

51. Gould to Bradstreet, December 13, 1760, T.P.C., 128/65; Namier and Brooke, *History of Parliament*, 3, 655; Gould to Bradstreet, December 13, 1760, T.P.C., 128/65;

Promptly the next day, Gould let Bradstreet know that some sort of personal recommendation was needed from Amherst before Pitt would act. As a result Bradstreet solicited the already-mentioned personal endorsement of Amherst and received in reply the General's statement of warm support, willingness to mention Bradstreet to Pitt, but reluctance to write a specific letter of recommendation. Armed with at least this limited recommendation, Bradstreet wrote to Gould on April 1 enclosing copies of Amherst's March 29 letter of approbation. Thankful for Pitt's "good opinion of me" and honestly pleased with Amherst's kind words, Bradstreet now assumed that by using Amherst's letter Gould would be able to secure his promotion. His confidence soaring, Bradstreet expressed himself agreeable to "the appointment of Quarter Master General for North America with British Rank of Colonel." These high hopes were soon shattered. Amherst's letter was placed before Pitt who, according to Wood, "read it & said it was very well"[52] but limited himself to a vaguely evasive answer on the matter of promotion. A disappointed Gould commented that "the Sight of this Letter has had its use, though it has not operated so forcibly, as I could have wished."

Determined to continue his lobbying efforts on Bradstreet's behalf, Gould urged his colonial friend to redouble his own efforts at securing even more favourable comments from Amherst. "The oftener you can be mentioned in Genl. Amherst's letters, the better," he argued. Furthermore, the cultivation of additional friends in Pitt's government was advisable. Thus a letter of congratulation to the recently appointed Secretary at War, Charles Townshend, who had attempted to aid Bradstreet's military rise during the Colonel's English sojourn in the early 1750s, might prove helpful. After cautiously feeling Townshend out concerning his interest and sympathy, more specific requests for his support could perhaps be made. On his part, Bradstreet faithfully executed each of Gould's suggestions. A letter to Townshend was sent off, as well as a note of thanks to Robert Wood "for his readiness to serve me." But most importantly, the fact that Bradstreet was, as he described it, "extremely well with the General," was to be milked for all it was worth. Bradstreet's optimism emerged once more as he received Amherst's personal assurance that "he never will fail making mention of me to Mr. Pitt and that tho he will not ask in direct terms for perferment he will do it in such a way as cannot fail of Serving me." Bradstreet fully expected that in this very batch of mail from the colonies was "further proof" of Amherst's desire for his promotion. Carried away by his own hopes, he urged Gould immediately to inform Wood of the kind words expected from Amherst and follow them up.

"The Memorial of John Bradstreet..." (c. 1761), T.P.C., 128/439; Robert Wood to Gould, January 9, 1761, T.P.C., 128/112.

52. Bradstreet to Gould, April 1, 1761, T.P.C., 128/68. The copies of the Amherst to Bradstreet letter of March 29, 1761, are numbered 128/113 and 128/114. Wood to Gould, June 10, 1761, T.P.C., 128/115.

Events seemed to be moving rapidly in Bradstreet's favour when suddenly all his carefully arranged solicitations and recommendations were rendered useless. The object of this lobbying campaign, William Pitt, fell from power. "A very unlucky Incident has happen'd" reported Gould in October, "Mr. Pitt upon some dissension in Council from the Measures, which appeared to him essential, has resigned the Seals." Quite clearly the ministerial regroupings necessitated by Pitt's departure precluded Bradstreet "being Served, at least for a time."[53]

Faced with the recurring frustration of his hopes for preferment in England, Bradstreet remained determined. Even the added burden of the constant shrinkage of his quartermaster responsibilities in North America failed to discourage him. Rather, these setbacks seemed only to spur him onward into more imaginative suggestions concerning his proper reward. At Albany, by early 1762, it was painfully clear that Bradstreet's quartermaster department was operating on a much reduced scale. Provisioning still had to be carried out, particularly to meet the western garrisons' needs, but the huge demands created by the earlier campaigns were now past. Departmental expenditures bear this out in that the greatly reduced total of £54,587 (N.Y.) was spent in 1760 while in 1761 Bradstreet did not expect expenses to "exceed much a quarter of what they were last Year."[54] Experiencing at first hand this gradual reduction of quartermaster activities and very aware of the failure of all his efforts to secure the higher appointment as Quartermaster-General for all North America, Bradstreet now moved beyond the confines of military provisioning in suggesting proper appointments for himself.

His new tack first emerged in a letter to Gould written in February 1762. Speculating about where the boundary of Canada eventually would be established, Bradstreet voiced his suspicions that the French wanted an arrangement allowing their continued connections with the "Nation of Indians which surround the Great Lakes." In this way an independent Indian power under French protection would rise west of the line and English traders would be completely shut out. To avoid such an unfortunate and dangerous development England should act quickly by forming "this Inland Country into a Government of it self and support it so effectually as to intimidate the Indians." Citing the Iroquois arrangement as an approach worthy of duplication further west, Bradstreet suggested that British sovereignty over the territory be asserted while at the same time a willingness to tolerate a continued Indian presence be demonstrated, so that the Indians realized it to be in "their interest to live well with and under the intire protection of England." Intimidation of the Indians was to be achieved by the posting of a strong military force at Detroit, which "would be a proper place

---

53. Gould to Bradstreet, June 12, 1761, T.P.C., 128/92; Bradstreet to Gould, August 10, 1761, T.P.C., 128/59; Gould to Bradstreet, October 9, 1761, T.P.C., 128/94.

54. Canedy, "An Entrepreneurial History Of The New York Frontier, 1739-1776," 320. This must have been New York currency. Bradstreet to Amherst, October 31, 1760, W.O. 34/57, 213, microfilm, Reel 154 (1).

for the principal seat of Government." Choice of Detroit was dictated by the good land in the area, its excellent geographic position in terms of trade with the Indians, and the existence there of an already established settlement consisting of between "2 & 300 French Families." The military force Bradstreet had in mind was 1,000 "good men" raised by "the best of the Provincial Field officers" and placed upon "the British establishment." What Bradstreet was really proposing was the creation of a new regiment and it was fairly obvious whom he had in mind as regimental colonel. With such protection guaranteed, "numbers of British Subjects" would be persuaded to move westward to develop the Detroit area. In addition the troops themselves could be given land thus allowing the regiment to be reduced in approximately five years when the colony would be self-sufficient and even able to provision any other garrisons which might be needed in the surrounding country. Bradstreet's proposed Detroit colony "will Secure the Frontier of our Colonies, give us the whole of the Indian Trade in safty, effectually put a stop to the great & dangerous French Plan of surrounding us with Inland Colonies."[55] The expansionist dreams of John Bradstreet which had first emerged in the mid-1750s had re-emerged with a new clarity and purpose.

The basic suggestions contained in the Detroit scheme were to be further refined and adjusted during the ensuing months and years as Bradstreet attempted to win their acceptance on both sides of the Atlantic. At times the idea of the colony itself was shelved in favour of emphasizing the formation of a new regiment or reviving his quest for the quartermaster appointment, but Bradstreet inevitably returned to the "Inland colony" suggestion, eventually seeing his own role as that of the territory's first governor. It was clear from the outset, however, that gaining support for even restricted versions of the basic plan was extremely difficult. The first adjustment of his proposals took place in May of 1762 when Bradstreet laid before Amherst a suggestion for the creation of a new regiment. Utilizing colonial officers, he proposed to raise a 1,000-man provincial regiment which was to be placed upon the British establishment for service only in North America. Bradstreet naturally suggested himself as the colonel of the new regiment and if Amherst approved the proposal he was ready to submit "a list of the Names for the Captains Lieutenants & Ensigns." Amherst's reply was quick and disappointing. Although he wished "to have it in My power to do Any thing to Serve you," the "Scheme" was unacceptable.[56]

---

55. Bradstreet to Gould, February 20, 1762, T.P.C., 128/95. It is noteworthy that in November of 1762 Amherst wrote to Secretary of State Egremont recommending that Detroit be made a separate government. See Clarence W. Alvord, *The Mississippi Valley in British Politics*, 1 (New York, 1959), 100. In view of his strong support for Bradstreet's Detroit proposals from 1765 onward, it is entirely possible that Amherst's 1762 recommendation was connected with Bradstreet's 1762 Detroit plan.

56. Bradstreet to Amherst, May 31, 1762, W.O. 34/57, 253, microfilm, Reel 154 (1); Amherst to Bradstreet, June 6, 1762, W.O. 34/56, 228, microfilm, Reel 153 (2); Bradstreet to Gould, June 13, 1762, T.P.C., 128/71.

Temporarily disheartened at this rejection Bradstreet was buoyed a few days later by word that a promotion, of sorts, finally had been granted him. In an April dispatch from Townshend to Amherst, Bradstreet was listed as promoted to the rank of colonel "by Brevet," thus removing the embarrassing qualification placed upon his colonel's commission up to this moment—namely, that he held that rank "in America only." In early June both Amherst and Gould congratulated him on his "promotion" although Gould went considerably beyond mere words of congratulation to suggest the possibilities presented by the new rank. Gould argued that one of Pitt's reasons for having refused in 1761 to recommend Bradstreet's appointment as Quartermaster General had been because Bradstreet had not as yet achieved the "Rank of Colonel in the Army." Since this obstacle had just been removed and Bradstreet's services now were well known to the "present administration," the time appeared ripe to seek "the Post of Q M General instead of Deputy." But clearly such an appointment could only be won with the full support of Amherst. Consequently Bradstreet phrased a probing letter to his commander, outlining the situation as well as asking for "a favorable mention" to the new Secretary of State, Lord Egremont, and guidance concerning how he should apply for the quartermaster position. Amherst, however, had reservations about Bradstreet's immediately seeking another office, pointing out that "too frequent Sollicitations, altho' Some times attended with Success, are in general wrong, and do not Answer the End proposed." Nevertheless, if Bradstreet wanted to make a "fresh application" he was free to do so, addressing himself to the Secretary at War. No doubt when Bradstreet repeated Amherst's reservations to Gould, as he promptly did,[57] his English friend realized that such a lukewarm recommendation was of little help and if presented might even hinder Bradstreet's quartermaster-general application.

Likewise realizing that his chances of promotion in the quartermaster department were slim, Bradstreet revived his other proposal, to raise a regiment "for the Inland service of this Country" or possibly even for service in Newfoundland. Any one of these three appointments was perfectly acceptable to him, he emphasized in letter after letter, as he urged Gould to seek which ever of them he thought most likely to succeed. The disgruntled Bradstreet was perfectly aware that a brevet colonel's rank brought none of the income or front-line action of a regimental colonel and would leave him "in a worse state now than at the end of the last war in point of pay." Only Gould could rescue him from this undeserved neglect. You are my "chief dependence" Brad-

---

57. Townshend to Amherst, April 10, 1762, M.G. 18, L4, Amherst Papers, Packet 38, 35, P.A.C.; Amherst to Bradstreet, June 9, 1762, W.O. 34/56, 229, microfilm, Reel 153 (2); Bradstreet to Gould, June 13, 1762, T.P.C., 128/71; Bradstreet to Amherst, June 13, 1762, W.O. 34/57, 255-56, microfilm, Reel 154 (1); Amherst to Bradstreet, June 20, 1762, W.O. 34/56, 231, microfilm, Reel 153 (2); Bradstreet to Gould, July 19, 1762, T.P.C., 128/72.

street reminded him, and without "bold pushes, there is no succeeding."⁵⁸

Gould was willing but the moment was not right. With the "prevailing opinion of Peace being very near at hand," he felt there was little chance of Bradstreet's "Schemes taking effect." To push for the quartermaster-general appointment at this time, for example, was unrealistic in that such a post was unlikely to be conferred at such a late stage in the war, and "if conferred, would end with the war." Instead, Gould recommended a two-pronged approach to Bradstreet. He should aim at securing "some government to be Established in America upon the Peace" and to this end an application to Lord Egremont was in order. In it "the affair of Frontenac shortly and modestly hinted at" might be helpful since there was the possibility that the deed was forgotten or, more likely, that it was assumed "something has been done for you in consequence thereof long before this time." In addition, Bradstreet should keep his military possibilities alive. He still had a captain's commission in the 60th Regiment and this, along with his brevet colonel rank, might "in time at least secure to you a Regiment." Charles Townshend, Secretary at War, should be addressed concerning military matters with "a warm acknowledgement of his former favours and of his Professions of Friendship" as well as some statement about the need for his "Protection and assistance." Of the two possibilities Gould believed the chances of success were greater and more immediate in the colonial government realm than in the military sphere.⁵⁹ His message was fairly clear but it remained to be seen whether a governmental appointment, once suggested, would prove acceptable to the ambitious and over-reaching Bradstreet.

While his search for preferment in England had made little progress, Bradstreet could take consolation that at least British officialdom indirectly had endorsed his quartermaster performance, in that his pre-1760 accounts had been approved. With the explanation and direction of Philip Schuyler, aided at all times by the knowledgeable Gould, the accounts slowly had wound their way through the various offices until by early June of 1762 they had been passed completely and Schuyler was able to return to New York.⁶⁰ Unfortunately for Bradstreet, on the American side of the Atlantic his quartermaster performance evoked few outward signs of approval. In Albany especially the criticisms continued to fly, while in New York even the usually patient Amherst seemed to weary of the constant turmoil.

Impressment to meet the army's transportation needs, the billeting of troops, and Bradstreet's arrogant actions continued in 1762 to create friction between the civil-military authorities in upper New York. Amherst still tended to back his Albany quartermaster in most matters,

---

58. Ibid., September 16, 1762, T.P.C., 128/74; October 19, 1762, T.P.C., 128/75; September 16, 1762, T.P.C., 128/73.
59. Gould to Bradstreet, October 5, 1762, T.P.C., 128/96.
60. Bradstreet to Amherst, April 18, 1762, W.O. 34/57, 245, microfilm, Reel 154 (1); ibid., August 9, 1762, W.O., 34/57, 269, microfilm, Reel 154 (1).

but on issues where the personality and private interests of Bradstreet, rather than the Crown's interests, seemed to be the nub of the problem, the commander was less willing to be guided by the Colonel's recommendations and descriptions. In the case of impressment, for example, Bradstreet's complaints appeared valid and won immediate support from Amherst.

Bradstreet reported that Volkert Douw, Albany's mayor, at least orally, although unwilling to repeat his statement in writing, had threatened "to order the constables to take up and put into jail the first of his Majesty's troops that should impress horses or carriages." This evidence of a lack of cooperation was further reinforced by a Captain Winepress' statement to Amherst that the civil magistrates were indeed frequently applied to for carriages. But instead of a positive response, they refused to act "or furnish any, and instead of assisting the officers in forwarding the service, they do every thing in their power to hinder and obstruct it." Evidently accepting Winepress and Bradstreet's description of the situation, Amherst urged New York's new Governor, Robert Monckton, to press for Assembly passage of quartering and impressment acts.[61]

Albany officialdom's uncooperative attitude, so often complained of by Bradstreet, was probably a factor in Amherst's decision to support the Colonel in the controversy concerning Albany's sheriff. Harmanus Schuyler's appointment to this office in 1761 had been arranged by Amherst on the advice of Bradstreet. Then in July of 1762 there was a move afoot to get Governor Monckton to turn Schuyler out of office, according to Bradstreet simply because the Sheriff had been "put in" by Amherst and was "exceeding obliging to all the Military." Rumour had it that "Genl Amherst made a point of keep[ing] in the Shiref" and Bradstreet's friend remained in office.[62] Nonetheless, in a number of other matters subdued hints of Amherst's displeasure at some of Bradstreet's actions emerged. The General made clear that he hoped a dispute between Bradstreet and a Mr. Matthews would not result in a "further law suit" and was relieved when the affair was "at last settled by Arbitration." Some of Bradstreet's quartermaster expenditures for 1762, which amounted roughly to £23,760 (N.Y.) in total, were questioned by Amherst. The summer expenses for teamsters, wagoners, wood cutters, and bateau-men seemed excessive to the General, while he also noted three items dating from 1756 which turned up in the accounts although they should have been long since settled.[63]

---

61. Bradstreet to the Mayor of Albany, May 31, 1762 and extract from a letter of Winepress to Amherst, May 31, 1762, in "Aspinwall Papers," M.H.S. *Collections*, 4th Ser., 9 (Boston, 1871), 455-57; Shy, *Toward Lexington*, 167.

62. Bradstreet to Amherst, July 19, 1762, W.O. 34/57, 265, microfilm, Reel 154 (1); William McCracken to Johnson, n.d., in Sullivan *et al.*, *Johnson Papers*, 3, 951-52; Shy, *Toward Lexington*, 167, 170. Brief descriptions of Bradstreet's involvement in Albany political battles are contained in Rogers, *Empire and Liberty*, 129-31; Alice P. Kenney, *The Gansevoorts of Albany: Dutch Patricians in the Upper Hudson Valley* (Syracuse, 1969), 73-74, 85.

63. Amherst to Bradstreet, December 19, 1762, W.O. 34/56, 269, microfilm, Reel

Several of the controversies concerning Bradstreet related to matters involving his private interests rather than his military service and Amherst attempted to steer clear of these. For example, Bradstreet was carefully gathering information concerning a land transaction made by the corporation of Albany in which, he alleged, the Mohawk Indians had been defrauded of land which had not been included in the original agreement. Such accusations of "Dutch roguery in regard to the Scorticoake Indians," which probably were aimed at allowing Bradstreet himself to purchase the land, only served to "raised another Dust in their Eyes" further alienating the good burghers of Albany.[64] In May of 1763 another piece of land became a bone of contention between Bradstreet and the city of Albany. A plot on which a broken-down provision storehouse was situated had been fenced in by one of Bradstreet's cohorts, a Mr. Wood. Promptly the Albany mayor, Bradstreet's old adversary V. P. Douw, and a number of supporters came and pulled the fencing down, arguing that the area was no longer being used for the King's provisions but rather for the private purposes of Wood. Since that "piece of Ground he has taken In is Wanted for the use of the Inhabitants of this City We have ordered our marshel to pull it [the fencing] Down," explained Douw. Maintaining that this was a deliberate interference with His Majesty's service, Bradstreet attempted to bring legal action against the Albany council, linking it with the still pending suit brought against him by the Dutch Church. As he sized up the situation, only two courses were open: either pay off the Dutch Church or defend against the suit in the strongest possible fashion. Assuming that Amherst would detest the former, Bradstreet argued that the best way to pursue the latter course was to "defend the Suit commenced by the Elders & Deacons and to Prosecute the Corporation for Cutting down His Majesty's Fence." Although at first Amherst agreed to this rather unusual approach, eventually Bradstreet's none too penetrating legal analysis was not accepted. While arrangements were made to defend against the Dutch Church, no prosecution of the corporation of Albany was launched. Bradstreet's complaints to Amherst concerning this failure to execute his courtroom strategems only produced the General's vague commitment to "Do the best I can in Behalf of the Crown & its Servants." Judging by an item of £1,000 for the elders and deacons, listed in Bradstreet's 1763 estimates,[65] the best

---

153 (2); April 17, 1763, W.O. 34/56, 283, microfilm, Reel 153 (2); "Account of monies paid by Colonel John Bradstreet... 1762," W.O. 34/57, 302-307, microfilm, Reel 154 (1); Amherst to Bradstreet, November 6, 1762, W.O. 34/57, 289, microfilm, Reel 154 (1).

64. Johnson to Bradstreet, January 4, 176[2?], in Sullivan *et al.*, *Johnson Papers*, 4, 4-5; Johnson to Bradstreet, December 17, 1762, in ibid., 3, 975; Bradstreet to Johnson, December 26, 1762, in ibid., 10, 603-604; Bradstreet to Johnson, January 12, 1763, in ibid., 10, 608; Bradstreet to Johnson, March 16, 1763, in ibid., 13, 284-85; Witham Marsh to Johnson, October 6, 1762, in ibid., 3, 887-88.

65. V. P. Douw to Bradstreet, May 20, 1763, W.O. 34/57, 332, microfilm, Reel 154 (1); Bradstreet to Amherst, May 23, 1763, W.O. 34/57, 328, microfilm, Reel 154 (1); ibid., June 29, 1763, W.O. 34/57, 353-54, microfilm, Reel 154 (1); Amherst to Brad-

Amherst could do in this case was adopt the course described by Bradstreet as detestable and attempt to pay off the Dutch Church.

Bradstreet's chronic squabbles in Albany certainly revealed him as far from the flexible diplomat who could adjust quickly to a sensitive peacetime situation. Rather, he had emerged as a somewhat embarrassing liability to the British army. But the Colonel would never have described himself as anything more than a bluff, straightforward soldier who thrived in a wartime situation. It was only then that his undoubted diligence, overpowering sense of duty, and willingness to cut through all obstacles in the execution of his orders took on virtuous overtones and made him an asset to the British cause. Possibly the moment was at hand when his unique talents would no longer "rust unburnished" but once more would "shine in use."

In the late spring of 1763 the British were given a pointed reminder that peace remained at hand but unachieved when war flared in the "Inland country." Egged on by the Seneca and the Illinois French, the Western Indians struck blow after blow throughout the Great Lakes region until by late June only Detroit, among the posts west of Niagara, remained in British hands.[66] Albany, and with it Bradstreet's quartermaster department, came alive as reinforcements and provisions flowed through on an ever-increasing scale. Once again the arrangement of bateaux, bateau-men, oxen, horses, carriages, and all manner of supplies were of crucial importance, and in letter after letter Amherst revealed his reliance upon Bradstreet in these matters. But immediately upon hearing of the first outbreak of hostilities Amherst hinted that an even more important assignment awaited Bradstreet. "I know that you are always ready" he wrote, however, in this particular instance he hoped the Colonel could move on only a moment's notice, since "if the Savages are not quickly reduced I believe I shall employ you on a Command, which, I am certain will be agreeable to you." Correctly assuming that leadership of a Great Lakes military expedition was to be entrusted to him, Bradstreet countered with the suggestion that construction of the necessary boats should commence immediately while also adding an expression of gratitude "for the honor you intend me."[67]

After a summer of discouraging reports it gradually became clear that Detroit and Niagara at least had held and that the Indian forces

---

street, July 20, 1763, W.O. 34/56, 302, microfilm, Reel 153 (2); Bradstreet to Amherst, August 21, 1763, W.O. 34/57, 367, microfilm, Reel 154 (1); Amherst to Bradstreet, August 28, 1763, Bradstreet MSS, A.A.S.; "Estimate of the Monies due for the Public Service under the Direction of Colonel Bradstreet Dy. Qr. M. General, from 25th December 1762 to November following... ," W.O. 34/57, 392, microfilm, Reel 154 (1).

66. Gipson, *The British Empire Before the American Revolution*, 9, 94, 95, 102.

67. Amherst to Bradstreet, June 22, 1763, W.O. 34/56, 297, microfilm, Reel 153 (2); July 20, 1763, W.O. 34/56, 302, microfilm, Reel 153 (2); August 7, 1763, W.O. 34/56, 307, microfilm, Reel 153 (2); September 18, 1763, W.O. 34/56, 315, microfilm, Reel 153 (2); Bradstreet to Amherst, June 26, 1763, W.O. 34/57, 352, microfilm, Reel 154 (1).

were melting away as winter approached. Nevertheless, for the proper reassertion of British control over the Great Lakes it was equally clear that decisive action would be needed in the spring of 1764. Determined to capitalize upon Amherst's mention of a western command, in early October Bradstreet openly requested such an assignment. A "Vigorous push" was needed "early the next Spring" he argued, in order to prevent the flames of rebellion from spreading and to recover immediately the lost posts. Should Amherst regard him as a "proper person to be entrusted with the execution" of this mission, Bradstreet pledged to "use my utmost endeavours to acquit my Self to Your Excellencys Satisfaction." Furthermore, he was ready with both figures and advice. With Amherst's permission he willingly would provide his opinions concerning the number of men and the type of preparations required for the expedition. There was need of an early decision on this matter, he stressed, since large quantities of provisions had to be moved to Lake Ontario and then on to Niagara if the operation was to be successfully attempted. An "extremely happy" Bradstreet soon discovered that his application had Amherst's full support. "Your Offers of Service are very agreable to me: Tis what I have already thought of" wrote his commander, although the final details of the spring expedition still remained to be worked out.[68] The conqueror of Fort Frontenac finally had received his long sought after front-line command, with all the dreams of glory that it presented.

At the same time as this American opportunity opened up, Bradstreet was also on the threshold of receiving the British recognition which had so long eluded him. However, while his western command was the immediate result of the fortuitous reopening of hostilities, his English reward represented the culmination of another faithful year's labour by Charles Gould. Throughout 1763 his English friend had kept energetic pressure on various ministerial figures, and by public petitions, private cajolery, and sheer persistence appeared on the verge of securing an appointment for Bradstreet. To a limited extent Gould was aided in these solicitations by Captain Mungo Campbell, whom Bradstreet dispatched to England in November of 1762 well laden with the colonel's various schemes,[69] and by Bradstreet's own alteration of his basic proposals in order to suit the changing American or British needs.

After receiving Gould's instructions of October 1762, concerning his greater chances for a governmental rather than a military appointment, Bradstreet began a limited adjustment. He now suggested that the governorship of his proposed Detroit colony would be gladly accepted although he still hoped for something more in the military line, such as quartermaster-general or a regimental command over "the

---

68. Bradstreet to Amherst, October 6, 1763, W.O. 34/57, 377-78, microfilm, Reel 154 (1); October 18, 1763, W.O. 34/57, 381, microfilm, Reel 154 (1); Amherst to Bradstreet, October 12, 1763, W.O. 34/56, 322, microfilm, Reel 153 (2).

69. Bradstreet to Gould, November 14, 1762, T.P.C., 128/77.

four New York Independent Companys." When Gould took up these suggestions with Robert Wood, who remained Undersecretary of State although now serving Lord Egremont, Wood made clear his continued concern for Bradstreet's cause but felt the regimental or quartermaster appointments were not "practicable." But he, like Gould, looked to "some good Government upon the Settling of North America" as an accessible reward. At the moment, though, changes within the administration made it difficult to push for any appointment. It was rumoured, according to Gould, that Egremont was about to be removed while Townshend had resigned as Secretary at War, having been replaced by Welbore Ellis.[70]

Keeping abreast of all these changes and directing his presentations to where they best served Bradstreet, Gould tenaciously continued his lobbying. Memorials on Bradstreet's behalf were addressed to George Grenville, First Lord of the Treasury, and to Lord Egremont, who continued as Secretary of State; while at the same time Bradstreet's prospects were discussed with the undersecretaries of the departments involved. The result was reassuring words but no action. Grenville was "perfectly well acquainted with Colo. Bradstreet's Character and shall most willingly concur, in whatever the rest of the King's servants shall think a proper acknowledgment of his Services." Lord Egremont mentioned Bradstreet's case "to the *King, who* is apprised of your Merit; and that some care will be certainly taken of you." Such encouraging comments could lead the optimist to assume the long-awaited rewards were at hand, but the realistic Gould was all too well aware that "many untoward circumstances happened, in the Changes & chances of publick affairs." In Bradstreet's case by now it was reasonably clear that any reward would come from the Secretary of State's department and it was this department which witnessed several important changes in the summer of 1763. In July the helpful and sympathetic Robert Wood retired from his office, while in August the obviously interested and well-memorialized Egremont died. Captain Mungo Campbell was now in England, having delivered Bradstreet's various communications to Gould and others, and he had watched with interest the progress of the Colonel's case, since he was earmarked for a subordinate position in any office Bradstreet gained. His comments appeared to summarize well his friend's plight at this moment. "The fluctuation of the Great, affect those in an inferior sphere" he observed, and then later he expressed the fear "that My Lord Egremont's death will greatly affect our Friend's interests."[71]

---

70. Ibid., December 9, 1762, T.P.C., 128/79; Note signed by Gould, January 26, 1763, T.P.C., 128/97; Gould to Bradstreet, January 7, 1763, T.P.C., 128/97.

71. "The Memorial of Colonel John Bradstreet . . . To the Right Honble Geo Grenville," May 12, 1763, T.P.C., 128/441; Gould to Egremont, July 12, 1763, T.P.C., 128/120; Gould to Bradstreet, May 20, 1763, T.P.C., 128/98; July 8, 1763, T.P.C., 128/99; Mungo Campbell to Gould, July 27, 1763, T.P.C., 128/104; Campbell to Gould, August 29, 1763, T.P.C., 128/106.

Indeed it did appear that ministerial changes threatened once more to undermine Bradstreet's cause. On this occasion though, Gould turned the changes to his friend's advantage. Determined to push for a definite decision, Gould enlisted the now-retired Wood in one more effort, this time directed at Egremont's successor, Lord Halifax. An explanatory note from Wood combined with Gould's repeated solicitations finally produced Halifax's agreement "to appoint Colo. Bradstreet either to the Lieut. Governmt. of Montreal or Trois Rivières, when Colo. Burton's choice is known."[72] Bradstreet's contribution to the conquest of Canada at last had earned him the possible lieutenant-governorship of whichever of the two Canadian towns Ralph Burton chose to decline.

But would the Lieutenant-Governor of St. John's, Newfoundland, regard the lieutenant-governorship of Montreal or Trois Rivières as an acceptable promotion, let alone the final settlement for his contribution during the entire war? The first mention to Bradstreet concerning the possible appointment openly acknowledged the award's limitations but strongly emphasized its acceptability as well. Gould stated that both he and Sir Richard Lyttleton, recently returned to London, "think it is by all means advisable for you to accept for the present though we are sensible you have reason to expect something better and will let no opportunity slip to promote it."[73] Despite such words of guidance the final decision remained with Bradstreet alone. And in the same months during which Gould's lobbying reached its "successful" conclusion, Bradstreet's correspondence with Gould and requests to Amherst revealed that his attention and desires now were firmly focused on the undeveloped "Inland Country" rather than on the recently conquered Quebec.

As the Great Lakes region burst into flames Bradstreet at first used this outbreak of hostilities merely as a personal vindication, pointing out to Gould that had his scheme of a strong Detroit colony been accepted such an Indian uprising would have been more effectively and immediately met. Then sensing that it was not too late to push his scheme, but rather that it was perhaps the ideal moment to attempt to win its acceptance in England, he resubmitted an only slightly altered version. With a force now increased in size to "three thousand good Men well officer'd," a well-defended Detroit settlement could be established as a base for operations against the Indians. "Perhaps Government may now See the reasonableness of that Plan and Adopt it," he suggested, "if so, I should be happy to be employ'd in it, and pray say so for me, it being the only way of keeping proper possession of that Country, punish & awe the Indians and Secure the Frontiers of the Colonies." Strangely enough, or perhaps not so strangely, Mungo Campbell at the same time took up the same themes that Bradstreet was

---

72. Edward Sedgwick to Gould, October 4, 1763, T.P.C., 128/110; Gould to Bradstreet, October 6, 1763, T.P.C., 128/101.

73. Ibid.

expounding. In letters to Gould and in a memorial placed in the hands of Stewart McKenzie, brother of the Earl of Bute, the merits of a plan for "Overawing the Indians by strengthening the Colony of Detroit" were developed at length.[74]

Consequently, even as Gould reported the possible reward of a lieutenant-governorship, he also responded to Bradstreet and Campbell's latest suggestions by admitting the continued potential of the Detroit proposals. He had persuaded Wood before his retirement to mention "that same scheme" to Lord Halifax and thus remained hopeful. But by early November the Detroit plan was abruptly shunted aside because of Amherst's designating Bradstreet as commander of the western expedition scheduled for the spring of 1764. Reporting this important assignment to Gould, before word of his possible lieutenant-governorship had reached him, Bradstreet's feelings of neglect clearly emerged. The Colonel petulantly commented "that altho no notice is taken of my particular Services in the last Wars, still my zeal & attachment for his Majesty's honor & wellfair of my Country is ever in my View & that my Ardour is not to be dampt tho unnoticed." He then proceeded to balance this brooding resentment by quoting some of Amherst's kind words of appreciation concerning his willingness to serve. The implication was that at least his commander was willing to reward meritorious service with encouraging comments and important assignments. Nonetheless, even while savouring this new appointment, largely gained on the strength of his own abilities and overtures, Bradstreet still could see the utility of Gould. He hoped his English friend now would seek on his behalf "a Commission as Brigr. General during this Service with the usual Allowance."[75] Gould's lobbying activities thus were redirected and linked up with the inland expedition. Even more than his friend's activities, however, Bradstreet's thoughts now were firmly fixed on the western command and the beckoning prospects of glory and advancement it seemed to offer.

Given Bradstreet's prevailing feeling that he had been overlooked for far too long, as well as his confident expectations that the western expedition was a golden opportunity to demonstrate anew his valuable services to the Crown, and thus push for even grander rewards, it was extremely unlikely that a minor lieutenant-governor's post would meet with any great enthusiasm from him. Yet on first hearing of the possible Quebec award he was properly thankful to Gould and, although letting slip the remark that "perhaps the Service I may be of in this Indian affair may merit some thing more than a Lieut. Government," advised Gould to accept for him "what ever I am appointed." Two days later, undoubtedly after some hard second thoughts on the

---

74. Bradstreet to Gould, July 12, 1763, T.P.C., 128/81, August 13, 1763, T.P.C., 128/82; Campbell to Gould, August 29, 1763, T.P.C., 128/106; October 24, 1763, T.P.C., 128/107. A copy of the memorial (128/442) was included with the latter letter to Gould. See also Campbell to Gould, August 20, 1763, T.P.C., 128/105.

75. Gould to Bradstreet, October 6, 1763, T.P.C., 128/101; Bradstreet to Gould, November 2, 1763, T.P.C., 128/86.

matter, what had been originally a slip re-emerged as a blunt, crisp expression of his real feelings. He begged Gould, "do not send me to Canada," arguing that once returned from this expedition with his years of seniority as lieutenant-governor and rank as brigadier-general, he would have considerably "more weight."[76] He had decided to let the Quebec appointment pass in favour of the greater honours which awaited him upon the successful completion of his western command. It was a gamble but to the long-neglected, under-rewarded, and overly confident Bradstreet, it was a gamble well worth taking.

Potentially Bradstreet now stood on the threshold of great achievements and rewards. In more concrete terms, however, he had little to show for his strenuous exertions from 1759 to 1763. To be sure, his financial position appeared to be far sounder than that expected of a person who earned under £500 sterling annually from all his offices combined. A 1760 gift of £350 and a 1761 loan of £1,000 to his friend Philip Schuyler[77] were but two of many indications that in strictly monetary terms these had been prosperous years for Bradstreet. Nevertheless, very little had been gained from his well-organized and shrewdly articulated campaign for higher military rank and further colonial appointments. He remained a deputy quartermaster-general and lieutenant-governor while his change in rank from lieutenant-colonel to brevet colonel still left him without the much desired regimental command.

But perhaps the potential of the western command and its possible rewards far outweighed these temporary failures and limited gains. Bradstreet had every reason to believe that with a continuation of the firm support of his commanding officer, Jeffery Amherst, and another brilliant military success, this time in the western interior, this pattern of neglect could be altered. The old hope revealed at Louisbourg in 1745 and Frontenac in 1758, of rescuing his stagnating military career by a dramatic triumph, emerged once more. What the dedicated efforts of his friends and patrons could not achieve in England he would win on the field of battle in America. Yet the essential ingredients in the achievement of this hope were a cooperative and sympathetic commanding officer and a clear military victory in the west. Already at least the first of these had vanished. In early November Bradstreet received from Amherst what he described as the "only letter I have received from Your Excellency which gave me pain, during the time I have had the honor to be under Your Command." Amherst wrote concerning his own imminent "return to England" which was to leave the "Command of the Troops" in the hands of Major-General Gage.[78] The "newer world" in which Bradstreet now found himself was to be the

---

76. Ibid., December 10, 1763, T.P.C., 128/89; December 12, 1763, T.P.C., 128/90.
77. Gerlach, *Philip Schuyler*, 78. This was probably New York currency.
78. Bradstreet to Amherst, November 7, 1763, W.O. 34/57, 390, microfilm, Reel 154 (1); Amherst to Bradstreet, November 1, 1763, W.O. 34/56, 327, microfilm, Reel 153 (2). See Shy, *Toward Lexington*, 122-23, for details of what amounted to a recall rather than merely a leave of absence.

coldly unsympathetic military command of Thomas Gage. In such a situation should the Colonel mishandle the inland expedition his military career would be in ruins. Bradstreet's gamble on a western command suddenly had become the greatest gamble of his entire career.

Chapter VIII

Preparations for Detroit

Pontiac's rising provoked a British military response and a more determined attempt to resolve Indian problems in the American interior. In military matters Thomas Gage, as acting Commander-in-Chief, was the final architect and director of operations, responsible for success or failure. Indian affairs, on the other hand, were Sir William Johnson's special responsibility, a fact reaffirmed by the British government's 1764 acknowledgment of his complete and virtually independent authority as Indian Superintendent in the Great Lakes region.[1] It was John Bradstreet's misfortune to have clashed with both of these men in the recent past, and even as his expeditionary force took shape there were signs that his ambitious and headstrong approach would create friction once again. These were powerful foes, dangerous officials to alienate, and constant confrontation would severely test the Colonel's abilities and ingenuity as well as the strength of his English connections. Indeed, disagreements and wrangling before the Detroit campaign was launched might fatally weaken the entire operation or at least considerably alter Bradstreet's perception of the expedition's basic purpose.

Preparations for the westward thrust were underway in November of 1763, at the very moment when the command of the British forces in North America passed from Amherst to Gage. Immediately there was disagreement between Bradstreet and his new commander concerning these preparations. The particular point at issue was the size of the force to be placed under Bradstreet's command, although tied in with this question were Bradstreet's own conceptions of what was necessary for his troops' proper equipment and success and what the expedition

---

1. See Peter Marshall, "Colonial Protest and Imperial Retrenchment: Indian Policy 1764-1768," *Journal of American Studies*, 5 (1971), 1-2.

actually was meant to achieve in the west. On all three matters Bradstreet's views were different from Gage's.

To a great extent these initial difficulties appear to have resulted from Amherst's giving one impression to Bradstreet and quite another to Gage. This was not a suprising development, since while the general outlines of the expedition had been decided upon by Amherst, and would have to be accepted and executed by Gage, specific details were left somewhat vague and open to alteration by the new commander. For example, in the matter of the force's size, Bradstreet had come away from a meeting with Amherst believing "every thing is agreed on; I am to have about 4000 Chosen Men well appointed." But it soon became obvious that the size and composition of Bradstreet's command was not, in fact, firmly settled upon. Several weeks later, in outlining to Gage the intended "Operations, by Niagara," Amherst hinted at a smaller number of troops and rather imprecisely spelled out how the force was to be made up. By this time, he informed his successor, he had asked New York to contribute 1,400 and New Jersey 600 men to the expedition. These were to be joined by any regulars who could be spared from Niagara. In addition there was the possibility of moving the 42nd Regiment, designated for garrison duty at Detroit and other inland posts, westward as a part of Bradstreet's force rather than having it advance by way of Fort Pitt. The decision concerning the 42nd's route was left up to Gage, however.[2] Hence by mid-November Bradstreet's expedition had quickly shrivelled from his optimistic estimate of 4,000 soldiers to an unspecified number of regulars, and a possible 2,000 provincials.

While the depleted strength of his assault force quickly was noted by Bradstreet, throughout the entire campaign he never seemed to understand the carefully restricted military mission actually intended for him. At this early point and throughout his movement to Detroit, Bradstreet persisted in believing that both the waging of war and the making of peace had been entrusted to him. His command's two-pronged task was outlined to Charles Gould in early November. The Colonel firmly believed that "our business is to drub those Nations of Savages at War with Us and endeavour to gain over to our interest such as have not declair'd by well tim'd presents at the head of a respectable Force it being idle to think of making War against all the Savages or making them presents but in the manner just mention'd." At this moment Bradstreet saw himself as both Indian fighter and Indian diplomat and, whether quite deliberately or out of careless inattention, failed to perceive that Gage was determined to limit him to a military role while allowing Johnson to handle all Indian negotiations. Evidently it was Amherst who gave Bradstreet the impression of this wider

---

2. Bradstreet to Gould, November 2, 1763, T.P.C., 128/86, N.L.W.; Amherst to Gage, November 17, 1763, Clarence E. Carter, ed., *The Correspondence of General Thomas Gage with the Secretaries of State, and with the War Office and the Treasury 1763-1775* (New Haven, 1933), 2, 211.

role, although in handing over authority to Gage this same Amherst carefully distinguished between Bradstreet's military operation and Indian matters. He explicitly advised Gage of his opinion that when "the Indians, who have Committed the Hostilities, are Sufficiently Punished, I would leave it to Sir William Johnson, who is the best Judge of the Manner of Treating with them, to Conclude a Peace with them."[3] Consciously ignoring or inadvertently overlooking this all-important distinction between his own military responsibilities and Johnson's authority as a peace-maker, Bradstreet dared to act in both capacities, thereby providing the basic grounds for Johnson and Gage's later criticisms of his western performance. Whether deliberate or not, his misapprehension concerning the scope of his responsibilities was at least consistent and complete.

This vision of responsibilities wider than the purely military remained serenely intact while Bradstreet's conceptions of the men and materials to be made available to him were being abruptly shattered by Gage. In November and December of 1763, as Gage settled into his new office, his scepticism about Bradstreet's demands and suggestions concerning preparations for his spring campaign became more and more pronounced. Sensing that his manpower and equipment needs were being underestimated by Gage and that his commander was lacking any sense of urgency about arranging the movement of provisions forward to Niagara in time for their spring use, Bradstreet moved to meet these problems in his usual tactlessly straightforward fashion. "Permit me, Sir, to say," he wrote Gage, "that when I offer'd my Self for this Service it was on condition I should be well appointed in Men & otherwise & nothing necessary for the Service grudg'd, which was promis'd me." Consequently the stockpiling of supplies and the construction of the number of bateaux needed, by a force which Bradstreet now expected to number 3,600 men, had commenced. But these activities were hampered by a lack of money to pay the carpenters, a shortage of provisions, as well as an apparent willingness to saddle him "with Battoes of all kinds so unfit for the Service as intirely to prevent its success for a saveing of four or five hundred pounds currency." Rather than use "this Rubbish of Battoes" Bradstreet was willing to pay the boat construction costs out of his own pocket. But he was "persuaded" that with Gage's approval and cooperation such an embarrassing outlay would be unnecessary. If Gage would approve his suggested preparations Bradstreet was confident that "I shall have the Satisfaction of being allow'd every thing necessary & proper for carrying on the Service and be sent of[f] the moment the Ice will permit."[4]

It was the usual Bradstreet attempt to bluster and intimidate by emphasizing the urgency of his assignment as well as his commander's implicit responsibility to carry through what was already well launched.

---

3. Bradstreet to Gould, November 2, 1763, T.P.C., 128/86; Amherst to Gage, November 17, 1763, Carter, *Gage Correspondence*, 2, 212.

4. Bradstreet to Gage, November 27, 1763, Gage Papers, A.S./9, U.M.C.L.

Such a high-pressure approach had achieved varying degrees of success with Shirley, Loudoun, Abercromby, and Amherst. It completely failed, however, with Gage. Obviously irritated at what he deemed to be Bradstreet's exaggerated manpower expectations and premature preparations, Gage crisply squelched every one of Bradstreet's major points. "I can't tell in what manner Sir Jeffry proposed making up 3600 Man having never talked of any such Numbers," he commented concerning the size of the force. Indeed, New York had consented to raise only 300 of the 1,400 men requested by Amherst, while New Jersey's 600 man commitment remained in abeyance until its Assembly determined whether the various New England colonies also were willing to contribute to the expedition. Moreover, Gage was at a loss to explain how "the other 1600 were to be compleated" although the "addition of Regular Troops to join them I am certain never could" make up the remainder. Summarily dismissed as well were Bradstreet's apprehensions about the state of his supplies and bateaux. "Common Sense tells Me," Gage sarcastically commented, "that if I fit out a Body of Troops for any Expedition, it behoves me to furnish every thing necessary to procure success." At the same time, however, preparations must be made with careful economy avoiding needless expenses. Possibly some new bateaux were needed "but I could not tell the King's Ministers that his Boats which have been used & found to answer for Eight Years together, were at length discovered to be good for Nothing." More importantly, until the colonial manpower contributions were clarified and finalized, Gage felt that "the immense preparations you talk of making immediately, must be postponed."[5]

Bradstreet was never one to let criticism pass unchallenged and a spirited rejoinder might have been expected. But Gage's strictures must have come as a bit of a shock to one accustomed to the far more hesitant and diplomatic reservations raised by his former commander, the compliant Amherst. No doubt as a result, Bradstreet's reply was rather subdued and took issue only with Gage's comments concerning the bateaux and "the immence preparation you take notice of." Regarding the former, Bradstreet begged "leave to observe I did not mean to say Battoes were good for nothing." On the contrary, they remained quite serviceable for the transportation of troops, but his point had been that in the service for which they were intended, the movement of provisions, they were of questionable adequacy. Turning to the matter of extravagant preparations, Bradstreet invoked his former commander's thoughts as justification. "Sir Jeffery Amherst was sensible of the necessity of leaving this Place [Albany] the moment the Ice would permit and that as little Stop would be made at the carrying place of Niagara as possible." Hence, provisioning preparations had to go forward "with Dispatch" so as not to delay the spring operations. Underlining the need for early and extensive preparations,

---

5. Gage to Bradstreet, December 12, 1763, Gage Papers, A.S./10.

Bradstreet strongly emphasized that "nothing can be done against Savages but by Surprise . . . which is one of the great reasons for getting over the Carrying place of Niagara and to Detroit before the Enemy can be appris'd of Us." Actually both Bradstreet's points appeared quite valid, but they brought forth only a further cold response from Gage. The General was very aware "that the Vessels were not Sufficient for the transportation of a large Stock of Provisions," but Bradstreet had to cope with this difficulty by employing "other Methods to get the Provisions to Niagara."[6] In effect Gage was allowing preparations for Bradstreet's spring campaign to continue, but on a much reduced scale and at a slower pace, and without all the additional bateaux Bradstreet felt were so badly needed. This initial exchange between the General and the Colonel provided an excellent indication of what their future relationship would be like. Bradstreet finally had come up against a commanding officer determined to bridle him once and for all.

Bradstreet never displayed any reluctance about criticizing the way in which American military campaigns were handled or mishandled. And on this particular occasion, with his own plans being stymied and his personal reputation at stake, he quickly informed his English friend, Charles Gould, of the several difficulties and disappointments his expedition had encountered up to that point. The colonies were damned for their "backwardness . . . in furnishing the Troops ask'd of them" which was delaying the entire operation, perhaps setting it back to "late next summer" before his forces could get underway. His command was "ill appointed," declining in potential size to "but three thousand Men," and of very poor quality since he estimated that approximately two-thirds of his troops would "go directly from the Plow to Engage the most Subtle Enemy on Earth." To rescue the situation he hoped Jeffery Amherst's timely arrival in England would provide "a true State of the Savages," which Bradstreet apparently assumed would influence "his Majestys Commands, respecting the Service to the Westward." It was his totally unwarranted expectation that these non-existent instructions from England also would contain "orders for my Endeavouring to make Strong Alliances with those Savages Inhabiting between the Mississippi & the Great Lakes."[7]

Reliance on Amherst and altered orders from home revealed either considerable naiveté or extreme subtlety on Bradstreet's part. By this point he must have realized that with Gage in command there was little chance of conducting the freewheeling operation he desired. Restrictions and restraints were clearly the order of the day rather than flexible cooperation and lenient attention to Bradstreet's suggestions and demands. Thus, the Colonel might very well have been attempting to by-pass Gage by securing orders from home allowing the sort of

---

6. Bradstreet to Gage, December 22, 1763, Gage Papers, A.S./11; Gage to Bradstreet, December 28, 1763, Gage Papers, A.S./11.

7. Bradstreet to Gould, December 5, 1763, T.P.C., 128/88; ibid., November 24, 1763, 128/87; ibid., December 25, 1763, 128/91; ibid., January 9, 1764, 128/22.

campaign which Bradstreet thought Amherst originally had in mind for him. One suspects, however, that his misplaced hopes were not a subtle ploy but merely another indication of how badly he had misread Amherst's thoughts on the expedition. In reality, there was no need for further instructions from England since Amherst had left Gage with the general outline of the campaign and his successor had received orders from home to adhere to these plans.[8] Furthermore, Bradstreet's hopes for the specific mention of his treaty-making powers already had been scotched by Amherst when he suggested to Gage that Johnson was best equipped to handle such Indian matters. Ironically, even if Amherst had been willing to involve himself in a reshaping of campaign instructions on Bradstreet's behalf, his efforts were unlikely to have met with any success because in England at that time it was Amherst who was receiving a great deal of the blame for the entire Indian rebellion.[9] Quite clearly the home authorities regarded Gage as perfectly competent to handle the American situation and Bradstreet could expect no English intervention to undermine Gage's authority.

By way of contrast there was no question of subtlety or naiveté involved when Bradstreet discussed his plans for the commercial development of the west. His continuing preoccupation with the economic potential of Detroit and the inland country were well-worn themes frequently repeated since 1755. Bradstreet clearly felt that economic and territorial gains in the Great Lakes region were vital corollaries to his military thrust. The "great advantage to the Nation" accruing from the encouragement of "two or three thousand Families to settle at Detroit" was emphasized for Gould's benefit along with the need for government control of the profitable Indian trade in the area. Of course a commander for the sizeable garrison to be stationed there was necessary[10] and, if a governor was ever required, what better choice could be made than John Bradstreet himself.

In succeeding letters variations of the basic scheme were articulated as different needs presented themselves. Even if the initial campaign should be totally unsuccessful, Bradstreet argued, further action was needed to guarantee the British hold on the west. Without "a respectable Force kept up in the Center of the Savages, namely Detroit, we shall never be in safty." The government may be tempted to postpone such an effective occupation but "believe me the longer it is put off the worse it will be." Now was the time to act. And since the number of regular troops needed for the country's proper security, protection of trade, and intimidation of the Indians was lacking, surely the wisdom and need of his plan for raising a regiment would be granted. In early January of 1764 rumours of French intrigue amongst the Indians were reported as another pretext for "having Sufficient Force in that up-Land Country as shall strike Terrour & amazement into them Both."

---

8. See Shy, *Toward Lexington*, 135.
9. Ibid., 122-24.
10. Bradstreet to Gould, November 2, 1763, T.P.C., 128/86.

When this situation was joined to "the badness of the Troops" raised for his expedition and the "Little time the Service is to last, Viz, five or six Months," it was clear to Bradstreet that more permanent and effective action was needed. He could only pray that a final solution would emerge soon in the form of word that "His Majesty had been Graciously pleas'd to order the Regiment to be rais'd & the Plan carry'd into execution which I first propos'd."[11] While his military campaign plodded slowly through its formative stages, the other side of it, namely the settlement of Detroit and the tapping of the economic potential of the Great Lakes empire, was already in well-articulated full flight.

During the early months of 1764, plans for the expeditionary force considerably accelerated as its numbers and composition began to take final shape. In fact, common problems linked with the formation of the western contingent created a rare and short-lived period of harmonious agreement between the Colonel and Thomas Gage. A tactfully deferential approach to his commander evidently contributed to this at least temporarily improved relationship. Bradstreet deplored the difficulties under which "His Majestys Service" laboured "as long as the Provincial Assemblys are to Judge of the propriety of the Commanders in Chiefs measures and act thereon as they please." Admittedly Bradstreet had the strength of his own expedition in mind as well when he supported Gage in his frustrating negotiations with the various colonial governments. But the criticism of the reluctant and ungrateful Americans, which continued to spew forth, no doubt coincided with the exasperated Gage's thoughts on the subject. It greatly disturbed the commander-in-chief that several of the colonies begged off contributing on the superficial pretext that the Indians were now seeking peace. Only a renewed outbreak of hostilities in the Detroit area, it seemed, would convince them of the continuing Indian menace and stimulate their support of Bradstreet's westward thrust. Such a "Disagreeable" situation was "enough to try your patience" Gage moaned to Bradstreet. The Colonel quickly joined this condemnation of faint-hearted and excuse-seeking colonials. "If the Eastern Governments, or Assemblys had common sense," he replied, "they would know that no safe & lasting peace can be made with Savages but at the head of a respectable Force."[12]

The continuing animosity which Bradstreet met in Albany and upper New York allowed him to demonstrate his own difficulties with the balky and uncooperative colonials. The still unsettled suit launched by the Dutch Church hung over his head, provoking a long explanation to Gage and predictable comments on Albany's general "Ingratitude to his Majesty" and "Knavery" in all such matters. The town's hostility was borne out by the violent incidents created by the civil-military friction which continued to occur. One such encounter took place immediately

---

11. Ibid., December 25, 1763, T.P.C., 128/91; January 9, 1764, T.P.C., 128/122.
12. Gage to Bradstreet, February 26, 1764, Gage Papers, A.S./14; February 13, 1764; Bradstreet to Gage, March 4, 1764, Gage Papers, A.S./15.

after a gathering of several officers at Bradstreet's abode. After drinking "pritty freely" and dining with Colonel Bradstreet, two lieutenants named Gillan and Godwin decided to seek "some Female acquaintance." Denied entry at the house where their lady friends lived, they enlisted some soldiers in support of their none too virtuous cause only to find a mob awaiting them on their return. Eventually both sides dispersed but later that night some of the soldiers returned and damaged the house in question which only further outraged the local citizenry.[13]

Unfortunately Gage offered neither Bradstreet nor posterity any official comment on this particular incident. But in cases where the military appeared to be on much safer ground in charging civilian harassment and lack of cooperation, the General revealed himself as being quite ready to support even an officer such as Bradstreet, about whom he had certain reservations. For example, early in 1764 the old problem of quartering troops arose and Gage was quick to take Bradstreet's side in the ensuing dispute. Some of the New York troops, journeying to German Flats, had to be billeted overnight in Schenectady; this chore was handled by the local justice who, by coincidence, turned out to be Bradstreet's assistant, John Glen. One resident, Ten Eyck by name, objected to the imposition and by using his fists and a gun managed to eject the three soldiers assigned to his home. The upshot was that John Glen found himself "indicted by the Grand Jury for giving the Billet" while the hapless troopers wound up in jail. Bradstreet argued that it was incumbent upon Gage to act quickly to protect Justice Glen. Otherwise should "these Reptiles" win their case against him, other justices "will give no assistance to His Majestys Service when requir'd" and "every thing will be obstructed." In view of the "perverse and obstinate Spirits of the Inhabitants," Gage was not at all surprised at the incident and promised to write the New York Lieutenant-Governor "in the Strongest Manner" complaining of the treatment meted out to Glen and the soldiers. The same day he provided Lieutenant-Governor Cadwallader Colden with an almost verbatim repetition of Bradstreet's argument that Glen's prosecution opened the way to further magistrate prosecutions which inevitably would "put a total Stop to the Publick Service" whenever troops had to move from one place to the next.[14]

Such quick and complete attention in the early months of 1764 to Bradstreet's complaints, as well as the Colonel's own confident reliance upon his cooperative commander, were destined to be elements of a passing phase in their relationship. As spring approached, Bradstreet's

---

13. Ibid., March 27, 1764, Gage Papers, A.S./16; R. Elliot to Gage, March 15, 1764, Gage Papers, A.S./15. This controversy was not resolved until the spring of 1766 when Gage authorized Bradstreet to pay off the Dutch Church. See Gage to Bradstreet, April 19, 1766, Gage Papers, A.S./50. For details of the actual charges, see J. T. Kempe to Bradstreet, September 9, 1765, Schuyler Papers, Box 9, N.Y.P.L.

14. Bradstreet to Gage, January 23, 1764, Gage Papers, A.S./12; Gage to Bradstreet, January 30, 1764, Gage Papers, A.S./13; Gage to Colden, January 30, 1764, ibid.

apprehensions re-emerged concerning the quality and size of his forces, as well as the delay in their dispatch to Detroit. But his complaints seemed only to further irritate Gage, bringing his biting sarcasm to the surface once again. By the end of March the General could definitely promise Bradstreet only that New York would contribute 500 men and New Jersey had voted 240 men, while 300 were expected from Canada, and he had heard Connecticut was to raise 260. A dejected Bradstreet by that time had discovered some of his recruits to be of dubious calibre since he had heard that "at least one half of the York Troops never Fir'd a Musket." Bluntly pessimistic at the way things were proceeding, he now felt "our Numbers fall much short of what is effectually necessary to push the Service intended" and placed increasing reliance on an early start to the campaign which would at least give him the advantage of surprise. Thus, the first feelers went out to Gage concerning exactly when orders would be issued officially placing the troops under his command, since "the sooner it is done the better it will be for the Service."[15]

His reservations and disappointments about the expedition arrangements were even more frankly stated to Charles Gould. The "Ingratitude of the Colonies" was discussed at length, since Bradstreet considered it particularly "vexatious to see the Nation put to great expence in the necessary preparations for bringing the Savages to reason & Securing the Inland Country and Men wanting to carry it into execution when they can be had with the least trouble & little or no expence divided amongst the Several Colonies." Dealing with the weaknesses of the force which was assembling, as well as the slowness with which it was being brought together, Bradstreet eschewed any responsibility for these problems since "every thing depending on Me ... is in excellent order." But the element of surprise was slipping away, the force's numbers were "unequal to the Task," and to cap it all "one half" of his troops "never saw a Gun fir'd at an Enemy and no time [remained] for amendment" of this rather major deficiency.[16]

Thanks to Gould's tireless lobbying, Bradstreet's British fortunes appeared reasonably well in hand in 1764, although nothing further in the way of concrete rewards had yet materialized. The Colonel's request for the rank of brigadier-general during the coming campaign, as well as his hope "not to be Sent a Lieut. Govr. to Canada," had been faithfully followed up by Gould. In the case of the Trois Rivières lieutenant-governorship Gould discovered additional reasons, besides Bradstreet's own reluctance, to decline diplomatically the possible appointment. After gathering further information concerning this office, he found it "considerably inferior" to his original expectations in terms of its "Value, [and] ... its Nature." There was also a residence requirement which he felt Bradstreet would find unacceptable.

---

15. Gage to Bradstreet, March 18, 1764, Gage Papers, A.S./15; ibid., March 26, 1764, Gage Papers, A.S./16; Bradstreet to Gage, February 27, 1764, Gage Papers, A.S./14.
16. Bradstreet to Gould, April 1, 1764, T.P.C., 128/123.

Moreover, Gould discovered that the recently arrived Amherst had another nominee, Colonel Frederick Haldimand, in mind for the appointment. Since Halifax already had promised Gould that the office would go to Bradstreet, Gould decided that Bradstreet's polite withdrawal would remove any possible embarrassment to Halifax and head off any possible displeasure on Amherst's part. In truth, Gould reasoned that such an approach could be used to put Bradstreet even more in Amherst's good graces. He decided "to wait upon Genl. Amherst, and to acquaint him of the Promise, which I had obtained in your favour before his arrival and at the Same time to pay him the Compliment of declining in favour of his Nomination, hoping for his Assistance in recommending you to something more immediately in your Profession."[17]

Such manoeuvres proved somewhat unnecessary in Amherst's case, since when Gould met with him it immediately became crystal clear that Sir Jeffery was extremely "well disposed" towards Bradstreet. Speaking of the Colonel with "great Justice" he informed Gould that he always had recommended Bradstreet in the strongest possible terms and remained ever ready to testify to his merit. The strategem of the diplomatic withdrawal, however, was not abandoned but was employed during Gould's next important meeting, a session with Lord Halifax. Gould reported that he "made his Lordship an offer of taking him out of the disagreeable Situation either of not performing his promise with regard to you, or of Setting aside the Genl's Nomination, by declining your Pretensions to the government in question relying on his Lordship's good Offices to reward your Services in Some other way." Well satisfied with this arrangement, Halifax expressed a very high opinion of Bradstreet's "Spirited behaviour" leading Gould to believe that if his Lordship continued as Secretary of State for any length of time they could expect "his Countenance and Assistance."[18] The disconcerting feature of Gould's lengthy report on his latest solicitations was that, when all was said and done, nothing significant had been gained except empty reassurances of support for Bradstreet and verbal recognition of his esteemed contribution.

In point of fact, Gould appeared to be dealing with a secretary of state who was able but unwilling to do anything and a returned general who was willing but unable to do anything further for Bradstreet. When Halifax finally was forced, because of Gould's repeated reminders, to answer Bradstreet's request for rank as a brigadier-general, he revealed his reluctance to act decisively on the Colonel's behalf. Owing to his fears that even such a temporary promotion might antagonize "two or three officers, whose Commissions bear elder date," Halifax refused the request. Interestingly enough a similar refusal, explained in a more revealing way, met Bradstreet's friend Mungo Campbell's

---

17. Ibid., November 24, 1763, T.P.C., 128/87; January 9, 1764, T.P.C., 128/122; Gould to Bradstreet, February 11, 1764, T.P.C., 128/132.

18. Ibid.

request for promotion from captain to major, which also was addressed to Halifax. Campbell wanted to secure the higher rank and then return to America for service in Bradstreet's command. Enlisting the support of Jeffery Amherst for his request, he received an audience with Halifax but his proposed advance in rank was flatly rejected. Halifax was concerned about the "injustices to Senior Captains" such a promotion would create but, in addition, explained that General Gage had "the Sole appointments of the Staff Officers for Colonel Bradstreet's expedition."[19] Here perhaps was the real stumbling block to Bradstreet's own advance. If a minor promotion such as Campbell's had to have Gage's approval surely Bradstreet's request for rank as a brigadier-general would only receive Halifax's approval if it was sanctioned and supported by his commander, Thomas Gage. Halifax's inaction on Bradstreet's behalf was merely another sign of the British government's determination not to undermine the authority of its new North American commander.

On the other hand, the former North American commander, Jeffery Amherst, in 1764 had virtually no influence on British politicians then in power. Even before Pitt had fallen from office, but more so after his departure, Amherst's personal recommendations frequently met with limited and delayed action. Now that the already-mentioned suggestions that his mistakes had precipitated the present Indian difficulties circulated in London, his reputation suffered accordingly. Furthermore, beset with personal problems and without any "taste for politics," he seemed content to withdraw from all battles, whether of a political or military nature. Thus, while his professions of support for Bradstreet were perfectly sincere, Amherst was simply not in a position to secure the rewards or advances his former officer-colleague sought. Complicating Bradstreet's cause even further was the equally powerless position of the individual who had been such an important patron in earlier years, Sir Richard Lyttleton. Now back in England, he frequently met with Gould to discuss Bradstreet's predicament, but Gould frankly felt that Lyttleton's "Connections with Mr. Pitt I believe prevent him from Serving you by his Influence." Sensing that sympathies and reassurances were no substitute for concrete actions, Gould himself was driven to a harshly realistic assessment of his activities and Bradstreet's cause. "Unluckily both for you and me," he confessed, "I stand single without a Second in your Service."[20] As the spring of 1764 approached, it was fairly obvious that Bradstreet could place only limited reliance on his British friends and patrons in his search for immediate military and political advancement. Solutions to this impasse perhaps could be found only through success in the west and the support and approbation of General Thomas Gage.

---

19. Ibid., March 6, 1764, T.P.C., 128/133; Mungo Campbell to Gould, March 3, 1764, T.P.C., 128/135.

20. Long, *Lord Jeffery Amherst*, 157, 188-89, 197-98; Gould to Bradstreet, February 11, 1764, T.P.C., 128/132.

Prospects for a rapprochement with Gage and a triumph against Pontiac were dimming instead of brightening, however. Although officially receiving his orders and command early in April of 1764, it was to be mid-June before Bradstreet finally left Albany to take to the field. The late arrival of the provincial troops was a major factor in this delay, although the state of Bradstreet's health and a series of spirited exchanges with Gage over the inadequacies of the expeditionary force and related problems no doubt contributed as well. In any case, it was because of Bradstreet's exhortations for early action that General Gage issued his official orders on April 2. These detailed instructions[21] were to be extremely significant in the later wrangles between Bradstreet and Gage, when the question was hotly debated as to whether the Colonel had exceeded their terms or merely followed them to the letter. They began with the standard references to the expedition commander's "Experience . . . Abilities . . . and Zeal for his Majesty's Service," as well as an outline of the expedition's general purpose: "to chastize the Savages who still continue in Arms, &, thereby obtain a Secure and lasting peace and restore Tranquility to the Country." In this opening statement, did the "thereby" mean that Bradstreet's military campaign was merely the preliminary to treaty-making by Johnson or was the Colonel to be both soldier and diplomat? Here was the first of several ambiguous statements which Bradstreet interpreted as confirmation of his hopes that both the waging of war and the making of peace were entrusted to him. Undoubtedly chastisement of hostile Indian nations was a major priority of the expedition, since Gage went on to spell out the specific offending tribes and their geographic locations. Bradstreet was directed to attack the "Wiandots of Sandusky" in order to "destroy & break upp that nest of thieves." He also was to fall upon "the Delawares and Shawnese who are retired upon the *Muskingham* and the *Scioto* Rivers." Likewise with the Detroit Indians, should it happen that they renewed hostilities, Bradstreet was to "use your best endeavours to destroy and extirpate them, by every means in your power."

The warlike nature of his expedition was certainly stressed, but also scattered through the instructions were equally clear references to peace-making activities which confirmed Bradstreet's reading of the opening general purpose and his own desires. At one point Gage expressed his hope "that the Savages in every part will be brought to Reason, and Oblig'd to submit, and that a sure and lasting peace will be concluded with them by the end of the Campaign." Obviously Bradstreet was to secure their submission but was he also to conclude the peace? This masterful imprecision went on and on. Gage further obscured matters when he reminded Bradstreet: "You will give the Savages in general to understand that you don't go to flatter or caress them, that you go with a Body of Troops to chastise such nations who

---

21. See Gage to Bradstreet, April 2, 1764, Gage Letters, H.H.L.; Gage's instructions to Bradstreet, April 2, 1764, Gage Papers, A.S./16.

shall continue in Arms against Us, to offer peace & his Majesty's Protection to those who shall chuse to conclude a lasting Peace, and live in Amity, and Friendship with Us." By implication this particular section would allow even the openly hostile Wyandots, Delawares, and Shawnees to escape military punishment if they expressed a desire and willingness for peace. Concluding the orders was Gage's frank recognition that the nature of Bradstreet's foray into the wilderness necessitated a great many matters being left to his own initiative. Since "you will be at such a distance as not to make it possible to send for Orders, and Circumstances may change many things which can't be foreseen at this Distance," Gage wrote to Bradstreet, "You must take upon yourself to manage them to the best adantage for his Majesty's Service: You will be upon the Spot, and I must trust for the execution of every thing to your Discretion and Judgement." Such wide-ranging discretionary powers, when linked with repeated hints of offering peace as well as threatening war, were loopholes wide enough to justify practically any action on Bradstreet's part.

Occasionally, to be sure, Gage did allow what may be regarded as his real intentions to emerge. There were two places in the instructions where he hinted at the limited nature of Bradstreet's mission and the role assigned Johnson in the campaign. In reference to the "Detroit Indians," Gage mentioned that Major Henry Gladwin, commandant at Detroit, had been ordered to instruct those tribes in the area desiring peace "to send their Chiefs to Niagara by the end of June, in order to conclude a formal peace with Sir William Johnson." Thus, in this case a distinction apparently was made between a temporary peace accepted by Gladwin and permanent peace negotiated by Johnson. Quite possibly the underlying message to Bradstreet was that he should operate in the same way. However, the positions of the two men were quite different in that the Major's beleaguered garrison had barely hung on to Detroit in a tenacious defensive action and he was clearly in no position to take the offensive or dictate terms to anyone. But Bradstreet was leading an offensive force which was, theoretically at least, of sufficient strength both to intimidate the Indians and to compel them to negotiate. Further evidence of Gage's thinking emerged in the fact that if Bradstreet was to conduct extensive negotiations then he had to be equipped with the lavish presents which normally were an integral part of such ceremonies. But Gage was of the opinion that Bradstreet should inform the Indians "that as you are on a Warlike expedition, you have brought no presents to bestow." Then, slightly contradicting himself, in order to appease those Indians who had remained friendly to the British cause, Gage allowed that "tho' you do not give them great presents, you may give them some tokens of your regard, by bestowing on them some pairs of Leggins & a few Bales of Strouds."

Admittedly, in a later letter to Bradstreet, Gage repeated his belief that "As you do not go, on the footing of making presents but to make War, there will be no occasion to carry Indian Goods, further than a few things," and advised the Colonel to send Indians desiring presents "to Sir William Johnson."[22] But to John Bradstreet, who for all his aspirations in Indian diplomacy was largely uninitiated in this subtle art, a lack of presents for tribes suing for peace presented no major obstacle. Should the Indians want to open negotiations and conclude a peace without the usual refinements of such transactions, the straightforward Bradstreet was not one to let the traditional approaches stand in the way of a quick achievement of what he felt to be one of the basic purposes of his expedition. Thus, it was unlikely that he regarded Johnson's responsibility for Indian presents as in any way handicapping him if the Indians indicated a willingness to discuss peace terms. Additionally, if Gage was attempting to imply that a lack of Indian presents meant Bradstreet was not to enter into peace negotiations, he was using a strangely convoluted if not singularly obtuse way of making his point. In reality, at the heart of the confusion surrounding the instructions was the simple failure of Gage honestly and openly to convey to Bradstreet an accurate statement of his assigned duties and the limits of his responsibilities. While Gage was willing to state clearly to Johnson that Bradstreet goes "on a Warlike Expedition" and in dealing with the Indians "must referr them to you for Settling all Affairs betwixt them and the English,"[23] no such direct attempt to distinguish between the responsibilities of Johnson and Bradstreet was made when Gage corresponded with the Colonel. Only twice, once in regard to recruitment of the Iroquois and then in the indirect discussion of Gladwin's Detroit orders, was Johnson specifically mentioned in Bradstreet's instructions. Without a more detailed mention and explanation of the Indian Superintendent's role it is little wonder that a state of acrimonious confusion ensued. Therefore, instead of charging Bradstreet with misconstruing the instructions[24] perhaps a stronger case could be made against Gage for misconstructing the orders, and then in a sense misrepresenting, or entirely failing to present to Bradstreet the vitally important role he intended Sir William Johnson to play in the expedition.

Such theorizing should not exclude the obvious. Sir William Johnson's expertise in Indian diplomacy and general responsibility for Indian affairs in the Great Lakes area were widely acknowledged and respected. Quite possibly it could be argued that for Gage to delineate Johnson's activities and responsibilities in Bradstreet's instructions was merely to offer an unnecessary restatement of the perfectly obvious. But the fact of the matter was that in dealing with John Bradstreet, Gage was attempting to direct an opinionated and independent indi-

---

22. Gage to Bradstreet, April 15, 1764, Gage Papers, A.S./17.
23. Gage to Johnson, April 22, 1764, in Sullivan *et al., Johnson Papers*, 4, 204-03. Earlier in this letter Gage complimented Johnson on his peace with the Senecas and commented: "Nothing remains but a proper Chastisement of the Delawares and Shawnese, which his Majesty expects as a Thing Necessary before a Genl. Peace, in order to Secure its Duration."
24. As Howard H. Peckham, *Pontiac and the Indian Uprising* (Princeton, N.J., 1947), 255, does.

vidual who possessed excessive ambitions and confidence in his abilities in all matters, even tricky Indian negotiations, and who in reality could only be controlled by precisely stated and pointedly restricted instructions. Quite ready to ignore the obviously extensive powers of Sir William Johnson, Bradstreet still regarded himself as the best judge of how the campaign should be conducted and how the Indians should be handled. Ironically, despite Gage's repeated encounters with the Colonel and early attempts to curb or impede some of his activities, when it came to the critically important instructions for the Detroit expedition the General failed to fashion the restrictive bridle needed if Bradstreet was to be restrained in the way desired by both Gage and Johnson.

Although this opportunity to do so was allowed to pass, in the interval between the issuing of the orders and the actual start of the movement westward there were any number of hints and indications that Johnson was regarded by Gage as the supreme authority in all Indian matters. Shortly after assuming office Gage had indicated his respect for Johnson's "Experience & Knowledge" concerning the Indians, and this confidence and reliance had continued to grow. The result was Gage's quick referral of all Indian questions to Johnson and usually a ready deference to Sir William's opinion. To give just one example, when Bradstreet reported rumours concerning the imminent renewal of hostilities by the Indians around Detroit, and that a force of 2,000 was preparing to attack the post, Johnson pooh-poohed the stories as "exaggerated" while Gage quickly joined the Indian Superintendent in dismissing such reports as "somewhat Incredulous." Furthermore, Johnson was quite willing to give Bradstreet what amounted to a crash course in how to handle his beloved Iroquois. While ostensibly opening his store-house of Indian experience for Bradstreet's benefit, his letters and comments also should have served as forceful reminders of his pre-eminence in this field. Bradstreet was informed about how to address the Six Nations, how to meet their clothing, arms, and liquor needs, their tradition of frequent councils, the importance of consultation with them before any sudden moves, the wisdom of careful cultivation of their chief warriors, and on and on, even to advice regarding the need for a careful watch over the troops' language so that "Curses" and "little indescretions" would not create unfortunate incidents.[25] There was, nevertheless, a deficiency in Johnson's comments to Bradstreet which was similar to that found in Gage's correspondence with the Colonel. While Sir William talked at length about how the Six Nations allies accompanying the expedition were to be treated, he never once referred to the question of how peace over-

---

25. Gage to Johnson, December 12, 1763, in Sullivan *et al.*, *Johnson Papers*, 10, 953; Bradstreet to Gage, April 23 and April 27, 1764, Gage Papers, A.S./17; Johnson to Gage, April 27, 1764, in Sullivan *et al.*, *Johnson Papers*, 11, 163; Gage to Bradstreet, April 30, 1764, Gage Letters; Johnson to Bradstreet, May 11, 1764, in Sullivan *et al.*, *Johnson Papers*, 11, 192-93; Johnson to Bradstreet, May 5, 1764, in ibid., 4, 415-17; "Heads For Colonel Bradstreet's Inspection," June 12, 1764, in ibid., 11, 231-33.

tures from the hostile Indians were to be handled. Consequently no illumination was shed upon the issue of whether peace with the warring Indian nations was totally Johnson's responsibility or whether Bradstreet could handle such negotiations if the need arose.

If Johnson expected that subtle indications of his mastery of Indian lore were sufficient to cause Bradstreet to avoid even the most limited transgression on the master's domain, he was to be sorely disappointed because the unsophisticated Bradstreet did not deal in such nuances. Furthermore, the Colonel refused to regard Johnson as the master of the Iroquois or as the only man who could successfully negotiate with the hostile tribes further west. While Johnson actively recruited among his loyal Six Nations friends because of the contribution they could make to the expedition, Bradstreet felt that the few Iroquois who would join his command would not do so out of loyalty and were likely to prove more a liability than an asset. It was his belief that reports concerning "a great Army going up the Country" were the real cause of the Iroquois becoming "so pliable," while he was quite concerned that once they joined his force at Oswego and Niagara, it would be only "to receive immence Presents, watch our Motions, & deceive us in everything, instead of assisting against the Enemy."[26] This lack of faith in Johnson's true ability to assess and deal with the Indians, which actually was closely linked with Bradstreet's own ambitions for appointment as Indian superintendent or at least a sharing of responsibility with Sir William, was not a criticism contrived on the spur of the moment. His reservations about Johnson and his own aspirations for Johnson's office had emerged as soon as Bradstreet had arrived in upper New York in 1755, and periodically re-emerged over the next twenty years until a last effort at gaining the appointment was made immediately after Johnson's death in 1774. Consequently if the Detroit expedition presented an opportunity allowing anyone to demonstrate a knack of dealing with the Indians, whether in a warlike or peace-making sense, the pattern of Bradstreet's career indicated that he would seize such an opportunity for himself rather than allow Johnson to gain further credit and a grander reputation. Unhobbled by precise orders closing off such a possibility, Bradstreet's major problem was the presence of Johnson. But Sir William intended only to be with the expedition as far as Niagara. It would appear that the point at which Johnson stopped accompanying Bradstreet, the end of Lake Ontario, was also the point at which his authority stopped, as far as Bradstreet was concerned. Bradstreet saw himself as the only, and in truth, the best judge of Indian affairs west of Niagara.

Although neglecting to treat in detail negotiations with the hostile tribes west of Niagara, Bradstreet's April 2 orders did make him the final judge in a number of other matters. After leaving Niagara in the best possible state of defense, and carrying out his military operations

---

26. Bradstreet to Gage, March 11, 1764, Gage Papers, A.S./15; Bradstreet to Gould, June 3, 1764, T.P.C., 128/125.

against the rebellious Wyandot, Shawnee, and Delaware tribes, he was to move on to Detroit. Its fortifications were to be strengthened while the Indians in the region were to be subdued if necessary. In addition Bradstreet was to make "proper examples" of any of "his Majesty's French Subjects" residing in the Detroit area who were themselves guilty of traitorous acts against the British crown or of encouraging the Indians "to commit hostilities." Then the Colonel was to push on to Michilimackinac for a repeat of his Detroit performance. Here also the fort was to be strengthened while those of the French inhabitants guilty of hostile actions were to be punished. "You will be the best judge when upon the spot," Gage commented, "whether it would not be for the advantage of the Service, to remove many of those French Renegades at Michillimackinack, and at several other posts, as likewise to send away all the Missionaries." Responsibilities relating to matters of commerce were also entrusted to Bradstreet. At Michilimackinac, as at other up-country posts, goods and furs belonging to "our Merchants," which had fallen into French hands, were to be returned to their proper owners. In addition, since "some Merchants at Montreal, have notwithstanding the proclamation issued to prohibit trade with the Savages, sent up Ammunition, & all manner of supplys," the Colonel was to seize all such goods and dispatch as prisoners any offending individuals to Montreal. As Bradstreet's force moved through the Great Lakes the garrisons at the various posts were to be re-established, or in some cases replaced, so Gage also spelled out the details concerning these arrangements.[27]

These particular instructions, unlike other sections of the April 2 orders, were relatively uncontentious. But there remained a few further comments by Gage which were to become an immediate bone of contention. These involved the precise number of troops destined for the western expedition, a matter on which the Colonel and the General had disagreed from the outset. Gage placed under Bradstreet's command the provincials raised by the colonies of Connecticut, New York, and New Jersey, a corps of Canadians, the 17th Regiment of regulars, and four companies from the 80th Regiment. In total Gage estimated that this provided "a Corps of near Two thousand Men." In addition Bradstreet was to be joined by a detachment of the Royal Regiment of Artillery with ten field pieces, and could hope for "a good body of faithfull Savages" as well. Over a month later, for Lord Halifax's benefit, Gage outlined the force in more specific detail. There were to be about 500 New York provincials, nearly 500 men drawn from Connecticut and New Jersey combined, 300 Canadians, the 17th Regiment which was to be "compleated by Draughts" from the 55th Regiment, the four companies from the 80th, and 50 artillery men. Once again Gage repeated his estimate of the total strength of Bradstreet's command as approximately 2,000 men.[28]

---

27. Gage's instructions to Bradstreet, April 2, 1764, Gage Papers, A.S./16.
28. Ibid.; Gage to Halifax, May 12, 1764, in Clarence E. Carter, ed., *The Correspond-*

On paper it looked a reasonably imposing force. In reality, in terms of quality and numbers, both the provincials and regulars turned out to be rather unimposing. Typically, Bradstreet used every device available to him in an attempt to increase the number of troops assigned to the expedition. These efforts, if successful, might have brought his force up to what Bradstreet assumed to be adequate strength. But such manoeuvres could not resolve the deeper problem of the unskilled, unhealthy, and unwilling nature of a good number of the soldiers. This difficulty perhaps could have been solved if he used his troops only to intimidate the enemy while he carefully avoided any potentially embarrassing pitched battles. As the force assembled and final preparations were made, it slowly became clear that the impetuous John Bradstreet of the Seven Years' War, ever thirsting for action and ready to lead into battle any soldiers, competent or incompetent, regular or irregular, was at least for the moment a creature of the past. The John Bradstreet preparing to move against Detroit in the spring of 1764 was a different man; he was cautious, totally lacking confidence in his troops, and seeking victory over the enemy by bravado and accommodation rather than by frontal assault.

This temporarily uncertain and hesitant Bradstreet only gradually emerged in April, May, and June of 1764 as he saw at first hand the calibre of his troops and experienced, as well, the wrath of General Gage at all his complaints and attempts to strengthen his command. The exchanges between the General and the Colonel during this period were spirited and blunt, usually resulting in the effective blockage of most of Bradstreet's moves or suggestions. Early in April the first disagreement arose when Bradstreet submitted his own estimate of what Gage was describing as a 2,000 man force. The Colonel "beg[ged] to know" if he could expect any more troops than the "314 including the draughts" of the 17th Regiment, a regiment which he described as possessing only about "140 Men fit to go on Service," some 300 Yorkers, 250 Connecticut men, 240 Jerseys, and 300 Canadians. Thus Bradstreet estimated that his total force numbered only 1,404. "I know not" he bitterly commented, "What Exploits may be expected from fourteen hundred Men, one half of them new Rais'd Provincials and the half of the other half but lately the Subjects of the French King acting in the Center of the Savages surrounding the Great Lakes known to be our inveterate Enemies." Even if the entire 1,400 "were of the best Troops His Majesty has, the number is far short of being equal to the service." However, since it was his "Duty to obey and to doe the best I can for the Service" he was determined to carry out his assignment with the available manpower. But in view of his force's limitations he suggested some juggling to Gage which would at least gain him a few more regulars. It was already intended that 174 men were to be drawn from the 55th Regiment to strengthen the 17th. Bradstreet now reques-

---

ence of General Thomas Gage with the Secretaries of State, and with the War Office and the Treasury 1763-1775 (New Haven, 1931), 1, 27.

ted permission to draft a further 100 men from the 55th, replacing them with an equal number of provincials. Initially Gage agreed to allow this exchange, but when Bradstreet pressed for even further drafts from the 55th a scorching refusal was the result. On no account were any further drafts to be taken from the 55th. Gage argued that these men were needed for garrison duty at various posts and while "You [Bradstreet] may be in the right to think of nothing but yourself... it's my Business to provide for every thing." Gage also was quick to take issue with Bradstreet's estimate of the size of his total force. The Colonel's calculations concerning the 17th Regiment were incorrect, he commented, since the entire regiment "must go on Service" rather than only 140 men. Furthermore he was surprised at Bradstreet's apparent misgivings about the provincials and the Canadians, since some of the former were experienced soldiers while at an earlier point Bradstreet evidently had expressed to Gage his confidence that the Canadians "would be extremely usefull in your operations." Finally, although Gage was willing to admit his inability "to procure as many Men as I endeavored," he remained convinced that Bradstreet still had "a Corps, equal to any Service you can undertake, and Superior to any Enemy you can meet."[29]

Bradstreet remained unconvinced, however, and by now had turned his attention to increasing the number of New York provincials consigned to the expedition. In this endeavour he was quick to take advantage of an opening provided by Gage himself. It was because of pressure from Gage that New York's commitment finally had risen to approximately 480 men, but the last 180 were only enlisted for service up to May 1. As a result, Gage instructed Bradstreet to get them enlisted for further service and then "find some Pretence to get them to Oswego or perhaps Niagara, where they can't move off." In this way they were to be forced into the campaign while, Gage promised, "we will find means to get them paid." Bradstreet immediately employed people to secure new enlistments as well as re-enlistments and, with the help of a promised pay rate of three shillings a day, soon had ample recruits. Indeed he had too many recruits achieved at too high a price. New York's Assembly had approved a 480-man contribution as well as a set amount for their subsistence and bounty money and refused to pay any more. Consequently Gage made clear that Bradstreet was to keep only this number and surplus recruits were to be "sent about their business." As to the additional pay promised by Bradstreet, Gage felt that he was not responsible for this but that "they must squabble it out with the province, for I can not pay a single Man." Although Bradstreet claimed that he would never dream of having a single man more than Gage approved of, regardless of "however Shocking the State of the Yorkers are & the number upon the whole insufficient," the additional bodies proved too tempting to pass up. Evidently 100 extra New

---

29. Bradstreet to Gage, April 6, 1764, Gage Papers, A.S./16; Gage to Bradstreet, April 15, 1764, Gage Papers, A.S./17; ibid., May 6, 1764, Gage Papers, A.S./18.

Yorkers were kept by him, served in the campaign, and then discovered that the New York Assembly was unwilling to pay them.[30] This question of paying the additional Yorkers remained unresolved for several years, and it contributed greatly to the bitterness between Bradstreet and Gage as well as between Bradstreet and the New York Assembly. More immediately, however, Bradstreet's attempted circumvention of Gage's orders and the New York Assembly's desires demonstrated yet once more his desperate conviction about how undermanned his expedition was.

As if a growing uneasiness about his troops and a pronounced lack of cooperation by his commander were not sufficient burdens, Bradstreet's health also failed him in late May. As the fiftieth year of his life neared completion, sickness had become almost a chronic companion of the Colonel. He had missed the last major campaign under Amherst because of illness and now as another campaign approached he was stricken again. Already in January of 1764 he was indisposed for a period, but in late May he really was hit hard by sickness. It was a continually recurring bout rather than a temporary illness which lingered on through June and well into July. As a result, the once energetic and indefatigable Bradstreet found himself unable to ride a short distance to converse with Johnson in June; he was carried on and off boats on the Great Lakes in July and towards the end of that month was as yet unable to walk.[31] The active John Bradstreet, who had thrived on such exhausting expeditions as that against Frontenac in 1758, was no longer physically capable of enduring the exertions demanded by wilderness campaigning. Clearly the deteriorated state of his health is a factor too long ignored in the explanation of his 1764 performance.

To Bradstreet's credit, in spite of his ailments he remained eager to get the expedition moving. By June 3, with the last of his provincial troops arriving at Albany and having entrusted his quartermaster duties to his close friend Philip Schuyler, he was straining to get underway. Several days later he began the move to Lake Ontario, reaching Schenectady on June 10 and arriving at Oswego approximately two weeks later. Unforeseen delays continued to plague him,

---

30. Gage to Bradstreet, April 2, 1764, Gage Letters; Gage to Bradstreet, May 6, 1764, Gage Papers, A.S./18; Bradstreet to Gage, May 11, 1764, Gage Papers; Gage to Bradstreet, December 9, 1764, Gage Letters; Gage to Bradstreet, May 15, 1764, Gage Papers, A.S./18; Bradstreet to Gage, November 29, 1764, Gage Papers, A.S./27; Dirck Ten Broeck to Bradstreet, November 29, 1764, Gage Papers; Gage to Bradstreet, December 9, 1764, Gage Letters.

31. Johnson to Bradstreet, January 10, 1764, ref. # 3421, N.Y.S.L.; Gage to Bradstreet, May 27, 1764, Gage Papers, A.S./19; Bradstreet to Johnson, June 10, 1764, in Sullivan *et al.*, *Johnson Papers*, 11, 231; "Papers Relating to the Expeditions of Colonel John Bradstreet and Colonel Bouquet In Ohio, A.D. 1764," *Western Reserve and Northern Ohio Historical Society*, 1 (1873), Tract 13, 2; "The Montresor Journals," *Collections Of The New-York Historical Society For The Year 1881* (New York, 1882) 269; James Dow to Henry Bouquet, July 22, 1764, in Sylvester K. Stevens and Donald H. Kent, eds., *The Papers of Col. Henry Bouquet* (Harrisburg, Pa., 1943), Series 21650, Part 2, 35.

however. Although he hoped his Oswego stop would be extremely brief, merely allowing time for a link-up with the Indians recruited by Johnson before pushing on, the fitting out of his Iroquois allies turned into a long drawn out affair and it was July 3 before the Colonel left Oswego for Niagara. Bradstreet rationalized this delay with the explanation that if he was to lose time anywhere it was better to do so at Oswego than Niagara, since at the latter place any lengthy stopover would be highly visible, allowing the quick report of his expedition's movements and strength to the enemy.[32]

There were other matters that were not so easily rationalized and, indeed, there were open signs of Bradstreet's reluctant acceptance of the fact that his expedition was incapable of an effective performance against the western Indians. With provincials "deserting every day from the fear of the Service they are going on" and the disappointing total size of his command making it "a very trifling" army, he now believed that the hostile Indians had the upper hand and could either attack the expedition or keep out of its way, whichever suited them. Delays had robbed him of the element of surprise, the uncooperative colonies had deprived him of the needed manpower; and so Bradstreet felt that the harsh reality was that he faced "the sad mortification of acting mostly on the defensive" instead of bringing the enemy "under a proper dependence."[33] As Bradstreet launched his western offensive the constant delays and deficiencies of his force, undoubtedly coupled with the precarious state of his health, had taken a deadly toll on his usually positive and optimistic attitude. He headed for Niagara firmly convinced that he could not mount an adequate offensive thrust and resigned to the fact that his grand expedition would be nothing more than a grandiose defensive operation. Against this background, Bradstreet's reluctance to wage war and his willingness to arrange a peaceful resolution of the difficulties with the rebellious tribes may be viewed in a far more sympathetic light.

---

32. Bradstreet to Gould, June 3, 1764, T.P.C., 128/125; Bradstreet to Schuyler, June 2, 1764, Schuyler Papers, Box 9; Bradstreet to Gage, July 2, 1764, Gage Papers, A.S./21; ibid., June 9, 1764, Gage Papers, A.S./19.
33. Bradstreet to Gould, June 3, 1764, T.P.C., 128/125; May 7, 1764, T.P.C., 128/124.

Chapter IX

The Great Lakes Campaign

As John Bradstreet's command moved to Detroit and then back to Fort Niagara, in the summer and fall of 1764, he found himself threatened both by hostile Indians and by hostile colleagues. His pretentious peace-making attempts were to be severely criticized by Thomas Gage and Sir William Johnson and momentarily capitalized upon by Pontiac and his allies. Ever ready to defend all his actions, Bradstreet produced detailed, point-by-point refutations of the various allegations concerning his misconduct.[1] Such a strenuous defense was necessitated by the threat to his reputation posed by Gage and Johnson's charges as well as by his own economic and territorial aspirations, since strong indications emerged at this time of his plans for the proper development of the Detroit area and his own appointment as the region's first British governor.[2]

---

1. For critical treatments of Bradstreet's campaign against Pontiac, see Francis Parkman, *The Conspiracy of Pontiac*, 10th ed. (New York, 1962), 388-91, 394-95, 401-403; Peckham, *Pontiac*, 255-57, 260-64; Alden, *General Gage in America*, 96-100. Gipson, *The British Empire Before the American Revolution*, 9, 118-23, is far more sympathetic to Bradstreet while arguing that he erred seriously in negotiating various Indian treaties. Shy, *Toward Lexington*, 136-37, 224-25, is one of the few historians perceptive enough to hint at another side to the military campaign by briefly mentioning the possibility of Bradstreet's illicit trading activities. Furthermore, after an objective analysis he maintains that "Militarily, the campaign of 1764 was a success."
2. Nelson V. Russell, *The British Regime in Michigan and the Old Northwest, 1760-1796* (Northfield, Minnesota, 1939), 65-66, 76-77, briefly mentions Bradstreet's 1764 interest in Detroit's development. But he fails to tie Bradstreet's proposal in with his activities throughout, and prior to, the 1764 campaign. Moreover, he refers only to the Bradstreet proposal contained in the Shelburne Papers, which was the tip of the iceberg, since elaborate refinements of this suggestion are contained in several other documentary collections. Alvord's, *The Mississippi Valley in British Politics*, 1, 244-45, mentions a Detroit plan submitted by "Major Thomas Mant" in May of 1765, but credits Amherst with first conceiving this project in 1762 and entirely overlooks Bradstreet's role. Indeed, in

To the Colonel's chagrin a further month-long delay awaited him after his July 7 arrival at Niagara. A "very ill" Bradstreet had sailed on the *Mohawk*, ahead of his troops, promptly followed the next day by Sir William Johnson on board the *Johnson*. Sir William had summoned all the Great Lakes Indian chiefs to a conference scheduled to take place at Niagara in July, and it was this meeting which necessitated Bradstreet's long stop-over. As the spokesmen for nineteen tribes and their many followers drifted into Niagara, there was considerable anxiety about the possibility of parties of disloyal Indians being present among the 2,000 who eventually assembled. Because of this possible threat to Niagara, Bradstreet and Johnson agreed to keep the expeditionary force at the post until the conference ended. While recognizing the necessity of this decision, Bradstreet was annoyed at the additional disruption of his campaign. Seizing this opportunity, he quickly pointed out to Gage that, had he originally been allowed an adequate number of troops, both the protection of Niagara and the continuation of his expedition could have been handled easily. As matters now stood, he found it "disgraceful & disagreeable ... to see a Body of English Troops, intended to Command respect every where in these Regions, so few in numbers as to be oblig'd to stop as it were before they enter danger to prevent a post of importance falling into the hands of Savages by treachery." Gage also received a taste of Bradstreet's pessimistic expectations concerning the expedition's outcome. It was disappointingly clear to the Colonel that the "train of Evils" he had encountered thus far, the lateness of the season, and an adversary well aware of his force's movements left "little hopes of our success" unless the hostile Indians chose to openly "give us battle."[3]

Actually the number of the hostile Indians had decreased considerably by means of the Niagara conference, since only the Potawatomis, Delawares, and Shawnees had failed to send delegates. During the meeting Johnson's persuasive powers were at their best as peace agreements were concluded with all the nations in attendance. In addition, their willingness to cooperate with the British against the remaining rebellious tribes was obtained. In concrete terms of aid to Bradstreet's expedition this commitment was translated into "500 Savages of all sorts of Nations" who were to accompany his force. This additional support failed to buoy Bradstreet's spirits, however. He remained suspicious of his new-found allies because, as he put it, "there are few who think Savages will kill Savages on our account." Nevertheless, "As it is thought best I should have them I take them let the

---

summarizing Mante's career Alvord erroneously identifies his commanding officer in 1763 as "Colonel Dudley Bradstreet." Quite possibly Bradstreet was behind Amherst's 1762 proposal and quite clearly it was on Bradstreet's behalf that Mante made the 1765 submission.

3. "The Montresor Journals," N.Y.H.S., *Collections 1881*, 269-70; Parkman, *The Conspiracy of Pontiac*, 381-87; Bradstreet to Gage, July 12, 1764, Gage Papers, A.S./21, U.M.C.L.

consequence be what it will."[4] Thus, as the conference wound to a successful conclusion early in August, the reluctant warrior prepared to resume his westward thrust, setting August 7 as the date for his departure from Niagara.

Suddenly, shortly before his departure, the old confidence and optimism returned to Bradstreet. Certainly they were not regained because of any last-minute strengthening of his command. Bradstreet counted his force as 1,500 regulars and provincials along with 500 Indians, and his estimated number of soldiers was the same as the figure offered by Lieutenant James Dow two weeks earlier.[5] Thus, he marched with a force that he still felt to be grossly undermanned. If his change in mood was not caused by any improvement in his manpower situation perhaps it can be explained by his discovery that his force no longer had to do battle immediately with the enemy. Letters from Gage and Gladwin opened the possibility of Bradstreet's postponement of the attacks upon the Wyandots, Shawnees, and Delawares, which originally had been outlined in his April 2 orders. In a letter from Detroit, which reached Bradstreet as the Niagara conference concluded, Major Henry Gladwin offered the encouraging news that "The Wiontots of Sandusky have sued for peace & brought in five prisoners." Then, in an interesting hint that Bradstreet was not the only one finding Gage's orders somewhat ambiguous, Gladwin explained that he felt Bradstreet should be informed immediately of this development since "the general seems desirous to make peace with those who ask." Elated at this news Bradstreet promptly forwarded Gladwin's letter to Gage and attempted to convey the impression that he was not at all pleased at the prospect of a good battle vanishing at such an inopportune moment. Had he not been required to stop at Niagara, he commented, "I should not have receiv'd that letter, & perhaps might have had the good fortune to cut up that Band, which I think would have been more for the Public good than making peace with them."[6] The prospects of peace rather than war apparently had revitalized and transformed Bradstreet into the willing warrior of old, although his strained heroics were of questionable sincerity.

If the Wyandots were ready for peace there remained the Shawnees and Delawares to be disposed of. In the same letter to Gage which passed on Gladwin's news, Bradstreet revealed how and why he intended to avoid confronting these nations at this time. Combining suggestions made several weeks earlier by Gage with some "very good Information" recently received, the Colonel proposed to push on directly to Detroit in "Hopes of falling on Mr. Pondiac's Friends" who

---

4. Gipson, *The British Empire Before the American Revolution*, 9, 118-19; Bradstreet to Gould, August 6, 1764, T.P.C., 128/126, N.L.W.

5. Ibid.; Dow to Bouquet, July 22, 1764, in Stevens and Kent, *Bouquet Papers*, Series 21650, Part 2, 35. Dow wrote that "we will have besides Indians about 1500" and that Bradstreet's provincials were "the poorest wretches ever I beheld."

6. Gladwin to Bradstreet, July 12, 1764, Michigan Papers, U.M.C.L.; Bradstreet to Gage, August 5, 1764, Gage Papers, A.S./22.

remained openly hostile. In mid-July Gage had suggested to Bradstreet that the "Rascal Pondiac" was "at the Bottom of the whole" Indian problem and that emissaries sent to the Illinois country might counteract his evil influence. Furthermore, the General informed Bradstreet of the delays encountered by Colonel Henry Bouquet's expedition which was to strike at the Delawares and Shawnees from the south while Bradstreet hit them from the north. It now appeared that Bouquet could not set out from Fort Pitt until the beginning of October. Thus if Bradstreet was "at that Time in a situation to go up the Sandusky, as far as you can, and entrench there, it will be a very good Divertion in his Favor." There is no doubt that in suggesting this October diversion and the major role of Pontiac in fomenting discord, Gage did not intend that Bradstreet should by-pass entirely the Delawares and Shawnees in favour of an immediate move to Detroit. The same day as his letter to Bradstreet, he wrote Johnson concerning his hopes for Bradstreet's "Attempt upon the Scioto and the Muskingham" area and a "good blow upon the Delawares &ca."[7]

But to John Bradstreet, who was in reality not at all spoiling for any pitched battles, Gage's suggestions could be distorted somewhat and, once blended with additional information, used to justify his own inclinations. Hence, the Colonel explained to his commander that reliable reports had reached him making clear that it was "impossible to get to the Siotio River by Water," but instead a roundabout trip by way of Fort Pitt would be needed. Such an excursion was too time-consuming to be attempted. Also even if he could make it to the Scioto River, Bradstreet's Indian informants felt the Delawares and Shawnees were not in the immediate vicinity and a much longer march would be necessary before contact could be made with them. Eventually, he assured Gage, he would march against the Delaware and Shawnee nations, perhaps at "about the time" in October when Bouquet also was moving against them. For the moment, however, he had decided to head directly for Detroit.[8]

This decision considerably upset Gage when he heard of it but it paled into insignificance when compared with the alleged "blunder" made by Bradstreet as his force moved over Lake Erie. By August 12 the Colonel and his command had reached L'Ance aux Feuilles, slightly to the east of Presqu'Isle. On the morning of that day there arrived at Bradstreet's Lake Erie encampment two canoes "with 10 Savages Chief Warriors & deputies from the Castles of the Hurons of Sandusky—Delawares, Shawanese & 5 Nations inhabiting the Plains of Scioto to treat for a peace." The enemy with whom he had taken such careful pains in order to avoid doing battle, apparently now delivered themselves into his hands in order to secure peace terms. Would and should Bradstreet negotiate with them? In view of the Colonel's

---

7. Gage to Bradstreet, July 15, 1764, Gage Letters, H.H.L.; Gage to Johnson, July 15, 1764, in Sullivan et al., *Johnson Papers*, 4, 483.
8. Bradstreet to Gage, August 5, 1764, Gage Papers, A.S./22.

already-established inclinations as an Indian diplomat and his equally obvious disinclinations as a soldier bent upon battle, it was predictable that he would seize such an opportunity for a peaceful settlement with the Delawares and Shawnees. Whether he should have done so, however, actually raises two intriguing questions. Did he have the authority to engage in peace negotiations and, secondly, was it wise to open negotiations with this particular ten-man delegation? Regarding the latter question, as Francis Parkman has pointed out, there were several rather disconcerting features involved in this Indian visit and their request for peace. They brought with them only "one small belt of wampum," when the traditional confirmation of every treaty article required additional belts of wampum, providing a clue that proper peace negotiations were not intended. They also did not present any clear evidence that they had been deputized to carry out peace discussions. Furthermore, within Bradstreet's command, according to Parkman, there was a clearly stated distrust and suspicion of the delegation. The Colonel's Indian allies apparently wanted to kill the intruders while "many of the officers believed them to be spies." Finally, Bradstreet himself was very aware that the Shawnees and Delawares had openly refused to treat with Johnson at Niagara and were past masters of the fine art of deception. Surely it must have dawned on him that their convenient capitulation only a few weeks after a refusal to negotiate at Niagara could serve to ward off any blow by Bradstreet's force and might be a useful delaying tactic.[9] Thus, quite probably their pretended overtures were designed to dupe Bradstreet.

Yet Bradstreet was so determined to avoid needless provocation and a possibly fatal confrontation that he was quite willing to overlook some of the delegation's questionable aspects. Certainly, he placed little confidence in the advice or opinions of his Six Nations allies, of whom half had melted away by this point,[10] and likewise his personal vanity caused him to feel himself to be a far better judge of Indian matters than his largely inexperienced officer corps. Furthermore, in the actual discussions and final treaty, there is clear evidence that the major uncertainties raised by Parkman were appreciated by Bradstreet and met in a reasonable fashion, given the pressures of the moment under which he acted.

Commencing negotiations, the Indians mouthed the usual compliments, which were interspersed with the presentation of one belt and three strings of wampum; they then explained their decision to seek peace. After receiving intelligence that "You were coming against us with an Army," they claimed, "we immediately called in all our Warriors, who were out against your Frontiers, and determined to meet you on this Lake, and beg for Mercy, and Peace." Apparently accepting this argument that a fear of his advancing army motivated their sur-

---

9. "The Montresor Journals," N.Y.H.S., *Collections 1881*, 280; Parkman, *The Conspiracy of Pontiac*, 389-90; Alden, *General Gage in America*, 97.

10. Bradstreet to Gould, August 14, 1764, T.P.C., 128/127. He reported his Indian contingent now numbered 250 instead of the original 500.

render, although at the same time Bradstreet was "surprized to find you begging Peace so soon after" the recent impertinences, the Colonel agreed to treat with them. But he clearly stated that the nine-point peace arrangement he was about to dictate was conditional. It rested on the proviso "that you are fully empowered from the Nations above mentioned, and that the Chiefs of those Nations will Ratify it, and that you name the Chiefs." Thus, Parkman's charge that the delegation was not properly deputized was a very real apprehension to Bradstreet, and he attempted to resolve it by forcing a clarification from them. Their answer was that "We are fully empowered to Conclude, and sign a Peace, if we can obtain one," and they proceeded to name the Chiefs of the Shawnee, Delaware, Sandusky Huron, and the Five Nations of the Scioto plains who "will certainly Ratify it." Satisfied with this outline of their authority the Colonel presented the terms of peace. After all, how far could Bradstreet push any investigation into the legitimacy of the delegation's credentials?

Some of the treaty articles again drove home the point that Bradstreet regarded the peace as purely provisional until final agreement was received from all the chiefs. All prisoners held by the Indians were to "be delivered up" at Sandusky; all the chiefs were to accompany the prisoners and ratify the peace at Sandusky; six of the deputation were to remain with Bradstreet as hostages while the remaining four, accompanied by one Indian and one officer from the expedition, were to acquaint the various nations of the peace. All Indian claims were relinquished to English forts and posts and immediately adjacent land presently occupied in Indian territory, while the British government could construct any additional outposts deemed necessary. An inspection team of eighteen was to be dispatched, with Bradstreet holding eighteen balancing hostages, to make sure that all the prisoners had been released and adequately provided for during their journey. Indians committing any further offences against Englishmen were to be taken to Fort Pitt for trial and punishment before a jury to be half-Indian in composition. Arrangements would be made to prevent Bouquet's expedition "Proceeding against you—but you may be assured, that should you ever be guilty of the like bad behavior, you will never be forgiven, but on the contrary you shall be cut off from the face of the Earth." If any nations violated the peace the other nations were obliged "to punish the Offenders, by Carrying on War either Separately, or Jointly with the English, and their Allies against them." And to avoid any great delay in the treaty's ratification, which might cause Bradstreet to "lose the Season for Acting against the above Indians," in other words to circumvent the delaying tactics which worried Parkman, the Colonel allowed the Indians a twenty-five day period, at the end of which the Chiefs with all the prisoners had to meet him at Sandusky. If they failed to arrive, the peace was void and the Indians "may expect to find us Warriors, instead of Brothers, and friends."[11]

---

11. "Copy of the Peace made by Col. John Bradstreet with the Indians of Scioto dated

The treaty appeared both strongly cautious in its approach to the Indians and yet reasonably generous in its terms. Bradstreet's articles concerning the delivery of all prisoners and the attendance of the chiefs within twenty-five days for final ratification, as well as his intimidating threats, left the way open for future action if they did mislead him. However, such suggestions as a half-Indian jury for future offences and a strange failure to gain compensation for the deaths and damages committed by the warring tribes were sure to be interpreted as overly generous and unsatisfactory. By way of comparison, Colonel Henry Bouquet, in May of 1764, had submitted to General Gage the sort of peace terms he considered as suitable to be offered to the Delawares, Shawnees, Wyandots, and Mingoes. Generally they followed much the same lines as those dictated by Bradstreet, with two major exceptions. Indians who were guilty of the murder of traders and one William Clapham, land speculator and soldier, were to be handed over and put to death. As well, compensation in furs for the losses "our Traders have suffered in their property" had to be paid within seven years.[12] Thus, Bradstreet's terms possibly could have been tougher. But at least they revealed his awareness of the risks involved in negotiating with this particular delegation, as well as his attempt to hedge on the treaty by incorporating a number of provisions and threats demonstrating that failure to adhere fully to its terms would provoke a military attack. Yet the original question must be considered: should Bradstreet have negotiated with this delegation? J. R. Alden suggests he should have seized the "pretended emissaries" and held them as captives. But this would have accomplished precisely nothing. Bradstreet already had decided to strike out for Detroit without bothering about the Delawares and Shawnees, so that the argument that by dealing with them he was being duped into postponing his attack[13] is unacceptable. In reality, the peace overtures were regarded by Bradstreet as a fortunate windfall and the terms he arranged, while possibly too generous, did attempt to guard against Indian deception. Moreover, they postponed the outbreak of hostilities between the Indians and Bradstreet's untried, and in his mind inadequate, troops and altered not one iota his already-established plan of by-passing the Delawares and Shawnees. Negotiating the treaty was admittedly a risky affair but, given Bradstreet's plans and the nature of the articles of peace, it was a treaty by which he lost little and, if it did hold, by which he stood to gain a great deal. It was, in short, a risk well worth taking, and he took it.

The additional question of whether Bradstreet was empowered to negotiate with the Indians can be dealt with more briefly. It will be recalled that by his original April 2 orders, while he was not specifically authorized to grant peace, neither was he instructed not to do so.

Lake Erie Camp at L'Ance aux Feuilles August the 12th 1764," in Sullivan *et al.*, *Johnson Papers*, 11, 328-33.

12. "The Montresor Journals," N.Y.H.S., *Collections 1881*, Appendix 4, 527.

13. Alden, *General Gage in America*, 97.

Indeed, vague suggestions, latent implications, and discretionary powers combined to leave considerable room for such activities. Although J. R. Alden argues that Bradstreet "had no power to sign treaties," this being Johnson's responsibility, even the generally critical Francis Parkman finds the Colonel's "instructions were not explicit" concerning this point.[14] Bradstreet's own complete confidence in the legitimacy of his action and unwavering faith in his interpretation of the orders was revealed in the open summary of his actions which was dispatched to Gage two days after the negotiations and treaty making.

After resuming his journey and reaching Presqu'Isle, Bradstreet sat down and in several letters unequivocally explained his actions. To Gage he wrote: "Agreeable to your Instructions to grant Peace & His Majesty's protection to such Savages who shall lay down their Arms & beg for it; I enclose you what has pass'd between me & the Deputys of all the Nations who Inhabit the Lands of Sandusky, the Sciotio Plains, Muskinham, the Ohio, Presque Isle &ca &ca and your Excellency may depend on my marching to the plains of Siotio if I find they intend to play me the least trick." A letter and a copy of the peace also went off to Colonel Bouquet with the explanation that the treaty was "Agreeable to Gen. Gages Orders" and the advice that perhaps Bouquet should delay his advance upon the Delawares and Shawnees until new directions, occasioned by the arrival of Bradstreet's "Letters and Articles of Peace," were received from General Gage. Furthermore, there was no hint of wrongdoing or overstepping his authority when, on the same day, Bradstreet informed his British friends of what he clearly regarded as a personal triumph. "Having at last got the better of all disappointments, [and] got into the Field of Action," he glowingly reported to Charles Gould, "and began with making a Peace & humbling a proud & troublesome Set of Savages, I enclose you a Copy of the Peace." Gould was urged to send a copy on to Sir Jeffery Amherst, excusing Bradstreet's own failure to write as caused by "the hurry I am really in, finding I have nothing to ensure Success but uncommon dispatch, having to do with other Nations soon."[15] Undoubtedly Bradstreet believed it to be within his power to make Indian treaties and he acted accordingly. Judged only on the basis of Gage's instructions and comments to the Colonel prior to the treaty, such a course was theoretically justifiable and perfectly understandable.

Completely oblivious to the outraged reaction and immediate disavowal his treaty of peace was to provoke from both Bouquet and Gage, Bradstreet pressed on towards Detroit. Along the way further meetings were held with other hostile tribes such as the Wyandots, Ottawas, and Miamis. By threatening to attack them Bradstreet extracted their

---

14. Parkman, *The Conspiracy of Pontiac*, 391; Alden, *General Gage in America*, 97.
15. Bradstreet to Gage, August 14, 1764, Gage Papers, A.S./23; Bradstreet to Bouquet, August 14, 1764, "Papers Relating to the Indian Wars of 1763 and 1764," in Franklin B. Hough, ed., *Diary of the Siege of Detroit in the War with Pontiac* (Albany, 1860), 282-83; Bradstreet to Gould, August 14, 1764, Amherst Papers, Packet 45, 21 P.A.C., and also in T.P.C., 128/127.

commitments to meet with him at Detroit to sign a final peace treaty. Carried away by the exhilarating success which appeared to be meeting every peace overture extended to the Indians, Bradstreet chose to attempt what amounted to a grandiose pacification of the entire midwest. On August 26, 1764, he issued orders to Captain Thomas Morris, who was to be accompanied by a twenty-three man party, to strike out for Fort Chartres in the Illinois country. The long instructions drafted for Morris assigned him the onerous, and indeed impossible, chore of persuading any French and Indian inhabitants of the area with whom he might come in contact that it was foolish "to obstruct the English coming up the Mississippi or by any other Route to take possession of the Illinois Country." The French residents were to be reminded that once they took the oath of allegiance, which Morris could administer, they could expect to "enjoy in every respect the same privileges and immunities with His Majesty's new Subjects of Canada." The Indian inhabitants were to be informed that there now was "a General peace and tranquility" between the English "and all the Savages with which they were at War." If they truly were inclined to live "in peace and Brotherly love with the English," they could depend "on His Majesty's favour and protection." On his return to Detroit Morris was to provide Bradstreet with a full report of his activities and his observations concerning "the people and Country."[16] Although Bradstreet demonstrated no awareness of it when he first launched Morris on this dangerous mission into potentially hostile territory, part of which remained very responsive to Pontiac's war cry, the Captain's journey and reports were to be a useful acid test as to whether the peace treaties negotiated, and to be negotiated, were indeed taking effect. Morris' journey, and a confrontation with the elusive Pontiac himself, were soon to provide Bradstreet with one of the first warnings concerning the imminent collapse of his hastily erected house of cards.

After Morris' August 26 departure the expedition's westward movement resumed and, the next day, the end of the journey, at least for Bradstreet, arrived. They reached Detroit, and after the cannon of the fort and those on Bradstreet's "Gun Boats" boomed out an exchange of greetings, the troops disembarked to make camp above the town on the north side. During the next few days the Detroit garrison was relieved, the French inhabitants "took the Oath of allegiance," Captain William Howard was dispatched to Michilimackinac with a 100-man detachment, and the construction of barracks and wharves, as well as a general examination of the fort's defenses, commenced. While these activities constituted a faithful execution of Gage's April 2 orders, Bradstreet, with considerable anticipation, looked forward to his approaching additional coup in what was to become the more contentious matter of his Indian negotiations. It was his optimistic expectation

---

16. "The Montresor Journals," N.Y.H.S., *Collections 1881*, 281-84; Alden, *General Gage In America*, 97; Parkman, *The Conspiracy of Pontiac*, 391; Bradstreet's instructions to Captain Thomas Morris, August 26, 1764, Gage Papers, A.S./23. See Peckham, *Pontiac*, 256-60, for a fuller discussion of the progress of Morris' mission.

that the imminent Detroit conference would lead not only to a "general Peace" marked by compliance with all his demands, but that it would cause even the great Pontiac "to be given up to be sent down to the Seacoast & maintain'd at his Majesty's Expence the Remainder of his Days."[17] Apparently, to Bradstreet, not only did the heroes of His Majesty's wars deserve pensions and preferment but even the villains of the piece could expect some form of kind consideration.

The much-awaited conference, with the Ottawas, Hurons, Chippewas, and Potawatomies in attendance, but Pontiac conspicuously absent, commenced on September 5 and concluded on September 7 with a treaty of peace, which was slightly amended on September 10 to accommodate the late arriving Mississaugi-Chippewas. The chiefs present were completely submissive, totally apologetic, and obligingly willing to explain that even the missing Pontiac was now in the same peace-seeking mood. Indeed, "he was hea[rti]ly Ashamed of what had happened, and if he could be forgiven he would be very thankfull; and do all the Service in his power to the English." Accepting their desire for peace as perfectly sincere, Bradstreet on September 7 presented them with a six-point treaty. They were to acknowledge themselves to be "the Subjects and Children of... George the third" who had "Sovereignty Over all and every part of this Coun[try] full and as ample a manner as in any part of his [ ]Dominions whatever." There followed what could be described generally as a repeat of several of the terms earlier extended to the Delawares and Shawnees. Violators of the treaty were to be punished by the other nations; Indians committing offences against Englishmen were to be delivered up to the Detroit commandant for punishment; all prisoners and deserters were to be sent to the nearest English post; authorized settlers were to be welcomed as "friends and Brothers," and French land grants within their villages were to be rescinded and the inhabitants removed. Quite different from the earlier arrangement was a clause which Bradstreet included for Pontiac's benefit. Because of a request from Captain Morris and "also on account of Pondiac's Submission & promise of future good behaviour and Friendship to the English, I do hereby Pardon and For[give] him and he may meet me in the utmost safety at Sandusky."[18] Acceptance of these terms by the chiefs in attendance theoretically brought an end to hostilities in the area of Detroit.

---

17. "The Montresor Journals," N.Y.H.S., *Collections 1881*, 284-87; Bradstreet to [Gage], August 28, 1764, in Sullivan et al., *Johnson Papers*, 11, 340.

18. "Congress With The Western Nations," Detroit, September [7-10], 1764, in Sullivan, et al., *Johnson Papers*, 4, 526-30; Peckham, *Pontiac*, 261-62. Parkman, *The Conspiracy of Pontiac*, 393, further breaks down the nations in attendance, listing the participants as the Ottawas, Ojibwas, Pottawattamies, Miamis, Sacs, and Wyandots. Likely by this time Bradstreet had received the early optimistic reports of Morris concerning his journey. He had discovered the tribes encountered thus far to be "not averse to peace," some actually courting it, while Pontiac appeared to him "quite tractable." Bradstreet was further advised that "kind treatment will infallibly open a way into the Illinois Country." See Morris to Bradstreet, August 31, 1764, T.P.C., 128/143 and September 2, 1764, T. P.C., 128/148.

Agreement with the treaty, moreover, opened Detroit and the entire midwest, in an equally theoretical sense, to the sort of settlement and development which Bradstreet had long advocated. This was achieved by the treaty's opening article which, upon first glance, represented a significant and unexplainable departure from prevailing British Indian policy. Bradstreet had forced the Indians into an acknowledgment of British sovereignty over their territory and also defined their position as dependent subjects of the Crown. They were viewed as sons of the "King your Father," rather than as independent nations who looked to the British monarch as their brother. L. H. Gipson feels that the change must have been "unwittingly" accepted by the Indians while Francis Parkman claims that Bradstreet's use of such terms was "impolitic and absurd." But there was method in Bradstreet's madness which completely escapes both historians. Throughout the treaty he repeated several times the Indians' new status and carefully explained to the tardy Mississaugi-Chippewas the importance of their appreciating this change. The Colonel observed that "they made use of the word Brother[s] instead of Subjects and Children of the King of England," and he informed them "nobody were to be admitted into the aforementioned Submission and Articles of Peace, but such as acknowledge themselves to be Subjects and Children of the King of England."[19]

The explanation for Bradstreet's determined definition of the Indians' status is found in an attempt made on his behalf, if not directly by him, to follow up the treaty, as well as in several of his actions while still at Detroit. An undated and unsigned memorial was eventually submitted to the British government suggesting a grant of land at Detroit as well as approval of the formation of a settlement and separate government. After summarizing the September 7 treaty, the memorial proceeded to argue that "From the Right acquired by the above Treaty the Col. [Bradstreet] thinks that His Majesty may in Justice and the ordinary Exertion of his Prerogative make what Grants of those Lands he pleases, & erect such Governments as in His Royal Wisdom he sees meet." The document then went on to repeat almost every one of the arguments used by Bradstreet late in 1763 when he presented his case for Detroit's development to Charles Gould and concluded: "the Col. [Bradstreet] therefore in his Memorial prays that Detroit may be erected into a separate Government and offers to transport and settle 600 Families in that Country, upon Condition of a Grant of 150 Acres of Land on the Banks of the River for each Family, and what over and above for Himself and His Associates may be thought reasonable for them."[20]

---

19. Gipson, *The British Empire Before the American Revolution*, 9, 121; Parkman, *The Conspiracy of Pontiac*, 394; "Congress With The Western Nations," Detroit, September [7-10], 1764, in Sullivan et al., *Johnson Papers*, 4, 532-33.

20. "A Short Abstract of the Proceedings at a Congress held at Detroit the 7th Septr. 1764, by Col. Bradstreet with the Deputies of the Indian Nations who inhabit that Country, and also of his Memorial for a Grant of Lands to form a Settlement there and a separate Government," n.d., M.G. 23, A4, Shelburne MSS, 50/144-46, P.A.C.

There is considerable evidence that this scheme was very much on Bradstreet's mind during and after the Detroit treaty negotiations. In the treaty itself, Article IV forewarned the Indians of the settlers with whom, Bradstreet hoped, they soon would have to contend. They were reminded that "when any Families come to Settle by permission of the King you are to esteem them friends and Brothers." Positive steps towards the fulfillment of his plan were taken the same day that this treaty was signed. Immediately after its ratification on the morning of September 7, Bradstreet proposed to his officers that they apply "for Grants of Lands here, for the advantage of the Crown & this new Colony." Evidently his proposal met with considerable approval at Detroit since a few days later Lieutenant-Colonel John Campbell, who was to remain at the post as commandant, was instructed not to impede the project. Since "many officers" had now applied "for Lands upon the Banks and the Islands of this Streight," Bradstreet explained, "You are therefore not to Grant Lands to any Person or Persons whatever untill the Kings pleasure shall be known thereupon." For the moment, Bradstreet contented himself with a one sentence suggestion to his English friends concerning his Detroit plans. He briefly commented to Gould "that it is absolutely necessary to support what is done by having more & good Troops in these parts."[21] In any case, his Detroit scheme had been set in motion once more and Gould was soon to be swamped with materials in support of it, designed for use in his solicitations.

In addition to Bradstreet's routine military duties, the delicate task of making peace, and the planning and pushing of a settlement scheme, the Colonel had other matters to deal with in Detroit. There is some evidence that he used his position of authority to engage in his own trading activities. This is particularly ironic in view of the fact that during his movement to and return from Detroit, the one feature of the entire campaign which earned Gage's consistent and unqualified support was the way in which Bradstreet seemed to clamp a heavy lid upon the Indian trade. As early as April of 1764 Gage had reminded Bradstreet that until peace was achieved with the Indians, trade was to be entirely suspended. In order to get around this restriction, firms such as "Duncan, Stirling & Campbel of Schenectady" approached the General, requesting special passes, but were abruptly rebuffed.[22] Obviously Gage intended Bradstreet to take the same hard line with aspiring traders, and in reporting his handling of trade matters Bradstreet did not disappoint his commander. In fact, he went to considerable lengths to harass one of the partners in the above-mentioned company, a Mr. Sterling, who like many others dispatched his goods westward

---

21. "Congress With The Western Nations," Detroit, September [7-10], 1764, in Sullivan et al., *Johnson Papers*, 4, 529; "The Montresor Journals," N.Y.H.S., *Collections 1881*, 289; Bradstreet's instructions to John Campbell, September 10, 1764, Gage Papers, A.S./40, and also in Bradstreet MSS, A.A.S.; Bradstreet to Gould, September 12, 1764, T.P.C., 128/128.

22. Gage to Bradstreet, April 30, 1764, Gage Letters.

behind Bradstreet's expedition in expectation of an eventual reopening of trade.

Along the route Bradstreet made sure that Gage was aware of the continuing problems presented by the eager traders with goods at the ready, only awaiting an official freeing of the trade or an illicit opportunity to evade the restrictions. As soon as he had arrived at Schenectady Bradstreet noted that "This Town is now full of Indian goods," and he was concerned that "the owners would do every thing they could to get them up the Country." Once he had reached Niagara, with the agreement of Johnson, a carefully controlled trade was allowed. This arrangement was accepted by Gage as "judicious and right," but it clearly failed to satisfy the more enterprising traders such as Mr. Sterling. He was busily engaged in getting his goods moved over the Niagara portage along with the army's provisions, and then conspiring with one of Bradstreet's officers, a Captain Egshaw, to stow fourteen of his barrels on one of the boats bound for Detroit.[23] It was at Detroit that Bradstreet caught up with both Sterling and Egshaw. Although he attempted to curb the trading speculation occurring there by calling in "All current paper money made by the Merchants," he endeared himself to the traders by ordering "an open free Trade as before with the Savages" the day after the September 7 peace was concluded. But he was still concerned about the way in which "his Majesty's service has been greatly obstructed this summer by Traders constantly smuggling goods in the Kings Vessels," and was determined that the few individuals apprehended while engaged in this nefarious practice, among whom were Sterling and Egshaw, should not escape punishment. Thus, he instructed Lieutenant-Colonel John Campbell to have the master of every vessel report his cargo to the town major, and should traders' goods be found accompanying the military supplies, they were to be confiscated. Furthermore, "such Goods as were lately smuggled here ... belonging to Mr. Sterling and by my order put into the Kings Store do remain there untill General Gage may think proper to give his Directions about them." At the same time, Bradstreet "dismissed Captain Egshaw from the service."[24]

All this gained the complete concurrence of General Gage. Bradstreet was, he wrote, "very right" in abolishing the paper currency,

---

23. Bradstreet to Gage, June 10, 1764, Gage Papers, A.S./19; Equivalents in barter established by John Bradstreet, July 19, 1764, in Sullivan et al., *Johnson Papers*, 4, 490-91; Gage to Bradstreet, August 16, 1764, Gage Letters. Because of the adverse impact Pontiac's rebellion had upon the New York traders and their desire to recoup their losses as soon as possible, Canedy, "An Entrepreneurial History Of The New York Frontier, 1739-1776," 194-97, 296, discusses Bradstreet's attempts to control them during the Detroit expedition. Unfortunately, in dealing with Bradstreet's own trade involvement he does not go beyond the comments in Shy's *Toward Lexington* and thus sheds no new light on exactly who Bradstreet's New York trading allies were and the extent of his involvement.

24. "The Montresor Journals," N.Y.H.S., *Collections 1881*, 288; Canedy, "An Entrepreneurial History Of The New York Frontier, 1739-1776," 297; Bradstreet's instructions to John Campbell, September 10, 1764, Gage Papers, A.S./40.

while Captain Egshaw should be "tried and publickly disbanded" and Sterling should be prosecuted by "the laws of the Province." What Gage certainly would not have condoned were the activities of Bradstreet, which were graphically pictured by one of the frustrated Montreal traders, Henry Bostwick. He outlined the "maney Oppossisions by Bradstreet and his underlings" which met his own trading attempts. While applying such restrictions, he charged, that same Bradstreet, allied with "Gallans & Company, Com[missary] Loring & Vancake & Com," was allowing "Severil Thousands of Pounds of Goods to Detroyet," some of it marked as naval stores, and all of it "Stored in kings Stores" and "Carryed in king carridis [carriages?]." The prospect of such unfair competition was bad enough, but even the chance to compete had been denied Bostwick. "I went to Broadstret at Detroyet," he reported, "and beged might have my small things brought forward in the next vessels, but the first Sallautation, was God-Dam you All for a Parsel of Raskels, I will have some of you hanged, and was for hanging Every Boddy in Traid."[25]

Bostwick's picture of Bradstreet and the Indian trade was, to say the least, substantially different from Gage's conception of the Colonel's activities in this area. It is difficult to reconcile the quite different versions. Was this a case of an overly zealous officer doing his job all too well, as the explanatory letters to Gage and the approving comments of his commander seem to indicate? Was Bradstreet an officer whose dedication to duty merely provoked a hostile reaction from a frustrated and thoroughly antagonized trader? Or were Bostwick's claims quite accurate indications of the Colonel's personal involvement in trading activities? Were these activities shrewdly concealed by Bradstreet's orders and comments to his commander, which portrayed himself as the ever vigilant opponent of illicit traders and smugglers? Certainly Bradstreet was no stranger to commercial ventures of this sort where his military position could be used for his personal financial profit. The fine line between the service of the Crown and the service of John Bradstreet himself always had been blurred or non-existent. Likewise, Bradstreet's tendency to try to cover his tracks and vindicate himself by the exaggerated action and the well-timed, over-inflated expression of

---

25. Gage to Bradstreet, October 15, 1764, Gage Letters; Henry Bostwick to James Beekman, December 10, 1764, in Philip L. White, ed., *The Beekman Mercantile Papers 1746-1799* (New York, 1956), 2, 953-53. This is the document on which Shy, *Toward Lexington*, 224-25, bases his comment that "Bradstreet seems to have had several thousand pounds worth of Indian trade goods with him, labeled 'King's stores,' with which he, Commodore Joshua Loring of the Navy, and several others planned to make a killing." It is interesting that in this scheme Bradstreet was linked with Joshua Loring. They were old colleagues since Louisbourg days but their relationship was soon to be rather strained. After the Detroit expedition, Bradstreet claimed that Loring had overcharged for some rum. As a result, Loring suggested that while he would never be guilty of such a deed, "there is an old Proverb in English, that the old woman would never have looked for her Daughter in the oven if She had not been there her self." See Joshua Loring to Philip Schuyler, April 1, 1765, Schuyler Papers, Box 23, N.Y.P.L.

a sense of duty and loyalty to the Crown were by now pronounced features of his approach to his patrons and superiors. Thus, there is a strong possibility that Bostwick was quite accurate. That being the case, the irony of the Bradstreet-Gage relationship becomes clearer. On a good number of the contentious questions which arose between the two men, Bradstreet had a reasonable position and was essentially in the right. Yet he frequently suffered stinging rebukes from his commander concerning the incorrectness of his actions. In this case, on one of the matters where there was some evidence of wrongdoing and calculated deception on Bradstreet's part, he gained the unwitting plaudits of General Gage.

As Bradstreet prepared to depart for Sandusky, however, in the distance and unknown to him a storm of abuse and criticism was about to break. Colonel Henry Bouquet had received word of Bradstreet's August 12 Lake Erie treaty on August 27 and promptly recoiled in horror and indignation. Immediately he wrote to the still uninformed Gage expressing his utter 'astonishment" at Bradstreet's action. These terms of peace contained "not the least satisfaction" for the massacres and damages committed by "those Infamous Murderers," the Delawares and Shawnees. Furthermore, their "horrid perfidies" had not ceased, since their raiding parties continued to ravage the frontier, killing and taking captives. Thus, the peace clearly was not being observed. Moreover it came at the worst possible moment since it was only now that both armies were ready to penetrate "into the Heart of the Enemies country." In addition, Bouquet pointed out the personal affront inflicted upon himself "by a younger officer in the Department where you have done me the honour to appoint me to Command" concluding a peace without referring the Indian deputies to him, but instead telling them "that he shall send and prevent my proceeding against them." For all these reasons, Bouquet felt that he must ignore this peace and push on to the Ohio where he hoped to receive further orders from Gage. Boiling with anger at this "scandalous Treaty," his outrage was expressed not only to Gage but to Benjamin Franklin and Governor John Penn of Pennsylvania. But it was not until September 5 that he gently explained to Bradstreet himself his reservations about Gage's willingness to ratify such a peace and about the terms of the treaty itself. Meanwhile Gage, in a September 2 letter, quickly replied to Bouquet's complaints. He too expressed "astonishment" that Bradstreet would take it "upon himself" to conclude such an unsatisfactory peace. He was in total agreement with Bouquet's disavowal of the treaty, commenting:

> You do well to proceed in your operations. I annull and disavow the Peace. Attack and use every means to extirpate the Shawnees and Delawares and listen to no Terms of Peace till they deliver the Promoters of the war into your hands to be put to death and send their deputys to Sir William Johnson to sue for Peace.

Gage was sending a more elaborate disavowal to Bradstreet via Bouquet while a duplicate was dispatched via Niagara.[26] By early September the rumours of Bradstreet's folly gained momentum as his August 12 peace became identified as a discredited failure.

At Detroit the Colonel remained totally unaware of the repudiation his initial treaty had received from his superiors as well as the Indians' failure to honour it by faithful adherence to its terms. On September 10 he entrusted the command of Detroit to Lieutenant-Colonel John Campbell with the confident assertion that "Peace is now concluded with all the Nations and Tribes of Savages who were at War." Two days later, in remarks to Charles Gould, the same certainty that all was well prevailed. "If I have done too much," he commented, "excuse me to my friends, saying, that I have assur'd You, nothing less than a determin'd resolution to oblige the Savages to such a Submission would have answer'd." But that very day the first of a series of long-delayed letters from Gage reached him and should have raised immediate uncertainties in his mind about the wisdom of his actions. In the first letter, written on August 16, Gage was replying to Bradstreet's decision to by-pass the Delawares and Shawnees. Disappointed at such a course, Gage pointed out that all the reported Indian peace gestures were completely tentative and uncertain, and that the heartland of the Delawares and Shawnees, at least in terms of their crops "planted on the Scioto," was not that distant or difficult to reach. Since he was presented with a "fait accompli," however, it was impossible to alter Bradstreet's decision. But in dealing with the Detroit Indians, Gage ordered him "without delay either to bring those nations to such a peace, as shall, to appearance, be sincere and lasting, or in failure of that, to attack them and do your best endeavors to extirpate them." Once this was accomplished, Bradstreet was to turn his force against the Delawares and Shawness, and in coordinated timing with Bouquet's expedition and by the route outlined in his original orders, or a better one if such could be discovered, strike hard at these defiant tribes. Gage now was extremely precise in his directions as he ordered Bradstreet to "use every means in your power to destroy them; Nor will you suffer yourself to be amused by those nations, the Shawnese & Delawares, by Offers of peace unless they immediately deliver into your hands Ten of the Chief promoters of the War, to be put to Death and agree to go, in a proper manner to Sir William Johnson to sue for peace."[27]

---

26. Bouquet to Gage, August 27, 1764, "The Montresor Journals," N.Y.H.S., *Collections 1881*, Appendix 4, 528; Gage to Bouquet, September 2, 1764, in ibid., 529; Bouquet to Benjamin Franklin, August 27, 1764, in Labaree et al., *Franklin Papers*, 2, 326; John Penn to Bouquet, August 31, 1764, in Stevens and Kent, *Bouquet Papers*, Series 21650, Part 2, 110; Bouquet to Bradstreet, September 5, 1764, Gage Papers, A.S./24.

27. Bradstreet's instructions to John Campbell, September 10, 1764, Gage Papers, A.S./40; Bradstreet to Gould, September 12, 1764, T.P.C., 128/128; Gage to Bradstreet, August 16, 1764, Gage Letters.

Too late, Gage had spelled out the sort of temporary peace terms desired and designated Johnson as the man to handle the final negotiations. Taken aback by these statements, Bradstreet defended his own peace negotiations and expressed his faith in these arrangements. Since "the Peace I have granted the Shawnes, Delawars . . . is agreable to your Instructions," he argued in apparent reference to the original orders, then he could only conclude that Bouquet's expedition by now had been stopped. Furthermore, "as I have no reason to think, as yet, they will not continue the Peace and comply with the Engagements of their Deputies I can only assure Your Excellency if they do not my utmost abilities will be exerted to punish them severely." Promptly the next day the first of many signs emerged that Bradstreet's peace had not held. A bateau arrived from Niagara with word that about "800 Warriors" were assembling at Sandusky not for purposes "of ratifying the treaty" but instead "to oppose our troops from disembarking." Orders immediately were issued for the troops to decamp and embark the next morning for Sandusky.[28] It was slowly dawning on Bradstreet that the final feather in his cap which he had hoped to find at Sandusky might be replaced by the greatest humiliation of his entire military career.

By September 18 the Lake Erie journey had been completed and the expedition reached the point on Sandusky Lake where an English fort once had stood. Bradstreet settled down in shaken but still hopeful expectation that the Delawares, Shawnees, and other tribes involved in the August 12 treaty would soon appear. Rumours abounded of their imminent appearance but each proved unfounded. Extensions of the time allowed were officially granted but the new deadlines passed unheeded. The chiefs who were supposed to ratify the treaty did not arrive. What did arrive were several further blows completely disabusing Bradstreet of any final hopes he might have had about the success of his August 12 negotiations. On September 21 a letter and the journals of Captain Thomas Morris reached him. Although at first the wandering Captain had been optimistic about the peaceful intentions of the various tribes, and even of Pontiac, he soon discovered this to be a false façade. The Shawnees and Delawares, it turned out, were particularly anxious to continue the war against the English and openly gloated over their deception of Bradstreet. This turn of events was revealed to Bradstreet in Morris' journals while in an accompanying letter the Captain stated his fears that "a mine is Laid, & the Match Lighted to blow us up. The Senecas, Shawnese, & Delawares, have sent their war belts to all the Nations; who only wait the signal for a General Attack."[29]

---

28. Bradstreet to Gage, September 12, 1764, Gage Papers, A.S./24; "The Montresor Journals," N.Y.H.S., *Collections 1881*, 291.

29. Peckham, *Pontiac*, 258-59; Morris to Bradstreet, September 18, 1764, Gage Papers, A.S./28. Heavy reliance has been placed upon "The Montresor Journals," N.Y.H.S., *Collections 1881*, 291-96, for the basic chronology and background of events at Sandusky during this period.

In a masterful understatement Captain John Montresor commented that at this point our "affairs do not wear the best appearance." In reality, Bradstreet was greatly alarmed by Morris' reports and was particularly fearful of his own exposed position at Sandusky. As a result, on September 23, he ordered a retreat to the carrying place between Lakes Sandusky and Erie, where his troops entrenched themselves, expecting the worst. It was here on September 25 that "an Express from General Gage to Col Bradstreet by the way of Niagara" arrived,[30] delivering the final crushing blow to his peace negotiations. Gage expressed his "great astonishment" at Bradstreet's August 12 treaty since it contained not "the smallest satisfaction" for the "traiterous proceedings, or the horrid and Cruel Massacres, these Indians have been guilty of." At considerable length Gage then went on to point out that Bradstreet had absolutely no authority to engage in peace negotiations. Admittedly, the General conceded, his August 16 letter allowed Bradstreet to negotiate with the Detroit Indians, but the Shawnees and Delawares were a different matter. Bradstreet had been specifically ordered to attack them in his original instructions and, in addition, they were definitely not included under the authority given the Colonel in that same document "*to offer peace, and his Majesty's protection &ca.*" Not only was it a mistake on Bradstreet's part to think this passage applied to the Shawnees and Delawares, but the Colonel also had misinterpreted what "to offer Peace" meant. Gage explained: "*To offer Peace* I think can never be construed a power to *conclude*, and *dictate the articles of peace*." The only person so empowered was Sir William Johnson, "his Majesty's sole Agent and Superintendent for Indian Affairs." These distinctions and divisions of responsibility were very illuminating but also very late, and one wonders why such precise explanations were not offered to Bradstreet in his original orders and in Gage's comments prior to the launching of the expedition. In any case, now that Bradstreet had stumbled into an allegedly unauthorized and unworthy peace, Gage stated that he could not "approve," "ratify," or "confirm" any treaty so "derogatory," "unsafe," and "so apparently productive of future wars." Accordingly Bradstreet was ordered to "break the peace you have made" and proceed against the Delawares and Shawnees in the manner outlined in Gage's earlier August 16 letter.[31]

Actually, as Gage himself realized, breaking the peace could be a ticklish proposition. If done without careful explanation and justification, it could create fears among the Indians that the British tended to make and break treaties at will. Concerned at this possibility, Gage, after ordering Bradstreet to go ahead and do it, turned to Sir William Johnson for guidance on this delicate question. After sending Johnson a copy of the treaty, repeating many of the harsh observations about it already offered to Bouquet and Bradstreet, Gage followed this up with

---

30. "The Montresor Journals," N.Y.H.S., *Collections 1881*, 298.
31. Gage to Bradstreet, September 2, 1764, Gage Letters.

another letter seeking Johnson's counsel. Gage felt that there were some suspicious signs that the peace was made without the full authority and knowledge of all the nations supposedly involved. It seemed strange to him that a delegation was not sent to the Niagara meeting if these tribes were truly desirous of peace. Furthermore, they came to Bradstreet rather inadequately equipped with wampum belts if peace discussions were their real intention, and their hostile actions since August 12 pretty clearly revealed their true inclinations. Nevertheless, there remained the remote possibility that they might appear at Sandusky and ratify the treaty. Should this occur, Gage wondered "what Effect it might have in Respect of us, with other Nations; and particularly with those, with whom you have lately concluded a regular Peace, should we break it on our Part?"[32]

This inquiry also allowed Gage to ascertain Johnson's own opinion of Bradstreet's action. But Sir William at the moment did not appear willing to indulge in denunciations of Bradstreet. Indeed, in late August he had expressed some of the same reservations that Bradstreet had repeatedly muttered about the chances of the expedition's success. The "lateness of the Season, & the disposition of the Inds. in general will I believe leave little to be done offensively," he commented to Cadwallader Colden, "& Coll. Bradstreet is well convinced of the absurdity of attempting to go to extreames with them." Even when confronted with the treaty and Gage's open criticisms, Johnson withheld judgment. Admitting that he "was concerned to hear" about the treaty, he seemed willing to attribute it to Bradstreet's possible unawareness that Bouquet was about to move to the attack. Turning to Gage's query about breaking the peace, Johnson admitted it could create problems, but he felt a number of reasons could be used to justify such an action. Contradictions and inconsistencies found in the Indian statements made during the August 12 negotiations could be cited, such as their commitment to call in their war parties, which clearly had not been executed. But above all he felt Gage had no need to worry, because the Indians were notoriously slow in surrendering prisoners and, no doubt, would fail to show up at Sandusky "within the time proposed." Apparently satisfied with this response, Gage selected one of Johnson's rationalizations—namely, the continuation of hostilities after the Indians had promised Bradstreet that they would cease—and instructed the Colonel to use it to justify his breaking of the peace. "You will please to make all the nations round you acquainted with their infamy, by this traiterous infraction of their pretended pacifick overtures to you," he wrote, "and give this for reason of your proceeding again against them, to obtain a proper satisfaction."[33]

---

32. Gage to Johnson, September 2, 1764, in Sullivan et al., *Johnson Papers*, 11, 342-44; September 4, 1764, in ibid., 4, 524-25.

33. Gage to Bradstreet, September 15, 1764, Gage Letters; Johnson to Colden, August 23, 1764, in Sullivan et al., *Johnson Papers*, 4, 513; Johnson to Gage, September 11, 1764, in ibid., 534-35.

At Sandusky, meanwhile, Bradstreet was not seeking excuses to proceed against the Delawares and Shawnees but was discovering reasons why it was impossible to do so. Before and during the campaign he repeatedly had voiced his lack of confidence in his troops and now that Gage expressly had ordered him to the attack there were others who apparently shared Bradstreet's reservations. This became evident at a September 27 Council-of-War which was convened to consider Gage's orders. At this meeting the expedition's guides were cross-examined concerning the distances involved in any move against the enemy, the state of the route, and the amount of supplies needed. From this testimony it was learned than an estimated journey of 225 miles was required to make contact with the Delawares and Shawnees. If the troops made 10 miles a day it would take "Forty two days to go and return." Without horses and carriages, provisions would have to be carried on the men's backs and, in view of the distances and time involved, it appeared an impossible burden. In addition, the troops were considered to be "so fateagued with hard Service" and those remaining "so reduced" in numbers that they could not take such an exhausting campaign. Consequently all the officers commanding the various military units involved in the expedition signed the report of this meeting, which offered as a conclusion their considered opinion that "Genl. Gages orders to Colonel Bradstreet are not practicable, nor the troops in a Condition to attempt so long a March."[34]

Confirmation of the expedition's inability to carry out Gage's orders is found in an admittedly convenient letter from the Sandusky camp, dated October 5, which appeared in the November 19 issue of the Newport *Mercury*. The writer, an officer in the expedition, argued that since the rivers which they were to use in moving against the Shawnees and Delawares were impassable because of low water, their only recourse was to convert their boats "to make them sail upon dry ground." The "impracticability of a march into that country 300 miles from home" was strongly emphasized and linked with the "incapacity of the troops to attempt it," more than one-half of them being "in the Condition of Fallstaff's." The approach of winter and rapidly declining provisions also sapped any willingness to do battle, since the letter concluded with the author's heartaches "at the apprehension of snow and ice, as my poor kegg is almost out; so it is with us all." This picture of the difficulties facing the expedition and the resultant reluctance to execute Gage's orders is quite different from that offered by Francis

---

34. "At a meeting of the Commanding Officers of Corps at the Camp near the carrying place of Sandusky Lake Sept. 27, 1764," Gage Papers, A.S./28. This document was signed by Colonel John Bradstreet, Lieutenant-Colonel Israel Putnam commanding the Connecticut battalion, Major Peter Daley of the light infantry, Major George LeHunte of the light infantry, Major William McDonald of the Jersey battalion, Major William Hogan of the New York battalion, Major J.B.M. des Berges de Rigauville of the Canadian volunteers, Captain James Grant of the 80th Regiment, Captain Joseph Walton of the Royal Artillery, and Lieutenant George McDougall commanding a detachment of the 60th Regiment.

Parkman. It is his judgment that the army was "ready for the attempt" upon the Shawnees and Delawares and that the limited "difficulties could not have deterred a vigorous commander."[35] But unless Bradstreet had intimidated virtually his entire officer corps and was stage-managing a brilliant deception, a possibility not so remote as it might seem, it would appear that by this point the morale of the Colonel's force was at such a low ebb and the obstacles to the penetration of enemy country were substantial enough to provoke an outright challenge to General Gage's orders, in the form of an openly stated incapacity to meet the Delawares and Shawnees.

Despite such superficially convincing evidence that the expedition was not in a position to carry out Gage's orders, the possibility should not totally be discarded that Bradstreet guided the Council-of-War to this verdict and encouraged such letters of vindication to appear in the press. Two days after this meeting a "Court of Enquiry" was held at Sandusky and then the conclusions reached at these meetings, along with Bradstreet's analysis of the orders and correspondence which had been received from Gage, were rolled into one long vindication of his conduct. Possibly these and all the expedition's future moves were about to be carefully reshaped into defensive justifications of John Bradstreet's general conduct and particular actions. Quite clearly it was with vindication in mind that Bradstreet ordered the September 20 examination under oath of Captains Henry Montour and John Johnson. Both men were questioned concerning what orders Sir William Johnson had given the Iroquois when they joined Bradstreet's army at Niagara. Both men gave essentially the same answer. According to the response attributed to John Johnson: "Sir Wm Johnson always told them, with the Belts He gave the Five Nations, that they were to Join the Army Commanded by Col: Bradstreet, in order to give Peace to every Nation of Indians who demanded it, they Complying with such Terms as Colonel Bradstreet Should propose, And if they persisted in carrying on the War, they were Immediately to take up the Hatchet against them."[36] Thus, Bradstreet's Indian allies allegedly joined the expedition with the same understanding of its basic purpose as that held by Bradstreet himself. Moreover, Sir William Johnson was portrayed as also acknowledging, by his instructions to the Iroquois, that Bradstreet's expedition was to offer and grant peace to those Indian nations requesting it, while waging war only on those who continued hostilities.

With such convincingly arrayed evidence, Bradstreet, on the same day as the enquiry, penned a long response to Gage's September 2 disavowal of his peace-making activities with the Delawares and Shaw-

---

35. "Papers Relating To The Expeditions Of Colonel John Bradstreet And Colonel Bouquet In Ohio, A.D. 1764," *Western Reserve and Northern Ohio Historical Society*, 1, (1873), Tract 13, 4-5; Parkman, *The Conspiracy of Pontiac*, 402.

36. "Examination By Israel Putnam And Others," September 29, 1764, in Sullivan et al., *Johnson Papers*, 4, 549-50; "Copy of a Court of Enquiry," September 29, 1764, Gage Papers, A.S./25.

nees. "I shall prove from your Instructions and other papers" Bradstreet explained to his commander, that "I therein not only acted agreeable to your Instructions but also to your Excellency's first Intentions." Selecting the various articles in Gage's original instructions which mentioned the power "to offer Peace and his Majestys protection" along with the concluding general discretionary power, Bradstreet combined these quotations with extracts from Gage's August 16 letter, which clearly had ordered him to conclude a peace with the Detroit-area Indians. Thus, he argued:

> By these Instructions I never doubted my having power to grant Peace and his Majestys protection to all Nations of Indians, without exception, that should ask it of me, and surely Sir, your own Words of 16th. August shows it was your first Intention that I should construe the words *To Offer Peace* 'To make a formal and regular Peace that shall have the appearance of being sincere and lasting' tho' by your Letter of the Second Septemr. you think otherwise.

Bradstreet was torturing the evidence at this point, since he well knew that Gage's August 16 letter carefully had distinguished between the Delawares-Shawnees and the Detroit Indians, with peace being offered only to the latter and war waged on the former. He would have been on far safer ground if he had argued his case purely on the basis of the original orders, but he persisted in attempting to combine these with the August 16 statement, which resulted in an unconvincing distortion of Gage's intentions. Continuing on this rather unfortunate tangent, he pointed out that in his orders he was to attack the Wyandots, Shawnees, and Delawares while in Gage's August 16 letter the General assumed he was going to make peace at Detroit with the Wyandots. With far from impeccable logic Bradstreet then asserted: "certainly, if I had power to grant it to the Wendots of Sandusky, which you clearly infer I had, by supposing I was gone to do it, I assuredly, had the same power to grant it to the Shawanese and Delawares, as your order respecting them, in your Instructions to me is the same."

Other parts of Bradstreet's argument were more convincing and more honestly presented. Any doubts he might have had about his peace-making authorization vanished, he claimed, when he learned of Johnson's instructions to the Iroquois at Niagara. At this time the expedition's chore of both warring and offering peace was spelled out clearly, and Bradstreet, for purposes of verification, enclosed "the Affidavit of two Captains in the Indian Service [Johnson and Montour] respecting the same." Dealing with Gage's accusation that he had usurped a power which rightfully belonged to Johnson, the Colonel succinctly spiked the General's gun. Bradstreet pointed out that while at Niagara he had talked with Johnson about "making Peace with the Savages," but he did so "not in consequence of any Instructions from you, as you in a Letter, only desire me to correspond with him." Again when answering Gage's charge that he should not have acted without consulting his superior, Colonel Bouquet, Bradstreet crisply pointed out that Gage had completely failed to give any directions concerning his relationship with Bouquet. If he, Bradstreet, had been informed "by Letter or otherwise, that I was to have concerted matters with Col. Bouquet and not have acted without his participation, I certainly should have endeavoured to have done it, altho' I have not been nearer him than the distance of Three hundred Miles."

When he considered Gage's strictures concerning the terms of the peace treaty, Bradstreet relapsed into his unfortunate habit of making a valid point and then wandering off on a tangent of questionable validity. It was his opinion that there was "not one Officer that I have the Honor to Command but thought, as well myself" the treaty terms to be "honorable to his Majestys Arms and advantageous to the Nation." Judging from the day-by-day report on the expedition offered by Captain John Montresor this appeared an accurate observation. Montresor was in the habit of interrupting his narrative of the expedition's progress with pithy comments when noteworthy incidents or setbacks occurred. Yet while the treaty and other of Bradstreet's negotiations were faithfully recorded, never was there a note of doubt or criticism concerning the terms extended to the Indians.[37] Furthermore, the response of Bradstreet's officers to his scheme for a Detroit settlement and their more immediate and virtually unanimous agreement at Sandusky, with what were probably Bradstreet's own inclinations, revealed their continuing confidence in his actions. But the Colonel then proceeded to obfuscate this reasonable argument by drifting into an indictment of one of the treaties negotiated by Sir William Johnson. His own peace, Bradstreet charged, stood up very well, especially if it was compared with the July treaty negotiated with the Seneca at Niagara. At the same time as this nation was negotiating with Johnson they were sending war belts to other nations, and he enclosed papers from Captain Morris to prove that this was the case. Added to this was the fact that his own peace might have held if Bouquet immediately had halted his advance. The Shawnees, Bradstreet had heard, now explained that their failure to appear at Sandusky at the appointed time had been caused by Bouquet's army "continually advancing against them." The indirect attack on Johnson's treaty-making abilities and the quite direct, but completely implausible, argument that but for Bouquet his peace would have held did more damage than good to his defense.

Turning his attention to Gage's recent orders to move against the Delawares and Shawnees in coordination with Bouquet's expedition, Bradstreet explained that it was "absolutely impossible" for his troops to do so. While referring Gage to the "enclosed meeting of the Commanding Officers of the Corps," he also explained some of the many reasons why his force was incapable of conducting such a campaign. Low water in the Sandusky River and Cayahoga Creek would block the bateaux transportation of the troops. Moreover, his men were "more

---

37. "The Montresor Journals," N.Y.H.S., *Collections 1881*, 252-321.

than half worn out, ill, or rather not at all provided to encounter the inclemency of the approaching Season, the distance we have to return great, and what is still worse, more than half the Men in their best days were fitter to be in a Hospital than to come on the Service." Consequently all that Bradstreet could do in support of Bouquet was to remain at Sandusky until mid-October, thus posing at least a potential threat to the enemy while at the same time preventing any other tribes from joining the Shawnees and Delawares. In addition, he hoped to persuade "these Western Indians to war against them." In this way Bouquet's chore would be made a bit easier and the unruly Delawares and Shawnees would be brought to heel.

In the midst of this elaborate explanation and personal vindication, Bradstreet let slip what was probably his real evaluation of the entire tempestuous affair. "I am so far happy, that his Majestys Service has not suffered from my Peace, as you say Colonel Bouquet writes you, he will take no Notice of it." Thus, when all was said and done, an attempt at peace had been made and apparently had failed but no significant damage had resulted from the effort. This was totally in keeping with Bradstreet's attitude when he first negotiated the August 12 peace. With no intentions of battling the Shawnees and Delawares, owing to the ineptness of his troops, the opportunity for their easy pacification was eagerly snatched. Matters had not turned out according to his more optimistic expectations, but then again no military setback had been inflicted upon his troops or those commanded by Bouquet. The olive branch, to forgive a perhaps rash action and forget a far from disastrous attempt at peace-making, all in all an inconsequential incident, in this way was hesitantly extended to Gage. Nevertheless, Bradstreet's concluding words made clear that should criticisms and insinuations mount concerning his performance, he would battle unceasingly for personal vindication. "To end this long and disagreeable Letter Sir, I shall only add that I did not expect to receive such a Letter from you, as that of the Second September," he informed his commanding officer. "I have done my Duty to my King and Country and am ready to defend my Conduct, the sooner I am called on the more pleasure it will give."[38] The reluctant front-line warrior certainly had not lost his taste for the behind-the-lines battling which had characterized his entire career. What he had lost, however, was the convincing brilliant victory or unquestionably outstanding performance which at earlier stages of his career had contributed to successive vindications and the silencing of his behind-the-lines detractors.

As he had mentioned to Gage, Bradstreet remained at Sandusky for almost three further weeks. During this time he relayed word to Lieutenant-Colonel Campbell at Detroit and to the various Indian nations now allied with Great Britain concerning the need for war parties to harass the Shawnee and Delaware nations. Bradstreet him-

---

38. **Bradstreet to Gage, September 29, 1764, Gage Papers, A.S./25.**

self launched a number of such parties out of Sandusky, drawing upon the friendly Ottawas, Chippewas, and Hurons who were in the region. To his disgust, and in a rather ill-timed confirmation of his previously voiced suspicions, his Six Nations allies refused to participate in these raids. During several meetings with the Colonel they offered a variety of excuses for their non-participation. This failure to cooperate provoked Montresor's bitter comment that "By the Behaviour of the 6 Nations in General now with us, I sincerely apprehend them to be the greatest Ennemies to his Brittanic Majesty in North America." At the same time as the war parties were being dispatched, Bradstreet occasionally sent out detachments of regulars in feints against the enemy. It was hoped that such manoeuvres would persuade the ever-observant Shawnee and Delaware spies that a full-scale attack was about to be launched. Instead, these probes, such as that of October 15 on which 130 regulars marched, halted at concealed encampments not far distant from Sandusky, in this case 12 miles, for only a short stay and then made a quick return to the main camp. Time and supplies were running low, however, and on October 17, with the remark "tis necessity, absolute necessity that obliges me to turn the otherway,"[39] Bradstreet hinted to Bouquet that his departure was at hand.

Early the next morning the army abruptly broke camp as the "1400 men besides 150 Indians—59 Long Boats, one Barge & 9 Birch Canoes" set out for Niagara. As if the expedition had not met with enough deception and misfortune, the elements were about to take their toll, combining with human carelessness to turn the entire return journey into a nightmarish rout. After all the boats, except for one straggler, had been pulled up on a sandy beach, where the encampment for the first night was located, the weather changed. A violent storm suddenly broke, lashing the beach with high waves and destroying twenty-five of the boats, along with sizeable amounts of ammunition, provisions, and baggage. To Parkman, blame for the disaster rested squarely with Bradstreet, since it was his decision to camp on this "open exposed beach" when the safe refuge of a large river was not far distant. Bradstreet's explanation was that the "fear & laziness" of the provincials and the Canadians allowed the boats "to go adrift" since they failed to haul "up their Boats when order'd." This accusation was supported by Montresor who attributed "this unfortunate accident . . . to the entire negligence of the Troops."[40] Regardless of who bears the greater burden of guilt, the expedition's return journey had commenced with a major setback.

---

39. Ibid., October 5, 1764, Gage Papers, A.S./25; Bradstreet to Campbell, October 18, 1764, Gage Papers, A.S./26; Bradstreet to Bouquet, October 17, 1764, in Stevens and Kent, *Bouquet Papers*, Series 21651, 24; Indian Conference, October 5, 1764, in Sullivan et al., *Johnson Papers*, 11, 373-74; Meeting of October 10, 1764, Gage Papers, A.S./27; "The Montresor Journals," N.Y.H.S., *Collections 1881*, 302, 310.

40. "The Montresor Journals, N.Y.H.S., *Collections 1881*, 311-12; Parkman, *The Conspiracy of Pontiac*, 402; Bradstreet to Gage, November 4, 1764, Gage Papers, A.S./26.

Faced with the destruction of almost half of his boats, and a good number so badly damaged as to be beyond repair, Bradstreet had to make major adjustments to squeeze his force into the remaining vessels. As a result the artillery pieces, twelve guns in total, were buried to make room and to lighten the load. Even so, there was not enough space for all the potential passengers. In a predictable Bradstreet decision, in view of his unconcealed animosity towards the Iroquois, it was the Indians who suffered first; "115 of our Savages" were equipped with some powder and ball and ordered to strike out overland for Niagara. Progress was slow over the next few days as violent gales and generally tempestuous weather conditions continued to churn the lake, forcing the expedition into frequent rushes for shore and time-consuming delays. Boat after boat was found wanting and was abandoned, along with ammunition supplies, which were buried along the route, and more and more troops were forced ashore to march the remaining distance. By October 27 the main force went on half-rations while the approximately 500 men dispatched overland were "without a morsel of Provisions." Finally on November 5 Little Niagara was sighted by the main body of the troops and the following day, after traversing the portage route, Niagara itself was reached. For at least the relatively fortunate troops allowed the luxury of a cramped bateau journey, the ordeal was over. But the return in triumph once experienced by the hero of Fort Frontenac and reported in the public press was replaced by pictures of dejection and disaster such as those offered by the Newport *Mercury*.

> The distressed, struggling army are now daily crawling homeward. Many left their carcasses in the woods and along the lake, a prey to the wolves and other vermin, through mere fatigue and want. Some Indians and a few of the Indian officers are arrived in a shocking condition, having been in the woods twenty-six days without a morsel but what they killed, which was a trifle for this number.[41]

In sharp contrast to Bradstreet's Lake Erie humiliation was Bouquet's "well-planned and faultlessly executed expedition" launched out of Fort Pitt. Early in October he began the push into Delaware-Shawnee territory and, at almost the same time as Bradstreet's hasty departure from Sandusky, he opened peace negotiations with the hostile nations. During a conference which commenced on October 17 and concluded on October 20, Bouquet vociferously expressed his outrage at the way in which the warring tribes had failed to adhere to the terms of the original peace so generously granted them by Bradstreet. For this, Bouquet explained, they deserved the "severest

---

41. "The Montresor Journals," N.Y.H.S., *Collections 1881*, 312-18; Charles Whittlesey, "Col. Bradstreet's Misfortunes on Lake Erie in 1764," *Western Reserve and Northern Ohio Historical Society*, 2 (1886), Tract 66, 361-63; Newport *Mercury*, December 31, 1764, as quoted in "Papers Relating To The Expeditions Of Colonel John Bradstreet and Colonel Bouquet In Ohio, A.D. 1764," *Western Reserve and Northern Ohio Historical Society*, 1 (1873), Tract 13, 2.

Chastisement" but since "the English are a merciful, and generous People," they were to be given one last opportunity to prove their sincerity. Within twelve days all prisoners held within their villages had to be released; once that had been done he would offer peace terms. Determined to keep an intimidating pressure on the enemy, Bouquet used the period of grace to march into the heart of hostile Indian territory where he solidly entrenched himself. He was now clearly ready to do battle or accept their submission, whichever the Delawares, Shawnees, and Senecas chose. Realizing their exposed position, the Indians selected the latter and the surrender of their prisoners commenced. By November 12 temporary peace terms had been offered by Bouquet and accepted by the Indians. Fourteen hostages were handed over to the British forces, and the Delawares, Shawnees, and Senecas were to send fully empowered deputies to Sir William Johnson in order to negotiate a permanent peace.[42] By November 28 Bouquet's force had safely returned to Fort Pitt, where the applause and approval of Gage, as well as votes of thanks from the Pennsylvania and Virginia Assemblies, awaited this wilderness victory.

Notwithstanding the quite different notes on which the Bradstreet and Bouquet expeditions ended, both had contributed to what could be considered a successful campaign. Of course no decisive military defeat over, or any savage revenge upon, the hostile tribes had been gained. Indeed Pontiac remained unmolested, although with a diminished following. But the rebellious Indians generally had been pacified and the British hold on the inland country had been effectively re-established. Bradstreet's contribution consisted in the long-awaited relief of Gladwin's beleagured Detroit post, an expansion of the pacification of the Indians residing in the Detroit vicinity which Sir William Johnson earlier had commenced at Niagara, and the reopening of the various posts on the upper lakes. To be sure, his performance was blemished by a hasty peace which did not hold, his October failure to attack the Delawares and Shawnees, and the disastrous return from Detroit. But the peace, as it turned out and as J. W. Shy has pointed out, did not materially affect "the military outcome of the campaign."[43] Again, Bradstreet's inability to move against the Delawares and Shawnees when ordered did not delay or hinder their submission to Bouquet. On the contrary, Bradstreet had at least provided indirect aid to the southern thrust by arranging war parties, conducting some deceptive feints, and, luckily enough, delaying his return journey until Bouquet was in a sufficiently strong position to dictate terms to the hostile tribes. On the basis of the available evidence, moreover, Bradstreet appeared quite correct in not inflicting upon his demoralized

---

42. Gipson, *The British Empire Before the American Revolution*, 9, 124-26; Conferences held with the Senecas, Delawares and Shawnees, October 17 and 20, 1764, in Sullivan et al., *Johnson Papers*, 11, 438-44; Parkman, *The Conspiracy of Pontiac*, 412-32.

43. Peckham, *Pontiac*, 264; Parkman, *The Conspiracy of Pontiac*, 403; Shy, *Toward Lexington*, 136-37.

and tired troops the travails and dangers of a late fall overland campaign. As to his force's final setback while returning to Niagara, obviously the unpredictable weather and simple bad luck combined with human error, on the part of both Bradstreet and his troops, to produce an accidental tragedy.

While such a balancing of the Detroit expedition's successes and failures places Bradstreet's performance in a more favourable light than it has hitherto received, it should not be allowed to obscure the more immediate and painful realities surrounding his activities. If there was a hero who had righted and rescued the entire 1764 campaign, it certainly was not John Bradstreet. It was Colonel Henry Bouquet who quite rightly basked in the public's praise and complete approval of the Commander-in-Chief. Bradstreet's contributions, on the other hand, slid into the background to be largely overlooked, while the only memorable events of his entire effort seemed to be his blundered peace attempt and the tragic retreat of his broken army. Further complicating his position was the fact that Bradstreet had dared to lock horns with his commanding officer on so many occasions during the campaign that their previously poor relationship now had completely deteriorated. This was a time to tread carefully, to admit mistakes honestly, and to outline with modest understatement the limited contributions which had been made. Above all it was not the time to make new enemies by an outspoken defense of one's actions coupled with accusations and insinuations that the real guilt for any alleged blunders rested elsewhere. Unnecessary vendettas and unceasing efforts at total vindication were perhaps the worst possible tactics for Bradstreet at this moment. But these were the very tactics which had seen him through many an earlier crisis and these were the tactics he chose now.

In actuality, the man who Bradstreet regarded as his worst critic, General Thomas Gage, while blistering Bradstreet in his private letters to the Colonel, demonstrated a more considerate attitude in his official correspondence with the home authorities. Reporting to Lord Halifax concerning the ill-fated August 12 negotiations, he portrayed Bradstreet as "betrayed" into them when he unfortunately "was at too great a Distance to be acquainted with the Falsehood of their ['the Indians'] Assertions." This picture of Bradstreet as the victim of Indian deception was followed by letters revealing an apparent acceptance of the Colonel's other actions. The Detroit negotiations appeared to be more successful in terms of Indian sincerity and the chances of this peace being observed, and had been transmitted to Sir William Johnson for his more knowledgeable judgment. When Bradstreet returned to Sandusky and discovered the Shawnee and Delaware treachery, Halifax was told, the Colonel was quick to inform the Indians now at peace concerning this development and the need for their cooperation against those tribes who remained at war. Bradstreet's failure to mount an October offensive against the Delaware-Shawnees was the result of his "not finding the Troops under his Command in a Condition to march to the Plains of Scioto." Compensating for his failure to attack, he had "kept the Enemy in awe, by remaining encamped at Sandusky as long as the Season would permit, and Spiriting up the Indians with whom He had lately made Peace, to declare War, and send out Partys against them." The expedition's difficulties during the return over Lake Erie, according to Gage, resulted from "Misfortune" and "Accident" which had led to the troops' suffering "greatly in their march."[44]

Naturally it was to Gage's personal advantage to put the best possible gloss on the first major campaign conducted under his North American command; this was particularly the case when these various reports, including those concerning Bouquet, led up to his concluding assessment that by means of the campaign "the Country is restored to it's former Tranquility." To engage in any lengthy discussion of Bradstreet's failures and blunders might arouse speculation that the expedition was not the satisfactory success pictured. Thus Gage's not unkind treatment of Bradstreet in the official dispatches should not necessarily be interpreted as a sign of his emerging endearment and deepening respect for the Colonel. In a mid-October letter to Bradstreet, he was willing to express his approval of the Colonel's Detroit actions and his handling of the Indian trade problems; but when it came to the matter of the August 12 peace treaty, his old animosity again asserted itself. "They have negotiated with you on Lake Erie, and cut our Throats upon the Frontiers," he commented, while pointing out that with regard to Bradstreet's assuming that he had the right to make peace, "I must say that I can not find what you mention, either in my Instructions, or my Letters."[45]

On his part, it is clear that Bradstreet was unwilling to let the issue of the peace die a quiet death by at least granting Gage's point that the Indians were insincere in their peace overtures and by softening his claims that he was fully empowered to grant peace. When he received Gage's October 15 letter he in turn put the best possible gloss on it while making clear that nothing short of total vindication would satisfy him. It "gives me some satisfaction to find You approve of all my conduct except my mistaking your intentions in making a formal peace," he wrote, but he hoped that even Gage's reservations about the latter issue soon would be removed when a full explanation, his long statement of September 29, finally reached the General. Instead, when his carefully documented Sandusky letter defending all his actions reached Gage, it evidently removed none of the General's doubts and did not alter his basic criticisms of Bradstreet. It puzzled Gage how Bradstreet could possibly argue that his peace would have held if Bouquet had stopped his advance when there were so many readily available indications that

---

44. Alden, *General Gage in America*, 100; Gage to Halifax, September 21, 1764, in Carter, *Gage Correspondence*, 1, 38; October 13, 1764, in ibid., 40; November 9, 1764, in ibid., 43; December 13, 1764, in ibid., 46.

45. Gage to Bradstreet, October 15, 1764, Gage Letters; Gage to Halifax, December 13, 1764, in Carter, *Gage Correspondence*, 1, 46.

the Delaware-Shawnees were insincere and continued actively to wage war. As to Bradstreet's copious quotations from Gage's August 16 letter and April 2 instructions in support of his argument that he was empowered to grant peace, Gage sharply countered: "I am glad you make every thing so clear to your own Satisfaction, and wish I could agree with you."[46]

Other than this general comment, however, Gage appeared to be backing away from a detailed rebuttal of the legitimacy of Bradstreet's peace-making powers. Instead he focused on the Colonel's much weaker argument relating to the possibility of the Delawares and Shawnees honouring the August 12 peace. This attempt to deflect Bradstreet's attention from his stronger case to a weaker one apparently worked. In his next letter, Bradstreet entirely dropped the argument concerning his instructions and once more attempted to prove that the Shawnees and Delawares had been on the verge of submission when he returned to Sandusky in September. Obviously Gage much preferred to debate this issue, since the weight of the evidence was so clearly on his side. The treaty remained "a perfidious peace" to the General "tho' you seem resolved," he pointed out to Bradstreet, "notwithstanding the most glaring proofs of their perfidy, to be still deceived." If the Colonel honestly expected the Delawares and Shawnees to hand over their prisoners in September he was completely mistaken, since "you might have waited till Doomsday at Sandusky before you would have them delivered to you."[47] Thus the hot debate continued. Bradstreet's claims about his right to act had a certain validity while Gage's claims about the deliberately deceptive actions of the Delawares and Shawnees had equal validity. The battle had been joined and neither man would yield.

These written broadsides were being fired in November as Bradstreet moved from Niagara to Oswego and then down to Albany. This was perhaps fortunate since, no doubt, a face-to-face confrontation between the General and the Colonel would have provoked an even angrier exchange. Safely ensconced in his New York City headquarters Gage was spared this sort of disagreeable encounter, but Sir William Johnson was not. Loudly proclaiming his innocence of any wrongdoing, Bradstreet stormed into a meeting with Sir William. Up to this point Johnson had refrained from making any overly critical comments on Bradstreet's Detroit expedition. Even when pressed about the acceptability of the Colonel's Detroit peace, which contained a redefinition of the Indians' status and an open extension of British sovereignty over their territory, Johnson was very understanding. Admitting that an attempt to enforce such claims probably would set off even "greater Calamities" with the Indians than previously experi-

---

46. Bradstreet to Gage, November 4, 1764, Gage Papers, A.S./26; Gage to Bradstreet, October 26, 1764, Gage Letters.
47. Bradstreet to Gage, November 20, 1764, Gage Papers, A.S./27; Gage to Bradstreet, November 20, 1764, Gage Papers, A.S./27.

enced, Sir William still was unwilling "to censure the insertion of these Words done by any Officer Commanding an Army, as probably his Motive might be well intended."[48] This mellow mood abruptly altered when the fuming Bradstreet descended upon him.

Producing "many Papers" relating to the expedition, which Johnson apprehensively commented to Gage "plainly shew a good deal of design," Bradstreet proclaimed that "he would vindicate his conduct to the utmost, and shew the World he acted up to his Instructions." At first Johnson attempted to persuade Bradstreet that openly "publishing" his complaints would only make matters worse. But the Colonel, working himself into "a verry high Strain," answered that he must defend himself when attacked, particularly when attacked by Gage, whom he assumed "had wrote a great deal home to his disadvantage." Altering his approach, Johnson then tried to point out some of the weaknesses in Bradstreet's own position, but these comments on the Colonel's alleged "unfair Steps" seemed only to further incense Bradstreet. He responded with the infuriating suggestion that perhaps Johnson should be concerned about defending his own actions. By now angered and alienated, Sir William answered that "I could easily clear my conduct, that my verry Instructions would do that." When the swirling smoke of accusation and counter-accusation cleared, Bradstreet had managed to convert a previously cautious critic into a totally outraged opponent.

Johnson's description of this meeting quickly was passed to Gage, "that you may know the Design & guard against it" he explained,[49] and it was soon to be joined by what was intended as an even more damaging indictment of Bradstreet's conduct. Already completely upset by the tone and content of Bradstreet's arguments, as well as by the suggestion of his own negligence, Johnson's disgust and disrespect for the Colonel mounted over the next few weeks as the remnants of the Six Nations contingent which had served under Bradstreet's command struggled home from Sandusky. Greatly disturbed at the way "our Brother Skana" [Bradstreet] had treated them during the campaign, they poured out a story of insulting incompetence which totally differed from Bradstreet's own description of his conduct. Johnson proved a patient listener to their tale of woe, taking note of their major grievances and apologizing for "the commanding Officer's [Bradstreet's] want of Knowledge in their way of waging War &c." After his angry meeting with the Colonel Johnson had set down, on November 24, a fourteen-point critique of the Bradstreet expedition,[50] and it must have given him considerable satisfaction when a good number of his suspicions and reservations about Bradstreet's conduct were confirmed

---

48. Johnson to Gage, October 31, 1764, in Sullivan et al., *Johnson Papers*, 11, 394-96.
49. Ibid., November 20, 1764, in Sullivan et al., *Johnson Papers*, 11, 471-73.
50. "Indian Proceedings," December 2-16, 1764, in Sullivan et al., *Johnson Papers*, 11, 500-508; "Johnson's Remarks On The Conduct of Colonel Bradstreet," November 24, 1764, in ibid., 4, 599-604.

during these early December sessions with the returning Indian allies. On December 6 a pared version of this original critique, buttressed now by the Iroquois' observations, was sent to Thomas Gage in order "to mention a few points which appear necessary for yr. private Observation and which friendship compels me to lay before you."[51]

Actually Sir William's charges contained substantially the same points made in his November 24 critique, although the latter document was replete with more colourful details. For example, Bradstreet's disobliging attitude to the Six Nations was revealed when he ordered them to march overland because of a lack of boats. Questioned by the Indian officers concerning how they could get along without boats, Bradstreet apparently answered that they could "Swim and be damned, or let them stay and be [damned &c]." On another occasion, during the Detroit negotiations, he had scandalized "all ye Inds." by cutting a wampum belt "to peices with a Tommahawk." Moreover, his sudden departure from Sandusky apparently left behind two New Jersey soldiers sent out on "his Orders to Catch Fish for his [Table]" as well as several Indians who were out hunting. Suggestions that the expedition's departure be delayed until these men returned resulted in the Colonel's answering with another damnation and the comment that "not a Boat should [stay one] Minute for them." More serious was Johnson's allegation that the September Council-of-War, which decided not to attack the Delawares and Shawnees, heard only the evidence Bradstreet wanted it to hear. The guides testifying concerning the distances and time involved in the proposed attack apparently were "Frenchmen (whom he [Bradstreet] had always in His Family, & at his Table and who are well paid)." It also was charged, that with the protection and cooperation of Bradstreet, "French Men" were allowed "to trade from Detroit" when English traders were denied the same privilege.[52]

While Johnson's criticisms of Bradstreet's conduct, as developed in his critique and refined in his letter to Gage, have been accepted and used by Francis Parkman as an accurate portrayal of the expedition,[53] almost every one of the points Sir William raised can be contradicted by other evidence or explained in a reasonably convincing fashion. Indeed Bradstreet, in his September 29 statement, had already defended himself against several of the charges. Johnson charged Bradstreet with contempt for his Six Nations allies, but this had never been concealed by the Colonel and his reluctance to accept their advice or to inform them concerning his negotiations and plans only increased as the expedition progressed, because of incidents such as their October

---

51. Johnson to Gage, December 6, 1764, in Sullivan et al., *Johnson Papers*, 11, 491-95.
52. "Johnson's Remarks On The Conduct of Colonel Bradstreet," November 24, 1764, in Sullivan et al., *Johnson Papers*, 4, 599-604.
53. See Parkman, *The Conspiracy of Pontiac*, 394-95 and 401-402, for examples of his tendency to base some of his strongest criticisms of Bradstreet, as well as his general description of the expedition, on this document, which he cites as "MS. Remarks on the Conduct of Colonel Bradstreet—found among the Johnson Papers."

refusal to attack the Shawnees and Delawares. Gage must have been fully aware of this from the tone of Bradstreet's letters and his reports concerning the meetings at which the Iroquois excused themselves from participating in war parties against the Shawnee-Delawares. Bradstreet's tendency to negotiate in French, another Johnson complaint, was not unusual in that this was a language the western Indians were more likely to have understood than English and it was also a language that the Anglo-Acadian Bradstreet understood. His abandonment of the Sandusky position came immediately after Morris' alarming reports of a possible Indian attack reached him, and the withdrawal appeared a reasonable precaution. The testimony at the Sandusky Council-of-War and Bradstreet's explanation to Gage concerning the state of his troops, which Gage by now had accepted and transmitted to Halifax, were quite different from Johnson's view, but a report signed by all the expedition's major officers probably would outweigh the statements of Johnson's informants. That the guides might have given false testimony was a possibility, yet it had proved acceptable to Bradstreet's officer corps who themselves had introduced no contradictory witnesses or testimony. The Detroit peace had been specifically ordered by Gage and while the wording used by Bradstreet represented a change in Indian status, it was a quite deliberate change on Bradstreet's part and one for which he would have been quite willing to argue the need. In view of Bradstreet's instructions to Lieutenant-Colonel Campbell not to grant land at Detroit until the British government had ruled on the proposed settlement, it was highly unlikely that Bradstreet, according to another Johnson allegation, had officially granted land. Unofficially, land might have been promised to individual officers and residents, but such promises were contingent upon the approval of his Detroit scheme. Johnson spoke of reliance on a villainous pilot which, if true, was a mistake in judgment and litte more, while Bradstreet had already argued that he had ordered the boats to be hauled up but some of the troops had neglected to do so. Involvement with French cohorts in the Indian trade at Detroit was a serious charge, but here Gage would have to balance Johnson's accusation against Bradstreet's description of his vigilant watch on illegal traders, a vigilance which Gage, once again, had already approved.

In summary, there was no one criticism advanced by Johnson which was incontestably proven. Many were contradicted by evidence already placed in Gage's hands while almost all could be justified or explained in a convincing fashion by Bradstreet. Various and conflicting interpretations could be rendered on almost every incident cited by Johnson. To give just one further example, the Six Nations reported to Johnson that Bradstreet's destruction of a wampum belt at Detroit had horrified all the Indians present at the conference. Yet according to Captain John Montresor's description of this incident, the belt was sent by the insolent Pontiac, who refused to come in to make peace himself. Thus, it was chopped to ribbons, Montresor did not specify by whom, and then "thrown piecemeal in the river by the 6 Nations." Yet the Iroquois now reported the incident as very insulting, without hinting at the reason for the action or their own complicity. Furthermore, a newspaper such as the Newport *Mercury* was inclined to credit Bradstreet with a heroic defiance of Pontiac by the destruction of the belt. "Colonel Bradstreet broke the wampum and sent back the messenger to acquaint him [Pontiac] that he must come himself or send his son," according to its report.[54] Johnson's straightforward portrayal of the Six Nation's disgust at Bradstreet's insulting deed could be bent into a haughty action in which the Iroquois themselves cooperated, or even further transformed into a heroic gesture on Bradstreet's part, insulting only to the villainous Pontiac.

Not only was Johnson presenting rather inconclusive charges against Bradstreet, but he had also completely failed to challenge what he himself had acknowledged as the main argument in Bradstreet's vindication. While he was willing to rhyme off many examples of Bradstreet's misconduct and misjudgment, he never once suggested that Bradstreet had distorted or disobeyed Gage's orders when he offered peace to the hostile Indian nations. Yet this was the major issue on which Bradstreet's misconduct had to be established if his actions during the campaign were to be discredited completely. Like Gage, Johnson backed away from what would have been a truly devastating accusation, perhaps realizing that on this all-important question Bradstreet was on solid ground. Without such a challenge Johnson's case against Bradstreet was reduced to some miscalculations and some admittedly outrageous, but difficult to prove, actions on the Colonel's part. If this was the best, or worst, that Sir William could do against Bradstreet, it was not enough to turn the Detroit effort into a totally discredited expedition.

By early December it was gradually becoming clear that Bradstreet had battled both Gage and Johnson to a standoff on the major issue of his authorization to act as he did in turning the expedition into a peace-seeking rather than a war-waging foray. On other less important but still controversial aspects of the campaign, he had strong and weak positions, but none of his glaring weaknesses was sufficiently significant to discredit him completely. It had been a speedy and decisive recovery from what appeared to be the nadir of his military career, reached when Gage's harsh disavowal of his actions stunned him at Sandusky. The rapid transformation was nowhere more pronounced than in the optimistic tone and confident expectations which quickly returned to his correspondence with his English confidant, Charles Gould.

At the end of September a dejected and uncertain Bradstreet had informed Gould of Gage's "severe letter" and enclosed for Gould's

---

54. "The Montresor Journals," N.Y.H.S., *Collections 1881*, 287; Newport *Mercury*, December 19, 1764, as quoted in "Papers Relating To The Expeditions Of Colonel John Bradstreet and Colonel Bouquet In Ohio, A.D. 1764," *Western Reserve and Northern Ohio Historical Society*, 1 (1873), Tract 14, 1.

perusal his own September 29 answer to that letter along with "many papers." After reading this material, he trusted Gould would take the appropriate action, namely: "If I am right defend me to the great & my friends—if otherwise say nothing in my favor." By early November, although bewailing the fact that "The Public Service suffers much for want of Sir Jeffy. Amherst in America," Bradstreet's mood had altered considerably. By now he assumed that Gage had "inform'd the Ministry I made a peace with the Shawnees & Delawar Indians contrary to his Orders." Also he assumed that the ministry would not condemn him unheard, and that Gould would argue on his behalf that "Genl. Gages orders to me on that head are clear; that I have obay'd them; that he has disavow'd them." Bradstreet remained ready with additional papers and explanations should the ministry desire them. "So much for Genl. Gage" he remarked, in apparent satisfaction that his vindication and defense were well in hand. Confident that the weight of the evidence and any final judgment rendered by the ministry would be in his favour, Bradstreet decided the moment had arrived for another attempt at the achievement of his long-delayed Detroit scheme.[55]

The advantage that the Colonel often had enjoyed in the past over other colonial schemers, however, was his record of military triumphs, which he used both to establish his impeccable loyalty to the Crown and hopefully the Crown's responsibility to recognize his contributions. His performances at Louisbourg, Oswego, Ticonderoga, and Frontenac had been presented in the best possible light and harnessed to his claims for offices and preferment. Could his Detroit expedition in its turn be employed in this way? Not really, because while Bradstreet's Detroit campaign was eminently defensible, his defense of it was somewhat indefensible. The state of his health, the limitations of his force, the vagueness of his orders, the lateness of his move westward, the deception of the Delaware-Shawnees, the simple bad luck so frequently encountered all combined to hamper, or to remove even before the expedition got underway, the chances of its being a grand success. Yet in spite of the difficulties, deceptions, and indeed disasters, endured by the expedition, it had contributed to the re-establishment of the British hold on the interior and the relatively successful pacification of the Indians. A defense conducted on the basis of an honest admission of the serious problems encountered, and the limited contribution made by the expedition despite these problems might have allowed Bradstreet to emerge with his reputation blemished but intact. Instead he chose to construct a defense based to a certain extent on a distortion and manipulation of several of the facts relating to the campaign; it was an approach replete with accusations and allegations that the real blame for the expedition's lack of total success rested on other individuals. It was an unconvincing performance which only

---

55. Bradstreet to Gould, September 30, 1764, T.P.C., 128/129; November 4, 1764, T.P.C., 128/130.

further damaged his reputation by throwing into question every one of his actions during the Great Lakes campaign.

Since Bradstreet was dealing with men such as Johnson and Gage, who possessed pronounced animosities and suspicions towards him, such an aggressive quest for total vindication only strengthened their belief in his misconduct. Granted that the Colonel's outspoken and excessively documented defense did force both men to back down on the important question of his authorization to grant peace, the same tactics further convinced them that Bradstreet must be engaged in calculated deception and concealment of many other irregularities relating to the expedition. Thus Johnson was moved to suggest the need for "an impartial Detail of the Proceedings of the Campaign" so that the public no longer would be "greatly deceived by partial representations of matters they are unacquainted with." General Gage was of a similar mind with Johnson on the general question of Bradstreet's conduct, since he condemned the Colonel's tactics; he suspected Bradstreet's real motives and assumed a design to deceive. "People sometimes write too much, and it may very likely be the Colonel's Case," he commented, while expressing his opinion that Bradstreet's "Jealousy, envy, and above all an immoderate vanity and self-opinion, and the pleasure to puff and bluster away a sort of Reputation amongst the Vulgar" probably outweighed his concern for "the Interest of the Publick, and a real sincere desire to use the most zealous Efforts for Her Service." Moreover, to the leery Gage, many of Bradstreet's defensive precautions in justification of his deeds and decisions revealed "too much Design and of a bad Nature too."

Bradstreet's victory on the point of his instructions thus turned out to be a hollow triumph, in that he might have won this point but further damaged his reputation and integrity in the process. Rumours of irregularities and hints of personal misconduct always had surrounded him, but they usually had been outweighed by his own convincing explanations of his actions and his clearly outstanding achievements on the field of battle. Both were conspicuously lacking on this occasion. In England his friends could try to defend him against the rumours circulating concerning absurd peace terms which were "contrary to the Opinion & approbation of General Gage" as well as the charge that "the Savages had duped" him "by obtaining a cessation of hostilitys,"[56] but, as in America, it was clearly going to be an uphill battle for any sort of vindication. John Bradstreet, who had always been so concerned that the dispatches of his commanding officers, the comments in the public press, and the published commentaries on North American military activities should do justice to his contributions and further enhance his reputation, for the first time discovered that reports of the rather unsavoury side of his more unfortunate actions were transforming his

---

56. Johnson to Cadwallader Colden, December 11, 1764, in Sullivan et al., *Johnson Papers*, 4, 616; Gage to Johnson, November 29, 1764, in ibid., 605; Mungo Campbell to Gould, November 14, 1764, T.P.C., 128/138.

fame and reputation into an infamous record of irregularity and misconduct. Bradstreet's hopes that a successful Detroit campaign would be the key to the opening of the west and further rank and honour for himself had been completely disappointed. In both instances the gamble had failed, leaving his reputation and western dreams shattered.

Chapter X

The Last Decade

"An Idea is revived, that a Government will be erected at Detroit" wrote Charles Gould to General Thomas Gage in 1774; "Should it take place, I am hopeful my Friend Genl. Bradstreet may be thought of."[1] Ideas, dreams, hopes quite frequently die a reluctant death, particularly if their possessor sees in them his only salvation from a totally unacceptable situation. His record and reputation tarnished after the 1764 expedition, John Bradstreet seemed left with little more than empty hopes and unattainable dreams. Yet both he and his friends in England, Amherst and Gould specifically, persisted in their expectations that his Detroit scheme and quest for higher rank and further offices eventually would succeed. Unfortunately for Bradstreet, both his military and colonial aspirations were to be frustrated by a combination of poorly placed friends at "home," well-placed foes in America, and the prevailing hesitancy and instability within British administrations during this period.[2] But in view of General Thomas Gage's unconcealed hostility towards Bradstreet's military pretensions and the way in which suggestions offered by American interest groups were being isolated and placed "beyond the pale" in Great Britain,[3] it is not surpris-

---

1. Gould to Gage, June 11, 1774, Gage Papers, English Series/25, U.M.C.L.
2. See Peter Marshall, "Imperial Policy and the Government of Detroit: Projects and Problems 1760-1774," *Journal of Imperial And Commonwealth History*, 2 (1974), 153-89, for an excellent examination of the British government's attempts to grapple with the Detroit proposals during which, as he so aptly puts it, "ministerial views remained obstinately indecisive." Marshall utilizes some of the same T.P.C. sources, available at the N.L.W., used by this writer and reaches similar conclusions. However, he is more concerned about the broader context of Whitehall policy-making relating to Detroit, while this study examines the Detroit schemes and other office-seeking proposals from Bradstreet's vantage point on the periphery of empire.
3. See Michael G. Kammen, "British and Imperial Interests in the Age of the American Revolution," in Alison G. Olson and Richard M. Brown, ed., *Anglo-American Political Relations, 1675-1775* (New Brunswick, N.J., 1970), 150.

ing that his proposals were not accepted. What is surprising is that some of them almost succeeded in gaining approval. Even at a moment when American suggestions were viewed with mounting suspicion and disfavour, some of Bradstreet's military and colonial schemes were carried to the very brink of success. The effectiveness of his connections with Gould, Mante, Amherst, and indirectly Lord Shelburne, was apparent even in failure. Nevertheless, the last decade of John Bradstreet's life and military career was a lost decade in the sense that his unceasing battle for vindication, recognition, and preferment was one long losing struggle. But it was very much a struggle and not a gentle decline into neglect and oblivion.

In the last months of 1764, having countered, at least to his own satisfaction, the charges of Gage and Johnson, Bradstreet felt the moment was right for the revival of his Detroit project. It now emerged as a "sketch" of his general observations on the administration of trade, settlement, and Indian matters in the American interior as well as a specific proposal for the settlement and development of the Detroit area. The proposal was in the form of a memorial, signed by sixty of the officers who had served under Bradstreet's command, requesting permission to settle "639 Families at Detroit." On behalf of "the subscribers" and himself, Bradstreet offered Gould the position of "Agent manager for us at home." This was the basic scheme, to which almost immediately a number of wrinkles were added. Since the officers involved were all half-pay men or former provincial soldiers, a sufficient number of them might be willing to continue their military careers by serving as officers in a regiment, if permission was granted to raise one "for the Service of that Country." In an additional submission Bradstreet suggested a fascinating experiment in Indian affairs which could be attempted at Detroit. Arguing that the "£5000 Sterling for presents to the Six Nations with £1000 to the Superintendent" was largely wasted money, he contended that it could better be used to pay for plowmen, overseers, plows, sets of harness and horses, which could be brought into Indian territory and used to provide the natives with a "Secure Subsistence" in place of the "want of provisions" from which they frequently suffered. It was emphasized that the "whole of these transactions should be an Affair of the Crowns and not of the Colonys, the latter being unable to manage the Indians." In a further memorandum, dovetailing with the original memorial, the necessity of yet another Crown intervention was argued. "It remains for the Petitioner, with all duty and respect, on behalf of himself and his associates, to pray, your Majesty would graciously cause the settlement of Detroit to be erected into a species of distinct government."[4] Obviously the

---

4. Bradstreet to Gould, November 4, 1764, T.P.C., 128/130, N.L.W.; December 4, 1764, T.P.C., 128/131; An untitled paper written by Bradstreet, c. 1764, T.P.C., 128/450; "Memorandum Concerning Detroit," according to the N.L.W. dated c. 1763, but judging from the several references in the document to the proposals contained in the memorial it clearly was drafted after the expedition and, thus, was probably c. 1764, T.P.C., 128/451.

suggested Detroit government and the experiment in Indian affairs, as well as the raising of a regiment, all opened possible further appointments tailored to the talents and qualifications of John Bradstreet.

The Colonel's general observations on the state of the American interior were presented at length in a statement which, when boiled down, appeared to be little more than an additional elaborate justification of his Detroit proposals.[5] It was his considered opinion that in order "to fix the [Indian] trade with equil Advantage to all his Majesty's Subjects" it should be restricted to designated posts. Geographically these posts must be chosen carefully to avoid, for example, a restriction of the trade to a post such as Niagara which would only allow the fur trade to flow into Spanish and French hands. Listing several such advantageously situated posts, Detroit was clearly the most important. If it were "properly settled," and made a "strong barrier," the provision needs of the Indian trade could be met, expensive transportation costs could be cut, and effective protection of the fur trade, and indeed British mastery of the entire region, could be guaranteed. The excellent geographic position of Detroit, in both a military and economic sense, the fertility of the soil thereabouts, the presence there of inhabitants who "have great influence over the Savages" were all presented as arguments in its favour. The French residents in the interior should be brought together at Detroit where, with the already-established French inhabitants, they would form the core of a successful settlement. Since it "will take a great length of time before they become properly English Subjects; it is therefore humbly submitted if it would be best to permit & Encourage Subjects to Settle there as the Increase of the latter would be so great in a few years that they must soon become one people by Marriages &ca." The support such a settlement scheme would receive was demonstrated by the "Memorial of Sixty Officers Serving in the upper Lakes this Campaign, praying His Majesty would be graciously pleas'd to permit them to settle Six hundred & thirty nine families at their own expence with such Marks of the Kings Royal favor as His Majesty may think proper."[6]

The other side of Bradstreet's military campaign now shone forth in abundant detail. Not only was his westward thrust designed to bring the rebellious Indians to heel, but it also was intended to lay the foundation for an economic and territorial expansion into the heart of the Great Lakes region. This expansion of empire could prove im-

---

5. A copy of Bradstreet's general observations is not contained in the N.L.W., T.P.C. material, although Bradstreet's own comments concerning his sending it and a summary of the statement in the handwriting of Charles Gould (See T.P.C., 128/449) establishes that it was sent and received in England. The version I have used is "Colonel Bradstreet's opinion of Indians and their affairs," December 4, 1764, Gage Papers, A.S./28. Although incorrectly dated and identified as "Gen. Bradstreet's Statement, December 17, 1764," it also is found in Hough, *Diary of the Siege of Detroit*, 141-57. A shortened version appears as "Colonel Bradstreet's thoughts on Indian Affairs," December 4, 1764, in O'Callaghan, *N.Y.C.D.*, 7, 690-94.

6. "Colonel Bradstreet's opinion of Indians and their affairs," December 4, 1764, Gage Papers, A.S./28.

mensely rewarding to Bradstreet if it was carried out along the lines he suggested. The detailed observations and specific suggestion he now offered were the culmination of his frequently repeated views of western development. Since 1755 his vision of a "dominion of the lakes," a Great Lakes empire, a tantalizingly attractive "Inland Country," had been directly expressed in his correspondence with Lyttleton, Gould, and others, as well as made theoretically accessible by the campaigns he proposed, and in some cases executed, on the Lakes. In late 1764, with his appetite freshly whetted by a firsthand experience of the region's potential wealth, Bradstreet mounted his most concerted effort towards the achievement of his own version of a properly developed American interior.

His letters, submissions and memorials were further reinforced by the dispatch to England of Thomas Mante, aide-de-camp in the Detroit expedition and "a very deserving Man" in the Colonel's view, who was to work with Gould to secure acceptance of the colonial scheme. Bradstreet even dared to hope that a combination of calculated pressure exerted on Thomas Gage, along with a full explanation of the Detroit proposal, might win the General's support for the project. Although worried that Gage "will not do me the Justice I deserve," copies of Bradstreet's memorial and observations were sent to him, the former "at the request of Sixty officers serving under my command" who hoped that Gage would favourably present the proposal to the ministry. The totally uncooperative and coldly unsympathetic Gage wasted neither time nor words in squelching Bradstreet's cherished Detroit aspirations. He curtly refused "to transmit Home the officers Petition concerning the lands at Detroit." Furthermore, Bradstreet's general observations were dismissed with the comment that "the Board of Trade has already to[o] many schemes and Projects about Indian Affairs upon which they have formed their present Plan." Unwilling to be rebuffed in this way, Bradstreet attempted to pressure Gage by hinting at an adverse reaction from the officers involved. "I suppose I am at liberty to let the officers know," he wrote, that "You do not choose to transmit Home their Petition concerning the Lands at Detroit." An unimpressed and unmoved Gage answered that Bradstreet certainly was free to inform the officers. Moreover, he reminded the Colonel that a "King's Proclamation" existed which forbade "the settling beyond certain Limits" and that there were established procedures and agencies to handle such matters. The officials charged with the administration of the west were guided by laws and conditions which they "will not alter for any body."[7]

Despite the General's failure to forward and support Bradstreet's proposals, the copies sent directly to England eventually received gov-

---

7. Bradstreet to Gould, December 4, 1764, T.P.C., 128/131; Bradstreet to Gage, December 4 and 7, 1764, Gage Papers, A.S./28; Gage to Bradstreet, December 15, 1764, Gage Letters, H.H.L.; Bradstreet to Gage, December 24, 1764, Gage Papers, A.S./29; Gage to Bradstreet, December 31, 1764, Gage Papers, A.S./29.

ernmental consideration. But Gage's comments proved quite accurate. The Board of Trade deferred action on the Detroit scheme with the explanation that if adopted it might interfere with the "general plan" under consideration with respect to the Indian trade. It was also questioned whether the lands mentioned in the petition could be granted in view of their "being beyond the Limits prescribed by His Majestys Proclamation." A particularly ironic final reservation, in view of Bradstreet's frequent professions of loyalty to the Crown, involved the Board members' fears that a Detroit settlement might weaken the Empire. Lacking a staple commodity, they reasoned, the settlers would be unable to purchase many "Necessaries" and might turn to manufacturing them on their own while attempting "to do without" items which they could not produce themselves. Consequently the settlers would be of no benefit to the state "and would have it in their Power, from the difficulty of Access, to throw off all dependance on their Mother Country, and instead of being beneficial by an Increase of People, they would lay a Foundation for future Empire."[8]

Gage's rejection of the scheme was not unexpected but rejection, or at least deferral, in England for reasons of incompatibility with prevailing British policy and a possible threat to the Empire was both distressing and surprising. Distressing to Bradstreet was the fact that in this presentation, as in others, he always had attempted to convey the impression that he was laying the foundation for an expansion and not an erosion of the Empire. It was surprising in view of Bradstreet's unique ability in earlier years to tie in so many of his schemes and suggestions with prevailing British policies and desires as well as with American realities and aspirations. On this occasion, the Colonel seemed very much out of step with the British desire to limit the westward expansion of the American colonies and very much in step with the mounting colonial pressure to push towards the Pacific the vaguely defined western boundary.[9] At a moment when the two worlds were drifting further and further apart, he found himself identified with the emerging American position and increasingly unable to function in the linchpin role he had assumed on earlier occasions. Like

---

8. Summary of the Board of Trade's consideration of "A Memorial ... presented to the King and Council, and from thence referred to the Board of Trade, signed by Sixty Officers who had served in the Campaign of 1764, on the upper Lakes under Colonel Bradstreet ... ," C.O. 5/67, 56-59, P.A.C. Unfortunately the document does not contain the precise date of the Board's consideration of the proposal. Alvord, *The Mississippi Valley in British Politics*, 1, 244-45, mentions that this plan, which he credits to Thomas Mante, was submitted on May 8, 1765, and the Board's decision was rendered in November of that year. The progress of the proposal is given detailed attention in Marshall, "Imperial Policy and the Government of Detroit," 166-68.

9. The research of Jack M. Sosin provides a solid background for a comprehension of the increasing colonial pressure on Britain to open the west, which took the form of such elaborate proposals as the Vandalia colony. Minor schemes such as that offered by Bradstreet are largely overlooked by Sosin or if considered are identified as the handiwork of Thomas Mante. See Jack M. Sosin, *Whitehall and the Wilderness* (Lincoln, Nebraska, 1961), 138-39, and *The Revolutionary Frontier, 1763-1783* (New York, 1967), 32.

other American land speculators and prophets of western development, he would refuse to accept the finality of the 1763 Proclamation and would continue battling in a vain attempt to achieve his Detroit scheme.

Restriction of the colonies and contraction of mother-country expenses were also the order of the day in other spheres. With the passing of Pontiac's threat, a desire for retrenchment and careful controls over all British military expenditures in North America manifested itself. Thomas Gage found himself dealing with a British ministry bent upon keeping a tight rein on his army's costs and willing to disallow or question any number of items.[10] Faced with rigid Treasury Board guidelines, excess officers and posts became expendable. Bradstreet and Albany were evidently high on the General's list of unnecessary expenditures.

From its important wartime position as a centre of military operations in the northern theatre, Albany had quickly declined into a mere "way-station between New York and Montreal." The Great Lakes posts could now be supplied more conveniently via the St. Lawrence-Lake Ontario route and thus a gradual abandonment of the upper New York posts commenced. In this way expenses and duties previously handled by Bradstreet's quartermaster department at Albany were greatly curtailed. Furthermore, the limited amounts expended in Albany were more carefully controlled. Instead of Bradstreet's issuing certificates and keeping annual accounts with wagoners and bateaumen, officers paid directly for necessary and authorized services and then passed on receipts to Bradstreet to be processed and forwarded to headquarters. With Albany's decline and the new expenditure methods, what C. R. Canedy describes as Bradstreet's "patronage empire" quickly shrivelled.[11]

At least one other Deputy Quartermaster-General in America, James Robertson, found his department and responsibilities undergoing the same shrinkage. Robertson had the discretion to withdraw from America and return to England in search of a new assignment, thereby allowing Gage to strike his name from the "established Staff." Bradstreet refused to follow Robertson. Although prodded by Gage about rejoining his regiment, the 60th, in which he still held rank as a captain, and about rumours of his impending departure for England, the Colonel refused to budge from Albany. Instead, he vainly attempted to fight the erosion of his quartermaster authority, but managed barely to cling to office as Gage agreed to return him each year as acting Deputy Quartermaster-General. This meant a squabble with the home authorities over his pay, since only one Deputy Quartermaster-General,

---

10. Dora M. Clark, "The British Treasury and the Administration of Military Affairs in America, 1754-1774," *Pennsylvania History*, 2 (1935), 202; Shy, *Toward Lexington*, 241-42.

11. Shy, *Toward Lexington*, 271; Canedy, "An Entrepreneurial History Of The New York Frontier, 1739-1776," 321.

Sir John St. Clair, was listed on the American establishment,[12] but it also gave Bradstreet at least a temporary office while he scrambled to secure another appointment.

While returning Bradstreet as acting Deputy Quartermaster-General, despite questions raised by Secretary at War Barrington, Gage relentlessly went about closing down the quartermaster department at Albany. This contraction of services threatened to sweep Bradstreet's closest cohorts, John Glen and Philip Schuyler, out of their lucrative employments. Bradstreet fought back but to no avail. He attempted to arrange another job for Glen but Gage was adamant on this point, dictating that if Bradstreet wanted to employ Glen he could place him in charge of the boats at Schenectady, but nothing else. Philip Schuyler also came under fire from Gage. The General bluntly refused to do the business of Bradstreet's quartermaster department with Schuyler. No longer would he "transact the King's Business on a footing to be insulted by Mr. Schuyler, or any other person, Whom you may think proper to employ."[13]

With his department crumbling around him Bradstreet at various times attempted to persuade Gage about the inadvisability of several of his decisions and actions. But the obvious military and geographic realities under which Albany laboured deprived Bradstreet of any convincing arguments, forcing him instead to emphasize the insults to his own honour and integrity caused by the throttling of his department. In this vein he protested against the new method of expenditures which allowed junior officers to pay directly for bateau-men and carriages which Bradstreet had arranged. The Colonel felt that such an approach amounted to rather "contemptuous treatment" particularly in view of his own "Rank in the Army" and "Services as an Officer." Pushing this argument to the limit Bradstreet wondered if, in light of this insult to his integrity and withdrawal of his authority, he now stood "dismiss'd" and "no longer" able "to act ... in the Department of Q.M. General." At the same time as he hinted at his possible dismissal as quartermaster, Bradstreet attempted to manufacture another office for himself and inquired whether this also was lost. Professing to believe that he "still Command[ed] the Western District," the Colonel requested Gage "to inform me if You have dismiss'd me from that Command also." Gage quickly countered that Bradstreet's "Command of the whole Western District" ended with the close of his Detroit

---

12. Gage to Barrington, September 13, 1766, in Carter, *Gage Correspondence*, 2, 373; Gage to Bradstreet, September 30, 1765, Gage Papers, A.S./43; Bradstreet to Gage, May 10, 1766, Gage Papers, A.S./51; Gage to Bradstreet, October 14, 1765, Gage Letters; Bradstreet to Gage, December 23, 1765, Gage Papers, A.S./46.

13. Barrington to Gage, September 13, 1766, and Gage to Barrington, November 9, 1766, W.O. 1/7, 167-68 and 241-42, P.A.C.; Gage to Bradstreet, March 3, 1766, Gage Papers, A.S./49; March 17, 1766, Gage Papers, A.S./49; Canedy, "An Entrepreneurial History Of The New York Frontier, 1739-1776," 238-39; Gage to Bradstreet, April 19, 1766, Gage Papers, A.S./50; June 9, 1766, Gage Papers, A.S./51; October 31, 1766, Gage Papers, A.S./58.

expedition. Furthermore, he was very "Surprized at your Idea of contemptuous Treatment." Certainly, he explained, Bradstreet remained acting Deputy Quartermaster-General at Albany but, in keeping with the new regulations from home, the old system of issuing certificates to secure needed men and materials, which opened the way to delays in payment and possible abuses, had been replaced by the officers on the spot offering cash payment. "Neither Contempt or Disrespect" was intended for Bradstreet or any one else, only that the "King's Service" be carried on "as effectually and with as little trouble as it can be done." If Bradstreet interpreted this as notice of dismissal, Gage commented, "You might therefore with the same Justice ask whether the King had dismissed you."[14]

Over the years the reassurance that Bradstreet remained acting Quartermaster at Albany was small comfort to the Colonel as his departmental expenditures were cut to the bone and he was periodically reminded by Gage that he remained in office only because of his commander's generosity. In June of 1767 the General pricked Bradstreet with the reminder that he could not continue to return him forever as acting Quartermaster. It was high time Bradstreet secured "counter orders" from home clarifying his status. On a later occasion Gage more pointedly humbled Bradstreet when he explained the continuation of his quartermaster service as due to Bradstreet's being "return'd entirely thro' Indulgence, and with a Risk of my receiving a Reprimand for so doing." Bradstreet's constant defense against these comments was that he lived "in dayly expectation of being employ'd in another way" and, hopefully, soon would no longer be so dependent on Gage. Further aggravating Bradstreet's embarrassment was the miniscule amount of money which now passed through his hands in the operation of his department. His departmental expenditures in 1767 amount to only approximately £717 while it has been estimated that between 1769 and 1772 "the Quartermaster Corps disbursed only £226/12 in Northern New York." This was a far cry from the freewheeling expenditures of the Seven Years' War when in one year, 1759, Bradstreet's department spent £157,779 (N.Y.).[15]

Faced with virtually dormant quartermaster duties and a commander who demonstrated no particular appreciation for his idle talents, Bradstreet could always turn to the touchy question of the civil-military relationship in Albany in order to demonstrate his continuing utility to the Crown. Several years earlier his activities in this area invariably had won the support of Amherst and Gage. Now when he attempted to

---

14. Bradstreet to Gage, May 10, 1766, Gage Papers, A.S./51; April 22, 1766, Gage Papers, A.S./50; Gage to Bradstreet, May 5 and 19, 1766, Gage Letters.

15. Ibid., June 21, 1767, Gage Papers, A.S./66; September 30, 1768, Gage Papers, A.S./81; Bradstreet to Gage, June 28, 1767, Gage Papers, A.S./66; "John Bradstreet's Account," December 24, 1768, in Sullivan et al., *Johnson Papers*, 12, 676-79 (probably New York currency); Canedy, "An Entrepreneurial History Of The New York Frontier, 1739-1776," 321 (also probably New York currency); "Account of Money paid by Colo. John Bradstreet... Ending the 24th December, 1759," T.P.C., 128/416.

portray himself as the vigilant defender of the Crown's rights against the attacks of Albany upstarts, he discovered Gage's response to be decidedly hesitant and cool. Indeed, the General seemed to feel that Bradstreet's abrasive tactics brought on needless confrontations between the town and Crown. As a result, when the ticklish question of the disposal of superfluous barracks and storehouse buildings, some of which had been erected in the streets and were a very real nuisance to the town, had to be threshed out with the Albany authorities, Gage entirely by-passed Bradstreet. To the Colonel's considerable displeasure, and in spite of his complaints, Captains John Montresor and Harry Gordon handled the negotiations with the Albany Council as well as the choice and sale of the useless buildings. Moreover, several of the Colonel's rather over-zealous applications of the controversial Quartering Act received only token support from Gage and were immediately softened by the General's explanations and concessions to the Albany officials. For example, in November of 1765 when troops from the 60th Regiment were about to march into Albany, Bradstreet was worried that the barracks he had in mind for their accommodation might be torn down by the corporation. Acting quickly, he put part of the garrison into the building to guard it until the troops arrived. Instead of winning Gage's applause the action provoked the General's pained explanation that Bradstreet was in the wrong. Gage had already promised the mayor of Albany that the barracks in question would be turned over to the city and in return the corporation would repair the hospital, making "it habitable for the Troops." Bradstreet's hasty action had jeopardized this neat little transaction since it "may have Occasioned some Suspicion in the Corporation, that we intend keeping the Barracks." To rectify matters Gage ordered Bradstreet to transfer the troops to the hospital while explaining to the mayor that the barracks still were to be handed over to the corporation as soon as some further formalities were completed.[16]

Once extricated from this confrontation Bradstreet promptly headed for another. He now pressed the mayor and corporation for adequate bedding and fuel for the troops as well as "a quarters allowance for the officers." Although Gage had specifically ordered him to seek bedding and fuel he had also explained that the New York Assembly had not acted on the Quartering Act one way or the other but appeared inclined only "to make Provision after Expences are incurred," and went on to hint that the entire matter should not be pushed too hard. Moreover, Gage seemed to feel that the officers' allowance

---

16. Gage to Welbore Ellis, May 5, 1765, W.O. I/6, 275-76; "Att a Common Councill held at the City of Albany at the City Hall of the said City on Saturday the 27th of April 1765," Gage Papers, A.S./35; Bradstreet to Gage, September 17, 1765, Gage Papers, A.S./43; Montresor to Gage, September 20, 1765, Gage Papers, A.S./43; Gage to Bradstreet, September 25, 1765, Gage Papers, A.S./43; Gage to Montresor, September 25, 1765, Gage Papers, A.S./43; Bradstreet to Gage, November 23, 1765, Gage Papers, A.S./45; Gage to Bradstreet, November 25, 1765, Gage Papers, A.S./46.

was not a vital necessity in any case. Unfortunately Bradstreet's unyielding quartering demand only served to provoke an official Albany explanation that the town could not act until the Assembly had dealt with the quartering question.[17] Thus, his actions exacerbated rather than solved the Crown's problems in Albany and were executed in the face of Gage's reservations about their propriety or need.

Fortunately for Gage, with only fifty British troops permanently stationed in Albany and with Bradstreet's quartermaster department reduced to an empty shell and virtual sinecure appointment, the opportunity for further headaches in this area was considerably reduced. Nevertheless, there was one outstanding and very thorny problem which remained unresolved and continued to create bitterness between Bradstreet and Gage throughout the 1765 to 1770 period. This involved the payment of the additional Yorkers enlisted by Bradstreet for service in his 1764 expedition. During the winter of 1764-1765 it became clear that the New York Assembly refused to pay them, and the unpaid soldiers turned on Bradstreet threatening a legal action to secure their money. The Colonel immediately turned to Gage and urged him to pay the troops and then press the New York government for reimbursement of the claim, which amounted to over £3,000 (N.Y.). Not surprisingly Gage refused to do so, arguing that the New York government had valid reasons for refusing payment and that Bradstreet had brought these difficulties on himself by a failure to follow orders. The basic problem appeared to be that Bradstreet had recruited troops on his own to bring the New York contingent up to its designated strength while the Assembly appointed its own officers who did their own recruiting for the same purpose. The latter men were then included in the New York battalion while Bradstreet's volunteers wound up serving as bateau-men, at a special pay rate, and were not "Muster'd or Return'd a part of the New York Battallion."[18]

With his usual prolific explanations and documentation Bradstreet set about proving that he had a solid case. Gradually the main thrust of his argument shifted from the position that he had merely been following Gage's orders in enlisting the recruits to the safer and more acceptable proof of the fact that the men had served in the campaign and in simple justice deserved payment. His presentations were convincing enough to allow Gage, while still privately criticizing him for originally disobeying orders, to complain to the New York Lieutenant-Governor

---

17. Bradstreet to V. P. Douw and Magistrates, December 31, 1765, Gage Papers, A.S./48; Shy, *Toward Lexington*, 251; Gage to Bradstreet, December 24, 1765, Gage Papers, A.S./46; D. Silvester (Clerk) to Bradstreet, January 23, 1766, C.O. 5/84, 163. For a fuller discussion of New York and the Quartering Act, see Gipson, *The British Empire Before the American Revolution*, 11, 36-69.

18. Shy, *Toward Lexington*, 250; Bradstreet to Gage, February 2, 1765, Gage Papers, A.S./30; Gage to Bradstreet, February 18 and March 4, 1765, Gage Papers, A.S./31; Colden to Gage, October 17, 1765, Gage Papers, A.S./44; Bradstreet to Gage, February 25, 1765, Gage Papers, A.S./31; Gage to Bradstreet, August 19, 1765, Gage Papers, A.S./41.

that it was "hard that Colonel Bradstreet should be troubled with vexatious Suits on this Account."[19]

When the General's personal intervention as well as the troops' petitions to the governor and assembly failed to move the New York authorities, Bradstreet sounded out Gage on the possibility of his support for a petition to the home authorities. Although initially reluctant to approve such a submission, Gage eventually yielded to Bradstreet's pleas and agreed to forward the Colonel's petition to the Treasury Office seeking permission for Gage to pay off the Yorkers. Early in May 1766, with a covering letter from Gage, the memorial was sent to England and by July had begun its journey through the maze of English bureaucracy where it was soon to be lost from sight. Meanwhile Bradstreet plunged ahead on the assumption that his claim would receive treasury approval. Accordingly he paid off the demanding Yorkers and then requested Gage to reimburse him. Surprisingly, Gage went along with this request. Gabriel Maturin, the General's secretary, calculated that Bradstreet's £3,456/3/0 claim equalled £2,003/11/3 sterling and explained that Gage "proposes only taking a Temporary Receipt for So much money being advanced You, 'upon account of Expenses in your Department' till such time as He shall receive Answers from the Treasury respecting Your Memorial."[20] There the matter rested, with Bradstreet having satisfied the Yorkers and Gage anticipating word that the expenditure was legitimate and had been approved.

No such immediate approval arrived. It turned out that "the Memorial and other Papers were mislaid before His Majesty's Pleasure could be taken thereupon." Discovering this in the winter of 1766-1767, Charles Gould immediately submitted another memorial on Brad-

---

19. Bradstreet to Gage, February 25, 1765, Gage Papers, A.S./31; August 12, 1765, Gage Papers, A.S./41; Gage to Bradstreet, February 3, 1766, Gage Papers, A.S./48; Gage to Colden, October 15, 1765, Gage Papers, A.S./44.

20. Colden to Gage, October 17, 1765, Gage Papers, A.S./44; Bradstreet to Gage, January 26, 1766, Gage Papers, A.S./48; Gage to Bradstreet, February 3, 1766, Gage Papers, A.S./48; April 7, 1766, Gage Letters; "The Memorial of Colonel John Bradstreet," April 29, 1766, C.O. 5/84, 280-81; Gage to Charles Lowndes (Secretary to the Treasury), May 7, 1766, C.O. 5/84, 287-88; Grey Cooper (Treasury Secretary) to Richard Stonehewer (at the Duke of Richmond's office, Richmond being First Lord of the Treasury), July 1, 1766, C.O. 5/84, 278; Bradstreet's account of enlistments in New York in 1764, November 2, 1766, Bradstreet MSS, A.A.S.; Gabriel Maturin to Bradstreet, December 4, 1766, in ibid. Alden, *General Gage in America*, 72-73, is somewhat misleading in his treatment of this transaction. He states: "When the province failed to pay, Bradstreet insisted that Gage should compensate him; and when Gage continued to refuse, Bradstreet used monies advanced for current bills to reimburse himself." Alden overlooks the fact that Gage did advance money to compensate Bradstreet for paying off the Yorkers. Alden also states: "Gage then cut off all supplies of cash intended for Bradstreet's department." Actually this action was taken several years later when a Treasury Board decision still had not materialized. Then in a totally inaccurate assertion Alden claims that Gage's action forced Bradstreet "to send Philip Schuyler to London to straighten matters out." Schuyler made no such journey. Alden is confusing Schuyler's 1761 trip to England, which was made to settle Bradstreet's quartermaster accounts, with this incident.

street's behalf, outlining the fate of the first submission and urging quick action on the matter. So the wheels began to turn again. The Treasury Office reached a decision, passed on word to Secretary of State Lord Shelburne, and he in turn ordered Governor Sir Henry Moore of New York to instruct the Assembly to make provision for the payment of the Yorkers. But the Assembly postponed consideration of the question and as 1768 dragged on it became clear that the New York legislators intended to refuse payment. Early in 1769 a totally exasperated Gage moved against Bradstreet, attempting to force him to repay the money advanced to him or get his friends at home to arrange a resolution of the question once and for all. The General simply refused to "advance any more Money to your Department till the sums already advanced to your Department are accounted for therein." Thus, until the £3,456 was repaid by Bradstreet his departmental funds were to be cut off and he would have to cope with unpaid creditors by evasion and delay or by dipping into his own pocket. An obviously upset Gage explained, "I have waited Packet after Packet, expecting Orders about the Affair of the Provincials to no Purpose; and I can neither answer it to myself, or my Family, to let this Burthen lye on my Shoulders any longer, and am determined not to do it." After first trying to argue that the money advanced for the Yorkers was a quite separate matter from his departmental accounts, which only further enraged Gage, Bradstreet finally solicited Gage's support for yet another memorial home which would seek a treasury order clearly allowing Gage "to pass" the item in his accounts. This Gage agreed to do and in May of 1769 another memorial, along with a covering letter from the General outlining the history of the problem and urging favourable treasury consideration, was sent to England.[21]

Although Bradstreet implored Charles Gould "to use your endeavours to forward the finishing this Affair by obtaining the Order from the Treasury... ," a year later the matter still was unsettled. Despite Gould's frequent visits to the Treasury Office, other more pressing matters commanded their attention and Gould could only report that a decision was imminent but not as yet reached. By this point Bradstreet was well aware of the fact that this long-standing squabble with Gage certainly was no help to his pursuit of other military offices and appointments. No doubt his disinclination to continue this tiresome and embarrassing struggle was behind the February 1770, meeting between Philip Schuyler and Lieutenant-Colonel Robertson at

---

21. "The Memorial of Charles Gould on the behalf of Colonel John Bradstreet," received by the Treasury Board, February 6, 1767, C.O. 5/85, 39-40; Cooper to Richard Sutton, February 10, 1767, C.O. 5/85, 35; Bradstreet to Gage, November 12, 1767, Gage Papers, A.S./71; Bradstreet to Gould, April 30, 1769, T.P.C., 128/286; Bradstreet to Gage, April 15, 1769, Gage Papers, E.S./15; Gage to Bradstreet, March 26, 1769, Gage Letters; March 13, 1769, Gage Papers, A.S./84; Bradstreet to Gage, March 18, 1769, Gage Papers, A.S./84; April 2, 1769, Gage Papers, A.S./84; April 15, 1769, Gage Papers, A.S./85; Gage to Bradstreet, May 8, 1769, Gage Papers, A.S./85; Gage to Thomas Bradshaw, May 12, 1769, Gage Papers, E.S./15.

which "a mode of Settlement between General Gage and Colonel Bradstreet relating to a disputed account" was discussed. Apparently an arrangement of some sort was reached between the Colonel and the General, since in October of that year Bradstreet informed Gould "not to trouble your self any further for the present to apply to the Treasury for the order to Genl Gage." That the Yorker question was now a thing of the past was revealed in June of 1770 when Bradstreet wrote to Gage in the friendliest possible terms. "It is a real pleasure to my friends at Home as well as to my self" he over-enthusiastically reminded the General, "that all disputes are at an end between Your Excellency and me, and that the friendship which subsisted between Us during the War is return'd; nothing will be ever wanting on my part for a perfect continuance of it."[22]

While the dispute raged, however, more than one office had slipped through Bradstreet's fingers because of Gage's objections to him. The most obvious example was an appointment as American Deputy Quartermaster-General for which Bradstreet was a logical choice both on the basis of seniority and experience. The Colonel had eyed this office in 1765 and was disappointed when it was awarded to Sir John St. Clair. But in November of 1767 St. Clair died and immediately an all-out effort was launched to secure the appointment for Bradstreet. Letters outlining his qualifications flowed in on Gould from John Montresor, Philip Schuyler, Thomas Mante, and Bradstreet himself. When Gage was questioned by Bradstreet about the appointment, the General assured him that "being the Eldest in that Department" Bradstreet could expect to be appointed. Nevertheless in writing to the War Office concerning a successor to St. Clair, Gage made no mention of Bradstreet's claims or cause. Instead he discussed at length Lieutenant-Colonel Robertson's aspirations for the office, making clear his "satisfaction" with Robertson's performance and the pleasure it would give him at Robertson's "nomination for any station under my order." Having clearly committed himself to Robertson's cause, Gage then attempted to cloak his position in impartiality. Because of the many applicants for the post, he proceeded to explain to Barrington, "I have recommended nobody, leaving it entirely to His Majesty's Decision."[23]

---

22. Bradstreet to Gould, April 30, 1769, T.P.C., 128/286; Bradstreet to Gage, February 25, 1770, Gage Papers, A.S./90; April 30, 1770, Gage Papers, A.S./91; May 13, 1770, Gage Papers, A.S./92; Gage to Bradstreet, May 21, 1770, Gage Papers, A.S./92; Bradstreet to Gould, October 25, 1770, T.P.C., 128/304; Bradstreet to Gage, June 25, 1770, Gage Papers, A.S./93; Schuyler to ?, February 5, 1770, ref. #2676, N.Y.S.L. This letter was probably to William Smith in the light of a further explanatory letter from Schuyler to William Smith, April 9, 1770, Miscellaneous, U.M.C.L.

23. Montresor to Gould, November 26, 1767, T.P.C., 128/206; Schuyler to Gould, November 27, 1767, T.P.C., 128/207; December 2, 1767, T.P.C., 128/208; Thomas Mante to Gould, January 18, 1768, T.P.C., 128/271; Bradstreet to Gould, November 30, 1767, T.P.C., 128/180; December 2, 1767, T.P.C., 128/181; June 14, 1768, T.P.C., 128/254; Bradstreet to Gage, September 2, 1768, Gage Papers, A.S./80; Gage to Barrington, April 25, 1768, W.O. I/8, 192-93.

Gould, meanwhile, impatiently awaited the arrival in England of a letter from Gage which he fully expected would nominate Bradstreet as Deputy Quartermaster-General. In mid-June of 1768 as soon as he heard that correspondence from Gage had reached the War Office, Gould presented Bradstreet's claims for the appointment to the Marquis of Granby, Commander-in-Chief of the British Army.[24] To his utter amazement Gould was informed that Granby had decided that the choice must be left up to Gage himself, and the General had just recommended "a person for it" other than Bradstreet. When word of this decision was relayed to America Bradstreet was outraged and furiously turned on Gage. In the light of Gage's previous comments and Bradstreet's long service as a quartermaster, he informed the General, his action in recommending another to the vacant post could only be interpreted as the severest "Sensure" of his performance. For the sake of Bradstreet's reputation, Gage must provide the ministry with some solid indication of his confidence in the Colonel. A logical solution, according to Bradstreet, was for the General to write both Granby and Barrington recommending the Colonel's appointment to a position of even greater consequence, possibly that of third brigadier-general on the North American staff if an additional brigadier was to be added. As might be expected, Gage could see no reason to apologize for his recommendation and proceeded to peck away at Bradstreet's argument. The Colonel's seniority claim was not as clearly established as Bradstreet thought, since he had been returned only as an acting quartermaster at Albany and the home authorities allegedly interpreted this as removing him from the active service establishment. Moreover, Gage offered the rather lame excuse that Bradstreet had not been precise enough in presenting his desire for the appointment. The General claimed that if Bradstreet had asked him to make clear to the Secretary at War that he, Gage, had no objections to Bradstreet's appointment and that he applied with his commander's approval, he willingly would have done so. "It is now too late" Gage concluded, while promising that if an additional brigadier was to be appointed and if no "colonels elder than yourself come out" to America, then he would "mention you for a Brigadier."[25] These were big and safe "ifs" since the War Office had no intention of appointing another brigadier and

---

24. Granby commanded from August 1766 to January 1770 and took control of army patronage when he assumed office as Commander-in-Chief. See John Brooke, *The Chatham Administration 1766-1768* (London, 1956), 16.

25. Gould to Bradstreet, April 16, 1768, T.P.C., 128/266; Gould to the Marquis of Granby, June 13, 1768, T.P.C., 128/275; Thomas Thoroton (for Lord Granby) to Gould, June 14, 1768, T.P.C., 128/276; Gould to Bradstreet, July 4, 1768, T.P.C., 128/267; Bradstreet to Gage, September 2, 1768, Gage Papers, A.S./80; Bradstreet to Gage, September 16, 1768, Gage Papers, A.S./80; Bradstreet to Gage, September 16, 1768, Gage Papers, A.S./81; Gage to Bradstreet, September 30, 1768, Gage Papers, A.S./81; Bradstreet to Gould, September 16, 1768, T.P.C., 128/257. There were already two brigadiers on the American staff, Frederick Haldimand appointed in 1767 as southern brigadier and Guy Carleton appointed in 1765 as northern brigadier. See Shy, *Toward Lexington*, 286, 288.

regiments with at least one colonel senior to Bradstreet were already bound for America. The appointment as deputy quartermaster general had eluded Bradstreet as would that of brigadier, and it is hard to escape the conclusion that Gage's clearly stated preference for others and unconcealed dislike of Bradstreet were the major reasons.

To be sure, there were occasions and applications on which Gage appeared to support Bradstreet wholeheartedly. In the aftermath of the Stamp Act crisis, Bradstreet's alarm at the deteriorating American situation was no doubt shared by Gage and the Colonel's eventual proposal, addressed to Sir Jeffery Amherst and Charles Townshend in England, won the General's approval. Although Bradstreet explained to the Albany opponents of the Stamp Act "that he valued Liberty as much as any of them," in reality the Stamp Act furore convinced him that England must bring the colonies into line immediately and a strong military presence was the most effective way to do so. Every colony seemed "desirous to out do each other in insolence & disrespect, or rather in shewing their resolution to Rebel before they will Submit to the execution of the Act," he reported. It seemed to him that the only solution was found in "Troops ... in considerable numbers" leading to "a Military Establishment as that in Ireland, and I relly cant see how it can be avoided long."[26] Gradually his dismay at American disloyalty and his desire for strong action by the British government, combined with the possible personal advantage which might be derived from the conflict between mother country and colonies, produced a proposal to raise an American regiment to shore up the English military position.

This suggestion was offered to Gage in early December of 1766, a rather opportune moment in terms of their relationship, since the General at this time was advancing Bradstreet the money needed to pay off the Yorkers. To both Gould and Amherst, Bradstreet privately commented that his relationship with Gage definitely had taken a turn for the better; he had "been receiv'd by General Gage in so obliging a manner as to put an end to all resentment upon the old affair." Consequently, he presented to Chancellor of the Exchequer Charles Townshend a proposal which General Gage "approves of" and recommended as worthy of "being carry'd into execution, seeing it to be of public benefit." Repeating exactly the same proposal to Amherst, Gould, and Townshend, the Colonel argued that more military manpower was needed in America. To meet this need, he, "with other officers," was willing to raise a regiment of 1,000 men. Regimental commissions, except for the field officers, should be "given to the Sons of the best Families in the Several provinces." Gradually, as openings occurred, members of this officer corps were to be "Shifted into Regiments at Home." In this way these American officers eventually would become "a pledge for the Loyalty of their friends & Families in America

---

26. Beverly McAnear, "The Albany Stamp Act Riots," *William and Mary Quarterly*, 3d. Ser., 4 (1947), 496; Bradstreet to Gould, September 8, 1765, T.P.C., 128/157; August 7, 1765, T.P.C., 128/156.

& be the means in a great measure to quiet the minds of the people on future Political occasions."[27] Despite Gage's support and the apparent timeliness of the ingenious suggestion, it failed to gain acceptance. For reasons Gould did not choose to spell out, he reported that "the Plan of the Regiment will not do, and it is in vain to push the Nail, that will not drive."[28]

Gage's displeasure could block Bradstreet's proposals but clearly his approval did not guarantee their acceptance either. Furthermore, as the fate of the Detroit scheme revealed, at least some of Bradstreet's plans were neither victimized nor helped by his commander's position but were at the mercy of the ever-changing attitudes of ever-changing English ministries. When the 1764 Detroit proposal was submitted it was presented to Secretary of State Lord Halifax. Gould then proceeded to badger Halifax concerning the plan and the long-awaited reward which his lordship had promised to Bradstreet. These efforts were totally unsuccessful and in mid-October of 1765, by which time Halifax had left office, Gould could only comment, with great disappointment, that "the hold I flattered myself, that I had upon Lord Halifax with regard to you is of course at an end." If this avenue was closed, however, new avenues were being opened by the activities of Thomas Mante. After serving in the campaign against Pontiac, he had been dispatched to England by Bradstreet to lobby for the creation of the Detroit colony. At times his activities and solicitations were to prove extremely embarrassing, but in April of 1765 he had enlisted the support of George Grenville, First Lord of the Treasury from April of 1763 to July of 1765, who had agreed to "put the Government of Detroit in such a Channell as to appear before the King in Council." However, these activities only led to the referral of the scheme to the Board of Trade and its November 1765 decision to defer action on the question. At this point support for the scheme emerged in another quarter from a person who was soon to be an important architect of tentative colonial policies. In September of 1765 Sir Jeffery Amherst wrote Gould concerning his support for the proposed Detroit government and offered his assurance that "Colonel Bradstreet has not been out of my mind, or will he be on this, or any other occasion, when I may have an opportunity of speaking for him."[29] Apparently the cloud

---

27. Bradstreet to Charles Townshend, December 3, 1766, T.P.C., 128/200; Bradstreet to Gould, December 3, 1766, T.P.C., 128/170; Bradstreet to Amherst, December 3, 1766, T.P.C., 128/202. See William J. Eccles, "The Social, Economic, and Political Significance of the Military Establishment in New France," *Canadian Historical Review*, 52 (1971), 1-22, in which the Canadianization of the French officer corps serving in New France had the sort of political repercussions Bradstreet hoped for in the English colonies.

28. Gould to Bradstreet, March 13, 1767, T.P.C., 128/188. Marshall, "Imperial Policy and the Government of Detroit," 169, explains Gage's change in attitude as perhaps more due to political considerations than anything else since Gage was aware of Bradstreet's strong connection with Amherst and could see the rise of Amherst, and his friend Shelburne, in England.

29. Sedgwick to Gould, April 11, 1765, T.P.C., 128/195; Gould to Bradstreet, A-

surrounding the last moments of Amherst's American service had dissipated and within the year, as a new ministry took shape, Bradstreet's old friend and colleague was to emerge as a respected advisor on colonial matters.

Encouraged by Gould's reports that achievement of the Detroit proposal remained within the realm of possibility, Bradstreet now corresponded at length with Amherst, pressing the case for Detroit and western development and offering his observations on the distressing American situation. Shortly thereafter he wrote to Gould concerning an interesting combination of the American emergency with the opening of Detroit. Suggesting that the raising of a regiment might meet with colonial opposition, Bradstreet felt that it could still be carried off "under pretence of Establishing a great settlement at Detroit" for which it could be explained as providing protection. An even more interesting combination involving the identical western perceptions of Bradstreet and Amherst emerged in the spring and summer of 1766. In the early spring rumours circulated in America that the English government was considering the withdrawal of "all the Troops from the upper Lakes." Without a British military presence and "proper management" of the American interior, Bradstreet firmly believed that such an ill-considered manoeuvre could only have immensely "bad consequences." In truth, just such a proposal was being considered, and in May of 1766 Secretary at War Barrington submitted a plan for the American west, involving a British military withdrawal from the interior to the major seaboard centres. Sir Jeffery Amherst was among those who raised their voices in opposition to this withdrawal. His opposing arguments were in complete accord with Bradstreet's western thoughts and aspirations. The interior must not be abandoned, Sir Jeffery argued, but instead England must capitalize upon her western conquests. And the best way to do so was by establishing three interior colonies: one on the upper and one on the lower Mississippi, and, of course, one at Detroit.[30]

The opportunity for Amherst to offer his views to a receptive ministry soon presented itself. In July of 1766 George III asked William Pitt, soon to be Lord Chatham, to form a government. Amherst was still identified with the Pitt interests but it was not to be through the good graces of Chatham but rather through the interest and cooperation of the new Secretary of State for the southern department, Lord Shelburne, that Sir Jeffery almost brought to fruition Bradstreet's Detroit

---

pril 12, 1765, T.P.C., 128/123; Gould to Halifax, June ?,1765, T.P.C., 128/196; Gould to Bradstreet, October 11, 1765, T.P.C., 128/185; Mante to Gould, April 4, 1765, T.P.C., 128/190; Sosin, *Whitehall and the Wilderness*, 138-39; Sosin, *The Revolutionary Frontier*, 32; Amherst to Gould, September 18, 1765, T.P.C., 128/198.

30. Bradstreet to Amherst, October 24, 1765, T.P.C., 128/199; Bradstreet to Gould, December 23, 1765, T.P.C., 128/159; March 16, 1766, T.P.C., 128/162; "Barrington's Plan For The West, May 10, 1766," in Clarence W. Alvord and Clarence E. Carter, eds., *Collections Of The Illinois State Historical Library*, 11 (Springfield, 1969) 234-43; Gipson, *The British Empire Before the American Revolution*, 11, 439-40.

plan. Elated at the news of the new ministry, Bradstreet at first hoped that Chatham himself, who had "been much my friend," could be persuaded to act on his behalf. But Chatham's soon-to-emerge physical and mental incapacity made this unlikely, particularly when, in addition, Bradstreet's old vital link with the Pitt of the past, Sir Richard Lyttleton, proved to be no longer in favour with the new Lord Chatham. Encouraged by Gould and Mante's suggestions that another of the ministerial figures, Charles Townshend, expressed renewed interest in his cause, Bradstreet turned to the cultivation of the new Chancellor of the Exchequer. But Townshend's views concerning the need for a withdrawal from the west[31] were diametrically opposed to Bradstreet's and, in any case, Townshend's meteoric rise within the ministry ended with his sudden death in September 1767. Especially to Mante and Gould who were on the spot, it seemed clear that Amherst and Shelburne were now Bradstreet's best potential patrons.

Once Lord Shelburne was in office and exposed to the solicitations of various American interests, as well as the comments of advisors such as Jeffery Amherst, his own policies for the proper management of the American interior gradually emerged. Although his formal plan was not submitted to his cabinet colleagues until September 1767, already in the spring of that year some of its essential points were rumoured in America. In April Bradstreet heard with pleasure that "it was likely three Governments would shortly take place—Detroit, Fort Charters & another on the Mississippi, between the Confluence of the Ohio & the River Iberville." In addition, Amherst continued to encourage Bradstreet with several letters stating, in the Colonel's words, that "the Affair of Detroit is not over" and that "it would soon take place." As Shelburne's plan took final form, Amherst's importance in its shaping was clearly revealed. Shelburne apparently had decided upon only two new interior colonies, one at Detroit and one on the Illinois, but after further consultation with Amherst a third government on the lower Mississippi was added. In this form Shelburne's colonial expansion plan went before the Lords of Trade in October 1767.[32]

Once the word was out concerning the proposal, Mante and Gould quickly set to work to complete what Amherst had initiated so well. Mante personally visited Sir Jeffery to be reassured that the Detroit

---

31. Alvord, *The Mississippi Valley In British Politics*, 1, 315; Bradstreet to Gould, n.d., T.P.C., 128/166 (from the context of the letter, it probably was written in September 1766); Note written by Gould, August 8, 1766, T.P.C., 128/186; Bradstreet to Gould, October 4, 1766, T.P.C., 128/167; Gould to Bradstreet, March 12, 1767, T.P.C., 128/188; Bradstreet to Gould, March 24, 1767, T.P.C., 128/172; R. A. Humphreys, "Lord Shelburne and British Colonial Policy, 1766-1768," *English Historical Review*, 50 (1935), 261.

32. Humphreys, "Lord Shelburne and British Colonial Policy," 258-64. Sosin, *Whitehall and the Wilderness*, 164, has a different view of Shelburne's attitude towards western expansion: "It does not seem that he [Shelburne] was legitimately convinced of the desirability of western expansion. He was merely trying to finance a program for the West." Bradstreet to Gould, April 13, 1767, T.P.C., 128/173; June 28, 1767, T.P.C., 128/174; October 15, 1767, T.P.C., 128/177.

government was definitely intended for Bradstreet, while Gould submitted to Lord Shelburne a memorial on the Colonel's behalf. Reaching back to the heroic capture of Fort Frontenac, outlining his faithful service in the quartermaster department, reciting the promises of rewards from personages such as Lord Halifax, arguing that Bradstreet's strong sense of duty detained him in America, depriving him of the advantage of personal solicitations, the memorial ended with the plea that "As an opinion now prevails that a Government will be erected at D'Etroit I must humbly beg leave to intreat your Lordship, in that case, to recommend him to his Majesty as Governor." Detroit appeared at last to be within Bradstreet's grasp. A triumphant Gould wrote his colonial friend, "I am not yet able to give you any certain account about the intended Government, but it seems now on the point of being determin'd; and I think in your favour."[33]

In the winter of 1767-1768 Bradstreet confidently assumed that his Detroit appointment was at hand and began plans for the administration of his new colony. He informed Gould that his English confidant was to be appointed the colony's London agent. Then he proceeded to speculate on a variety of questions concerning Detroit. He wondered what its form of government would be, how the Indian lands were to be granted, how many civil officers he would have the right to appoint, what troops would be stationed there, and how the colony's major potential industry, the production of hemp, could best be encouraged. Continuing his long discourse, he emphasized the need for the construction of a proper governor's residence and the establishment of an Indian "Seminary" for their religious conversion, proper civilization, and also as a useful guarantee for "the Fidelity" of the students' parents.[34]

His expectations soaring, Bradstreet even hoped that his imminent Detroit triumph might reunite him with at least one member of his estranged family. Several years earlier, evidently in 1764 or 1765, his wife Mary had departed from Boston with his daughters Agatha and Martha and stepdaughter Elizabeth, bound first for Ireland and then for England. Tired of the Colonel's constant absence on military campaigns and obvious tendency to make his Albany quartermaster department rather than his Boston family and home the centre of his life, she took leave of the Colonel and America never to return. No doubt her decision was helped as well by the rumours circulating concerning the Colonel's Albany mistress[35] and his pronounced endearment for Catherine Schuyler, wife of his close friend and colleague Philip Schuyler.[36] Once arrived in England Bradstreet's family proved a con-

---

33. Mante to Gould, October 24, 1767, T.P.C., 128/193; n.d. T.P.C., 128/194; Gould to Shelburne, October 27, 1767, T.P.C., 128/204; Gould to Bradstreet, November 13, 1767, T.P.C., 128/189.
34. Bradstreet to Gould, January 26, 1768, T.P.C., 128/250.
35. Alden, *General Gage in America*, 73.
36. Arthur Pound's sketch of "John Bradstreet" in his *Native Stock: The Rise Of The American Spirit Seen In Six Lives* (New York, 1931), 69, mentions the "gossip" and "slimy

stant drain on his finances as his wife quickly used the funds she took with her and went through an additional "Eleven hundred pounds," according to the Colonel's estimate, by the spring of 1768. A good portion of this amount came directly from Charles Gould, who provided Mary Bradstreet with a basic support allowance of £230 in December of each year, in addition to meeting other of her obligations and debts, all of this money naturally being taken from Bradstreet's account with him. Although Bradstreet periodically ordered his wife to return to Boston, by 1768 he had abandoned any hope of reconciliation and was in the process of arranging a £230 yearly annuity to be paid for the remainder of her life. Nonetheless, he retained a particular fondness for his youngest daughter, Martha, and used his Detroit appointment as a reason for his at least being reunited with her. Expecting a sizeable income and permanent home at Detroit, Bradstreet hoped his wife would allow Martha to return to America. A tender letter was addressed to Martha, "the only Child I love" according to Bradstreet, expressing his expectation that once the Detroit appointment was finalized she would join her father.[37]

But the Detroit appointment, and the many dreams that went with it, were not to be. In early January of 1768 Gould wrote Bradstreet concerning "Another Change ... in the Departments of State" which he interpreted as temporarily delaying the "Settlement of D'Etroit." In reality, this change ended any chance of Bradstreet's proposal and appointment. Already strong opposition to Shelburne's proposed three interior colonies had emerged at the Board of Trade, and before the winter of 1767-1768 passed his plan was in ruins. Furthermore, the January 1768 change created a new secretaryship for colonial affairs, thus curtailing Shelburne's department, stripping him of the initiative in American matters, and leaving him in an increasingly uncomfortable position within a ministry which was embarking upon American policies substantially different from his own. Undaunted by ministerial

---

inferences" concerning Bradstreet and Schuyler's wife. Dismissing the rumoured affair as total nonsense, Pound vehemently defends the happy family life enjoyed by both the Schuylers and Bradstreets. Concerning Bradstreet he writes of his "consistent record in matrimony which makes philandering at the age of fifty seem out of character in his case. Happily married, he fathered a large family; amid the suspicions roused against him in early life, he had shown himself a devoted husband." As on so many occasions in his sketch of Bradstreet, what Pound lacks in evidence he compensates by exaggeration. It is clear that Bradstreet was far from happily married. Concerning the rumours of Bradstreet's attachment to Mrs. Schuyler, one of Bradstreet's descendants made the interesting comment that "the Eldest Son of Schuyler Jno. Bradstreet Schuyler was the picture of Gen. B. and it was from his attachment to Mrs. S. that he treated his Wife and Daughters most cruely and never saw them for many years before his death." See "A Book, containing an account written in the hand of Major Christopher Aldridge giving information for the benefit of Sir Charles Morgan relating to the financial affairs of the Bradstreet family," c. 1809, T.P.C., 128/1730.

37. Bradstreet to Gould, October 15, 1767, T.P.C., 128/175; January 27, 1768, T.P.C., 128/251; April 29, 1768, T.P.C., 128/252; Bradstreet to Martha Bradstreet, April 29, 1768, T.P.C., 128/273; Bradstreet to Mary Bradstreet, April 29, 1768, T.P.C., 128/272.

fluctuations Gould continued to press Bradstreet's case, presenting to the new American secretary, Lord Hillsborough, an only slightly revised version of the petition earlier presented to Shelburne seeking the Detroit government for the Colonel. But during his years in office from 1768 to 1772, Hillsborough was to demonstrate constant opposition to western expansion. To him, "western colonies meant Indian war" and consequently any number of such schemes were to be unequivocally rebuffed. By June of 1768 a disappointed Bradstreet had learned that "the affair of the Detroit & establishing the two other Governments intended are laid aside." Moreover, by mid-October of this year of disappointment Amherst's resignation as Governor of Virginia had been forced by the ministry's demand that he take up residence in the colony; in addition Shelburne's resignation from the government had been demanded, and Chatham himself resigned, citing reasons of health, but also lamenting "the removal of Sir Jeffery Amherst and that of Lord Shelburne."[38] When the world collapsed around Bradstreet, it completely collapsed!

At the same time as these critical setbacks were occurring, the Colonel was being denied the appointment as Deputy Quartermaster-General for America because of Gage's manoeuvres. Thus by the end of 1768 Bradstreet's search for both a colonial governorship and a higher military office were completely frustrated. It is not surprising that his career underwent a shift in emphasis at this point. It was the summer of 1768 when Sir William Johnson commenced preparations for the finalization of an interior Indian boundary and word reached the colonies that imperial regulation of the Indian trade was to be abandoned, with control over it reverting to the various colonial governments. All eyes were turned to Sir William's approaching October and November Indian conference at Fort Stanwix which was to open, to the dismay of the home authorities, a considerable amount of Indian territory for speculation and expansion.[39]

Although not present at the Fort Stanwix discussions, Bradstreet quickly negotiated his own land deal with representatives of the Six Nations and by July of 1769 had purchased approximately 300,000 acres between the Susquehannah and Delaware Rivers from the Oneida Indians.[40] Both the Lords of Trade and American Secretary

---

38. Gould to Bradstreet, January 8, 1768, T.P.C., 128/263; Humphreys, "Lord Shelburne and British Colonial Policy," 264, 271; Gould to Hillsborough, June 20, 1768, T.P.C., 128/277; Shy, *Toward Lexington*, 283; Peter Marshall, "Lord Hillsborough, Samuel Wharton and the Ohio Grant, 1769-1775," *English Historical Review*, 80 (1965), 717-39; Marshall, "Imperial Policy and the Government of Detroit," 177; Bradstreet to Gould, June 15, 1768, T.P.C., 128/255; Brooke, *The Chatham Administration*, 366-67, 381-83.

39. For the background of events leading to the Fort Stanwix treaty and a fuller consideration of Johnson and the English government's positions on the controversial boundary finally drawn, see Peter Marshall, "Sir William Johnson and the Treaty of Fort Stanwix, 1768," *Journal of American Studies*, 1 (1967), 149-79.

40. "Copy of Coll Bradstreets Indian Deed for Lands . . . ," July 2, 1769, ref. #13357, N.Y.S.L. See also T.P.C., 128/317.

Hillsborough, along with the Hardenburgh proprietors who claimed a part of the same land, opposed the transaction. Supported by Governor Moore initially and by a series of favourable decisions from the New York Council, Bradstreet fought on over a several-year period. While never abandoning the basic claim, to begin development of the larger tract, he refined his proposal, aiming first at 20,000 acres and then by the time of his death at 5,000 acres.[41] More successful were the several land deals in which he cooperated with, and at times financed, Philip Schuyler. For example, in 1772 Bradstreet was a partner with Schuyler, Rutger Bleecker, Jacob Ten Eyck, and Volkert Douw in the purchase of two blocs of 16,950 and 21,850 acres in upper New York.[42] Unfortunately the true extent of his landholdings is uncertain since, after being warned by Gould that land speculation activities might hurt his quest for public offices, Bradstreet often operated as a silent, or invisible, partner in deals. Indeed, because Gould feared it did not "perfectly coincide with your Application for Preferment," he refused to handle the English end of Bradstreet's Indian land purchase, forcing his old friend to recruit Colonel Thomas Howard to try to secure Crown approval for the scheme.[43] Further obscuring matters is the possibility that as American executor of Bradstreet's estate, Philip Schuyler for his own benefit might well have underestimated the amount of land actually owned by his departed partner. This was the allegation of Bradstreet's heirs and, as a result, tangled legal actions would stretch out over a fifty-year period after Bradstreet's death.[44] In any case, if Schuyler's report on Bradstreet's landholdings at the time of his death is accepted as a bare minimum, he owned at least 15,212 acres and when this is added to his estate worth £15,000 sterling, including his English investments, by the standards of the day Bradstreet was a wealthy man in both money and property.[45]

---

41. See "The Claims of Col. John Bradstreet To Lands In America," *Transactions and Collections of the American Antiquarian Society*, 11 (Worcester, 1909), 101-31; *New York Council Minutes*, 26, 238-38, 240-44, and 31, 77-78, N.Y.S.L.; Bradstreet to Governor William Tryon, December 27, 1771, ref. #11544, N.Y.S.L.; Representation of the Lords of Trade to the Committee of the Privy Council, July 1, 1773, in Edmund B. O'Callaghan, ed., *Documents Relative to the Colonial History of the State of New York*, 8 (Albany, 1857), 378-80.

42. Don R. Gerlach, *Philip Schuyler and the American Revolution in New York, 1733-1777* (Lincoln, Nebraska, 1964), 218-19.

43. Gould to Bradstreet, June 6, 1769, T.P.C., 128/309; Bradstreet to Johnson, August 14, 1769, in Sullivan et al., *Johnson Papers*, 7, 94-95; "Memorandum of an Agreement between Colonel John Bradstreet of the Town of Albany & Province of New York and of Colonel Thos. Howard of the City of Westminister in England," Nov. ?, 1771, T.P.C., 128/794.

44. "A Bundle of Old Papers... 1894," Misc. MSS, Taber, 1-72, N.Y.H.S.; Richard Peters, *Reports of Cases Argued and Adjudged In The Supreme Court Of the United States January Term 1831*, 5 (Philadelphia, 1831), 402-50; Joseph L. Wendell, *Reports Of Cases Argued And Determined In The Supreme Court of Judicature And In The Court For The Correction Of Errors, Of The State Of New York*, 12 (New York and Albany, 1896), 602-80.

45. "Acct. of Genl. Bradstreets real Estate in America," by Philip Schuyler, November 29, 1774, T.P.C., 128/791. See also "Computation of the value of Gen Bradstreets

Nevertheless, he remained as alert as ever when opportunities or offices opened before him and was quick to attempt to grasp these elusive prizes. The old hopes and aspirations remained ready to spring to life when the moment appeared right. The applications and suggestions soon resumed their homeward flow, but now they were tinged with a deepening pessimism concerning their probable fate. Indeed, it appeared at times that a routine sense of duty compelled Bradstreet to apply for what he increasingly suspected he could never secure. Deprived of patrons at the centre of political power, lacking the complete confidence and support of his commanding officer, and unable to straddle convincingly and utilize the differing positions of mother country and colonies, the Colonel was slowly driven to a desperate acknowledgment that his chances for further military or governmental honours were at best emasculated and at worst non-existent.

The most pathetic chapter in his military and imperial career was now underway. Wildly scrambling for virtually any appointment, snatching at rumours and incidents and attempting to convert them into opportunities for his further service to the Crown, a bitter and despondent Bradstreet managed only to accumulate an impressive list of failures and near misses. One such occurred over the office of brigadier for the middle district. Watching the concentration of troops at Boston and the departure of two successive commandants, Brigadier-General John Pomeroy and Major-General Alexander Mackay, from the city in the summer of 1769, Bradstreet pressed Gage for an appointment as brigadier for the middle district to handle this trouble spot. Gage argued that there appeared no indication that the home authorities were willing to allow the appointment of an additional brigadier and he himself could not see the need. By now, however, petitions directed to Lord Granby in October of 1768, one of which he passed on to George III, appeared ready to bear fruit in that hints of a possible appointment were made to Gould who in turn relayed them to Bradstreet. Further pressuring Gage in January of 1770, Bradstreet claimed that he had heard from England that upon "a favourable mention of me to my Lords Granby & Barrington for Brigadier of the Middle District it was expected His Majesty would grant it to me." Pointing out that he still felt a greater need for a major-general, rather than a brigadier, Gage agreed at least to mention Bradstreet to Barrington. This he did in a February 1770 letter explaining that if a brigadier for the middle colonies was to be appointed, then "I must in Justice to Colonel Bradstreet beg leave to recommend him, as the only Colonel resident in this Country." At approximately the same time Bradstreet wrote directly to Lord Granby soliciting the appointment as brigadier and informing his Lordship that Gage was writing to Barrington in support of his application. The Granby connection had been carefully cultivated by Gould, but it was already at an end. It turned out that Granby had resigned as Commander-in-Chief of the army in January of 1770; thus, as Gould put it, "that Channel is Diverted." Consequently in April of 1770 Gould forewarned Bradstreet that, despite Gage's recommendation of him as a possible brigadier over the middle district, an answer was about to be sent to America "that no such appointment is at present intended."[46] It had been a near miss but Bradstreet had failed again.

It appears that many of the channels which Bradstreet persisted in employing had been "diverted" or completely dried up by 1770. The Colonel's "very good friend" Sir Richard Lyttleton passed on in October of that year, while other possible patrons whom Bradstreet continued to badger were powerless. For example, in April of 1770 Bradstreet reminded Lord Chatham of his wartime services and loyal performance of peacetime duties, neither of which had gained him any rewards. As a result he hoped "my Noble Patron" could possibly "recommend me to his Majestys favor that I shall not much longer remain thus neglected." But Chatham himself was now into the last decade of his life, experiencing his own "years of disappointment, frustration, and tragedy" when his "advice was not asked, his warnings were ignored, his co-operation was rejected."[47] Equally futile was Bradstreet's attempt in December of 1770 to enlist the support of Lord Halifax for a campaign which the Colonel proposed to launch down the Mississippi. At this time there existed a possibility of war between Britain and Spain over the Falkland Islands and so Bradstreet solicited Halifax's support for his plan to raise a 4,000-man force in America and lead it down the Mississippi to capture New Orleans. "The People of this Country are so Sensible of the Advantage of taking New Orleans that they would gladly contribute towards it," he argued. But Halifax had long since ceased to play an active role in politics and by June of 1771, according to Gould, was "dangerously ill" and not likely "to hold it long." By that time, as well, the war scare had ended. Although the military strike

---

Estate in Britain and America at the time of his decease," by Philip Schuyler, n.d., Schuyler Papers, Box 9, in which Schuyler calculated the estate was worth approximately £32,662 (N.Y.). Included in this amount were Bradstreet's English investments and savings which Schuyler estimated at £21,000 (N.Y.) or equivalent to about £12,000 sterling. Gould presented a slightly lower estimate of Bradstreet's English fortune, calculating that the General left a total of £10,787 sterling in principal money, reduced bank annuities, and old South Sea annuities. See "The Estate of the late Major General Bradstreet at the time of his decease, so far as came to the hands or knowledge of his Executor in Great Britain," n.d., T.P.C., 128/809. Thus, the estate was probably worth at least £15,000 sterling.

46. Shy, *Toward Lexington*, 310-11; Bradstreet to Gould, October 24, 1768, T.P.C., 128/260; Bradstreet to Granby, October 24, 1768, T.P.C., 128/282; "To the King's most Excellent Majesty The Petition of Colonel John Bradstreet," n.d. (but judging from the similarity between it and the petition to Granby, and Bradstreet's mention of a petition to the King which he sent to Granby, it probably also was drafted in October 1768), C.O. 5/114, 101-102; Bradstreet to Gage, August 13, 1769, Gage Papers, A.S./87; Gage to Bradstreet, August 21, 1769, Gage Papers, A.S./89; January 14, 1770, Gage Papers, A.S./89; Gage to Barrington, February 20, 1770, W.O. I/9 pt. 1, 74-75; Bradstreet to Granby, January 19, 1770, T.P.C., 128/326; Gould to Bradstreet, February 6, 1770, T.P.C., 128/313; April 4, 1770, T.P.C., 128/314.

47. Bradstreet to Gould, December 5, 1770, T.P.C., 128/305; April 20, 1770, T.P.C., 128/300; Bradstreet to Chatham, April 20, 1770, T.P.C., 128/327; Brooke, *The Chatham Administration*, 385.

against New Orleans had been very much on the mind of American Secretary Lord Hillsborough, his plan differed in important respects from Bradstreet's. In September and December of 1770 he had warned General Gage concerning the chance of war between England and Spain and on January 2, 1771, before Bradstreet's suggestion had reached England, he instructed Gage concerning preparations for such an eventuality. Should hostilities commence Gage was ordered to attack New Orleans. The augmented regular regiments were to be used in the campaign and it was "the King's present intention" that "you should command upon this Expedition in Person."[48] The Colonel still had the knack to perceive what was in the air and attempt to turn it to his advantage, but his once precise timing was slightly off and, more importantly, the individual to whom he addressed his proposal was too far removed from political power to drive the scheme home. Furthermore, the stumbling block of Gage had re-emerged for neither the first nor the last time.

Potential governorships also eluded Bradstreet and in at least one case it was again Gage who carried off the prize rather than the Colonel. With keen interest Bradstreet watched the dismaying course of events in unruly Massachusetts and tried to capitalize upon them. In July 1769, hearing of Governor Sir Francis Bernard's intention to return home, he suggested to Gould the possibility of securing the office for himself. It was Bradstreet's opinion that Bernard needed "Cash and for five hundred pounds would possibly give his Interest for a Successor and timely notice; please to think of this." The attempt to buy his way into office failed, but Bradstreet continued to urge Gould to press his claim to the appointment since it was the Colonel's feeling that the person intended for the office, Lieutenant-Governor Thomas Hutchinson, did not want it at all. Nevertheless, Hutchinson received the appointment. No curbing of Massachusetts' rebelliousness ensued, however, so that by mid-1773 Bradstreet felt that the situation had so far deteriorated that it cried out for his appointment and his solution. "I have long thought the day would come when the Independency of the Colonys would be made a question, but I did not think it so near," he commented. Strong action was needed to take the "firebrands" behind the agitation in hand, but the scholarly Hutchinson, in Bradstreet's judgment, was not the man to do it. The English government had "for some time past, try'd Pen & Ink men to Govern that Province [Massachusetts], which has not succeeded; perhaps they may now think it best to try a Soldier." Ironically the home administration did feel a soldier was needed to govern Masachusetts and soon appointed one. But it was not the soldier either Bradstreet or Gould had in mind who

---

48. Bradstreet to Halifax, December 1770, T.P.C., 128/329; Shy, *Toward Lexington*, 292; Gould to Bradstreet, June 5, 1771, T.P.C., 128/358; Hillsborough to Gage, September 28 and 11, 1770 and January 2, 1771, in Carter, *Gage Correspondence*, 2, 117-18. For further details concerning this war scare, see Gipson, *The British Empire Before the American Revolution*, 12, 3-11.

received the appointment. It was Thomas Gage who was called upon to serve as Governor of Massachusetts, "a department," Gould complained to Bradstreet, "in which I could have wished to have Seen you."[49]

Other governorships were eagerly eyed by Bradstreet but his pretensions were equally as unsuccessful as his Massachusetts efforts. When Governor Sir Henry Moore of New York died in 1769 the Colonel quickly expressed his willingness to accept the vacant position, but instead it went to Lord Dunmore. When plans were being made to shift Dunmore to the Virginia governorship, Gould knew the Colonel's desires before they even were voiced. Thus, he explained that Dunmore's shift was to be coupled with William Tryon's appointment to the New York position. By 1770 a residence in inhospitable Canada, which Bradstreet had declined in 1764, now took on a certain attraction. Thus, the rumour that Brigadier-General and Governor Guy Carleton was about to leave for England, and contemplated "never returning" to Quebec, awakened the Colonel's interest and brought the inevitable application. Gould was urged to secure both offices for Bradstreet, but he soon discovered that Carleton intended to "return to America and continue his appointments." Owing to Carleton's lengthy four-year absence Bradstreet continued to hope that this English sojourn was permanent, but his inquiries produced the repeated answer from Gould that the offices were not going to be vacated and that Carleton's return to Canada was near.[50]

As might be expected Bradstreet's consistent failure to secure a higher military or colonial appointment left him a bitter and desperate man. In August 1771 he lamented to Gould, "To tell you the truth, my Dear friend, my situation is almost grown intolerable; after so many years faithful Service, and some in high rank too, still to find myself unemploy'd equal to that Rank but left so many years with a paltry Emolument to Subsist on." He was now reduced to the suggestion that he was willing to give up his "Employments" as acting Deputy Quartermaster-General at Albany and Lieutenant-Governor of St. John's in Newfoundland in return "for a thousand pounds Sterling a year for life" which could be paid from the New York quit-rents or other provincial revenue if they refused to pay it at home. While offering to surrender these two offices he wanted to keep his rank as colonel and his captain's commission in the 60th Regiment. As one last alternative to this proposal, in view of possible future disturbances in Boston, he wondered about the possibility of his appointment to com-

---

49. Bradstreet to Gould, July 22, 1769, T.P.C., 128/287; April 1, 1770, T.P.C., 128/297; March 15, 1773, T.P.C., 128/343; July 25, 1773, T.P.C., 128/349; Gould to Bradstreet, April 6, 1774, T.P.C., 128/373.

50. Bradstreet to Gould, September 17, 1769, T.P.C., 128/289; Gould to Bradstreet, December 5, 1770, T.P.C., 128/299; Bradstreet to Gould, June 3, 1770, T.P.C., 128/302; Gould to Bradstreet, January 2, 1771, T.P.C., 128/356; Bradstreet to Gould, July 18, 1772, T.P.C., 128/337; Gould to Bradstreet, April 6, 1774, T.P.C., 128/373.

mand Castle William. Perhaps "if I gave up all my Employments I might be appointed Military Govr. of that Island."

By this point, however, Gould himself was ready to call a halt to such constant and fruitless applications. Accordingly in September 1771 he advised Bradstreet to come to London "and see what you can effect by a personal application." His advice was accepted and in the spring and fall of 1772 the fifty-seven year old Colonel busily sorted out his American affairs in preparation for the journey to England. But the settling of his "Public & Private Business" proved more complex and time consuming than initially assumed and by late September 1772 it became clear that he would not be able to leave America before the coming spring. Moreover, his spirits were by now so low that he really questioned whether personal solicitations would help him at all. "After all, my friend," he explained to Gould, "long experiences have shewn me, that the power of real and repeated Service, the respectable application of friends at the Times and the promises of the great have not as yet been sufficient to obtain me Bread at the expence of the Public—what hopes then can I flatter my Self with from my personal and weak application; surely none—and to live on beging & expectation all a mans Life is hard indeed."[51]

Suddenly in the last months of 1772 Bradstreet's gloom and doom were pierced by rays of hope as a series of events combined to create what appeared to be an extremely favourable situation for the advancement of his claims. His last campaign was about to be mounted. Motivated by the course of events occurring in both America and England Bradstreet and his friends were spurred to one more effort. News reached America in late September that Colonel John Bradstreet was among those profiting from a general promotion of the "Colonels appointed before the end of the year 1762" and, as a result, he now held rank as a major-general. In late November, moreover, word leaked out that General Thomas Gage had "requested leave to return Home from his Command." At the same time, in England, Sir Jeffery Amherst completely shook off the "royal disfavour" created by his unwillingness to accept what was regarded as adequate compensation for the loss of his Virginia governorship. He was wooed openly by the North administration and before 1772 ended had agreed to an office and reward which healed the old wound and earned George III's approval. Furthermore, in August 1772 the resignation of American Secretary Lord Hillsborough had been forced and at least one factor in his removal was his opposition to the schemes for colonization of the American west. Finally, in late 1772 Thomas Mante proved his value to Bradstreet in that his history of the American war was published in London, weighted with vindication and praise for the Colonel's role

---

51. Bradstreet to Gould, August 1, 1771, T.P.C., 128/331; November 30, 1771, T.P.C., 128/333; Gould to Bradstreet, September 30, 1771, T.P.C., 128/361; Bradstreet to Gould, May 10, 1772, T.P.C., 128/335; August 23, 1772, T.P.C., 128/339; September 28, 1772, T.P.C., 128/340.

both in the Seven Years' War and in the campaign against Pontiac.[52] In this way the stage was set with a variety of new possibilities which might lead to a triumphant conclusion of Bradstreet's quest for preferment.

Only one of these several occurrences was fated to bring any satisfaction to Bradstreet, however. There is no doubt that he craved an historical vindication of his Detroit performance and Mante provided it. Gould had periodically reported the progress of Mante's proposed history which, it was promised, would make "particular mention" of Bradstreet and, in order to ensure that this would be the case, would be read by Gould prior to publication. True to his word, in October of 1772 Mante passed on sections of the book for Gould's perusal so that he could "expunge any part" which might "appear to contain any thing contrary to the Interest of General Bradstreet." The reception and reading audience which the book received is of course uncertain but at least an historical vindication of Bradstreet's performance now existed.[53]

This attempted restoration of Bradstreet's military reputation proved of little help when he tried to follow up the other opportunities presented in late 1772. One by one these various openings closed before him. Gage's rumoured departure for England when coupled with Bradstreet's new rank as major-general, it was assumed, left him in an excellent position for some sort of appointment. This was Gould's reasoning when, in February 1773, he revised his earlier advice and now urged Bradstreet to remain in America since "perhaps after General Gage's arrival something further may be determined with respect to the American Staff." Succeeding Gage as Commander-in-Chief might appear a rather lofty aspiration but to Philip Schuyler it was a possibility. In the event of Gage's not returning to America, Schuyler suggested that "General Bradstreet's friends in this Country who are respectable and numerous would be vastly happy to see the Command of his Majesty's troops Conferred on him." While professing to believe such an application was of "little use," Bradstreet himself still hoped for it, since he pointed out that Gage's logical successor was Frederick Haldimand but he might be disqualified because he was "a foreigner." By April Gould had investigated the situation and informed both Bradstreet and Schuyler that there was no chance of Bradstreet's replacing Gage. The Commander-in-Chief fully intended to return to America and in his absence General Frederick Haldimand was to

---

52. A. Charrier to Amherst, May 25, 1772, Amherst Papers, Packet 72, 9, P.A.C.; *Nova Scotia Gazette and the Weekly Chronicle* (Halifax), September 29, 1772; Bradstreet to Gould, November 29, 1772, T.P.C., 128/341; Long, *Lord Jeffery Amherst*, 212-13, 220-21; Shy, *Toward Lexington*, 325; Thomas Mante, *The History Of The Late War In North-America, And The Islands Of The West Indies, Including The Campaigns Of MDCCLXIII And MDCCLXIV Against His Majesty's Indian Enemies* (New York, 1970; originally published London 1772), 62-63, 152-55, 506-35.

53. Gould to Bradstreet, March 31, 1772, T.P.C., 128/365; Mante to Gould, October 29, 1772, T.P.C., 128/382. Alden, *General Gage in America*, 100; and Parkman, *The Conspiracy of Pontiac*, 39 dismiss Mante's work as prejudiced.

command by reason of his seniority. Nevertheless, Gould assured Bradstreet that he intended to meet with Sir Jeffery Amherst to present his case.[54]

Bradstreet himself left no stone unturned in this last effort to achieve some mark of honour. Several petitions were addressed to Secretary at War Barrington, the support of Gage was solicited, and Amherst's help was requested. Before Gage's departure Bradstreet wrote to him seeking his "kind assistance" and requesting that he allow Charles Gould to meet with him when he reached England so that a possible position could be discussed. Unfortunately Bradstreet expressed a willingness to serve anywhere except in the southern district. Gage seized upon this slip claiming, quite accurately in view of Haldimand's shift northward to replace him but also quite conveniently, that at present service there "is the thing most likely to offer." After shutting the door in this way, Gage did grant that "other Projects" might materialize in England, but he obviously was in no mood to encourage Bradstreet's solicitations. The petitions to Barrington emphasized the long neglect suffered by Bradstreet and suggested the need for a regiment or any mark of favour. Barrington laid one of these before his Majesty but he did it in such a noncommittal fashion that Gould was pessimistic about the result. "If any thing arises from it, you will owe it to H. Ms. goodness," he observed, "for I must think his Ministers have not greatly importuned him in your favour." At least Bradstreet's complaints to Amherst brought a more sympathetic response, although Sir Jeffery's comments to Gould concerning Bradstreet's predicament revealed that he felt the strongest case for preferment lay in the colonial rather than the military sphere. Asserting his willingness to serve Bradstreet in any possible way, Amherst was of the opinion that "he has been unlucky in not having a Government established, which would have been of great Advantage to the Publick, and an appearance of reward to him by appointing him the Governor as he wished."[55] One after another the

---

54. Gould to Bradstreet, February 3, 1773, T.P.C., 128/367; Schuyler to Gould, February 8, 1773, T.P.C., 128/384; Bradstreet to Gould, February 14, 1773, T.P.C., 128/342; March 30, 1773, T.P.C., 128/444; Gould to Bradstreet, April 6, 1773, T.P.C., 128/368; Gould to Schuyler, April 6, 1773, Schuyler Papers, Box 9, N.Y.P.L.

55. Bradstreet to Gage, April 25, 1773, Gage Papers, A.S./118; Bradstreet to Gould, May 16, 1773, T.P.C., 128/348; Bradstreet to Barrington, May 10, 1773 (in the Bradstreet MSS at the American Antiquarian Society a copy of this letter is erroneously identified as addressed to Shelburne), T.P.C., 128/387; October 9, 1773, T.P.C., 128/392; Gould to Bradstreet, January 3, 1774, T.P.C., 128/371; Bradstreet to Amherst, May 16, 1773, T.P.C., 128/389; Amherst to Gould, August 1, 1773, T.P.C., 128/391. Even when Bradstreet learned of Sir William Johnson's death and sought his office as Indian superintendent, he was blocked again, this time by the dead Johnson. In June 1773 Sir William hinted that his office should remain in the family and not fall into the hands of "a person nowise qualified for it, but who has Confidence enough to pass for a man acquainted with these matters, & a few friends to Countenance & recommend the Application, tho' incompetent Judges of the necessary qualifications." This might very well have been a thinly veiled reference to Bradstreet. See Bradstreet to Gould, July 14, 1774, T.P.C., 128/355; Johnson to Gage, June 2, 1773, in Sullivan et al., *Johnson Papers*, 7, 814.

potential opportunities had vanished until Bradstreet was left with only Amherst's implication that a colonial government was best for him. In that case, the natural colonial government to seek was that of a new Detroit colony.

Detroit seemed all that remained to Bradstreet and he hoped for it, while Gould pursued it, to the bitter end. The moment seemed opportune, since Hillsborough left office in August 1772 to be replaced by Lord Dartmouth in the position of American secretary, and the advocates of the far more elaborate Vandalia scheme of western colonization appeared at long last on the verge of success.[56] Once more rumours circulated both in America and England concerning the soon-to-be established interior colonies, although Bradstreet suspected his own Detroit proposal to be well down the list. In mid-July 1772 he heard of possible governments at Fort Pitt and on the Mississippi, and proceeded to outline the disadvantages of both. "If Inland Governments are to be Established," he claimed, "there is no part of No. America so proper as the Detroit." For his part Gould waited, listened, and prepared to move when the time was right. In June 1774, ironically at the very time when legislation precluding a Detroit colony was being passed by Parliament, Gould acted. He urged both Sir Jeffrey Amherst and General Thomas Gage, by then in England, to mention Bradstreet to Lord Dartmouth for an appointment as Governor of Detroit. This was followed in August by a long petition to John Pownall, Undersecretary to Dartmouth, outlining Bradstreet's valued services and unwarranted neglect, and requesting Pownall to place before Dartmouth the Major-General's desires for the governorship of any new colony to be established in America. There was to be no new colony created. Coincident with Gould's final submission the administration's "final decision" concerning the American west was being rendered by means of the Quebec Act.[57] Detroit was within the boundaries of Canada and Bradstreet's quest was at an end.

The embattled warrior was spared the news of this final failure as well as the spectacle of the open revolution he long expected. For several months in 1774 Bradstreet had been bothered by what he described as a "debilitated Stomach" and no significant improvement in his health occurred as the year progressed. By September he lay sick and dying at New York City. A combination of cirrhosis of the liver and a dropsy condition snuffed out his life on Sunday, September 25, 1774.[58] He was three months short of sixty years of age. According to a

---

56. Sosin, *Whitehall and the Wilderness*, 181-210, devotes a chapter to the Vandalia project's rising and declining fortunes.

57. Bradstreet to Gould, December 27, 1771, T.P.C., 128/334; Gould to Bradstreet, March 31, 1772, T.P.C., 128/365; Bradstreet to Gould, July 12, 1772, T.P.C., 128/336; Gould to Bradstreet, December 2, 1772, T.P.C., 128/366; March 1, 1774, T.P.C., 128/372; Gould to Gage, June 11, 1774, Gage Papers, E.S./25; Amherst to Gould, September 4, 1774, T.P.C., 128/398; Gould to Bradstreet, July 2, 1774, T.P.C., 128/374; Gould to John Pownall, August 2, 1774, T.P.C., 128/397; Sosin, *Whitehall and the Wilderness*, 239; Hilda Neatby, *The Quebec Act: Protest and Policy* (Scarborough, Ontario, 1972).

58. Bradstreet to Gould, May 10, 1774, T.P.C., 128/354; Schuyler to Mrs. Agatha

newspaper account: "After having settled his affairs, and taken leave of his friends, he left the world with the most perfect and heroic resignations." Philip Schuyler was at his side as death approached and, apparently at the urging of his close friend, the General made a gesture of reconciliation with his absent family. Schuyler was allowed to destroy a will made by Bradstreet which treated the General's wife and children rather cruelly. In its place a will was substituted which made financial provision for his wife Mary, children Agatha and Martha, and stepdaughter Elizabeth, and which also contained bequests for Philip and Catherine Schuyler and two of their children, John and Margaret. On Monday, the day after his death, amidst an elaborate funeral cortège Bradstreet's body was borne to its final resting place.[59] With full military honours Jean-Baptiste Bradstreet, born in Annapolis Royal, Nova Scotia, was laid to rest in Trinity Church, New York City, as Major-General John Bradstreet.

Buttar and Miss Martha Bradstreet, October 2, 1774, Schuyler Papers, Box 9; Schuyler to Gould, October 2, 1774, Schuyler Papers, Box 9. Schuyler bluntly described the cause of death to Bradstreet's daughters as "a Seirrosis Liver which occasioned a dropsy," while he more discreetly explained to Gould that the General was carried off by "a dropsy and disorder in the Liver."

59. *Rivington's New York Gazetteer*, September 29, 1774; Schuyler to Gould, October 2, 1774, Schuyler Papers, Box 9; "This is the last will and Testament of John Bradstreet...," September 23, 1774, T.P.C., 128/467; Gerlach, *Philip Schuyler*, 240.

Conclusion

History has been described as "the record of an encounter between character and circumstance"[1] and, in a very real sense, John Bradstreet both shaped and was shaped by the course of mid-eighteenth-century Anglo-American relations. His colonial and military aspirations stood the best chance of success when they dovetailed English and colonial desires and needs. But his deeds and suggestions were occurring during a period in Anglo-American history when such a harmony of interests was becoming increasingly rare. His own position was further complicated by his mysterious background, since the uncertainty about his Acadian-Nova Scotian birth and childhood made him suspect both as an Englishman and as an American. During the 1745 Louisbourg campaign and its aftermath, Bradstreet discovered how easy it was to fall between the two stools and to be victimized by the similar suspicions and quite dissimilar Louisbourg intentions of Old and New England.

Determined to avoid a repetition of such a situation, Bradstreet attempted to anchor firmly his position and reputation in both worlds. During his years in England in the early 1750s he carefully cultivated the "Easie Access" to the great and near great which was so necessary for the aspiring colonial. Upon his return to North America in 1755 he also went to great lengths to curry favour with his commanders in the field while at the same time building a formidable reputation for himself among the provincials, both military and civilian. With his interests thus protected at "home" and abroad and with colonies and mother country, at least temporarily and tenuously, united against a common foe, Bradstreet was in the crucial place at the crucial time. Added to what Donald Creighton would call this proper "position in time and space" was the undeniable military contribution made by

---

1. Donald G. Creighton, *Towards the Discovery of Canada* (Toronto, 1972), 19.

Bradstreet at Oswego, Ticonderoga, and Fort Frontenac. His actions, his connections, and the dynamic aura surrounding him thrust Bradstreet to the forefront as a figure of some significance in the conquest of New France.

The 1763 peace removed not only the common menace offered by New France; it also removed the common fears and goals so briefly shared during wartime by the colonies and mother country. Quickly swept away as well were Bradstreet's military utility and, after the 1764 expedition against Pontiac, a sizeable portion of his once-respected military reputation. Likewise in England, the tide of circumstances appeared to turn against him. William Pitt was out of power, Sir Richard Lyttleton had left for the continent, Robert Wood had retired from office, and once-sympathetic patrons, such as Lord Halifax, now turned a deaf ear to the unceasing solicitations offered by Charles Gould on behalf of his friend. Bradstreet was caught in what Richard M. Brown would describe as "a decline of standing" within both his English and his American constituencies.[2] He attempted escape from this possibly fatal predicament by a rather paradoxical approach.

In the military sphere he attempted to turn to his advantage the Americans' increasing restlessness within the empire. Diverting campaigns, new regiments, additional military offices, strategically located posts, military governorships were all suggested as possible solutions to the rising American problem. All such solutions were basically military approaches and all involved appointments or activities for which Bradstreet felt himself eminently qualified. While most of these suggestions revealed his willingness to view the widening gulf between England and America as largely caused by unfortunate rebellious tendencies on the part of the colonials, in another sphere Bradstreet's sympathy for the emerging American position was demonstrated. On the question of western development, Bradstreet was in total agreement with colonial expansionists and very much at odds with the mother country's restrictive policies. Although his dreams of new colonies in the west had been articulated as early as 1755, and repeated on many occasions since then, his western schemes received their clearest, most detailed, and most dedicated presentation from 1764 onward. There might be disagreement with other western prophets concerning the proper location of the new colonies, with Bradstreet naturally emphasizing his cherished Detroit proposal, but he was in general agreement with them concerning the need to open the west by means of new colonies.

Bradstreet was not to be alone in failing to achieve offices, the creation of new colonies, or title to vast tracts of land. While his failure bore some resemblance to that suffered by others, such as patrons reduced to impotence in the face of ministerial instability or, worse yet, ministerial opposition to and suspicion of colonial schemes, the charac-

---

2. See Richard M. Brown, "The Anglo-American Political System, 1675-1775: A Behavioral Analysis," in Olson and Brown, *Anglo-American Political Relations*, 20.

ter of Bradstreet must be matched with the circumstances of the moment for a more complete understanding of his predicament. He was at times haughty, overbearing, and overconfident while at other times his deference, humility, and abject dependence on others shone through. He could be brutally honest in assessing his commanders but on occasion he could be evasive and strangely uncritical. He possessed an abrasive and prickly personality and yet he could be quite persuasive and quietly patient when the need arose. When he was attacked or criticized, however, perhaps the real man emerged. He never admitted a mistake or wrongdoing but went to considerable lengths to show the correctness of all his actions. By long and at times distorted arguments, by historical justifications penned after the event, by endless repetition of his contributions and his innocence of any evil deed he continually sought, and sometimes gained, a vindication of sorts. Yet this overly defensive reaction and the shrill pitch of his pleas of innocence revealed the essential Bradstreet. An aggressive opportunist ever grasping for further honours and economic gains, Bradstreet was at the same time very insecure and possessed few really close friends. He was an Anglo-Irish-Acadian, neither English nor American, and this left him vulnerable and dependent. The handful of people he had trusted with his friendship were all staunch defenders of his interests—individuals who compensated for his own uneasiness within two societies which were, to a certain extent, equally alien to him. The victim of his own self-inflicted amnesia, he was for all his interests and connections, a rootless wanderer. His fictionalized "home" in England and his final resting place in New York were forced upon him by opportunity and necessity. He was a man constantly on the move and on the make with neither the time nor inclination to plant deep and permanent roots.

But his uniqueness must not be over-emphasized to the neglect of his typicality. Bradstreet was one of a good number of office-seekers drawn from marginal parts of the Empire and destined to find more frustration than satisfaction in the post-1750 trans-Atlantic world. To retain a masterful grasp of the political intricacies of two diverging worlds, while viewed with suspicion in England and an increasing resentment in America, was a virtually impossible task. In 1752, after a long-time residence in America and retirement to Massachusetts, Paul Mascarene well demonstrated the cautious uncertainty of many "colonial" seekers of imperial favour. Elaborate instructions were drawn up for his son John as he was dispatched to England to seek a proper reward for his father's services. He was to seek out William Shirley, then in England, and "if you find him inclin'd to do me Service & I can not butt think he will be You may communicate to His Excellency my Memorial." Lacking Shirley's support perhaps through "Mr. Kilby" or "Mr. Lane" an audience with Lord Halifax could be secured. If received by his lordship "in a kind manner and with openess shewing a regard to Your father," John was to "begg . . . his countenance" and guidance as to how to proceed with the memorial. If "failing there," the younger Mascarene was to try Sir John Ligonier and then Edward Cornwallis and so the list continued. It all came to naught for Mascarene.[3]

Even such a well-connected English colonial administrator as William Shirley, protégé of the powerful Newcastle, could find himself friendless. Acclaimed as the last royal governor "able to harmonize ... the interests of the mother country—imperial in nature—with those of the vigorous corporate colonies—local in nature,"[4] by 1758 this same Shirley begged for an appointment of any sort. Do "not discard me" he implored Newcastle, "after having spent so many years in faithful Services to the Crown." Halifax sympathized with Shirley's plight since the charges which brought his downfall were unproven, he was a "poor old Servant of the Crown" now "reduced to want," and an appointment would at least spare Newcastle "further Solicitations from the poor old Man." Thus the governorship of the Bahamas was granted, "a narrow sphere, where he may End his Days in Quiet & Repose."[5] Then there were those who could be described as essentially "mid-Atlantic" men, of whom William Knox is one of the best-documented examples. Irish-born and always on "the margins of the territorial aristocracy which dominated eighteenth-century British society," he was never able to exert the influence he desired on the dominant English elite and possessed an imperial vision that "found even less favour in America."[6] Bradstreet's career bears some striking similarities to that of Knox although by 1766 Bradstreet spoke of and identified with the rising American dislike of outside office-holders imposed upon the colonies. He hinted to Charles Townshend that he should be perceived as an American and rewarded with offices since the Americans have a "general complaint, that Government makes great difference between them & the Scotch & Irish by giving & granting to the two last posts & Employments & none to them"[7] What he failed to acknowledge was the American perception, like the British perception, of him as an outsider. His services, like those offered by many others, were needed to head off the revolutionary drift of the colonies, but he was not heeded or appreciated in England or America. On the other hand, perhaps the

---

3. Paul Mascarene to John Mascarene, October 21, 1752, Papers Relating to Nova Scotia, 1720-1791, Add. MSS 19,071/60, B.M.; John Mascarene to Grenville, October 27, 1764, Grenville Papers, Add. MSS 57,823/103-104, B.M.; Maxwell Sutherland, "Paul Mascarene," in Francess G. Halpenny et al., *Dictionary of Canadian Biography*, 3 (Toronto, 1974), 439; Barry M. Moody, "'A Just and Disinterested Man': The Nova Scotia Career of Paul Mascarene, 1710-1752" (Ph.D. dissertation, Queen's University, 1976), 391.

4. Gipson, *The British Empire Before the American Revolution*, 6, 240, as quoted in Richard B. Morris, "The Spacious Empire of Lawrence Henry Gipson," *William and Mary Quarterly*, 3d Sr., 24 (1967), 174-75.

5. Shirley to Newcastle, April 1, 1758, Newcastle Papers, Add. MSS 32,879/15-16, B.M.; May 12, 1758, in ibid., 32,880/48-49; Halifax to Newcastle, September 14, 1758, in ibid., 31,883/448-49.

6. Leland J. Bellot, *William Knox: The Life and Thought of an Eighteenth-Century Imperialist* (Austin, 1977), 216.

7. Bradstreet to Townshend, December 3, 1766, T.P.C., 128/200, N.L.W.

apparent success such outside office-seekers had enjoyed for so long in the colonies, which Americans found so distasteful, meant that any further generous accommodation of the Bradstreet-types would have hastened, not slowed, the final rupture.

Bradstreet's position as the vulnerable outsider, always defending and justifying his conduct, frequently finding his reputation clouded with rumours and suspicions, made him somewhat of an irregular regular. Serving in an officer corps which, particularly at the colonel's level and above, was dominated by men drawn from social strata well above his own,[8] Bradstreet discovered that others could capitalize upon their offices and remain above reproach. Or they could move from undistinguished service in one disaster after another and still aspire to and achieve an office such as Commander-in-Chief in America. At the same time, any suggestion of his own involvement in illicit trading activities, corruption within his quartermaster department, or privately profitting from a wilderness triumph such as that at Frontenac in 1758 seemed sufficient to block his advance and any chance of further honours. It is of some significance that in reporting Bradstreet's Frontenac victory to the King, Newcastle concluded his brief summary with the remark: "The plunder is said to be worth seventy Thousand pounds Sterling."[9] Time and again such rumours and suspicions were to surface to temporarily disadvantage if not to discredit Bradstreet completely.

Offsetting such hints of excessive profiteering were his unique talents and acknowledged military triumphs and contributions. Several of his plans revealed an imaginative flair other officers sadly lacked, while his successful use of colonials, willingness to undertake lightning-like strikes, and rapport with the bateau-men set him apart from other English regulars attempting, often unsuccessfully, to adjust to service alongside and over colonials. Moreover, when Bradstreet had successfully completed the tasks assigned, on the field of battle for example, his English supporters could use such virtuous performance of duty to counter the whispers concerning the unsavoury side of their client's activities. The lack of unquestioned triumphs, however, meant a stagnating career, since without the conclusive performance that cried out for reward his interests simply were not powerful enough. In this sense, also, the irregularity of Bradstreet emerges. Others could

---

8. See James W. Hayes, "The Social And Professional Background Of The Officers Of The British Army, 1714-1763" (M.A. thesis, University of London, 1956). For brief comments on the additional difficulties of officers serving overseas, see Eric Robson, "Purchase And Promotion In The British Army In The Eighteenth Century," *History*, 36 (1951), 58.

9. Newcastle to the King, October 30, 1758, Newcastle Papers, Add. MSS 32,885/126. Another example of gossip and rumour damage is found in the concern and hestiation about William Franklin's appointment as Lieutenant-Governor of New Jersey caused by his "unsavoury background, penchant for 'the good life,' and reputation for ribaldry." See Larry R. Gerlach, "Anglo-American Politics in New Jersey on the Eve of the Revolution," *Huntington Library Quarterly*, 39 (1976), 302.

rely on their interests alone to achieve their desired offices and appointments. He was very much a self-made man in that almost all his prizes were won by undeniable contributions, admittedly driven home at the right time and place by his friends "at home." When military triumphs and praise from commanding officers for conscientious service eluded him, little could be done on his behalf.

That merit was important in his rise should not preclude the possibility that there was much that was far from meritorious in his career. While, as might be expected, the evidence is far from conclusive and sometimes obfuscated by Bradstreet's obvious inclination to cover his tracks, he clearly was not above combining performance of public duties with private profit-making. Whether at Louisbourg, St. John's, Albany, or Detroit, the opportunities presented for personal enrichment were quickly seized. What must be questioned is the extent to which Bradstreet's conduct deviated from the norm. While it might appear at first glance a rather lame defence to cite the "sins" of others, the way of the world at the time appeared to accept that a colonel's rank, for example, guaranteed not only a colonel's salary but other profitable perquisites as well. This mid-eighteenth-century perception of public offices, whether military or colonial, as appointments to be discretely milked for all they were worth was widely held; modestly revealed in William Johnson's land dealings, blatantly demonstrated in Henry Fox's performance as Paymaster-General. Discretion seemed the watchword, however, except for those who were among the most powerful or had extremely strong and active connections with the mightiest, and discretion was one characteristic rarely linked with John Bradstreet. The periodic cautions of King and Charles Gould concerning reports of illicit trade, Charles Knowles's comments on profiteering at the expense of the Cape Breton garrison, the possible misappropriation of Albany quartermaster department funds, and the evidence placed in the hands of Gage and Johnson concerning trading activities all point to Bradstreet's consistent indiscretion. What he was doing was not all that unusual, but his unabashed way of doing it, his ungentlemanly approach to the spoils of office, meant that rumours concerning his excesses frequently circulated on both sides of the Atlantic.

John Bradstreet was an appreciative student of the way of the mid-eighteenth-century trans-Atlantic world, and his career reveals a definite ability to adjust to changing circumstances and, on many occasions, to profit from them. Although his fluctuating fortunes were, as he put it, in the hands of "a capricious goddess," he had received much in the way of "riches, honours & reputation." However, despite his expression of satisfaction "that whatever errors I have committed, or whatever faults can be objected to me, still I have always lov'd my country, & study'd to serve it,"[10] he was all too aware of the uncertainties about just which "country" was his own and whether the public's interests were

---

10. Bradstreet to King Gould, January 7, 1755, T.P.C., 128/4.

always his primary concern. Valued in a wartime emergency yet always kept slightly beyond the pale, Bradstreet remained an irregular regular. Ironically, some of the same traits which contributed to his irregularity, his rootlessness and knowledgeability of both sides of the Anglo-American world, for example, represented both his greatest asset and his most profound weakness.

Bibliography

I. Primary Sources

A. Manuscript

American Antiquarian Society.
    John Bradstreet Mss.
British Museum.
    Papers relating to Nova Scotia, 1720-1791. Add MSS. 19,071.
    Newcastle Papers. Add. MSS. 32,692-32,740; 32,771; 32,807-32,808; 32,811; 32,811; 32,821-32,822; 32,825-32,827; 32,831; 32,835; 32,852-32,959; 32,979-32,989; 32,992; 32,994; 33,004; 33,009-33,010; 33,028-33,030; 33,046-33,048; 33,054-33,057; 33,067-33,069; 33,071-33,072.
    Hardwicke Papers. Add. MSS. 35,409-35,416; 35,423; 35,479; 35,909-35,914.
    Grenville Papers. Add. MSS. 42,085-42,088; 57,808-57,817; 57,820-57,831; 57,835.
    Loudoun Papers. Add. MSS. 44,068.
    Holland House Papers. Add. MSS. 51,376-51,393; 51,422; 51,427-51,436; 51,468-51,469; 51,471A-51,471B, 51,821-51,828; 51,470B.
    Ligonier Papers. Add. MSS. 57,318.
Harvard University Houghton Library.
    Gage Letters. fms. Eng 106.
Henry E. Huntington Library.
    Abercromby Papers.
    Loudoun Papers.
Maine Historical Society.
    J. S. H. Fogg Collection. Vol. 7.
    Pepperrell Papers.
Massachusetts Historical Society.
    Belknap Papers.
    Parkman Transcripts.
    Pepperrell Papers.
    Wendell Papers.

New-York Historical Society.
    DeLancey Papers. Case 10.
    DePeyster Mss. Box 7.
    Gates Papers. Box 1.
    Lord Stirling, William Alexander, Mss. Vols 1 and 2.
    Miscellaneous Mss. Taber, S. R.
    Miscellaneous Mss. Louisbourg.
    Miscellaneous Mss. Bradstreet, John.
New York Public Library.
    Philip Schuyler Papers. Boxes 2, 9, 10, 13, 24, 39, 41, 43.
New York State Library.
    Items 2253, 2676, 3406, 3419, 3429, 3752, 4480, 5692, 6053, 6666, 6920, AV7002, 7118, 9691, BA9691, 11544, 12564, 13357, 13615, 13616, 13818, 14524.
    New York Colonial Manuscripts. Vol. 86, 1758-1759.
    New York Colonial Mss. Land Papers 1775-1776. Vol. 35.
    New York Council Minutes. Vol. 25. 1755-1764.
    New York Council Minutes. Vol. 26. 1765-1783.
    New York Council Minutes. Vol. 31. 1772-1776.
    Schuyler Mansion Documents.
    Van Vechten Papers.
Public Archives of Canada.
    M.G. 1. Series C^{11}B. Vols. 18-27.
    M.G. 1. Series F^3. Archives Nationales. Vol. 50, pt. 1.
    M.G. 1.Archives des Colonies. Series B. Vol. 74, pt. 3.
    M.G. 9. B. 8. Vol. 24-1.
    M.G. 11. C.O. 5. Vols. 1-28, 33-77, 83-208, 898-901.
    M.G. 11. C.O. 194. Vols. 1-26.
    M.G. 11. C.O. 199. Vols. 16-18.
    M.G. 11. C.O. 217. Vols. 1-9.
    M.G. 11. C.O., 218. Vols 1-3.
    M.G. 11. Nova Scotia A Series. Vols. 2-32.
    M.G. 12. A Adm. I. Vols. 3817-3818.
    M.G. 12. B 9. W.O. I. Vols. 1-9.
    M.G. 18. L 4. Amherst Papers. Packets 1-76.
    M.G. 18. O 9. Thomas Hancock Papers.
    R.G. 22. B 3. Louisbourg Restoration Project. Micro B-3311.
    M.G. 23. A. 2. Chatham Papers. Bundles 1-98.
    M.G. 23. A 4. Shelburne Papers, Vols. 38-39, 48-59, 57, 60, 66, 134.
Public Archives of Nova Scotia
    Vols. 5-26, 29-30, 34-35, 38.
Public Record Office.
    Chatham Papers. P.R.O. 30/8. Vols. 18, 48, 56, 73, 75-76, 95 pt. 1-98, 101, 121, 151-52, 177-78, 188.
University of Michigan Clements Library.
    Amherst Papers. Vols. 1-7.
    James S. Schoff Collection.
    Michigan Papers.
    Miscellaneous.
    Thomas Gage Papers. American Series. Vols. 1-129.
    Thomas Gage Papers. English Series. Vols. 1-29.
University of Michigan Graduate Library.
    British Manuscript Project. W.O. 34. Vols. 56-58, 101-102.

National Library of Wales.
  Tredegar Park Collection, 49/2, 49/74, 49/90, 79/24-79/54, 103/164-103/184, 103/757-103/782, 128/1-128/1739, Mss./255-262, Mss./272-279, Mss./284-287.

B. *Printed*

"A Journal Of An Expedition Against Canaday By Moses Dorr Ensin Of Capt Parkers Company Roxbury May 25th 1758." *New York History*, 16 (1935), 452-64.
Akins, Thomas B., ed. *Selections From The Public Documents Of The Province of Nova Scotia*. Halifax, 1869.
Alvord, Clarence W., and Clarence E. Carter, eds. *Collections of the Illinois State Historical Library*. Vol. 10: *The Critical Period 1763-1765*. Springfield, 1915.
―――――. *Collections of The Illinois State Historical Library*. Vol. 11: *The New Regime 1765-1767*. Springfield, 1916.
Balderston, Marion, and David Syrett, eds. *The Lost War: Letters from British Officers during the American Revolution*. New York, 1975.
Bass, Benjamin. "Account Of The Capture Of Fort Frontenac By The Detachment Under The Command Of Col. Bradstreet." *New York History*, 16 (1935), 449-52.
[Bradstreet, John]. *An Impartial Account Of Lieut. Col. Bradstreet's Expedition To Fort Frontenac*. London, 1759.
Canada, Department of National Defence. *History Of The Organization, Development and Services of the Military and Naval Forces of Canada From the Peace of Paris in 1763 to the Present Time*. Vol. 1, Ottawa, 1919.
Carter, Clarence E., ed. *The Correspondence of General Thomas Gage with the Secretaries of State, and with the War Office and the Treasury 1763-1775*. 2 vols. New Haven, 1931 and 1933.
Collections Of The Pioneer Society Of The State Of Michigan. Vol. 8, pp. 340-63. "The Conspiracy of Pontiac—Accounts of Eye-witnesses." Lansing, 1907.
Collections. Report Of The Pioneer Society Of The State of Michigan. Vol. 9, pp. 343-637. "The Haldimand Papers." Lansing, 1908.
Dalton, Charles, ed. *English Army Lists and Commission Registers, 1661-1774*. Vol. 6; *1707-1714*. London, 1960.
―――――. *George The First's Army 1714-1727*. Vol. 1. London, 1910.
DeForest, Louis E., ed. *Louisbourg Journals 1745*. New York, 1932.
―――――. *The Journals and Papers of Seth Pomeroy*. New Haven, 1926.
Documentary History of the State of Maine. Vol. 11. "Baxter Papers." Portland, 1908.
Doughty, Arthur G., ed. *An Historical Journal Of The Campaigns In America For The Years 1757, 1758, 1759 and 1760 By Captain John Knox*. 3 vols. Toronto, 1914-1916.
Fergusson, C. Bruce, ed. *Nova Scotia Archives IV: Minutes of His Majesty's Council At Annapolis Royal 1736-1749*. Halifax, 1967.
Government of Canada. *Report of the Public Archives for the Year 1929*. "Montcalm Correspondence." Ottawa, 1930.
Grant, William L., and J. Munro, eds. *Acts of the Privy Council of England Colonial Series*. Vols. 2-6. London, 1910-1912.
Great Britain, Public Record Office. *Calendar Of State Papers, Colonial Series, America and West Indies*. Vols. 25-44. London, 1924-1969.
―――――. *Journal of the Commissioners for Trade and Plantations*. Vols. 2-13. London, 1925-1937.

Gwyn, Julian, ed. *The Royal Navy and North America: The Warren Papers, 1736-1752.* London, 1975.

Hamilton, Edward P., ed. *Adventure In The Wilderness: The American Journals of Louis Antoine de Bougainville 1756-1760.* Norman, Okla., 1964.

Historical Collections Made By The Pioneer Society Of The State Of Michigan. Vol. 11, pp. 319-620. "Haldimand Papers." Lansing, 1908.

Historical Collections And Researches Made By the Michigan Pioneer And Historical Society. Vol. 27, pp. 605-80. "Gladwin Manuscripts." Lansing, 1897.

Hough, Franklin B., ed. *Diary Of The Siege Of Detroit In The War With Pontiac.* Albany, 1860.

Innis, Harold A., ed. *Select Documents In Canadian Economic History 1497-1783.* Toronto, 1929.

"Journal of Colonel John Winslow," in *Collections of the Nova Scotia Historical Society for the Year 1884.* Vol. 4, pp. 113-246.

Kimball, Gertrude S., ed. *Correspondence of William Pitt When Secretary Of State With Colonial Governors and Military and Naval Commissioners In America.* 2 vols. New York, 1906.

Labaree, Leonard W. et al., eds. *The Papers of Benjamin Franklin.* Vols. 8 and 11. New Haven, 1965 and 1967.

Lincoln, Charles H., ed. *Correspondence of William Shirley.* 2 vols. New York, 1912.

Lodge, Richard, ed. *Private Correspondence of Chesterfield and Newcastle 1744-46.* 1882.

MacMechan, Archibald M., ed. *Nova Scotia Archives II: A Calendar of Two Letter-Books and One Commission-Book in the Possession of the Government of Nova Scotia 1713-1741.* Halifax, 1900.

──────── . *Nova Scotia Archives III: Original Minutes Of His Majesty's Council At Annapolis Royal 1720-1739.* Halifax, 1908.

Massachusetts Historical Society. *Collections.* 1st Ser., Vol. 1, pp. 5-60. "Letters relating to the Expedition against Cape Breton." Boston, 1792.

──────── . *Collections.* 1st Ser., Vol. 7, pp. 67-163. "A Review of the Military Operations in North America, from the Commencement of the French Hostilities on the Frontiers of Virginia in 1753, to the Surrender of Oswego, on the 14th of August 1756." Boston, 1846.

──────── . *Collections.* 4th Ser., Vol. 5, pp. 305-589. "Niles's History of the Indian and French Wars." Boston, 1861.

──────── . *Collections.* 4th Ser. Vol. 9. "Aspinwall Papers." Boston, 1871.

──────── . *Collections.* 4th Ser. Vol. 10. "Aspinwall Papers." Boston, 1871.

──────── . *Collections.* 6th Ser., Vol. 6. "Belcher Papers." Boston, 1893.

──────── . *Collections.* 6th Ser., Vol. 10. "Pepperrell Papers." Boston, 1899.

New England Historic-Genealogical Society. *The New England Historical and Genealogical Register.* Vols. 16 and 24. Albany, 1862 and Boston, 1870.

New-York Historical Society. *Collections For The Year 1871.* Vol. 1. "The Lee Papers." New York, 1872.

──────── . *Collections For The Year 1876.* Vol. 1. "The Colden Letter Books." New York, 1877.

──────── . *Collections For The Year 1877.* Vol. 2. "The Colden Letter Books." New York, 1878.

──────── . *Collections For The Year 1881.* "The Montresor Journals." New York, 1882.

O'Callaghan, Edmund B., ed. *Commissary Wilson's Orderly Book.* Albany, 1857.

──────── . *Documents Relating To The Colonial History Of The State Of New York.* Vols. 7, 8, and 10. Albany, 1856-1858.

_____. *The Documentary History Of The State Of New York.* Vols. 1 and 4. Albany, 1850-1851.

Pargellis, Stanley, ed. *Military Affairs in North America.* New York, 1936.

Pease, Theodore C., ed. *Anglo-French Boundary Disputes In The West 1748-1763.* Springfield, 1936.

Peters, Richard. *Reports of Cases Argued and Adjudged in the Supreme Court of the United States January Term 1831.* Vol. 5, pp. 402-50. Philadelphia, 1831.

Pioneer Collections And Researches Made By The Pioneer Society Of The State of Michigan. Vol. 10, pp. 210-546. "The Haldimand Papers." Lansing, 1908.

Preston, Richard A., and Leopold Lamontagne, eds. *Royal Fort Frontenac.* Toronto, 1958.

Proceedings of the American Antiquarian Society. Vol. 20, 1909-1910, pp. 139-83. "The Journal of Sir William Pepperrell Kept During the Expedition Against Louisbourg Mar. 24-Aug. 22, 1745." Worcester, 1911.

"Records of the Reformed Dutch Church of Albany N.Y." *Year Book of the Holland Society of New York 1908.* pp. 1-62. New York, 1916.

Sabine, William H. W., ed. *Historical Memoirs from 16 March 1763 to 9 July 1776 of William Smith.* New York, 1956.

Shortt, Adam et al., eds. *Documents Relating to Currency, Exchange and Finance in Nova Scotia with Prefatory Documents 1675-1758.* Ottawa, 1933.

Stevens, Sylvester K., and Donald H. Kent, eds. *The Papers of Col. Henry Bouquet.* Series 21631, 21632, 21634, 21650 pt. II, 21651, 21653. Harrisburg, 1940-1943.

Sullivan James et al., eds. *The Papers of Sir William Johnson.* Vols. 1-13. Albany, 1921-1962.

Transactions and Collections of the American Antiquarian Society. Vol. 10. Worcester, 1909.

Webster, John C., ed. *The Journal of Jeffery Amherst.* Toronto, 1931.

Wendell, Joseph L. *Reports of Cases Argued and Determined in the Supreme Court of Judicature and in the Court for the Correction of Errors, of the State of New York.* Vol. 12, pp. 602-80. New York and Albany, 1896.

White, Philip L., ed. *The Beekman Mercantile Papers 1746-1799.* Vol. 2. New York, 1956.

Williams, E. G., ed. *The Orderly Book of Colonel Henry Bouquet's Expedition Against the Ohio Indians, 1764.* Pittsburgh, 1960.

Wrong, George M., ed. *Louisbourg in 1745: The Anonymous "Lettre d'un Habitant de Louisbourg."* Toronto, 1897.

C. *Newspapers and Magazines*

Boston Evening Post, February 9, 1756 to October 11, 1756 and June 26, 1758 to October 8, 1758.

Boston News-Letter, August 10, 1758 to November 2, 1758.

Boston Weekly Advertiser, August 21, 1758 to December 11, 1758.

Gentleman's Magazine, 1745, 1746, 1758, and 1774.

Halifax Gazette, March 23, 1752 to March 6, 1776.

London Gazette, October 31, 1758.

Nova Scotia Gazette and Weekly Chronicle, September 29, 1772 and September 6, 1774 to October 18, 1774.

Rivington's New York Gazetteer, September 29, 1774.

II. Secondary Sources

A. Books

Abernethy, Thomas P. *Western Lands and the American Revolution*. New York, 1959. Originally published Charlottesville, 1937.

Alden, John R. *General Gage in America*. Baton Rouge, 1948.

Alvord, Clarence W. *The Mississippi Valley in British Politics*. 2 vols. New York, 1959. Originally published Cleveland, 1917.

Andrews, Charles M. *The Colonial Background of the American Revolution*. New Haven, 1942. Originally published New Haven, 1924.

_____. *The Colonial Period of American History*. 4 vols. New Haven, 1954-1959. Originally published New Haven, 1934-1938.

Ayling, Stanley. *The Elder Pitt: Earl of Chatham*. New York, 1976.

Bailyn Bernard. *The Ideological Origins of the American Revolution*. Cambridge, Mass., 1967.

_____. *The Ordeal of Thomas Hutchinson*. Cambridge, Mass., 1974.

_____, and Jane N. Garrett, eds. *Pamphlets of the American Revolution*. Vol. 1: *1750-1765*. Cambridge, Mass., 1965.

Baker, Norman. *Government and Contractors: The British Treasury and War Supplies, 1775-1783*. London, 1971.

Baxter, W. T. *The House of Hancock*. New York, 1965.

Becker, Carl. *The History of Political Parties in the Province of New York, 1760-1776*. Madison, 1909.

Bellot, Leland J. *William Knox: The Life and Thought of an Eighteenth-Century Imperialist*. Austin, 1977.

Bell, Winthrop P. *The "Foreign Protestants" and the Settlement of Nova Scotia*. Toronto, 1961.

Bernstein, Barton J., ed. *Towards a New Past: Dissenting Essays in American History*. New York, 1969.

Bird, Harrison. *Battle for a Continent*. New York, 1965.

Bonomi, Patricia U. *A Factious People: Politics and Society in Colonial New York*. New York, 1971.

Brebner, John B. *New England's Outpost*. New York, 1927.

_____. *The Neutral Yankees of Nova Scotia*. Toronto, 1969. Originally published New York, 1937.

Bridenbaugh, Carl. *Cities in Revolt*. New York, 1955.

_____. *Cities in the Wilderness*. New York, 1955.

_____. *Mitre and Sceptre: Transatlantic Faiths, Ideas, Personalities, and Politics 1689-1775*. New York, 1962.

Brooke, John. *The Chatham Administration, 1766-1768*. London, 1956.

Brown, Gerald S. *The American Secretary: The Colonial Policy of Lord George Germain, 1775-1778*. Ann Arbor, 1963.

Brown, George W. et al., eds. *Dictionary of Canadian Biography*. Vol. 1. Toronto, 1966.

Brown, Robert E. *Middle-Class Democracy and the Revolution in Massachusetts, 1691-1780*. Ithaca, 1955.

Browning, Reed. *The Duke of Newcastle*. New Haven, 1975.

Burke, Bernard. *A Genealogical and Heraldic Dictionary of the Peerage and Baronetage*. 53rd ed. London, 1891.

Burt, Alfred L. *The Old Province of Quebec*. 2 vols. Toronto, 1968. Originally published Toronto, 1933.

Butler, Lewis. *The Annals of the King's Royal Rifle Corps*. Vol. 1. London, 1913.

Calnek, William A., and Alfred W. Savary. *History of the County of Annapolis*. Toronto, 1897,
Campbell, William W. *Annals of Tryon County or, The Border Warfare of New-York During the Revolution*. New York, 1831.
Carse, Robert. *The River Men*. New York, 1969.
Chalmers, Harvey. *Drums Against Frontenac*. New York, 1949.
Campagne, Roger J. *Alexander McDougall and the American Revolution in New York*. Schenectady, 1975.
Charteris, Evan. *William Augustus Duke of Cumberland and the Seven Years' War*. London, 1925.
Christie, Ian R. *Crisis of Empire: Great Britain and the American Colonies 1754-1783*. New York, 1966.
──────, and Benjamin W. Labaree. *Empire or Independence 1760-1776: A British-American Dialogue on the Coming of the American Revolution*. Oxford, 1976.
Clark, Andrew, H. *Acadia: The Geography of Early Nova Scotia to 1760*. Madison, 1968.
Clark, Charles E. *The Eastern Frontier: The Settlement of Northern New England 1610-1763*. New York, 1970.
Clark, Dora M. *The Rise of the British Treasury: Colonial Administration in the Eighteenth Century*. New Haven, 1960.
Clode, Charles M. *The Military Forces of the Crown: Their Administration and Government*. 2 vols. London, 1869.
Connell, Brian. *The Savage Years*. New York, 1959.
Corbett, Julian S. *England in the Seven Years' War: A Study in Combined Strategy* 2 vols. London, 1907.
Crane, Verner W. *Benjamin Franklin and a Rising People*. Boston, 1954.
Creighton, Donald G. *Towards the Discovery of Canada*. Toronto, 1972.
Cuneo, John R. *Robert Rogers of the Rangers*. New York, 1959.
Dangerfield, George. *Chancellor Robert R. Livingston of New York, 1746-1813*. New York, 1960.
Davis, Rose M. *The Good Lord Lyttleton: A Study in Eighteenth Century Politics and Culture*. Bethelehem, Pa., 1939.
Despres, Azarie C. *Charles de Saint-Etienne De La Tour, gouverneur, lieutenant-général en Acadie, et son temps, 1593-1666*. Arthabaska, Quebec, 1930.
Dickerson, Oliver M. *The Navigation Acts and the American Revolution*. Philadelphia, 1951.
Dillon, Dorothy R. *The New York Triumvirate: A Study of the Legal and Political Careers of William Livingston, John Morin Scott, William Smith Jr*. New York, 1949.
Eccles, William J. *France in America*. Toronto, 1972.
──────. *The Canadian Frontier 1534-1760*. Hinsdale, Ill., 1969.
Evans, Geraint N. D. *Uncommon Obdurate: The Several Public Careers of J. F. W. DesBarres*. Toronto, 1969.
Fairchild, Byron. *Messrs. William Pepperrell: Merchants at Piscataqua*. Ithaca, 1954.
Fitzmaurice, Edmond. *Life of William, Earl of Shelburne, Afterwards Marquess of Lansdowne*. 2 vols. London, 1875-1876.
Fortescue, John W. *A History of the British Army*. Vols. 1-3. London, 1910-1911.
Fox, Edith. *Land Speculation in the Mohawk Country*. Ithaca, 1949.
Frégault, Guy. *Canada: The War of the Conquest*. Toronto, 1969. Originally published Montreal, 1955.
──────. *Francois Bigot: Administrateur francais*. 2 vols. Montreal, 1948.

Gamble, Thomas. *Data Concerning the Families of Bancroft, Bradstreet, Dudley, Emerson etc. in England and America, 1277-1906.* Savannah, 1906.

Gerlach, Don R. *Philip Schuyler and the American Revolution in New York, 1733-1777.* Lincoln, 1964.

――――――. *Philip Schuyler and the Growth of New York, 1733-1804.* Albany, 1968.

Gipson, Lawrence H. *American Loyalist: Jared Ingersoll.* New Haven, 1971. Originally published New Haven, 1920.

――――――. *The British Empire Before the American Revolution.* 15 vols. New York, 1958-1970.

――――――. *The Coming of the Revolution.* New York, 1954.

Grant, Anne. *Memoirs of an American Lady with Sketches of Manners and Scenes in America as They Existed Previous to the Revolution.* 2 vols. New York, 1901.

Graymont, Barbara. *The Iroquois in the American Revolution.* Syracuse, 1972.

Griffiths, Naomi. *The Acadians: Creation of a People.* Toronto, 1973.

Gruber, Ira D. *The Howe Brothers and the American Revolution.* New York, 1975 ed.

Guttridge, George H. *English Whiggism and the American Revolution.* Berkeley, 1963.

Gwyn, Julian. *The Enterprising Admiral: The Personal Fortune of Admiral Sir Peter Warren.* Montreal, 1974.

Hale, R. W., Jr. *The Royal Americans.* Ann Arbor, 1944.

Halpenny, Francess G. et al., eds. *Dictionary of Canadian Biography.* Vols. 3 and 4. Toronto, 1974 and 1979.

Hamilton, Milton W. *Sir William Johnson: Colonial American, 1715-1763.* Port Washington, N.Y., 1976.

Hannay, James. *History of Acadia.* Saint John, N.B., 1879.

Hayne, David et al., eds. *Dictionary of Canadian Biography.* Vol. 2. Toronto, 1969.

Head, C. Grant. *Eighteenth Century Newfoundland: A Geographer's Perspective.* Toronto, 1976.

Henretta, James A. *"Salutary Neglect": Colonial Administration under the Duke of Newcastle.* Princeton, 1972.

History Division, National Museum of Man. *Papers and Abstracts for a Symposium on Ile Royale during the French Regime.* Ottawa, 1972.

Innis, Harold A. *The Fur Trade in Canada.* Toronto, 1962 ed.

Jacobs, Wilbur R. *Wilderness Politics and Indian Gifts: The Northern Colonial Frontier, 1748-1763.* Lincoln, 1966. Originally published Stanford, 1950.

Johnson, Allen, ed. *Dictionary of American Biography.* Vol. 2. New York, 1929.

Kammen, Michael G. *A Rope of Sand: The Colonial Agents, British Politics, and the American Revolution.* Ithaca, 1968.

――――――. *Colonial New York: A History.* New York, 1975.

――――――. *Empire and Interest: The American Colonies and the Politics of Mercantilism.* New York, 1970.

Katz, Stanley N. *Newcastle's New York: Anglo American Politics, 1732-1753.* Cambridge, Mass., 1968.

Kenney, Alice P. *Stubborn for Liberty: The Dutch in New York.* Syracuse, 1975.

――――――. *The Gansevoorts of Albany: Dutch Patricians in the Upper Hudson Valley.* Syracuse, 1969.

Knollenberg, Bernhard. *Origin of the American Revolution: 1759-1766.* New York, 1965 ed.

Kyte, Ernest C., ed. *An Impartial Account of Lieut. Col. Bradstreet's Expedition to Fort Frontenac.* Toronto, 1940.

Leach, Douglas E. *Arms for Empire: A Military History of the British Colonies in North America, 1607-1763*. New York, 1973.
_____. *The Northern Colonial Frontier 1607-1763*. New York, 1966.
Leder, Lawrence H., ed. *The Colonial Legacy: Some Eighteenth Century Commentators*. Vol 2. New York, 1971.
Lindsay, J. O., ed. *The New Cambridge Modern History. Vol. 7: The Old Regime, 1713-1763*. Cambridge, England, 1957.
Long, John C. *Lord Jeffery Amherst: A Soldier of the King*. New York, 1933.
Lossing, Benson J. *The Life and Times of Philip Schuyler*. 2 vols. New York, 1872-1873.
_____. *The Pictorial Field-Book of the Revolution*. Vol. 1. New York, 1851.
Lydekker, John W. *The Faithful Mohawks*. New York, 1938.
MacNutt, William S. *The Atlantic Provinces: The Emergence of Colonial Society, 1712-1857*. Toronto, 1965.
Main, Jackson T. *The Social Structure of Revolutionary America*. Princeton, 1965.
Malone, Joseph J. *Pine Trees and Politics: The Naval Stores and Forest Policy in Colonial New England*. Seattle, 1964.
Mante, Thomas. *The History of the Late War in North-America, and the Islands of the West-Indies, Including the Campaigns of MDCCLXIII and MDCCLXIV against His Majesty's Indian Enemies*. New York, 1970. Originally published London, 1772.
Martin, James K. *Men in Rebellion: Higher Governmental Leaders and the Coming of the American Revolution*. New Brunswick, N.J., 1973.
McCormac, Eugene I. *Colonial Opposition to Imperial Authority during the French and Indian War*. New York, 1971. Originally published Berkeley, 1911.
McLennan, John S. *Louisbourg from its Foundation to its Fall*. London, 1918.
Merritt, Richard L. *Symbols of American Community 1735-1775*. New Haven, 1966.
Morgan, Edmund S., ed. *The American Revolution: Two Centuries of Interpretation*. Englewood Cliffs, 1965.
_____. *The Birth of the Republic 1763-89*. Chicago, 1956.
_____, and Helen Morgan. *The Stamp Act Crisis*. Chapel Hill, 1953.
Morrison, Samuel E. *The Parkman Reader*. Boston, 1955.
Morris, Richard B., ed. *The Era of the American Revolution: Studies Inscribed to Evarts Boutell Greene*. New York, 1939.
Mullaly, B. R. *The South Lancashire Regiment*. Bristol, 1952.
Murdoch, Beamish. *A History of Nova Scotia or Acadia*. Vols. 1-2. Halifax, 1865-1866.
Namier, Lewis. *England in the Age of the American Revolution*. London, 1963 ed.
_____. *The Structure of Politics at the Accession of George III*. London, 1963 ed.
_____, and John Brooke. *Charles Townshend*. London, 1964.
_____. *The History of Parliament: The House of Commons 1754-1790* Vols. 1-3. London, 1964.
Nammack, Georgiana C. *Fraud, Politics, and the Dispossession of the Indians*. Norman, Okla., 1969.
Neatby, Hilda. *Quebec: The Revolutionary Age 1760-1791*. Toronto, 1966.
_____. *The Quebec Act: Protest and Policy*. Scarborough, Ont., 1972.
Norris, John. *Shelburne and Reform*. London, 1963.
Norton, Mary Beth. *The British-Americans: The Loyalist Exiles in England 1774-1789*. Boston, 1972.
Olson, Alison G. *Anglo-American Politics 1660-1775*. New York, 1973.
_____, and Richard M. Brown, eds. *Anglo-American Political Relations, 1665-1775*. New Brunswick, N.J., 1970.

Osgood, Herbert L. *The American Colonies in the Eighteenth Century.* 4 vols. Gloucester, Mass., 1958. Originally published New York, 1924-1925.
Palmer, Robert R. *The Age of the Democratic Revolution.* Princeton, 1959.
Pares, Richard, and A. J. P. Taylor, eds. *Essays Presented to Sir Lewis Namier.* London, 1956.
Pargellis, Stanley M. *Lord Loudoun in North America.* New Haven, 1933.
Packman, Francis. *The Conspiracy of Pontiac.* New York, 1962 ed.
———. *A Half-Century of Conflict.* 2 vols. Boston, 1903. Originally published Boston, 1892.
———. *Montcalm and Wolfe.* 2 vols. Toronto, 1906. Originally published Boston, 1884.
Parsons, Usher. *The Life of Sir William Pepperrell Bart.* Boston, 1856.
Peckham, Howard H. *Pontiac and the Indian Uprising.* Princeton, 1947.
———. *The Colonial Wars 1689-1764.* Chicago, 1964.
Pound, Arthur. *Native Stock: The Rise of the American Spirit Seen in Six Lives.* New York, 1931.
———, and Richard E. Day. *Johnson of the Mohawks.* New York, 1930.
Prowse, Daniel W. *A History of Newfoundland from the English, Colonial and Foreign Records.* London, 1895.
Quaife, Milo M. *The Siege of Detroit in 1763.* Chicago, 1958.
Rawlyk, George A. *Nova Scotia's Massachusetts: A Study of Massachusetts-Nova Scotia Relations 1630-1784.* Montreal, 1973.
———. *Revolution Rejected 1775-1776.* Scarborough, Ont., 1968.
———. *Yankees at Louisbourg.* Orono, Maine, 1967.
Ritcheson, Charles R. *British Politics and the American Revolution.* Norman, Okla., 1954.
Rogers, Alan. *Empire and Liberty: American Resistance to British Authority, 1755-1763.* Berkeley, 1974.
Rudé, George. *Hanoverian London 1714-1808.* Berkeley, 1971.
Russell, Nelson V. *The British Regime in Michigan and the Old Northwest, 1760-1796.* Northfield, Minn., 1939.
Sabine, Lorenzo. *Biographical Sketches of Loyalists of the American Revolution.* Vol. 2. Boston, 1864.
Savary, Alfred W. *Supplement to the History of the County of Annapolis.* Toronto, 1913.
Schutz, John A. *Thomas Pownall: British Defender of American Liberty.* Glendale, 1951.
———. *William Shirley: King's Governor of Massachusetts.* Chapel Hill, 1961.
Scouller, Raibeart E. *The Armies of Queen Anne.* London, 1966.
Severance, Frank H. *An Old Frontier of France.* Vol. 2. New York, 1917.
Sherrard, Owen A. *Lord Chatham: Pitt and the Seven Years' War.* London, 1955.
Shy, John. *Toward Lexington: The Role of the British Army in the Coming of the American Revolution.* Princeton, 1965.
———. *A People Numerous and Armed: Reflections on the Military Struggle for American Independence.* New York, 1976.
Smythies, Raymond H. R. *Historical Records of the 40th (2nd Somersetshire) Regiment.* Devonport, England, 1894.
Sosin, Jack M. *Agents and Merchants: British Colonial Policy and the Origins of the American Revolution 1763-1775.* Lincoln, 1965.
———. *The Revolutionary Frontier, 1763-1783.* New York, 1967.
———. *Whitehall and the Wilderness.* Lincoln, 1961.
Stacey, Charles P. *Quebec, 1759: The Siege and the Battle.* Toronto, 1959.
Stanley, George F. G. *New France: The Last Phase 1744-1760.* Toronto, 1968.

———, and Harold M. Jackson. *Canada's Soldiers 1604-1954*. Toronto, 1954.
Steele, Ian K. *Guerillas and Grenadiers*. Toronto, 1969.
Stephen, Leslie, and Sidney Lee, eds. *Dictionary of National Biography*. Vol. 22. London, 1890.
Stewart, Gordon, and George A. Rawlyk. *A People Highly Favoured of God: The Nova Scotia Yankees and the American Revolution*. Toronto, 1972.
Stone, William L. *The Life and Times of Sir William Johnson, Bart*. 2 vols. Albany, 1865.
Thomas, Peter D. G. *British Politics and the Stamp Act Crisis: The First Phase of the American Revolution 1763-1767*. Oxford, 1975.
Upton, Leslie F. S. *The Loyal Whig: William Smith of New York and Quebec*. Toronto, 1969.
Van Alstyne, Richard W. *The Rising American Empire*. Oxford, 1960.
Wade, Mason. *The French Canadians 1760-1967*. Vol. 1. Toronto, 1968 ed.
Wainwright, Nicholas B. *George Croghan: Wilderness Diplomat*. Chapel Hill, 1959.
Wallace, Nesbit W. *A Regimental Chronicle and List of Officers of the 60th, or the King's Royal Rifle Corps, Formerly the 62nd, or the Royal American Regiment of Foot*. London, 1879.
Waller, George M. *Samuel Vetch: Colonial Enterpriser*. Chapel Hill, 1960.
Ward, Harry M. *"Unite or Die": Intercolony Relations 1690-1763*. Port Washington, N.Y. 1971.
Whitworth, Rex. *Field Marshal Lord Ligonier: A Study of the British Army, 1702-1770*. Oxford, 1958.
Wickwire, Franklin. *British Subministers and Colonial America, 1763-1783*. Princeton, 1966.
———, and Mary Wickwire. *Cornwallis: The American Adventure*. Boston, 1970.
Wiener, Frederick B. *Civilians Under Military Justice: The British Practice since 1689 Especially in North America*. Chicago, 1967.
Willcox, William B. *Portrait of a General: Sir Henry Clinton in the War of Independence*. New York, 1964.
Williams, Basil. *The Whig Supremacy 1714-1760*. Oxford, 1962 ed.
Willson, Beckles. *The Life and Letters of James Wolfe*. London, 1909.
Wood, George A. *William Shirley: Governor of Massachusetts 1741-1756*. Vol. 1. New York, 1920.
Wood, Gordon S. *The Creation of the American Republic 1776-1787*. Chapel Hill, 1969.
Wright, Esmond, ed. *Causes and Consequences of the American Revolution*. Chicago, 1966.
Wright, Robert. *The Life of Major-General James Wolfe*. London, 1864.

B. Articles

Adams, Paul K. "Colonel Henry Bouquet's Ohio Expedition in 1764," *Pennsylvania History* 40 (1973), 139-47.
Anderson, F. W. "Why Did Colonial New Englanders Make Bad Soldiers? Contractual Principles And Military Conduct During The Seven Years' War," *William and Mary Quarterly* 3d Ser., 38 (1981), 395-417.
Bailyn, Bernard. "The Beekmans of New York: Trade, Politics, and Families," *William and Mary Quarterly* 3d Ser., 14 (1957), 598-608.

Barrow, Thomas C. "The American Revolution as a Colonial War for Independence," *William and Mary Quarterly* 3d Ser., 25 (1963), 452-64.

Basye, Arthur H. "The Secretary of State for the Colonies, 1768-1782," *American Historical Review* 28 (1922-1923), 12-23.

Browning, Reed. "The Duke of Newcastle and the Imperial Election Plan, 1749-1754," *Journal of British Studies* 7 (1967-1968), 28-47.

Buffinton, Arthur H. "The Canada Expedition of 1746: Its Relation to British Politics." *American Historical Review* 45 (1939-1940) 552-80.

———. "The Colonial Wars and their Results." In Alexander C. Flick, ed. *History of the State of New York*, Vol. 2, pp. 203-46. New York, 1933.

———. "The Policy of Albany and English Westward Expansion," *Mississippi Valley Historical Review* 8 (1921-1922), 327-66.

Burt, Alfred L. "The Tragedy of Chief Justice Livius," *Canadian Historical Review* 5 (1924), 196-212.

Burton, I. F., and A. N. Newman. "Sir John Cope: Promotion in the Eighteenth-Century Army," *English Historical Review* 78 (1963), 655-68.

Carter, Clarence E. "The Significance of the Military Office in America, 1763-1775," *American Historical Review* 28 (1922-1923), 475-88.

Christie, Ian R. "The Cabinet during the Grenville Administration, 1763-1765," *English Historical Review* 73 (1958), 86-92.

Clark, Dan E. "News and Opinion Concerning America in English Newspapers, 1754-1764," *Pacific Historical Review* 10 (1941), 75-82.

Clark, Dora M. "The British Treasury and the Administration of Military Affairs in America, 1754-1774," *Pennsylvania History* 2 (1935), 197-204.

Daniell, Jere R. "Politics in New Hampshire under Governor Benning Wentworth, 1741-1767," *William and Mary Quarterly* 3d Ser., 23 (1966), 76-105.

Eccles, William J. "The Social, Economic, and Political Significance of the Military Establishment in New France," *Canadian Historical Review* 52 (1971), 1-22.

Edmunds, R. David. "Pickawillany: French Military Power Versus British Economics," *Western Pennsylvania Historical Magaine* 58 (1975), 169-84.

Egnal, Marc. "The Origins of the Revolution in Virginia: A Reinterpretation," *William and Mary Quarterly* 3d Ser., 37 (1980), 401-28.

———, and Joseph A. Ernst. "An Economic Interpretation of the American Revolution," *William and Mary Quarterly* 3d Ser., 29 (1972), 3-32.

Ernst, Joseph A. "Ideology and the Political Economy of Revolution," *Canadian Review of American Studies* 4 (1973), 137-48.

Farrell, David R. "Anchors of Empire: Detroit, Montreal and the Continental Interior, 1760-1775," *American Review of Canadian Studies* 7 (1977), 33-54.

Gerlach, Larry R. "Anglo-American Politics in New Jersey on the Eve of the Revolution," *Huntington Library Quarterly* 39 (1976), 291-316.

Graham, Dominick. "The Planning of the Beausejour Operation and the Approaches to War in 1755," *New England Quarterly* 41 (1968), 551-66.

Grant, Charles S. "Pontiac's Rebellion and the British Troop Moves of 1763," *Mississippi Valley Historical Review* 40 (1953-1954), 75-88.

Grant, William L. "The Capture of Oswego by Montcalm in 1756: A Study in Naval Power," *Proceedings and Transactions of the Royal Society of Canada* 3d Ser., 8 (1914), 193-214.

Greene, Jack P. "The Plunge of Lemmings: A Consideration of Recent Writings on British Politics and the American Revolution," *South Atlantic Quarterly* 47 (1968), 141-75.

———. "The Seven Years' War and the American Revolution: The Causal Relationship Reconsidered," *Journal of Imperial and Commonwealth History* 8 (1980), 85-105.
Gwyn, Julian. "British Government Spending and the North American Colonies 1740-1775," *Journal of Imperial and Commonwealth History* 8 (1980), 74-84.
———. "Money Lending in New England: The Case of Admiral Sir Peter Warren and His Heirs 1738-1805," *New England Quarterly* 44 (1971), 117-34.
———. "Prize Money and Rising Expectations: Admiral Warren's Personal Fortune," *Social History* 4 (1971), 84-101.
Haffenden, Philip. "Colonial Appointments and Patronage Under the Duke of Newcastle, 1724-1738," *English Historical Review* 78 (1963), 417-35.
Hall, Hubert. "Chatham's Colonial Policy," *American Historical Review* 5 (1899-1900), 659-75.
Hamilton, Edward P. "Colonial Warfare in North America," *Proceedings of the Massachusetts Historical Society* 80 (1968), 3-15.
Harper, Lawrence A. "Mercantilism and the American Revolution," *Canadian Historical Review* 23 (1942), 1-15.
Hart, Harriet C. "History of Canso, Guysborough Country, N.S.," *Collections of the Nova Scotia Historical Society*, 21 (1927), pp. 1-34.
Humphreys, R. A. "Lord Shelburne and British Colonial Policy, 1766-1768," *English Historical Review* 50 (1935), 257-77.
Kelsey, Harry, "The Amherst Plan: A Factor in the Pontiac Uprising," *Ontario History* 65 (1973), 149-58.
Kenney, Alice P. "The Albany Dutch: Loyalists and Patriots." *New York History* 42 (1961), 331-50.
Kenyon, Cecelia M. "Republicanism and Radicalism in the American Revolution: An Old-Fashioned Interpretation," *William and Mary Quarterly* 3d Ser., 19 (1962), 153-82.
Kingsford, Peter W. "A London Merchant: Sir William Baker," *History Today* 21 (1971), 338-48.
Kirtland, J. P. "Disasters Attending the Expeditions of Major Williams and Colonel (Afterwards General) Bradstreet, Near the Present City of Cleveland," In Charles Whittlesey, ed. *Early History of Cleveland Ohio*, pp. 97-129. Cleveland, 1867.
Knollenberg, Bernhard. "General Amherst and Germ Warfare," *Mississippi Valley Historical Review*, 61 (1954-1955), 489-94.
Lawson, Philip. "George Grenville and America: The Years of Opposition, 1765 to 1770," *William and Mary Quarterly* 3d Ser., 37 (1980), 561-76.
Leach, Douglas E. "Brothers in Arms?—Anglo-American Friction at Louisbourg, 1745-1746," *Proceedings of the Massachusetts Historical Society* 89 (1977), 36-54.
Lemisch, Jesse. "Jack Tar in the Streets: Merchant Seamen in the Politics of Revolutionary America," *William and Mary Quarterly* 3d Ser., 25 (1968), 371-407.
Lounsbury, Ralph G. "Yankee Trade at Newfoundland," *New England Quarterly*, 3 (1930), 607-26.
Lower, Arthur R. M. "Lawrence H. Gipson and the First British Empire: An Evaluation," *Journal of British Studies* 3 (1963), 57-78.
Lunn, Jean. "The Illegal Fur Trade Out of New France, 1713-1760," *Canadian Historical Association Report* (1939), 61-76.

Mahon, John K. "Anglo-American Methods of Indian Warfare, 1676-1794," *Mississippi Valley Historical Review* 45 (1958-1959), 254-75.
Maier, Pauline. "Popular Uprisings and Civil Authority in Eighteenth-Century America," *William and Mary Quarterly* 3d Ser., 27 (1970), 3-35.
Marshall, Peter. "Colonial Protest and Imperial Retrenchment: Indian Policy 1764-1768," *Journal of American Studies* 5 (1971), 1-17.
————. "Imperial Policy and the Government of Detroit: Projects and Problems 1760-1774," *Journal of Imperial and Commonwealth History* 2 (1974), 153-89.
————. "Lord Hillsborough, Samuel Wharton and the Ohio Grant, 1769-1775," *English Historical Review* 80 (1965), 717-39.
————. "Sir William Johnson and the Treaty of Fort Stanwix, 1768," *Journal of American Studies* 1 (1967), 149-79.
McAnear, Beverly. "The Albany Stamp Act Riots," *William and Mary Quarterly* 3d Ser., 4 (1947), 486-98.
McLennan, John S. "Review of *Louisbourg Journals 1745*," *Canadian Historical Review* 14 (1933), 206.
McLoughlin, William G. "Essay Review: The American Revolution as a Religious Revival," *New England Quarterly* 40 (1967), 99-110.
Morgan, Edmund S. "The Puritan Ethic and the American Revolution," *William and Mary Quarterly* 3d Ser., 24 (1967), 3-43.
Morris, Richard B. "Class Struggle and the American Revolution," *William and Mary Quarterly* 3d Ser., 19 (1962), 3-29.
————. "The Spacious Empire of Lawrence Henry Gipson," *William and Mary Quarterly* 3d Ser., 24 (1967), 169-89.
Mullett, Charles F. "James Abercromby and French Encroachments in America," *Canadian Historical Review* 26 (1945), 48-59.
Olson, Alison G. "The Board of Trade and London-American Interest Groups in the Eighteenth Century," *Journal of Imperial and Commonwealth History* 8 (1980), 33-50.
"Papers Relating to the Expeditions of Colonel John Bradstreet and Colonel Bouquet in Ohio, A.D. 1764," *Western Reserve and Northern Ohio Historical Society* 1 (1870-1877), Tracts 13 and 14, 1-6 and 1-6.
Pares, Richard. "American Versus Continental Warfare, 1739-63," *English Historical Review* 51 (1936), 429-65.
Pargellis, Stanley. "Braddock's Defeat," *American Historical Review* 41 (1935-1936), 253-69.
Peckham, Howard H. "Speculations on the Colonial Wars," *William and Mary Quarterly* 3d Ser., 17 (1960), 463-72.
Pencak, William. "Warfare and Political Change in Mid-Eighteenth-Century Massachusetts," *Journal of Imperial and Commonwealth History* 8 (1980), 51-73.
Piers, Harry. "The Fighting Fortieth Regiment, Raised in Nova Scotia in 1717." *Collections of the Nova Scotia Historical Society*, Vol. 21 (1927), 115-83.
Preston, Richard A. "In Defence of Old Fort Frontenac and Its Founder," *Historic Kingston* 20 (1972), 49-64.
Reid, Allana. "Intercolonial Trade During the French Regime," *Canadian Historical Review* 32 (1951), 236-51.
Riker, Thad, W. "The Politics Behind Braddock's Expedition," *American Historical Review* 12 (1907-1908), 742-53.
Robson, Eric. "Purchase and Promotion in the British Army in the Eighteenth Century," *History* 36 (1951), 57-72.
Roy, Antoine. "Le Fort Frontenac ou Catarakoui sous le régime français," *Canadian Historical Association Report* (1950), 51-57.

Russell, Peter E. "Redcoats in the Wilderness: British Officers and Irregular Warfare in Europe and America, 1740 to 1760," *William and Mary Quarterly* 3d Ser., 35 (1978), 629-52.
Savelle, Max. "The Appearance of an American Attitude toward External Affairs, 1750-1775," *American Historical Review* 52 (1946-1947), 655-66.
Schutz, John A. "Imperialism in Massachusetts during the Governorship of William Shirley, 1741-1756," *Huntington Library Quarterly* 23 (1959-1960), 217-36.
―――――. "The Disaster of Fort Ticonderoga: The Shortage of Muskets during the Mobilization of 1758," *Huntington Library Quarterly* 14 (1950-1951), 307-15.
Shortt, Samuel E. D. "Conflict and Identity in Massachusetts: The Louisbourg Expedition of 1745," *Social History* 5 (1972), 165-85.
Smith, William H. "The Pelham Papers—Loss of Oswego," *Papers of the American Historical Association* 4 (1889), pt. IV, 369-79.
Sosin, Jack M. "The French Settlements in British Policy for the North American Interior 1760-1774," *Canadian Historical Review* 39 (1958), 185-208.
Stanley, George F. G. "Kingston and Oswego," *Historic Kingston*, 13 (1965), 76-83.
―――――. "The Defence of Canada during the Seven Years' War: A Military Appreciation." In Michael Cross and Robert Bothwell, eds. *Policy By Other Means*, pp. 53-75. Toronto, 1972.
Steele, Ian K. "The Empire and Provincial Elites: An Interpretation of Some Recent Writings on the English Atlantic, 1675-1740," *Journal of Imperial and Commonwealth History*, 8 (1980), 2-32.
Sutherland, Lucy S., and John Binney. "Henry Fox as Paymaster General of the Forces," *English Historical Review* 70 (1955), 229-57.
Thayer, Theodore. "The Army Contractors for the Niagara Campaign, 1755-1756," *William and Mary Quarterly* 3d Ser., 14 (1957), 31-46.
Thomas, Peter D. G. "Charles Townshend and American Taxation in 1767," *English Historical Review* 83 (1968), 33-51.
Trelease, Allen W. "The Iroquois and the Western Fur Trade," *Mississippi Valley Historical Review* 49 (1962-1963), 32-51.
Van Alstyne, Richard W. "Revolution and Patriotism in America, 1763-1775," *Canadian Review of Studies in Nationalism* 6 (1979), 152-74.
Varga, Nicholas. "Robert Charles: New York Agent, 1748-1770," *William and Mary Quarterly* 3d Ser., 18 (1961), 211-35.
Vitzthum, Richard C. "The Historian as Editor: Francis Parkman's Reconstruction of Sources in Montcalm and Wolfe," *Journal of American History* 53 (1966), 471-86.
Walkem, Richard T. "Notes on Fort Frontenac and the Old Fortifications of Kingston," *Queen's Quarterly* 4 (1896-1897), 290-300.
Wall, Robert E., Jr. "Louisbourg, 1745," *New England Quarterly* 37 (1964), 64-83.
Webb, Stephen S. "Army and Empire: English Garrison Government in Britain and America, 1569 to 1763," *William and Mary Quarterly* 3d Ser., 34 (1977), 1-31.
―――――. "The Strange Career of Francis Nicholson," *William and Mary Quarterly* 3d Ser., 23 (1966), 509-48.
Webster, John C. "Review of *Native Stock: The Rise of the American Spirit Seen in Six Lives*," *Canadian Historical Review* 12 (1932), 79.
Whittlesey, Charles. "Col. Bradstreet's Misfortunes on Lake Erie in 1764,"

Western Reserve and Northern Ohio Historical Society 2 (1877-1887), Tract 66, 361-63.

Wickwire, Franklin B. "John Pownall and British Colonial Policy," *William and Mary Quarterly* 3d Ser., 20 (1963), 543-54.

Willcox, William B., and Frederick Wyatt. "Sir Henry Clinton: A Psychological Exploration in History," *William and Mary Quarterly* 3d Ser., 16 (1959), 3-26.

Williamson, J. "General Samuel Waldo." *Maine Historical Society Collections* 9 (1887), 75-93.

Wood, Gordon S. "Rhetoric and Reality in the American Revolution," *William and Mary Quarterly* 3d Ser., 23 (1966), 3-32.

C. Dissertations

Canedy, Charles R. III. "An Entrepreneurial History of the New York Frontier, 1739-1776." Ph.D. dissertation. Case Western Reserve University, 1967.

Cooper, Johnson G. "Oswego in the French-English Struggle in North America, 1720-1760." D.S.Sc. dissertation. Syracuse University, 1961.

Foote, William A. "The American Independent Companies of the British Army, 1664-1774." Ph.D. dissertation. University of California, Los Angeles, 1966.

Fox, Edith M. "Williams Johnson's Early Career as a Frontier Landlord and Trader." M.A. thesis. Cornell University, 1945.

Graham, Dominick S. "British Intervention in Defence of the American colonies." Ph.D. dissertation. University of London, 1969.

————. "The Making of a Colonial Governor: Charles Lawrence in Nova Scotia." M.A. thesis. University of New Brunswick, 1963.

Guzzardo, John C. "Sir William Johnson's Official Family: Patron and Clients in an Anglo-American Empire, 1742-1777." Ph.D. dissertation. Syracuse University, 1975.

Hayes, James W. "The Social and Professional Background of the Officers of the British Army, 1714-1763." M.A. thesis. University of London, 1956.

Katz, Stanley N. "An Easie Access: Anglo-American Politics in New York, 1732-1753." Ph.D. dissertation. Harvard University, 1961.

MacLeod, Malcolm. "French and British Strategy in the Lake Ontario Theatre of Operations, 1754-1760." Ph.D. dissertation. University of Ottawa, 1974.

MacNutt, William S. "British Rule in Nova Scotia, 1713-1784," M.A. thesis. University of London, 1932.

Moody, Barry M. "'A Just and Disinterested Man': The Nova Scotia Career of Paul Mascarene, 1710-1752." Ph.D. dissertation. Queen's University, 1976.

————. "Paul Mascarene, William Shirley and the Defence of Nova Scotia, 1744-1748." M.A. thesis. Queen's University 1969.

Pothier, Bernard. "Acadian Settlement on Ile-Royale, 1713-1734." M.A. thesis. University of Ottawa, 1967.

Salay, David L. "The William Johnson—William Shirley Dispute: Origins, Course, and Consequences." M.A. thesis. Vanderbilt University, 1972.

Shy, John W. "James Abercromby and the Campaign of 1758." M.A. thesis. University of Vermont, 1957.

Varga, Nicholas. "New York Government and Politics During the Mid-Eighteenth Century." Ph.D. dissertation. Fordham University, 1960.

Index

Abercromby, James, x, 71n, 75, 78, 81-82, 84-85, 88, 91, 95-96, 115-41 *passim*, 143, 178; approval of Frontenac attack, 124-25; attitude towards John Bradstreet, 116-19, 124-25, 132; John Bradstreet's criticisms of, 119, 123, 125, 132-34, 141, 149; charges against William Shirley, 82-83; in Ticonderoga campaign, 120-23, 140; rift with John Bradstreet, 134-38

Acadia/Nova Scotia, xi, 7-11, 14, 16, 20, 23, 34, 56-58, 106; state of, 2

Acadians: recruitment of, 38

Admiralty Office, 23

Albany, 67, 69-71, 76-78, 80-82, 89-90, 94, 99, 101, 103, 106, 109-10, 116-17, 119, 124, 129, 132-33, 137, 142-43, 145-47, 149, 155-56, 162, 178, 186, 194, 225, 246-47, 251, 258, 269; civil-military difficulties, 152-54, 158-59, 165-67, 181-82, 240-42; quartermaster department at, 168, 238-40

Aldridge, Christopher Jr., 10, 15, 21n, 41, 47, 252n

Aldridge, Christopher Sr., 14-15, 21

Alexandria, 58

American provincials, 112, 119-22, 126-28, 141, 154-55, 163, 186, 192-93, 195, 198, 234; appointment to regular officer corps, 247-48; pride in, 137

Amherst, Sir Jeffery, x-xi, 51, 115, 138-39, 142-44, 150, 163-64, 178, 180, 184-85, 194, 203, 230, 247, 253, 259, 261; arrangements for Detroit expedition, 168-69, 172-73, 176-77, 180; doubts about John Bradstreet, 166-68; in 1759 campaign, 144-49; in 1760 campaign, 154-56; powerless position, 185; return to England, 173, 175, 179; support of Detroit colony, 248-51, 262; support of John Bradstreet, 148, 154, 158-61, 163-66, 184, 233-34, 240, 261

Annapolis Royal, 1-3, 5, 7-8, 10, 14-15, 21, 34, 263; precarious position of, 23

Anne, Queen, 2

Armstrong, Lawrence, 3n, 5, 7, 9n, 12n, 13; trade activities of, 18

Articles of War, 53

Avalon, 47-48

Babock, Henry, 126-27

Bahamas, 267

Baker, William: relationship with John Bradstreet, 40, 43-44, 46-47, 51

Baltimore, Frederick Calvert, Lord, 45, 51, 54; petition of, 47-49

Banyar, Goldsbrow, 71n, 73

Barrington, William Wildman Shute,

Viscount, 139, 239, 245-46, 249, 255, 261
Barton, Mary, 4
bateau-men, 11, 69, 107, 112, 116-17, 119-21, 126, 132-33, 143, 147, 151, 153, 155, 166, 168, 238-39, 242; John Bradstreet's command over, 76-82, 86, 90-93, 118
Bedford, John Russell, Duke of, 39, 45, 50
Belcher, Jonathan, 99, 104
Bernard, Sir Francis, 257
Bigot, Francois, 18-19
Bleecker, Rutger, 254
Board of Trade, 9, 20n, 48, 159, 236, 250, 252, 253-54; award to Agathe Campbell, 4; defers action on Detroit, 237, 248
Borland, Francis, 16
Boston, 7, 18-19, 21, 26, 30, 76, 78, 93-96, 101, 151-52, 155, 251-52, 255, 258; agent required in, 14; threat to its shipping, 23
Boston Evening Post, 137
Boston News-Letter, 137
Boston Weekly Advertiser, 137
Bostwick, Henry, 209-10
Bouquet, Henry: criticisms of John Bradstreet, 210; expedition of, 199, 201, 203, 211-12, 214, 217-24; suggested peace terms of, 202
Braddock, Edward, 49-50, 55, 60-61, 72; arrival in America, 58; defeat of, 67, 120
Bradshaw, Thomas, 244n
Bradstreet, Anna Elizabetha, 35n
Bradstreet, Edward, 1-3, 5
Bradstreet, Elizabeth, 10, 251, 263
Bradstreet, John:
    Albany difficulties of, 152-54, 158-59, 165-68, 181-82, 240-42
    as Anglo-Irish Acadian, xi, 50, 55-56, 112, 237, 265-66
    as client of King Gould, 15-17, 42-43, 45-47, 51
    as Deputy Quartermaster-General, 142-48, 150-52, 162, 165-66, 168, 238-40, 242
    as irregular, xi, 11, 49-50, 88, 99-100, 106-108, 112-13, 268-70
    captivity at Louisbourg, 20-22
    career overview, ix, x
    character of, 266
    command over bateau-men, 76-82, 90-93, 118
    connection with Sir Richard Lyttleton, 51-52, 99, 113
    death of, 262-63
    early years, 1-9
    family of, 10-11
    friendship with Charles Gould, 52-54
    friendship with William Pepperrell, 36, 40-42, 44-45, 55
    Indian superintendency aspirations of, 60-67, 72, 74, 85-89, 101, 190, 234, 261n
    land speculation of, 167, 253-54
    Louisbourg testimony of (1757), 97-98
    New Englanders' suspicions of, 11, 26, 28-31
    Newfoundland service and proposals, 44-49, 55
    opinion of Six Nations, 126, 135-36, 190, 197-98, 200, 220-21, 227-28
    patronage empire of, 142-43, 150-52, 238
    plans for Detroit, 162-63, 171-72, 180-81, 196, 206-207, 218, 228, 230, 234-38, 248-53, 262, 265
    possible corruption of, 95, 150-52, 268-69
    possible trade activities of, 89-90, 111-12, 114, 268
    proposals to Sir Richard Lyttleton (1757), 99-106, 135
    proposed campaign against Quebec (1746), 35-39, 55
    relationship with Charles Knowles, 36, 38, 42-44
    relationship with Sir William Johnson, 189-90, 196, 225-29
    relationship with William Baker, 43-44, 46-47, 51
    role in Louisbourg campaign (1745), 23-31, 49
    service under James Abercromby, 115-41 *passim*; attack on Fort Frontenac, 123-32; contribution in Ticonderoga campaign, 115-18, 120-24, 140; criticism of James Abercromby by, 119, 123,

Index

125, 132-34, 141, 149; rift with James Abercromby, 134-38
service under Lord Loudoun, 88-114 *passim*; adjustment to Lord Loudoun, 84-87; quartermaster duties under Lord Loudoun, 94-97, 99-100; suggestions to Lord Loudoun, 106-10; Lord Loudoun's support of, 90-93; survival despite Lord Loudoun's demise, 111-12
service under Sir Jeffery Amherst, 142-74 *passim*; appointment of to western command, 168-69, 172-73; role in 1760 campaign, 154-56; wins confidence of Sir Jeffery Amherst, 148
service under Thomas Gage, 175-263 *passim*; attempts at promotion under Thomas Gage, 245-47, 253, 255-57; conception of his western assignment, 176-77, 186-89, 195; defense of Detroit expedition, 196, 216-19, 224, 227-31; Detroit trade activities of, 207-10, 227-28; disagreements with Thomas Gage, 175-79; 183, 191-94; Great Lakes campaign of, 196-232, 260; instructions from Thomas Gage, 186-91, 202-203, 229, 231; lack of confidence in his troops, 192-95, 197; peace treaties of, 199-207, 210-14; preparations for Detroit expedition, 175-95 *passim*; quarrel over Yorkers, 193-94, 242-45, 247; retreat to Niagara, 220-23; Thomas Gage's criticisms of, 196, 210-14, 223
service under William Shirley, 57-87 *passim*; loss of William Shirley's support, 39-40, 55; Oswego activities of, 76-81, 92; role in Niagara campaign, 58-74, 86-87; wariness towards William Shirley, 68, 75-76, 78, 81-86, 93
supplanted by Simon Bradstreet, 33-34, 55, 74, 92
trade with Louisbourg, 12, 15, 17-20, 97
treatments of, ix

Bradstreet, John (Lieutenant): military career of, 9; death of and family of, 10
Bradstreet, Martha, 10, 155, 251-52, 263
Bradstreet, Mary, 10, 85, 155; health of, 39; relationship with John Bradstreet, 251-52, 263
Bradstreet, Samuel, 10, 159
Bradstreet, Simon, 3, 12, 33, 40, 55, 74, 92; death of, 35, 39; military service of, 4-6, 8, 34; relationship with King Gould, 7-8, 15-17, 46
British regulars, 11, 39, 49-50, 58, 99, 103-104, 112, 119-22, 126; attitude towards irregulars and provincials, xi, 11, 88, 106, 108, 268; stationed in Acadia/Nova Scotia, 2-3; used against Pontiac, 176, 178, 191, 198. *See also* Regiments.
Brouillan, St. Ovide de, 9n
Burton, Ralph, 171
Bute, John Stuart, Earl of, 52n, 172
Buttar, Agatha, 10, 155, 251, 263

Cabinet: divisions in, 39
Cadaraqui. *See* Fort Frontenac.
Campbell, Agathe (De Saint-Etienne De La Tour), 1, 2, 11, 18; land claims of, 4, 5; marriages of, 3; relationship with King Gould, 6-8
Campbell, Hugh, 3
Campbell, John, 207-208, 211, 219, 228
Campbell, Mungo, 169-72, 184-85
Canada. *See* Quebec.
Canso, 5, 6, 8-9, 16, 18, 31, 42, 44, 63; captured garrison of, 21-22; fishery at, 12-13; garrison and defenses of, 12-13, 20-21; rendezvous at, 26; taverns and trade of, 14-15, 17-19, 23
Cape Breton. *See* Ile Royale.
Carleton, Guy, 246n, 258
Cayahoga Creek, 218
Chauncy, Charles, 30n
Christie, Gabriel: clash with John Bradstreet, 146-48
Clapham, William, 202
Claus, Daniel, 71n
Colden, Cadwallader, 182, 214, 242-43

Company of Duncan, Stirling and Campbell, 207-208
Connecticut, 106; contribution to 1764 western expedition, 183, 191-92, 215
Conolly, Frances, 9n
Cooper, Grey, 243n
Cork, 50
Cornwallis, Edward, 267
Cotterell, Charles, 14
Cottnam, Samuel, 14, 21n
Council of Trade and Plantations, 2n, 4n, 9n, 12n
Coventry, George, 142, 151-52, 159
Croghan, George, 136
Cumberland, William Augustus, Duke of, 46-47, 49, 85, 97, 113
Cuyler, Cornelius, 151-52
Cuyler, John, 151-52

Daley, Peter, 215
Dartmouth, William Legge, Earl of, 262
DeLancey, James, 71n, 126-27, 136
DeLancey, Oliver, 71n
De La Tour, Charles De Saint-Etienne, 3
DeNoyan, Pierre-Jacques Payen, 128-31
DesBarres, Joseph F. W., 11n
Detroit, 62, 90, 102, 168, 175-76, 179, 196, 198-99, 203, 211, 219, 223-25, 229-30, 269; economic potential of, 180-81; establishment of colony at, 162-63, 169, 171-72, 233-63 *passim*; governorship of, 48; Indians at, 186-87, 189, 202, 211, 213, 217; orders concerning, 191; plans for development of, 196, 206-207, 218, 228, 265; trade at, 207-209, 227-28; treaty-making at, 204-205, 222, 227-28
Devonshire, William Cavendish, Duke of, 93
Dieskau, Jean Armand, Baron de, 67, 71
Douw, Volkert, 166-67, 242, 254
Dow, James, 153, 198
Drake, Francis William, 45
Du Chambon, Louis, 20n, 29n
Dunbar, David, 5
Dunmore, John Murray, Earl of, 258

Du Quesnel, Jean-Baptiste-Louis, 18-19, 21-22
Durell, Philip, 29n
Du Vivier, Joseph Dupont, 19

Egremont, Charles Wyndham, Earl of, 164-65, 170-71
Ellis, Welbore, 170
England, xi, 4-5, 32-33, 35, 39-40, 51, 54, 56, 59, 66-67, 76, 81, 85, 87, 93-94, 97-98, 101-102, 105-106, 110-12, 133, 138, 140, 155, 157-60, 162, 165, 169, 171, 173, 179-80, 231, 233, 238, 243-44, 246-49, 251, 258-59, 261-62, 264-67

Fairservice, James, 91
Falkland Islands, 256
Faneuil, Peter, 18
Forbes, John, 115-16, 118, 131, 134
Forts:
    Beausejour, 58
    Bull, 76, 128, 131
    Castle William, 259
    Chartres, 204, 250
    Crown Point, 58, 83, 103-104, 119, 144-45, 149
    Duquesne, 58, 102, 115, 131, 134
    Edward, 144
    Frederick, 5
    Frontenac (Cadaraqui), 9, 62, 67, 69, 82, 102, 114-15, 133-43, 145, 149, 156, 160, 165, 169, 173, 194, 221, 230, 251, 265, 268; attack on (1758), 123-32; John Bradstreet's proposal to attack (1758), 108-10, 112, 116-17, 119; possible French attack from, 65, 67-68, 81; proposed English attack on (1756), 69-70, 77
    Halifax (Maine), 58
    LaGalette, 130-31, 145-47, 149
    Michilimackinac, 70, 191, 204
    Newport, 128
    Niagara, 102, 131, 135-37, 140, 144-45, 153, 159, 168-69, 176-79, 190, 193, 195-96, 208, 211-13, 220-21, 223, 225; campaign against, ix, 56-74, 86; delay at, 197-98; meeting at, 187, 190, 197, 200, 214, 216-18, 222
    Ontario, 70

Pitt, 176, 199, 201, 221-22, 262
Pontchartrain, 70
Presqu'Isle, 70, 199, 203
St. Jean, 143
Stanwix, 147, 253
Ticonderoga, 103-104, 115, 127, 130, 140, 143-45, 149, 154, 230, 265; campaign against (1758), 115-17, 119-24, 138
Toronto, 70
William Henry, 100-101, 117, 123, 125
Fox, Henry, 33n, 40n, 43, 46-47, 51, 54, 73-74, 76, 80n, 81, 113, 269
France, 19, 20, 105
Franklin, Benjamin, 210
Franklin, William, 268n
Frey, Henry, 151-52
fur trade, 59, 70; John Bradstreet's thoughts on, 89-90, 101-102, 104-105, 162-63, 235; key to Sir William Johnson's success, 89

Gabarus Bay: landing at, 26
Gage, Thomas, x, 99n, 108, 119-20, 151, 198-99, 202-204, 215, 233, 262, 269; approval of John Bradstreet's trade controls, 207-10, 224; as Commander-in-Chief, 173-76, 179-80, 185; disagreements with John Bradstreet, 177-79, 183, 191-94; frustration of John Bradstreet's office-seeking attempts, 233, 245-48, 253, 255-58; instructions to John Bradstreet (1764), 186-91, 217-18, 229; involvement in Albany disputes, 181-82, 240-42; LaGalette campaign of, 145-49; opinion of Detroit scheme, 236-37; peacetime administrator, 238-40; problem of Yorkers, 193-94, 242-45, 247; reliance on Sir William Johnson, 189, 213-14, 223; repudiation of John Bradstreet's treaties, 196, 210-14, 223-25, 229, 231; returns to England, 259-60
Gentleman's Magazine, 40n, 122-23, 131
George II, 6, 17, 139, 268; dismissal of William Pitt, 97
George III, 170, 205-206, 248-49, 255, 257, 259, 261
German Flats, 182

Gerondequast, 62-63, 90
Gladwin, Henry, 187-88, 198, 222
Glen, John, 142, 151-52, 182, 239
Gordon, Harry, 241
Gould, Charles (Sir Charles Morgan), x, xi, 6, 43, 45, 64, 67, 73-75, 80, 83, 89, 91, 93-94, 100-101, 105, 109, 111, 116, 118-19, 123-24, 127, 131-34, 139-41, 143, 149-50, 154-57, 160-65, 176, 180, 203, 211, 229-30; career of, 52-53; embarrassment at trading rumours, 111-12, 269; emergence of, 51; faithful lobbying of, 169-73, 265; frustration of, 184-85; informed of western expedition's difficulties, 179, 183; support of Detroit scheme, 206-207, 233-63 *passim*; usefulness to John Bradstreet, 52-54
Gould King, xi, 45, 52, 56, 73, 75, 93; activities on behalf of Agathe Campbell, 6-8; as agent of 40th Regiment, 5, 9; relationship with John Bradstreet, 7, 15-19, 42-43, 45-47, 51, 54, 87, 269; relationship with Simon Bradstreet, 7, 8, 12, 15-17, 33-34; trade activities of, 14-15, 17
Granby, John Manners, Marquis of, 246, 255
Grant, James, 215
Great Carrying Place, 61, 124, 126, 132
Great Lakes Country, xi, 57, 59-61, 64-65, 102-105, 134, 138, 145, 175, 179, 188, 191-92, 194, 249; Indian uprising in, 168, 171; John Bradstreet's plans for, 61-63, 70, 86-87, 135, 137, 141, 159, 163, 169, 180, 235-36, 265; military expedition through (1764), 196-232
Grenville, George, 138, 170, 248
Guernsey, 52

Haldimand, Frederick, 184, 246n, 260-61
Halifax, 23n, 97-98, 101, 103
Halifax Gazette, 66
Halifax, George Montagu Dunk, Earl of, 105, 139-40, 171-72, 191, 223, 248, 256, 266-67; promise of, 184, 251; reluctance to act, 185, 265
Hamilton, Otho, 44n

Hardenburgh: proprietors, 254
Hardy, Sir Charles: criticisms of William Shirley, 71, 73
Harrison, Henry, 34
Haviland, William, 154
Herkimer, Johan, 90
Herkimer, Joseph, 151-52
Herkimer, Nicholas, 151-52
Heron, Patrick, 20n, 21n
Hillsborough, Wills Hill, Earl of, 253-54, 257; resignation of, 259, 262
Hogan, William, 215
Holburne, Francis, 98
Holdernesse, Robert D'Arcy, Earl of, 50
Home, William, Earl of, 75
House of Commons, 50, 52-53
House of Lords, 139
Howard, Thomas, 254
Howard, William, 204
Howe, George Augustus, Lord, 116, 120, 138
Hutchinson, Thomas, 257

Ile Royale (Cape Breton), 9, 17-18, 22-23, 34, 36, 38, 44, 47, 115
Indians:
    Chippewas, 205-206, 220
    Delawares, 186-87, 191, 198-203, 205, 210-13, 215-25, 227-28, 230
    Five Nations of Scioto, 201
    Huron, 201, 205, 220
    Iroquois. *See* Six Nations.
    Miamis, 203, 205
    Mingoes, 202
    Mississaugi, 61, 205-206
    Mohawk, 167
    Oneida, 253
    Ottawas, 203, 205, 220
    Potawatomies, 197, 205
    Sacs, 205n
    Seneca, 168, 212, 218, 222-23
    Shawnees, 186-87, 191, 197-203, 205, 210-13, 215-22, 224-25, 227-28, 230
    Six Nations (Iroquois), 59, 61, 72-73, 102, 126, 132-33, 135-37, 162, 190, 234, 253; service in Detroit expedition, 188-89, 195, 200, 216, 220; treatment by John Bradstreet, 221, 226-29
    Wyandots, 186-87, 191, 198, 202-203, 205, 217
Ireland, 5-8, 247, 251

Johnson, 197
Johnson, John, 216-17
Johnson, Sir William, x, 60-61, 63, 77, 89, 101, 126, 135-36, 145, 159, 186, 194-95, 197, 200, 208, 216, 253, 269; advisor of Thomas Gage, 189, 213-14; attempt to imitate by John Bradstreet, 89-90; criticisms of John Bradstreet by, 196, 218, 225-29, 231, 261n, 269; Crown Point campaign of, 58, 65, 67, 71; Indian Superintendent and negotiator, 175-77, 180, 187-90, 202, 211-13, 222; obstacle to John Bradstreet, 135-36; relationship with William Shirley, 61, 71-74, 87

Kennebec region, 58
Kilby, Christopher, 14
Kilkenny, 5, 6
Knowles, Charles, 40; arrival as governor, 36; relationship with John Bradstreet, 36, 42-45, 55, 269; perception of Louisbourg, 38, 44
Knox, William, x; as mid-Atlantic man, 267

Lachine, 130
Lakes:
    Champlain, 67, 119-20, 144-45, 154
    Erie, 135, 138, 199, 210, 212-13, 215, 221, 224
    George, 116-17, 119-20, 123, 132-33, 144-45
    Huron, 135
    Oneida, 128, 131
    Ontario, 59-61, 65-68, 76-79, 84, 102-103, 109-10, 115-16, 125, 127-29, 132, 135-37, 139, 146, 154-55, 169, 190, 194, 238
    Sandusky, 212-14, 216, 218-21, 224-28
    Superior, 135
L'Ance aux Feuilles, 199
Lawrence, Charles, 58
Lee, Charles, 133, 137n
LeHunte, George, 215

Lévis, Chevalier Francois Gaston de, 76, 121, 130
Ligonier, Sir John, 113, 267
Littlehales, John, 39
Little Carrying Place, 126
London, xi, 14, 40, 42-43, 56, 87, 93, 99, 105, 157, 171, 185, 251, 259; officialdom of, 53
London Gazette, 131, 139
Longueuil, Chevalier Paul Joseph le Moyne de, 126, 135
Loring, Joshua, 118, 121, 209
Loudoun, John Campbell, Earl of, ix, 24n, 25n, 33n, 37n, 51, 74-75, 78, 82-87, 94-97, 116-17, 140, 178; criticism of William Shirley by, 84, 88-90; John Bradstreet's service under, 88-114; Louisbourg campaign of, 97-99, 100; recall of, 110-11; relationship with John Bradstreet, 76, 90-93, 106-10
Louisbourg, ix, xi, 9, 11, 12, 22, 24, 33-36, 38, 40-42, 44, 49-50, 55, 57, 59, 63, 68, 85, 103-106, 115, 127, 134, 137-38, 140, 173, 230, 264, 269; abortive campaign against (1757), 97-99; attack on (1745), 26-28, 92; food shortage at, 21; Grand Battery of, 26-27; Island Battery of, 28; John Bradstreet's journal of, 45-47; return of to French, 39; state of (1744-1745), 23; surrender of, 29-32; trade with, 15, 17-20
Lovell, John Jr., 151-52
Lowndes, Charles, 243n
Lydius, John Henry, 72
Lyttleton, Sir Richard, xi, 74, 93, 127, 140, 149, 156-57, 159, 236; access to William Pitt, 94, 99, 101, 113; career of, 51-52; death of, 256; interventions on John Bradstreet's behalf, 52, 54, 99, 105-106, 111-12; John Bradstreet's proposals to (1757), 99-104, 135; leaves England, 157, 160, 265; powerlessness of, 185, 250; returns to England, 171

McDonald, William, 215
McDougall, George, 215
MacKay, Alexander, 255

Mackellar, Patrick, 77, 81, 83
McKenzie, Stewart, 172
Mante, Thomas, 196n, 197n, 234, 237n, 245, 248, 250; dispatched to England, 236; *The History of The Late War In North-America, And The Islands Of The West Indies, Including The Campaigns of MDCCLXIII And MDCCLXIV Against His Majesty's Indian Enemies*, 259-60
Mascarene, John: dispatched to England, 266-67
Mascarene, Paul, 6n, 34; colonial supplicant, 266-67
Massachusetts, xi, 26, 29, 37, 57-59, 61, 67, 71-73, 75, 85, 92, 106-107, 137, 257-58; battalions from, 126; Council of, 21, 25; credit for Louisbourg victory, 30; General Court of, 24, 137; ports of, 13; prisoners there, 21-22; threat to, 23; trade of, 18-20
Maturin, Gabriel, 243
Maurepas, Jean-Frédéric Phelippeaux, Comte de, 18
Mercer, James, 41, 70, 77
Minorca, 52
Mohawk, 197
Monckton, Robert, 166
Montcalm, Louis-Joseph, Marquis de, 76, 79, 82, 100, 130
Montour, Henry, 216-17
Montreal, 62, 103-104, 130, 146, 156, 171, 238; merchants of, 191, 209
Montresor, John, 213, 218, 220, 228, 241, 245
Moore, Sir Henry, 244, 254; death of, 258
Morgan, Jane, 52
Morgan, Thomas, 52-53
Morris, Robert Hunter, 78n
Morris, Thomas: pacification mission of, 204-205, 212-13, 218, 228
Mount Johnson, 60, 89
Mulcaster, John, 2n
Mutiny Bill, 53

Newcastle, Thomas Pelham-Holles, Duke of, 21n, 24n, 30, 35n, 36n, 42n, 43, 47, 49-50, 53, 98, 267-68
New England colonies, 32, 34-35; contribution to Detroit expedition,

178; view of Louisbourg, 36, 38, 55, 264. *See also* Massachusetts.
New Englanders, 35-36, 42, 44, 88, 92, 94
New France. *See* Quebec.
Newfoundland, xi, 8, 32, 34, 40, 43-44, 47-50, 55-56, 95, 164, 258
New Hampshire, 26, 106-107
New Jersey, 48, 99, 100, 104-105, 227; contribution to Detroit expedition, 176, 178, 183, 191-92, 215; troops of, 64-65, 67, 126-27
New Orleans, 35, 256-57
Newport *Mercury*, 215, 221, 229
Newton, Hibbert, 9n
New York, xi, 59, 61, 63, 71, 89, 108, 139, 143, 152, 156-57, 165-66, 182, 190, 238, 240, 258, 265; additional recruits from, 193-94, 242-45; Assembly of, 166, 193-94, 241-42; Council of, 254; currency of, 90-91, 240; Independent Companies of, 170; regiment from, 126-27; troops for Detroit expedition, 176, 178, 183, 191-92, 215
New York City, 96-98, 101, 165, 225, 238, 262-63
New York Mercury, 80
Niaouré bay, 79
Nicholson, Francis, 2
North, Lord Frederick, 259
Nova Scotia. *See* Acadia/Nova Scotia.

Ohio Valley, 57, 60, 64, 115
Ontario, 69
Oswego, 69
Oswego, 59, 62-63, 65-70, 72, 74, 87, 102-104, 109-10, 125, 128, 131, 137, 140, 146, 148-49, 154-56, 190, 193-95, 225, 230, 265; attack on, 78-79, 82-83; defenses of, 60-62, 74, 86; fall of, 83-85, 102, 108; implementation of William Shirley's instructions, 64; journey to, 61; relief of, 76-78, 80-81, 86, 92; trade at, 88-90

Parliament, 262
Pelham, Henry, 50
Pemaquid, 4-5
Penn, John, 210

Pennsylvania, 107, 137, 210; Assembly of, 222
Pennsylvania Gazette, 66
Pepperrell, Andrew, 44
Pepperrell, William, ix, 25, 32-39, 42, 49, 59, 70, 92; conduct of attack on Louisbourg, 27-28; relationship with John Bradstreet, 24, 26-30, 40, 55; thoughts of selling his regiment, 41; trade of with Newfoundland, 44-45
Philadelphia, 118
Philipps, Richard, 3, 5-7, 9, 12, 16, 34, 92; attitude towards Agathe Campbell, 4
Pitt, William (Lord Chatham), 39, 52, 74-75, 93-94, 97-99, 101, 103, 105, 110-13, 117-19, 121, 124, 127, 131-32, 138, 149, 154, 157, 160-61, 164, 256; fall from power, 162, 185; John Bradstreet's perception of, 113, 139; perception of John Bradstreet, 114, 116, 139; resignation, 253, 265; return to power, 249-50
Placentia, 3-5
Pomeroy, John, 255
Pontiac, 198-99, 229-38; capitalizes upon John Bradstreet's peacemaking attempts, 196, 204-205, 212, 222, 228; expedition against, x, 196-232, 248, 260, 265; John Bradstreet's plans for, 205; rising of, 175
Pownall, John, 262
Pownall, Thomas, 71n; expansionist hopes, 63, 138
Prendergast, Thomas, 21n
Prideaux, John, 144-45
Privy Council: committee of, 47, 254n
Putnam, Israel, 215

Quartering Act: application of, 241-42
Quebec (Canada or New France), xi, 35-37, 39, 42, 55, 57-58, 101, 104, 128, 130, 134, 143, 145, 149, 156-57, 162, 171-73, 258, 262, 265; contribution to Detroit expedition, 183, 191, 193, 220; John Bradstreet's plan for conquest of (1757), 102-103, 112-13; militia of, 121, 130
Quebec Act, 262

Quebec City, 37, 97-98, 105, 144, 148-49

Regiments:
  1st Massachusetts, 25
  17th, 191-93
  40th, 3, 5-6, 8-9, 12, 14, 34, 92, 159
  42nd, 176
  44th, 82-85, 121
  50th, 39-41, 70, 94
  51st, 33-34, 37n, 40-41, 49, 59, 70, 94
  55th, 192-93
  60th, 94, 121, 165, 215, 241, 258
  80th, 191, 215
  Royal Regiment of Artillery, 191, 215
Rhode Island: battalion from, 126; prisoners from, 22
Richmond, Charles Lennox, Duke of, 243
Rigauville, J. B. M. des Berges de, 215
Rivers:
  Chouaguen. *See* Oswego.
  Delaware, 253
  Hudson, 117-18, 130
  Iberville, 250
  Illinois, 199, 204
  Mississippi, 179, 204, 249-50, 256, 262
  Mohawk, 124-25, 127, 130, 135, 146, 151, 153-55
  Muskingham, 186, 199, 203
  Ohio, 134, 203, 210, 250
  Oneida, 128, 131
  Oswego, 70, 78, 128
  Richelieu, 143, 154
  St. Lawrence, 103, 130, 145, 148, 154, 238
  Sandusky, 186, 199, 201, 203, 205, 210, 212, 218
  Scioto, 186, 199, 203, 211
  Susquehannah, 253
Rivington's New York Gazetteer, 263n
Robertson, James, 238, 244-45
Robinson, Sir Thomas, 65-66, 68-69; John Bradstreet's observations to, 61-62, 86, 135
Rogers, Robert: rangers of, 119, 121
Rousby, 34
Ryal, George, 23

St. Clair, Sir John, 118, 239, 245
St. John's, ix, 40, 43-48, 63, 92, 99, 157, 171, 258, 269
Schenectady, 59, 70, 78-79, 82, 85, 109-10, 125, 127, 146-47, 153, 194, 207-208, 239; billeting problem at, 182
Schuyler, Catherine, 251, 252n, 263
Schuyler, Harmanus, 166
Schuyler, John, 252n, 263
Schuyler, Margaret, 263
Schuyler, Philip, 10n, 151-52, 239, 244-45, 256n, 260; friendship with John Bradstreet, 89-90, 142, 155, 173, 194, 251, 252n, 263; land deals with John Bradstreet, 254; to England, 159, 165, 243n
Scotland, 7
Seven Years' War, ix, 1n, 56, 57-174 *passim*, 192, 240, 260
Sharpe, Horatio, 78n
Shelburne, William Petty Fitzmaurice, Earl of, 234, 244; resignation of, 253; support of Detroit colony, 249-52
Shippen, Edward, 137
Shirley, William, ix, 21, 24-25, 29, 33-34, 36-39, 57-59, 71-74, 76-77, 87, 91-92, 100, 108, 127, 136, 140, 178, 266; accusations against, 82-84, 88-90; as expansionist, 63, 70; hard bargaining of, 21-22; Niagara campaign of, 56-74, 87; regiment disbanded, 94; relationship with John Bradstreet, 23, 25, 30, 39-40, 55, 74-75, 81, 84-86; relationship with Sir William Johnson, 61, 71-74, 87, 136; replacement of, 78, 93; support of Louisbourg campaign, 24; use of John Bradstreet in Niagara campaign, 59-61; as well-connected office-seeker, 267
Shirreff, William, 14-15
Smith, William, 245n
South Carolina, 108
Spain, 13, 256-57
Stamp Act, 247
Stanwix, John, 124, 126-27, 132, 136
Stonehewer, Richard, 243
Strahorn, William, 16

Ten Eyck, Jacob, 254
Thoroton, Thomas, 246n
Townshend, Charles, 108, 161, 164-65, 170, 250, 267; help of John Bradstreet, 49, 51, 54; John Bradstreet's proposal to, 247-48
Treasury Office, 152, 159, 238, 243-44
Trinity Church (New York City), 263
Trois Rivières: lieutenant-governorship of, 171-73, 183
Tryon, William, 258

Vandalia scheme, 138, 237n, 262
Vaudreuil, Francois-Pierre de Rigaud de, 79, 130
Vaudreuil, Pierre de Rigaud, Marquis de, 67, 126, 128, 130
Vaughan, William, 26, 27n; claims authorship of Louisbourg plan, 24
Vetch, Samuel, 2n
Villiers, Nicolas-Antoine Coulon, Sieur de, 78-80
Virginia, 58, 61, 108, 253, 258-59; Assembly of, 222

Waldo, Samuel, 40; letters of, 27
Waldron, Thomas, 26
Walton, Joseph, 215
War Office, 16, 53, 92, 111, 139, 245-46
Warren, Peter, 25, 29, 32-33, 36, 40, 42, 92; activities in Louisbourg assault, 26; comments on John Bradstreet, 24, 28, 30; description of Canso, 13, 20; trade activities of, 18
Webb, Daniel, 78, 82, 84-85, 91-92, 100
Wentworth, Benning, 24
West Indies, 13
West Temple, 13n
Williamsburg, 58
Williams, Israel, 126-27
Wolfe, James, 114-15, 144-45, 148-49
Wood Creek, 128, 131
Wood, Robert, 160-61, 170-72, 265
Wraxall, Peter, 71n

Young, Robert, 20n

www.ingramcontent.com/pod-product-compliance
Lightning Source LLC
Chambersburg PA
CBHW052013070526
44584CB00016B/1734